ABOUT THE AUTHOR

The Venerable Professor Obaro Ikime is a retired Professor of History of the University of Ibadan, where he served from 01 October, 1964 to 15 October, 1990. He became Professor of History on O1 October, 1973.

He is the acknowledged pioneer in the field of Inter-Group Relations in Nigeria. His other areas of specialisation are History of the Western Niger Delta; the British Conquest of Nigeria and its aftermath, British Colonial Rule in Nigeria. Professor Obaro Ikime is the single author of seven books, among them, *Merchant Prince of the Niger Delta: The Rise and Fall of Nana Olomu, Last Governor of the Benin River (1968. Reprinted 1994 and 2016); Niger Delta Rivalry: Itsekiri-Urhobo Relations and the European Presence 1884-19936, 1969)*; *The Isoko People. A Historical Survey (1972); The Fall of Nigeria: The British Conquest (1977); History, The Historian and The Nation: The Voice of a Nigerian Historian (2006, reprinted 2008).* He has contributed chapters to twelve books and is the Editor, *Groundwork of Nigerian History,* first published by the Historical Society of Nigeria in 1980, and co-Editor with Michael Crowder of *West African Chiefs: Their Changing Status Under Colonial Rule and Independence.*

While at Ibadan, Ikime served as Director, Institute of African Studies; two times as Head of the Department of History; and as Dean, Faculty of Arts. He was President, History Society of Nigeria, March 1984 – April 1988. While at Ibadan, Ikime was at different times Visiting Professor of African History, University of California, Los Angeles, and at Beckley; Harvard University Summer School and the University of Benin. He was National Secretary, University of Ibadan Alumni Association, November 1975 – November 1983. After retirement, he served as Professor of History (on contract), Bayelsa State University, Wilberforce Island, for three years.

Ikime joined the ordained ministry of the Diocese of Ibadan, Church of Nigeria, Anglican Commission, in December 1995, and served until 2007. Made a Deacon in December 1995, he was priested in 1996, preferred Canon, 2002 and preferred Archdeacon in December 2006. He lives in Ibadan.

PRAISE

The central argument in this impressive collection by Professor Obaro Ikime, an extraordinary scholar of conscience and a living legend, is the relevance of history to the nation-building project and trauma in Nigeria. Grounded in over half a century of practical experience, deep maturity, responsible scholarship, and intense passion, profound perspectives emerge on Nigeria and Nigerianisation in the larger context of Europeanisation, westernisation, and globalisation. The liquidity of historical narratives is set against the relative fixity of the structures of society, revealing the cogency of History as a discipline, history as a process, and recurring issues in reconciling Nigeria's exaggerated promise with its vulnerable reality. Ikime's thematic approach combined with the subtle emphasis on stability and progress will appeal to a new generation of students. The dramatic subject provides the requisite ground for scholarly debate, and the author's vivid style makes it a pleasure to read.

– Toyin Falola, University Distinguished Teaching Professor, and Jacob and Sanger Mossiker Chair in the Humanities, The University of Texas at Austin.

There has been a government policy flip-flop over the teaching of history in Nigerian schools. History was first being taught and later abolished and then restored. What informed the flip-flop in policy decision? By this book's title, the author poses the question and tries to answer. The author embarked on this publication in furtherance of his campaigns before the latest government decision that restored the teaching of history in schools.

The book provides the background to the author's life-long campaigns and that of the Association of African Universities and the Historical Society of Nigeria,for the indispensible values and relevance of history in nation building.The book points out that with eyes fixed on technological advancement many are tempted to believe that History is no longer relevant to the present world. This is erroneous. History is a major instrument in policy making and has to be conscientiously made to perform that task by being studied, understood and applied.

– Bukar Usman, D.Litt., M.IoD, OON

Can Anything Good Come Out of History?

Can Anything Good Come Out of History?

LECTURES AND PAPERS ON NIGERIAN HISTORY

Obaro Ikime

Ibadan

BOOKCRAFT

23, Adebajo Street, Kongi Layout, New Bodija,
GPO Box 16729, Ibadan, Nigeria
Tel/Fax : +234-2-7517153
Mobile : +234-803-344 7889; +234-803-722 0773;
+234-807-3199 967

E-mail: info@bookcraftafrica.com,
Website: www.bookcraftafrica.com

ISBN: 978-978-8457-85-5

DEDICATION

This book, the last of its type that will come out of me, is dedicated to my family:

To my wife of fifty-five years,
HANNAH ORITSẸGBUBẸMI.

I was nobody, 1 had nothing, when Hannah, at the age of twenty, rejected offers from medical doctors and other well-placed men who were introduced to her by a politician-uncle, and insisted it was me, a mere undergraduate of the University College, Ibadan, she wanted. We got married on 01 December, 1962, when I was working for my Ph.D. We have grown up together as husband and wife—and what a wife she has been to me! What a mother she has been to our children! For fifty five years, I and the children God has given us have been the beneficiaries of the talents and gifts of this extraordinary personage called Hannah—wife, lover, friend, mother, house-maker, house keeper ***par excellence,*** great cook, worshipper, intercessor. The impact of Hannah's talents and gifts on the lives of the children and myself cannot be adequately conveyed in words. In the last nine years that I have been afflicted with paralysis, Hannah has been my care giver—after God, my **Chief Care Giver—**and what a care giver she has been. I owe her more thanks than I can express.

Our daughter, MajirỌghẹnẹ Oritsẹtsemayẹ, and her husband, Steve Ahaneku, have been pillars of love and support always. But in the nine years of my affliction they have sacrificed their own comfort to ensure that Hannan and I do riot suffer lack. This dedication is my little way of saying "Thank You" to "Maj" and Steve. Oziọma, daughter to Majiro and Steve, and our first grand-child, is a wonderfully well raised young lady who loves her Grandpa and Grandma deeply, and has been a great source of joy and satisfaction to us. This book is also dedicated to her.

Our firstborn and son, Mazino lives in Ibadan. He and his wife, Toju, and two daughters, OkeỌghẹnẹteno; and Oghẹnẹkẹno, have always been available to and for us. They bore the pain of seeing Daddy and Baba lying helpless in bed for years; and they participated in nursing me. It is in appreciation of their love and services that I dedicate this book to them as well.

Our last born and son, Ọghẹnẹmaino, has been away in the United States for some twenty years, and so has not participated in any of our family activities here at home for years. Even so, my years of affliction have caused him deep pain. This dedication is to re-assure him that we appreciate his concern, love and prayers.

IT IS INDEED WITH GREAT JOY AND DEEP GRATITUDE THAT I DEDICATE THIS BOOK TO MY FAMILY!

CONTENTS

PREFACE

In 2006, I published a book titled *History, The Historian and The Nation: The Voice of a Nigerian Historian.* It was a book of lectures and papers in Nigerian History, just like the one in your hand. Although the 2006 publication had to be reprinted in 2008, I received no communication from anyone concerning their views about the book. The fact that, as I write this, the publishers of the 2006 book are planning to reprint it, is evidence that some Nigerians have read the book. What was my objective as I put the 2006 collection of lectures and papers together? My objective was to demonstrate that the historian does not ply this profession *in vacuo.* He or she does not write for writing sake! He or she writes knowing that what he or she writes is of value to his or her nation, in the first instance, and then to the wider world. The title of the 2006 book makes it clear that I was addressing myself to my nation – Nigeria. I was making the point that quite a number of my colleagues have made over the years, namely, that though history is not a profession like law, medicine, agriculture, accountancy, pharmacy and so on, it has a relevance for every nation, Nigeria included. How? Why? Because every nation of the world is the product of history. It is history that gives a nation its identity.

Permit me to explain what I mean. When I was a primary school boy, I was taught that Mungo Park discovered River Niger; that it was the Lander Brothers who discovered what is today the Niger Delta – the rivers, streams and creeks through which the River Niger empties itself into the ocean. But the River Niger existed long before Mungo Park saw it! How then could he have discovered what already existed? Mungo Park did not discover the River Niger! He was the first European to see what he described as the Majestic Niger and to write about it. And because he wrote about it, it became part of human history. The River Niger acquired an identity which it did not have before. It is in this way that history gives a people, an ethnic group, a nation, its identity. The world knows about Nigeria today because history created Nigeria over a period of time. What is true of Nigeria is true of every nation of the world.

As I began to put the lectures and papers in this book together, I was tempted to use the title of the 2006 book, and make this one a Volume II. I overcame that temptation and have chosen *Can Anything Good Come Out of History?* My plea to my Nigerian readers is that as they finish reading each chapter, they should ask themselves the question which is the main title of this book. I believe that if they do so consciously, they will be enabled to begin to grasp the value of History.

For some four decades now, the Historical Society of Nigeria, the bulk of the membership of which is made up of academic historians, has been drawing the attention of the Federal Government of Nigeria to the fact that the nation's policy on education is slowly killing History as a subject that should be taught to everyone who passes through our educational system. We contend that all who are in government should have knowledge of the history of the peoples over whom they exercise governance. We contend that over the years, government has made a number of mistakes, as local governments and states have been created, because no historian was in the body that made recommendations to government. Consequent on the mistakes made, there are villages or towns which are not large enough ever to produce a local government councillor, because the group concerned is in one local government, whereas the majority of their kith and kin are in another local government! As I write this, quite a number of students who are reading History at University level – and the numbers have reduced over the last four decades – were not taught History at secondary school! Most of them studied "Government". The consequence is that they have problems studying History. It is the position of the Historical Society of Nigeria that every child who goes through our primary and our secondary school system should study Nigerian History. We are persuaded that this will do them and the nation good.

Part of the problem we face as historians is that the claims we make for History are in the realm of ideas. The arguments which we have been developing in this preface are in the realm of ideas. History is not like

Medicine, Engineering, etc, where one can see the outcome of the labour of the medical doctor or engineer. Indeed it is my view that this is one reason why past governments have not been able to listen to us these many years. I am fully persuaded that if government hearkens to the Historical Society of Nigeria, the ideas we have been canvassing will ultimately produce results which will be beneficial to our country.

This preface had already been written, and the manuscript completed, before the federal government announced, through the Minister of Education, that History will be re-introduced into the nation's schools. I rejoice that the government has at last responded positively to the plea of the Historical Society of Nigeria – a plea in which I was involved when I served as the President of the Historical Society of Nigeria way back in the 1980s.* The announcement referred to above immediately raised a question in my mind: should I change the title of this book? It did not take me time to answer this question in the negative. The title of this book had been chosen to challenge the teachers of history at all levels to ply their trade in a manner which emphasises the value of history both for those who study it and for the nation as a whole. It is a book which, I am hoping, that even those who have never studied history can read and grasp the relevance of history for our nation – Nigeria.

This book consists of a preface, prologue, an introduction, fourteen chapters and a conclusion which I have titled "As We End". Of the fourteen chapters, six are lectures I was invited to deliver by different organisations. One is my Inaugural Lecture which I delivered in 1979 in fulfilment of requirements of the University of Ibadan: a professor was required to deliver an inaugural lecture based on his area of specialisation. As was the practice, the University of Ibadan Press published the lecture. Those who read the publication must have been limited to colleagues in the Faculties of Arts and Social Sciences. It is included in this book as Chapter Two. I believe that the reader will find that that lecture addresses quite a number of the issues that are raised in this book. Papers which I presented to academic bodies account for the other seven chapters in the book.

*Two memoranda which the Historical Society of Nigeria presented to Government when I was President of the Historical Society of Nigeria can be found on pp 297 and 302.

As I prepared these lectures and papers for publication, I knew that they could attract harsh reviews from some of my academic colleagues. What is the purpose of publishing a lecture delivered in 1979, in 2018 — thirty-nine years after? How much of what is in this book is new? Of what value is it? Let me begin by stating that my concern is to answer the question that constitutes the main title of this book. *Can Anything Good Come out of History?* Does History have any value for our peoples, our nation? The value of History is, in a sense, eternal. The issues which the historian decides to concentrate on are thrown up by the challenges which confront the society in which he/she lives, as well as the age in which he/she lives. When I began my professional career in 1964, History was regarded as a respectable discipline that had something to contribute to a newly independent Nigeria. By 1979 when I delivered my inaugural lecture as professor of history at the University of Ibadan, developments in our country had begun to challenge practitioners of History to ply their trade in a manner that would ensure the continued relevance of their discipline in the Nigeria in which they lived. This challenge was intensified as we entered into the 1980s, and developed into something of a crisis by the beginning of the present century. The lectures and papers in this book, like those in my *History, The Historian and The Nation (2006),* represent my contribution to answering the question: Has History any value for us Nigerians and for our nation, Nigeria? The spread in terms of time – 1977 to 2013 – is evidence of one's consistency in responding to the challenges faced by one's discipline over the years. Let me state here, that my hope is that even the non-historians will find this book useful, valuable.

Another criticism that some of my colleagues might raise is that a number of these lectures have no footnotes or bibliography. That is well taken. The circumstances in which the lectures were delivered, as well as the audiences to which they were delivered, partly account for that. I trust that my colleagues will agree with me that I have said nothing that cannot be backed by facts of history.

The majority of the chapters of this book were typeset courtesy of my dearly beloved "son" and friend, Professor C.B.N. Ogbogbo. Professor Ogbogbo has, in many other ways, demonstrated a great love for my family. I cannot thank him enough. May the good Lord reward him bountifully for his labour of love. My three granddaughters, Oziọma,

Oke Ọghẹnẹteno and Ọghẹnẹkẹno also did some of the typesetting. I am grateful to them for helping Baba!

In the last couple of years, Mrs. Eunice Onwuemeli, has done the bulk of typesetting of my works. This is the third book in the typesetting of which she has been involved. In nearly every case, I put great pressure on her, in the sense that I gave her little time to work. I apologise for always making her to work under pressure and I thank her very much indeed for putting up with my demands on her time. Not once have I seen a frown on her face. It is my prayer that the good Lord will continue to bless the works of her hands.

As usual when I get really busy, as I was while preparing these lectures and papers for publication, my wife Hannah, paid the price of loneliness while I spent long hours in my study. Yet she encouraged me, as she has always done, to go on till the work was ready. I am deeply grateful to her for her understanding and loving support. May the God, whose she is and whom she serves, meet her at every point of need—in the peerless name of our Lord Jesus Christ.

Obaro IKIME
October 2017

[illegible] and Nobody, [illegible] also did some of the typesetting. I am grateful to them for helping Gabe.

In the last couple of years, Mrs. Eunice Onwuachi has done the bulk of typesetting in many ways. This is the third book [illegible] [illegible]

[illegible]

PROLOGUE

Background

The Prologue which follows hereunder is titled "History and the Historian in the Developing Countries in Africa." It is a Keynote Address that I delivered at a workshop in 1977 on the "Teaching of African History in African Universities." Some may question my including it in this book that deals with Nigeria. I will answer that question later. Meanwhile, I draw the attention of the reader to the title of the address. The workshop was sponsored by the Association of African Universities. The theme of the workshop suggests that there was some concern about the teaching of African History in the developing countries of the continent. The reader will discover that nine years later, in 1986, the Historical Society of Nigeria organised a workshop on *The Teaching of Nigerian History from a National Perspective*. I was the president of the Historical Society of Nigeria at that time, and had to deliver the opening address at the workshop in February 1986. What I said in that address is Chapter 6 of this book. It is clear from these two workshops that we, as historians, have been conscious of our responsibilities to our nation and our continent. That consciousness constitutes evidence that we, the teachers of history, are mindful of the need to ensure that the history we teach should not be history for history sake, but history that serves a purpose in our countries, in our continent—without jettisoning the worldwide canons of our discipline. Most regrettably, the papers presented at these two workshops were never published, for reasons I cannot now recollect.

The paper which I presented at the 1986 Workshop, that is, apart from the opening address, is chapter 7 of this book. The only other thing that I consider necessary to say concerning the prologue is that the person, to whom the assignment was given to deliver the keynote address at the 1977 Workshop, could not attend the Workshop for health reasons. At about 5pm on the day before the Workshop, Professor J.F. Ade Ajayi, then Vice-Chancellor of the University of Lagos, who hosted the Workshop, asked me to stand in for Professor B.A. Ogot, my very senior colleague from Kenya, who was originally assigned the responsibility of delivering the keynote address, but who could not attend as was stated earlier.

Only two more points need to be made regarding the prologue. The subject of the keynote address was decided upon by the Planning Committee. So, when I was asked to stand in for Professor Ogot, at less than twenty-four hours' notice, I was not given the option of choosing any other topic. I had to speak on the subject that the Planning Committee had agreed on. The second point is why I have included my Keynote Address of 1977 which dealt with Africa in this book which deals only with Nigeria. My answer is that the reader will find that what the Historical Society of Nigeria did in 1986 was very similar to what historians of Africa gathered to do in 1977. As the reader will find in this book, historians are expected to ply their trade in a world that is constantly changing. Different epochs throw up different challenges. The historian must be conscious of this truth, and undertake his or her research and writing in the context of changing times and changing challenges. The two workshops were addressing a similar challenge. And it fell to my lot to deliver the Keynote Address at the 1977 Workshop, and the Opening Address at the 1986 Workshop. We go on now, to the prologue proper.

History and The Historian in the Developing Countries of Africa

It is now at least two clear decades since African History became accepted as a respectable subject, fit to be taught to the human species – black, yellow, white or colourless. While this is not to say that historians across the globe are agreed on the interpretations to be placed on the events which constitute African History, or the kind of issues which the African historian is entitled to raise is his historical inquiry, it is, I think, to say that the African historian needs not worry his head as to whether what he writes is acceptable to his colleagues outside Africa, or even to his non-African colleagues within Africa. For although the historian's craft may have certain universalist tendencies and rules of procedure, the purpose for which history is taught has always been, and continues to be, bound up within the context – geographical, social and political (meaning cultural) in which that history is written and taught. It is for this reason that African History written and/or taught by an African historian can be legitimately expected to be different in important respects from the same history written and/or taught by the non-African. If, therefore, there is need to justify this Workshop on the Teaching of African History in African Universities, this is the reason.

There is, I would like to suggest, another reason. We live in an increasingly technological world. The governments of the world, including the governments of African countries, are anxious to develop their technological capacities to the optimum. In our present situation, History can quite easily be seen as a useless, or at best a not-so-useful, discipline. Here in Nigeria, we are already faced with that kind of situation. Our History undergraduates and graduate students are beginning to find that governments do not think that History is a priority. While I am satisfied that this attitude is the result of a mistaken idea of what History can do, and has done, for nations and communities, it may also be that we the practitioners of History have not carried out our calling in a manner which makes it easy for our products to immediately see the value of the subject for their lives after they pass their examinations. And if our own products do not see the immediate value of History to them, then we can hardly blame government if it takes the view that History is a useless or near-useless discipline. This workshop should, I feel certain, give us the opportunity of engaging in that critical self-appraisal necessary from time to time for most human organisations. As has been pointed out earlier, African History is now acceptable and respectable. That very acceptability and respectability can become a veritable snare for the practitioner of African History, especially the African practitioner.

As we meet, therefore, to engage in a critical self-appraisal of how we have handled our calling, it is meet and right that one should say a few words about the role History can play in the developing countries of Africa. Only two days ago, I was being introduced by a friend to one of the coaches in the National Sports Commission. Said my friend to the coach, "This is Professor Ikime from the University of Ibadan. He is a historian. He is interested in our yesterday, so that we can plan our tomorrow." I was rather impressed by that statement, coming as it did from an expert in physical education. It is easy for us historians to say in defence of our discipline that no nation unaware of its past can hope to plan its future course successfully. It is indeed within this context that I have said on more than one public occasion, that any African government, which allows itself to be persuaded, at this stage of our development, to neglect historical research in pursuit of science and technology, will find that science and technology, excellent weapons as they are for the boosting of the national ego, do not on their own necessarily create the nation. For, a look at the really advanced technological nations of the world will reveal that these nations first attained true nationhood, before they set their tracks for rapid technological advancement. Britain, America, Japan, China – these all first had to go through the turmoil of nation-building before they attained their greatest heights in science and technology. And in the task of nation building – a task on which all African countries are still very much involved – History can be a major instrument. However, let it be said straight away that if History is to be a major instrument in the task of nation-building, it has to be deliberately made to perform that task. And the task of nation-building has to be seen in its full ramifications, not just in some self-deceiving effort at identifying the things which allegedly unite, while failing to give equal attention to such aspects as public morality, public accountability and consideration for human life. It is the totality of the nation-building process that we must be concerned with as we read and teach History, not just certain aspects of that process.

The writing of African History by African academics began at a time when most African countries were struggling to regain independence from colonial rule. Naturally, therefore, the first generation of African historians concerned themselves with seeking to demonstrate that Africa had a historical past of which we can be justly proud. This concern invariably involved a certain denunciation of the kind of history which had been written about Africa by European scholars, travellers and the like.

The kind of history which emerged from this generation was one which sought, more often by implication rather by direct statement, to inculcate in the African who read or was taught it, a certain pride in his race, in terms of how the African ordered his social and political life, in terms of the economic activities which supported the socio-political edifice, and in terms of the creative and adaptive genius of the African. Within the context in which they wrote and taught, that generation of historians was fulfilling an essential political, psychological and intellectual function. For it is a well-accepted tenet of historical scholarship that the historian can only work within the context of the expectations of his society at any given time. It was pleasant to be told as an undergraduate in 1959 by our host, Professor J.F. Ade Ajayi, that if Taubman Goldie founded anything, it was the United African Company, not modern Nigeria, an obvious reference to the then recently published *Sir George Goldie and the Making of Modern Nigeria* by J.E. Flint. It gave us joy to be told by K. Onwuka Dike about the political genius of Osei Tutu of Asante. Similarly, we learnt with joy and indeed pride about the nation-building genius of Shaka and Moshweshe. For us, undergraduates in the era of the struggle for independence, History was not just another subject which we learnt solely or even mainly for the passing of examinations; it was a process of re-education, after all the British Empire History that had been fed into us at grammar school. Additionally, it was a major factor in our equipment for coping with a world in which the African is still very much an under-dog. More than that, the historians of that generation were playing an important role in preparing our peoples to look to their past as they prepared to face the then present and future. And in doing so, they tended to concentrate on the nineteenth century history of Africa, anxious to demonstrate that even in that century, which can be seen as the century of intense European activity in Africa, our continent was not a *tabula rasa* on which Europe sketched what she pleased. The historians of that generation were responding to a need in their society, for as Henri Pirenne wrote in 1931,

> Historians are not conditioned in various ways solely by inherited qualities; their milieu is also important. Their religion, nationality, and social class influence them more or less profoundly. And the same is true of the period in which they work. *Each epoch has its needs and tendencies which demand the attention of students and lead them to concentrate on this or that problem.* (My emphasis)

If the historians of the decade 1956-1966 were primarily concerned with the task indicated above, a task that I consider crucial for the emergent African countries at the time, what have their successors been seeking to do? To answer this question we need to have a look at the type of history that has been produced by these later historians. I think that history can be divided into two broad areas. Some, especially our East African colleagues, have worked on the pre-nineteenth century history of our peoples. Others, to which I belong, have not only continued to explore the nineteenth century, but have attempted to study the colonial period of Africa's history. Have these two groups been guided by any ideals, any needs of the epoch in which they have been working? I would say Yes and No. Yes, with regard to those who have worked on the more ancient history of Africa, in the sense that one of the oft-repeated claims as to why newly independent African states are finding it difficult to forge really meaningful nation-states, is the fact that they are artificial creations of the colonial powers. The historians of Africa's more ancient past can, by their work, furnish evidence of links of a social and economic nature which bound many of the peoples who constitute quite a number of the countries of Africa. Put crudely, these historians can be said to be seeking to demonstrate that, while there may be many things in our past which are different for the various groups that now make up the different states of Africa, there is also a large number of factors which could be used to seek to unite. In fact, many in government see this as the only role which history can play in the Africa of today.

During FESTAC '77 we heard quite a great deal about this role which the historian was expected to play in the Africa of our time. No one can fail to see that there is a certain validity in this expected role of the historian. Yet one must warn against false unities and false autonomies. For in the nation-building process in Africa, there are not wanting many who seek to use History to build false autonomies within each African country, just as there abound many who seek to build false empires. It is my view that the historian must remain faithful to his evidence, and yet contribute to the nation-building effort, the supreme pre-occupation of most of the African states. If in his unearthing of the African past, the historian finds that the evidence points to divergences rather than unities, he owes a duty to say so and yet be contributing to the much desired nation-building effort. For I am persuaded that it is the function of the historian to demonstrate why things have happened the way they have happened. In doing so, he appeals to general as well as less general principles: he shows that, given certain circumstances, man does tend to behave in certain ways; at the same time he also shows that a particular group behaved in a particular way for reasons peculiar to its situation. In this way, the historian will be fulfilling his purpose which, in the words of J.H. Plumb (1971) "is to deepen understanding about men and society, not for its own sake, but in the hope that a profounder awareness will help to mould human attitudes and human action". In the Africa of today, the historian can only hope that by unearthing the history of the ancient past, the leaders and peoples of today will have material with which to appeal to all concerned for a sympathetic understanding of the problems with which society has to contend, for not infrequently, the attitudes of one group to another within the various states of our continent derive from a certain insularity, the result of inadequate knowledge about the other groups. This absence of knowledge, and the attitude which it generates, are just as important for the nation-building effort as the decisions and policies of the ruling elites. For those whose interest is the more ancient past of Africa, therefore, there is a valid role. For they study the past in a present beset with certain pre-occupations of which nation-building is decidedly major. The present thus informs the study of the past, as the knowledge of the past should illuminate the problems of the present. No doubt this is what E.H. Carr meant when he wrote (1961) "Great history is written precisely when the historian's vision of the past is illuminated by insights into the problems of the present."

Then there are those who have been working on the colonial period of African history. Strangely enough, although the colonial period of African history is in many ways crucial for our understanding of the many problems of African states as we know them today, it is one aspect of our history which has been little studied by African historians. Here in Nigeria, for example, the historians of the colonial period of Nigeria constitute a small group. And the same is true for many of the other African states. While one reason for this must be the fact that the records of the colonial period are only partially available, I fear that this cannot justify our failure to pay the kind of attention to this aspect of our history as it deserves. Whatever the differences which existed among different peoples on the African continent before the colonial period, I have no doubt in my mind that colonialism compounded the situation. Where before various groups had decided for what and how they co-operated, the colonial situation forced groups to co-operate in all sorts of ways, often without explanation. In the process, all kinds of inter-group tensions were built up which have continued to influence the politics of independent African states. Take, for example, the constitution of provinces or divisions or districts. Often this was done without sufficient knowledge of the existing political or social relations between the peoples brought together in such units. The fact that the colonial administrators thought that this was a good thing for the peoples concerned was seen as enough justification of the action. Yet that action could, and did, create disharmonies which have rankled till today. The historian of the colonial period owes it a duty to draw attention to the problems created by this attitude of the governors to the governed, in the hope that today's governors will take heed and take the trouble of explaining government measures to the people before they are implemented. The study of that aspect of colonial rule can thus be made relevant to the problems of today. The pity is that our study of the colonial period does not give enough emphasis to this type of problem, because we are so attracted by a study of various legislations and theories of colonial rule. I suggest that a thorough study of colonial boundary-making within each of the African states, in terms of the constitution of various administrative units will be a most rewarding venture, just as I am sure that a similar study of such boundary-making, in similar terms, in the independent states will reveal quite some explanations for a few of the problems with which these states have to cope.

There are other aspects of the colonial period, a study of which could furnish useful explanations for some of our other problems. The colonial period introduced into the various colonies all sorts of differentials. Indeed in some ways the colonial period is something of a paradox. It is usually credited with bringing African peoples together into new political units. Yet it not only underlined differences which already existed before colonial rule, but in some instances intensified these differences and introduced new ones. Thus differences in socio-political institutions between groups were often used as an index of development or lack of it, resulting in different treatments being meted to such groups, and creating new tensions which did not exist before colonial rule. It will be rewarding to find out how much of the stereotypes which we have come to accept in terms of various groups in different countries of Africa are traceable to the colonial period. Here in Nigeria, I have no doubt at all in my mind that the British attitude to the three main groups of the Hausa/Fulani, Yoruba and Igbo has been instrumental in creating the stereotypes, such that even the students we teach today already have their views about these peoples, and will contest those views with their teachers even in the face of evidence that contradicts their views. So invidious can the colonial inheritance become. Yet how many of the studies of the colonial period that exist concern themselves with such aspects of the colonial inheritance?

Or take the issue of the police in African states. The colonial police was not just a law enforcement agent. In the circumstances in which it was created, it had to be an instrument of intimidation and coercion. In fact, it can be claimed, with a great measure of truth, that in its early years the colonial police force was far more an instrument of intimidation then a law enforcement agency. Has the police force been successfully given a new image in independent African states? Has the training of the police been sufficiently modified to make the constable a friend of the public rather than a foe? And how often have tensions between the police and the public led to situations which could have been contained before getting out of hand? Have the successors to political power in Africa deliberately refused to change the image of the police force in order that they can use the force as an instrument of coercion? Do we, in or study of the colonial police, draw attention to these aspects, or are we more interested in the kinds of information which the documents provide? Or take the various civil services of the independent states of Africa. No one can question the role of these arms of government. Yet I am not aware of many studies of the civil services of African states by African historians. Is this because we do not think that we have a contribution to make by studying a body, the wranglings and struggles for places within which can throw the body politic completely off balance? The point I am seeking to make, is that a study of the colonial period of African history can throw up information and explanations relevant for many of the problems with which independent African states have to contend. And the more we can address ourselves to some of the issues which I have raised – and I have by no means exhausted them – the more we would make History relevant to national problems in many an African state.

But I must return to the query which I raised earlier, as to whether those historians who have worked on the more ancient past of our history as well as those who have worked on the colonial period have sought to meet the problems and demands of the age. I said the answer was Yes and No. Yes, to the extent that the history unravelled has provided material which the discerning reader and student can see as being immediately relevant to the understanding of some of the problems which beset us. No, to the extent that our historical studies have failed to draw attention to issues relevant to such problems. And since we can only play a meaningful role in so far as our studies have relevance to national needs, I am hoping that we shall, during this Workshop, be averting our minds to the kind of scholarship that we are engaged in, since the scholarship must necessarily inform and direct the teaching.

Let me draw this address to a close by borrowing from Professor A.E. Afigbo, who happens to be with us at this workshop. Earlier, I said that as undergraduates in the late 1950s, it was something of a pleasure and a pride to be taught about the nation-building genius of the Shakas and Moshweshwes of Africa. Even though we realised at the time that these and other great names in nineteenth century African History were in some ways extreme despots who bordered on the blood thirsty, we did not pay particular regard to that aspect of their lives. Indeed, we wrote essays in which we sought to explain away their weaknesses in this regard. In the Africa of the 1970s in which we had various degrees of despotisms, some bordering on the blood-thirsty, we must ask ourselves whether our failure to condemn the foibles in some of the great names of African History has not been reprehensible and partially contributory to the despotisms which exist on the continent in our time. For, surely, the view that the historian must content himself with the whys and the hows and the whens, and not constitute himself into a judge of the characters he studies, can hardly meet the function of the historian in our Africa of today. Perhaps if we made the point more pungently that those who draw the sword will die by the sword, those who are inclined to put their political opponents to the sword may think more about their deeds. Only recently, in Nigeria here, lawyers, some of whom had helped to draft legislation which had been made retrospective by the governments to which they then belonged, found it necessary to protest to the Federal Military Government that it is against the rule of law to punish a man for an offence which was not an offence when it was committed! It took those lawyers rather long to discover this important ingredient of the rule of law. If at some point in our history, we felt called upon to stress certain aspects of the deeds of the leading historical figures, perhaps the time has come to review our assessment of those same figures in the light of the crying need in Africa for just and humane governments with respect for human life and human dignity.

Similarly, I would like to draw attention to Professor Afigbo's reference to Mansa Musa's pilgrimage to Mecca when he was ruler of the Mali empire. That pilgrimage is one of the ingredients of Mansa Musa's greatness. Yet it was a display of extravagance which not only brought fiscal hardship on Egypt, but impoverished the Mali treasury. Yet little is Mansa Musa taken to task by the historians who have told this tale many times. If we will not condemn Mansa Musa, perhaps we cannot condemn Africa's new Emperor who has ordered 100 pairs of shoes fit for an emperor, even though it was less than a year ago that he ordered a similar number – but that was when he was a mere president of what has now become an empire without provinces! That same emperor is busy having a special crown and an equally special throne made for him in France. What is true for "His Imperial Majesty" is true in varying degrees for many an African ruler of today. You and I, as historians, can hardly afford to condemn these rulers of today, at the same time as we laud to high heavens equally extravagant rulers of yester years. The period during which the African historian felt called upon to engage in what amounted to indiscriminate glorification of the dramatic personae of that history must be seen as being very definitely over. We must usher in a new brand of historical scholarship which feels able not only to pass judgement where the evidence justifies such passing of judgement, but which also deliberately draws attention to the consequences which have attended certain weaknesses of character in the past. For, as someone once said, the weakness of a king is wickedness. Unless we can usher in this new brand of historical scholarship, the past may fail to inform the present, and our role in society may well be derided.

I am not sure that this address is the most suitable that could be given at the beginning of a workshop such as this. For one thing I have talked more about the material that should be taught, than about the method of teaching it. And there must be other inadequacies. If I have deviated from the exact assignment that I was given, I would plead that the circumstances in which I took on that assignment should excuse the deviation. I can only hope that some, at least, of the things which I have said would re-echo in the course of the next few days as we settle down to this workshop on the Teaching of African History in African Universities, bearing in mind the fact that the workshop is taking place in the Africa of the 1970s.

INTRODUCTION: ON HISTORY

The title of this book tells the reader the reason for publishing it. A question which arises from the title is: What is History? Below we provide a number of comments to do with that question. The aim is, as it were, to prepare the reader to seek to answer the question which constitutes the main title of the book. The reader will find that some of the comments given hereunder are found in various chapters and, in that sense, constitute repetitions. It is my view that despite such repetitions, this "foretaste" is useful.

1. According to R. G. Collingwood

(i) History is the science of *res gestae*, the attempt to answer questions about human actions done in the past.

(ii) Historical procedure, or method, consists essentially of interpreting evidence.

(iii) What is History for? According to Collingwood, "History is 'for' human self-knowledge. Knowing yourself means knowing, first, what it is to be a man; secondly, knowing what it is to be the kind of man you are; and thirdly, knowing what it is to be the man you are and nobody else is. Knowing yourself means knowing what you can do; and since nobody knows what he can do until he tries, the only clue to what man can do is what man has done. The value of History, then, is that it teaches us what man has done and thus what man is." Seemingly difficult, won't you agree? Simply put, what Collingwood is saying is that it is through what man has done in the past that today's man knows that such things are do-able! And History is a study of that past. – R.G. Collingwood, *The Idea of History*, London, Oxford University Press, 1946 (paperback, 1961), pp. 9 & 10.

2. "When all is said and done, a single word, 'understanding,' is the beacon light for our studies. Let us not say that the true historian is a stranger to emotion: he has that at all events. 'Understanding' in all honesty, is a word pregnant with difficulties, but also with hope. Moreover, it is a friendly word. Even in action, we are far too prone to judge. It is so easy to denounce. We are never sufficiently understanding. Whoever differs from us – a foreigner or a political adversary – is almost inevitably considered evil. A little more understanding of people would be necessary…in the conflicts which are unavoidable…" – Marc Bloch, *The Historian's Craft*, New York, Alfred Knopf, Inc., 1953 (Peter Putman's Translation), pp. 143 - 144.

3. (i)"Man, except perhaps in earliest infancy and extreme old age, is not totally involved in his environment and unconditionally subject to it. On the other hand, he is never totally independent of it and its unconditional master. The relation of man to his environment is the relation of the historian to his theme. The historian is neither the humble slave nor the tyrannical master of his facts. The relation between the historian and his facts is one of equality, of give-and-take. As any working historian knows, if he stops to reflect what he is doing as he thinks and writes, the historian is engaged on a continuous process of moulding his facts to his interpretation and his interpretation to his facts. It is impossible to assign primacy to one over the other.

The historian starts with a provisional selection of facts, and a provisional interpretation in the light of which that selection has been made – by others as well as by himself. As he works, both the interpretation and the selection and ordering of facts undergo subtle and perhaps partly unconscious changes, through the reciprocal action of one on the other. And this reciprocal action also involves reciprocity between present and past, since the historian is part of the present and the facts belonging to the past. The historian and the facts of history are necessary to one another. The historian without his facts is rootless and futile; the facts without their historian are dead and meaningless. My first answer therefore to the question 'What is history?' is that it is a continuous process of interaction between the historian and his facts, an unending dialogue between the present and the past.

– E.H. Carr, *What is History?* First published by Macmillan, 1961, published in Penguin Books, 1964, Hammondsworth, Middlesex, England, pp. 29-30.

(ii) "History, then, in both senses of the word – meaning both the historian and the facts of the past into which he inquires – is a social process, in which the individuals are engaged as social beings; and the imaginary antithesis between society and the individual is no more than a red herring drawn across our path to confuse our thinking. The reciprocal process of interaction between the historian and his facts, what I have called the dialogue between the past and the present, is a dialogue not between abstract and isolated individuals, but between the society of today and the society of yesterday. History, in Burchhardt's words is 'the record of what one age finds worthy of note in another'*. The past is intelligible to us only in the light of the present; and we can fully understand the present only in the light of the past. ***To enable man to understand the society of the past, and to increase his mastery over the society of the present is the dual function of history***" (my emphasis). E. H. Carr, *op.cit,*.55

4. (i) "For the historian history becomes only that part of the human past which can be meaningfully reconstructed from the available records and from inferences regarding their setting."– Louis Gottschalk, *Understanding History*, (2nd Edition) Alfred A. Knopf, Inc., 1969, p. 48.

(ii) "The Historian must be sure that his records really came from the past and are in fact what they seem to be and that his imagination is directed towards re-creation and not creation."– Gottschalk, *op.cit.*, p. 49.

*J. Burckhardt, *Judgements on History and on Historians,* (1959), p. 158.

5. "The Historian's purpose, therefore, is to deepen understanding about men and society, not merely for his own sake, but in the hope that a profounder knowledge, a profounder awareness will help to mould human attitudes and human actions." – J.H. Plumb, *The Death of the Past*, Boston, Houghton Miflin Company, 1971, p. 106.

6. (i) "HISTORY IS THE MEMORY of human group experience. If it is forgotten or ignored, we cease in that measure to be human. Without History we have no knowledge of who we are or how we came to be, like victims of collective amnesia groping in the dark for our identity. It is the events recorded in History that have generated all the emotions, the values, the ideals that make life meaningful, that have given men something to live for, struggle over, die for. Historical events have created all the basic human groupings – countries, religions, classes – and all the loyalties that attach to these." – Robert V. Daniels, *Studying History: How and Why* (2nd Edition) Prentice-Hall, Inc., Englewood Cliffs, New Jersey, 1972, p. 6.

(ii) "Professional historians do not have any monopoly on the thoughtful study of human affairs. All of the other social sciences and humanities are engaged in this, though people in each discipline work from their own particular standpoint. History, however, must be drawn upon by all other fields. It offers the raw record of what has happened and it sets the context of unique situations in the stream of time within which the other forms of specialised enquiry must operate.

This outward looking emphasis on the broad range of human affairs does not exhaust the value of history. The study of history is important not only for what it tells us about our world, but also for its value in developing our powers of thinking. Successful historical study forces us to train and exercise all the essential aspects of intellectual activity – it excites curiosity and the spirit of inquiry; it disciplines the faculty of reason; it cultivates the arts of self-expression and communication. Historical study is also fundamental in developing the attitudes of mind that distinguish the educated man – the habits of skepticism and criticism; of thinking with perspective and objectivity; of judging the good and the bad and the in-between in human affairs; of weighing the pros and cons and discerning the different shades of gray that lie between the white and the black".– Daniels, *op.cit.*, pp. 8-9

(iii)"History teaches judgment. It does this both by supplying a knowledgeable background and by training the technique of criticism and reasoned conclusions. Good judgment often depends upon asking the right questions and the knack for this depends upon the use of a disciplined imagination. Sometimes, in the absence of clear or consistent information, judgment must be reserved, as many an historical problem illustrates. A healthy skepticism, though never cynicism, should be one aim of all historical instruction." – Daniels, *op.cit.*, p. 10.

(iv) **"The ultimate virtue of the Historical approach is the detachment that enables the observer to rise above human conflicts and see all sides of a question, no matter which position he personally prefers** (my emphasis). Historical study teaches the recognition of legitimate differences of viewpoint and the difficulty of final judgments in human affairs. Historical thinking appreciates the mixture of motives and the balance of wisdom and error in any human situation.... Good historical study recognises how rarely, if ever, clear-cut conflicts occur between good or evil, black and white. It also recognises the differences among the many distinct shades of gray. This is the most important lesson that history can offer its students for coping with their own world." – Daniels, *op.cit.*, p. 13

7. (i) "There is no escape from the past. It is built into the concepts we employ to cope with the everyday physical and social world... The view we take of nation-states is inevitably influenced by our understanding of their past. The past gives our concepts concrete content." – P.J. Lee "Why Teach History?" in A.K. Dickson, P.J. Lee, and P.J. Rogers (Editors), *Learning History*, London, Heinemann Educational Books, 1984, p. 1.

"If our knowledge of the present world is never an 'instantaneous' knowldge, and brings with it willy-nilly some substantive conception of the past, then to be historically ignorant is just to be ignorant". – P.J. Lee, *op. cit.*, p. 4.

(ii) "Like the poor, the past is always with us; not because we choose to tolerate it (as we do poverty) but because we cannot escape it. Experientia docet [we learn from experience] because, as beings endowed with memory, we cannot have a perception of a present that is not strongly influenced by a version of the past – some sort of version – which we have internalised in the cause of growing up, and articulated in our adult lives. Such versions vary and matter because they determine how we understand and behave towards events that occur in our present world." – E.J. Rogers, "Why Teach History", in *Learning History*, p. 20.

"... the historian's knowledge encompasses not only the events of the past but their consequences. What enables him to discriminate an event as important is largely his hindsight, his knowledge of which events were fecund with important consequences... Important historical facts are those with consequences..., and only historical study can reliably isolate these". – E.J. Rogers, loc. cit. p. 22.

8. "Historical knowledge gives solidity to the understanding of the present and may suggest guiding lines for the future." – G.R. Elton, *The Practice of History*, London, Fontana Paperbacks, 1984, p. 67.

"...history, to be worthy of itself and beyond itself, must concentrate on one thing: the search for truth. Its real value as a social activity lies in the training it provides, the standards it sets, in this singularly human concern." – Elton, *op.cit*., p. 68.

The quality of an historian's work must, as I have said, be judged purely by intellectual standards; the same is true of his contribution to society.... It is not the problems they study or the lessons they teach that distinguish the historical sheep from the goats, but only the manner of their study, the precision of their minds, and the degree to which they approximate to the ultimate standards of intellectual honesty and intellectual penetration". – Elton, *op.cit*., p. 69.

I do not consider it necessary to comment on what you have just finished reading. But I do hope that as you go on to read the fourteen chapters that constitute this book, you may find yourself wanting or needing to link what you read in those chapters with the few selected comments on History and what service it can render to man, to nations, Nigeria and Nigerians included.

This is, as it turns out to be, the best place for me to say a few words about my choice of the main title for this work. In John 1:45 and 46, we read:

> 45. Philip found Nathaniel and said to him, "we have found Him of whom Moses in the law, and also the prophets wrote – Jesus of Nazareth, the son of Joseph";
> 46. And Nathaniel said to him, "Can anything good come out of Nazareth?" Philip said to him, "Come and see".

My experience as a historian has been that a large number of my fellow countrymen, including many in high offices in Government and Industry, know very little about the history of their country. The attitude of these otherwise educated people is rather like the attitude of Nathaniel in the passage quoted above. By their reactions to history, many of my countrymen are asking: Can Anything Good Come out of History? Philip said to Nathaniel, "Come and see". Through this book, I am saying to my countrymen, Come, Read and See – See whether anything good can come out of history.

1

HISTORY AND THE CHANGING CULTURES OF NIGERIA*

In 1976 I had the privilege of serving on the Academic Planning Committee of the National Universities Commission (N.U.C.) for a short while. The task of the Committee was, among others, to visit the then new universities and advise the N.U.C. as to which faculties and departments were to be established by these new universities. In carrying out our assignment we held discussions not only with the vice-chancellors and their respective staff, but also with leaders of the communities among whom the universities were located. That was why we visited Maiduguri, and held talks with leaders of the community there.

Alhaji Shetima Ali Munguno was one of the community leaders who attended that meeting. He was at that time pro-chancellor and chairman of council of this university, the University of Calabar. In his contribution to the discussion, Alhaji Shetima dwelt at length on the need to ensure that the University of Maiduguri reflected the culture of the people in whose locale it was situated. He expressed horror at what he had seen here at the University of Calabar. Students went about wearing all sorts of trousers and high-heeled shoes. And their teachers too. He hoped that no such evil would afflict the University of Maiduguri.

*This was a lecture delivered under the auspices of the Department of History, University of Calabar, Calabar, some time in 1977.

While the general point which the Alhaji was seeking to make was well taken, I found his disgust with the dressing style of the staff and students of the University of Calabar evidence of cultural intolerance, for it must be clear that the dress style of any group is tied up with the cultural influences to which that group has been exposed. The dress style of the people around Maiduguri, for example, (and most of them at the meeting were wearing the flowing robes typical of that region) is clearly a product of the cultural influence to which they have been subjected. And these cultural influences cannot but be a product of their history. Trite as it might seem, it is the incident narrated above, together with the tendency of many to speak disparagingly about the values and cultural traits of fellow Nigerians who belong to other cultural groups, that has decided me to choose as my subject for this talk, History and the Changing Cultures of Nigeria.

Nigeria is composed of a large number of peoples. I am not sure that there is yet agreement on just how many ethnic groups there are in the country. Whatever the number, the culture-groups would be even more, for there are culture groups within certain ethnic groups. The cultural diversity evident in the county is often one of the reasons advanced for our inability to unite and to function effectively as one nation. Also, cultural differences are sometimes used as an index of development, "civilisation" and progress. Thus, to take one obvious example, monarchical systems are seen as advanced; non-monarchical systems as backward. If "Advanced" and "Backward" referred just to the political systems described, perhaps one could defend the categorisation. Often, however, the description by implication also refers to the people who live under the systems. At that level the categorisation becomes, in my judgement, objectionable and productive of strife. Objectionable because the point at which the categorisation is made is usually hundreds of years removed from the point at which one group developed its monarchical institutions, and the other group did not. In the time span between that time and now, the peoples who live under the respective political systems have been subjected to varying or even identical or similar historical processes. To categorise them as "advanced" or "backward" is clearly inadequate.

Nor is that all. One of the greatest problems we face in our country is that of inadequate knowledge of the history and the ways of life of the various groups or peoples that make up Nigeria. Unable or unwilling to acquire such knowledge, we are content to make do with what Professor C.C. Ifemesia has described as "blatant misconceptions and alienating stereotypes."[1] Thus to many of us in the southern parts of Nigeria, the Hausa-Fulani is "gambari", by which we mean a fool, the Yoruba is tricky and untrustworthy; the Igbo is aggressively grabbing and fiercely ethnic; the Bini is wicked and dangerous; as for the Urhobo, he is "Sobo wayo," a trickster. As I have had cause to say elsewhere, these stereotypes prevent us from knowing the real peoples, make inter-group and even inter-personal relations difficult and so retard national development and the nation-building process.[2] If we are to rise above these "alienating stereotypes," we need to know the ways of life – the cultures – of the various groups that make up our country. Those cultures are a product of the peoples' history. What is more, culture is a dynamic entity; it is undergoing change nearly all the time – and that change is invariably the result of the historical experiences of the people concerned.

Enough of general comments. Let us proceed more specifically to our subject. In this regard, I wish to begin by going back to the story with which I began this talk. We were meeting in Maiduguri, Borno State. The people of that state are predominantly Kanuri. Without question there is today what can be described as a Kanuri culture. But just what does it mean to speak of a Kanuri culture? Although the debate about the beginnings of the Kanem-Borno empire will continue, the postulate now generally accepted is that the Kanuri are to be seen as an amalgam of peoples, some of whom were agriculturists others pastoral. It was not easy for the earliest rulers to forge a kingdom out of this amalgam of peoples. The early rulers had in fact to deliberately devise various ways of getting their people to accept the idea of belonging together. The deliberate cultivation of the idea of a divine kingship was one such devise. The arrangement whereby the Magumi ruling clan married only non-Magumi women for a period of time was another. There were other devises adopted in the task of building the Kanem kingdom. Clearly, the emerging Kanuri culture was being influenced by its history.

It is not intended to take you through the entire history of Kanem-Borno to prove the point made above. But it is necessary to draw attention to certain other important aspects of the history of that state that cannot but have left their mark on Kanuri culture. The coming of Islam into Kanem-Borno and her involvement with North Africa and the holy lands of Islam had a lasting impact on the emerging culture. Thus the building of mosques, the introduction and consolidation of Islamic law and jurisprudence, the place of the Mais and, after them, the Shehus of Borno in the social life of the people – all of these became important ingredients in the culture of the Kanuri and other peoples of the state. Similarly, the military reforms of Idris Aloma and of Muhammad al – Kanemi, have left a permanent mark on the social life of the people. The coming to the fore of Al-Kanemi's Shuwa supporters must also have led to an increasing Shuwa-risation of the Kanuri culture.[4] When Shetima Ali Munguno talked about the culture of the area, I wondered whether he was aware that the culture of which he was evidently so proud was indeed the end result of centuries of adaptation and borrowings; that the architectural styles of his people, for example, had been influenced not only by the environment but by contacts with North Africa and Arabia; that the dress style was similarly the product of environment and contacts with neighbours and other external agencies; that his and his peoples' attitude to women, for example, was a product of the Islamic religion, which religion is as foreign to Borno as Christianity is to Calabar and the rest of the old Southern Nigeria; that if his people had a dress style reminiscent of the Arabs, other peoples of Nigeria had the right to adopt dress styles that reflect their differing historical experiences. I wonder whether when as so often happens, we speak disparagingly of the cultures of other Nigerian groups, we bother to remind ourselves that the way of life of a people is the product of its total experience, the product of its history.

Let us move from Borno to Hausa-land. Whatever the origin of those who became known as Hausa, available evidence indicates that the emergence of the various Hausa states was assisted by migrations from areas outside these states. These migrations played an important role in the emergence of the Hausa *birni*, and the rise of certain dynasties, such as those of Kano and Zazzau. And it was the rise of the *birni* and the emergence of dynasties that led to the emergence of a distinct class of office holders, the *masu sarauta*. The *sarkin kasa* (king of the country, the title of the ruler of the Hausa *birni*) was himself a product of the activities of a mixed group of peoples who eventually evolved to be known as the Hausa. The culture of the Hausa *birni* was remarkably different from that of the Hausa *kauye* or hamlet.

Mahdi Adamu, himself a product of the Hausa in diaspora, has written: "throughout history, the Hausa ethnic unit has shown itself as an assimilating ethnic entity and the Hausa language a colonising one to the extent that many people who were not originally Hausa and did not use the Hausa language as their first language later became Hausa through assimilation."[7] He goes on to say that no non-Hausa language has survived within the boundaries of Hausaland and that "the extent of Hausanisation in the Northern part of Nigeria is...threatening the continued existence of many minor languages in the region."[8] In the context of my subject, a number of issues arise from Adamu's assertions and arguments. One, if the Hausa ethnic unit is an assimilating entity, that must mean that Hausa culture has borrowed some cultural traits from those assimilated, though Adamu does not consider this possibility. Adamu is from the Hausa state of Yawuri. This state is located in an area outside the original area of Hausaland, in what Adamu describes as Kabershen Bauchi, in what is known as the 'Middle Belt" zone of Nigeria. The first Hausa ruler of Yawuri established himself in the 14tth century. Adamu says that this was the result of "a small group of Hausa traders from the former kingdom of Katsina" settling "in the River Niger valley and gradually [establishing] their political rule over the Gangawa island dwellers." If this indeed is what happened, it is difficult to conceive of this 'small group of Hausa" not only imposing their language but also their entire culture. The chances are that the culture of the people of the area would have greatly influenced the Hausa culture, and that the resultant culture would reflect this admixing. Put differently, the point being made is that Adamu's claims for the assimilating capacity of the Hausa must be placed in a proper historical perspective, for it is history alone that holds the key to that capacity.

Two, when Adamu describes the Hausa language as "a colonising one' he should have proceeded to discuss the historical processes that have made it so, not write as if certain intrinsic elements in the Hausa language make it 'a colonising one'. For Adamu himself shows in the second chapter of the same work that there was considerable contact between the Hausa states and the people of the Middle Belt in the 16th and 17th centuries, especially in the realm of inter-state and inter-group trade and wars. This was the situation which led to the rise of Hausa dynasties in Yawuri and Kumbashi and to the settlement of Hausa populations in the same areas.[10] Secondly, the Sokoto jihad of the 19th century saw a great extension of Hausa influence to areas which had up to that time been free of such influence. Thirdly, when the British imposed their rule on the former "Northern Nigeria," a great effort was made by them to extend the emirate type of organisation to the Middle Belt region.[11] With this went the Hausa language which increasingly became the lingua franca of Northern Nigeria. So, if the Hausa language emerged as "a colonising one", it did so within a certain historical context. Any discussion of the matter outside this historical context is thus both inadequate and unsatisfactory. The essential role of history in cultural development, with particular reference to language, becomes even clearer when we examine developments that have taken, and are taking, place with the creation of states. The former middle belt area was virtually helpless in terms of the promotion of its own languages when it was part of the Northern Region. The creation of states has seen marked attention being paid to the languages of these areas. With time Hausa may well become of much less significance in these areas.

As with Borno so with Hausaland, Islam has been a major influence on Hausa culture. If we may quote Adamu again, "The traditional Hausa way of life and Islamic social values have been inter-mixed for such a long time that many of the basic tenets of Hausa society are Islamic. How far back in time this has been so cannot be said, though it has been so for centuries."[12] The coming of Islam into Hausaland has not yet been firmly dated. The present state of knowledge would suggest a date between the reign of Sarkin Kano Yayi (1349-1385) and Sarkin Kano Rumfa (1463-1499). Both S.A. Balogun and Peter Clarke[13] are inclined to prefer a mid 14th century date for the initial coming of Islam into Hausaland in Kano. Writes Clarke, "Prior to the second half of the 15th century Islam made very little progress in Kano. Indeed there is some indication that Muslims may have met with a considerable amount of opposition from the adherents of the traditional religions, and that there was great relenctuance on the part of the local people to support or recognise the authority of a Muslim ruler."[14] What this means is that it was not till the 15th century that Islam began to secure a strong footing in Hausaland. This would further mean, it seems to me, that it was even later before Islam would have made the kind of impact on Hausa culture about which Mahdi Adamu speaks in the passage quoted.

Let us, for the sake of argument, say that Islam began to affect Hausa culture in a significant manner as from the 16th century. That impact was still not as total as Adamu indicates by the end of the 18th century, for there can be no doubt that the conflict between Uthman Da Fodio and the Sarkin Gobir was cultural as it was religious. In other words, Hausa culture was undergoing change over a period of some three to four centuries. The culture about which Adamu writes is thus the product of the history of Hausaland over those centuries. That culture was to be further consolidated in the 20th century as a result of British attitude to the emirates that had constituted the Sokoto caliphate.[15] I wonder, however, whether the fact that Hausa culture is a mixture of indigenous and foreign elements is remembered by many of those who speak so proudly of the culture of the "Muslim North'.

From what has been said in the preceding paragraphs, it is clear that by the 1480s Islam was still finding its feet in Hausaland. By about that time, European traders were beginning to arrive in certain parts of Nigeria's coastal states. And European commerce and cultural influences were to remain in these areas from that time. Just as the Sokoto Jihad intensified and crystallized the nature of the Islamic impact on parts of the old 'Northern Nigeria," so did missionary activity in the 19th century deepen the impact of European, and especially British, cultural traits on the peoples of certain areas of Southern Nigeria. Hence the dress styles of the Efik, for example, hence the bowler hats which are a feature of funeral rites among some Ijọ. Hence the fact that the Delta States and Calabar imported pre-fabricated European-style houses which have left a permanent mark on the architecture of these parts. To speak of such cultural adaptations as if they represent a low level of development and yet glorify other and similar adaptations is, in my judgement, indefensible. For the issue here is not that of superior of inferior cultures. The issue is that of understanding how a people have come to live the way they do and so to learn to co-exist with such a people in a new nation-state.

Mahdi Adamu also discusses the issue of dress. He draws attention to the major differences between the forest dwellers and the savannah dwellers. "In the forest zone, the untailored rectangular one-piece garment characterised the traditional costume, while the tailored style was characteristic of the traditional dress of the savanna people.[16] Adamu then points out that while the sartorial tastes of the forest zone people have undergone considerable change due to commercial and cultural contacts both with Europeans and with the savanna belt, the savanna people have, by and large, retained their mode of dress. Hausa dress, in particular, he argues, has enjoyed wide publicity and circulation. We do not yet know just when the savanna people began to tailor their clothes rather than wrap themselves with the rectangular one-piece garment. The role of history in the culture change to which Adamu draws attention is, however, obvious. Note, for example, that Yoruba dress (especially for the male) is closer to Hausa dress than that of the Bini, Ijọ, Urhobo, Efik, Ibibio and Igbo. Yoruba dress may well have developed in situ; but it could also have been influenced by Hausa dress style as a consequence of centuries of commercial contact. On the other hand, there is a certain sameness (despite stylistic tailoring differences) in what is today regarded as the traditional dress of the delta peoples. This is clearly a product of their history – the kind of clothes that they bought from the Europeans as from the 16th century.

It is perhaps in this area of dress that our history has its greatest impact on us, even though we may not realise it. The wearing of trousers, shirts, ties and coats as well as frocks, to which some may take objection, is easy enough to explain. Observe, however, that many Igbo now wear flowing robes of the Hausa or Yoruba type; that here in Calabar one sees the Yoruba *iro* and *buba* in lace and other materials worn by Efik ladies; that the delta wrapper, blouse and head tie to match are worn by Efik, Yoruba, Igbo and occasionally even Hausa women; that many more men wear the Hausa and Yoruba style clothes than was the case, say at the beginning of the twentieth century. All of these examples are pointers to the fact that our closer interaction within the new Nigerian nation-state has been influencing us in the area of dress. In the heats and differences of national politics, some question the wisdom of the amalgamation of 1914 and wonder whether salvation may not be found in some degree of falling apart. Yet, imperceptibility and indeed inexorably, cultural adaptations and fusion are going on all the time, because we live and work under the aegis of a single nation-state. Our history draws us together despite ourselves. A Nigerian culture may not yet have emerged; strands of it appear to me to be visible in the areas of dress, of food, of law, and so on. And the very heterogeneity which poses such a problem and challenge in our political life cannot but enrich our national culture when that eventually emerges.

My discussion of dress has taken me slightly off my discussion of the Hausa-Fulani as a group. What I have been seeking to demonstrate is how the history of Borno and the Hausa states has affected their culture, their way of life. I cannot conclude that aspect of my talk without drawing attention to the central place of the Sokoto jihad. It was that revolution which made Hausa-Fulani society decidedly Islamic in culture. It is that revolution which makes the Hausa-Fulani so proud of his culture, of his religion, of his law, as witness the big debate about Sharia law during the writing of our present constitution. As a member of the Judicial Sub-Committee of the Constitution Drafting Committee, I was able, because of my awareness of the history of that part of the country, to enter into the thoughts of my colleagues from that part, though I also had my reservation about certain positions they took. Whatever the virtues of Hausa- Fulani culture as the jihad made it, it is true that that culture did become a problem in terms of the political evolution of Nigeria, in a situation in which Britain, not an Arab country, colonised us. Islamic education which Adamu says "was and still is almost universally compulsory for all Hausa children from Muslim homes,[17] may have prepared the Hausa children to be good Muslims. It certainly did not prepare the bulk of them to take jobs in the colonial civil service, in the business houses, in the banks and so on. It was, in retrospect, a great pity that the British did not see fit to broaden the scope of Muslim education so that its products were also exposed to aspects of Western European education needed in the colonial situation. For it must be clear, from what had happened elsewhere like Egypt and the other Arab countries, that Muslim education need not be to the exclusion of all other types of education. Unfortunately for us, that was how it was for the clear majority of the Hausa-Fulani, out of some misdirected concept of Islam and Islamic culture. The results of the educational backwardness of that part of the country, which backwardness is still being redressed today, (circa. 1977) are still very much with us, and were an important ingredient in the political imbroglio which produced our civil war. Such can be the impact of history on culture and of culture on political stability.

If I have dwelt at some length on the impact of history on the cultural development of the peoples of Borno and the Hausa state, it is because I believe that sometimes those peoples believe that Allah produced their culture, forgetful that they knew nothing about Allah before the 14th century. Pride in one's culture is certainly an attribute that should be cultivated, for culture helps to identify a people. We must, however, distinguish between pride in one's culture and cultural arrogance. I fear that often this distinction is not made. And cultural

> arrogance is not a monopoly of the peoples about whom I have spoken thus far. We find it all over the country, especially among those Nigerian peoples who developed monarchical institutions.

Let us take the Yoruba. These are probably Nigeria's most urbanized people. They lived in large towns and cities. They possess many kingdoms, the courts of which are centres of elaborate rituals. They have elaborate dances, songs and drums – the Yoruba talking drum being world famous, even though other Nigerian groups also had a system of talking – sending messages – with their drums. Today Yoruba poetry has found a new lease of life since *ewi* began to feature on radio. One historian has claimed that "qualitatively if not quantitively the Yoruba have produced the greatest number of works of art in Africa, south of the Sahara."[18] There is a great deal in Yoruba culture that they and indeed all of us Nigerians can be justly proud of. But there can be no doubting the role of history in bringing about this rich culture. As already indicated the Yoruba developed into a number of kingdoms, except in the north-east where a different culture developed. The emergence of kingdoms is determined by a number of factors – the environment, the economy, the challenges to which a people are subjected, especially in terms of relations with surrounding peoples, etc. Unfortunately, we do not really know enough about the evolution of the various Yoruba kingdoms to engage in a detailed discussion of this aspect of their history. But once established, the courts of Yoruba rulers became the centres of Yoruba civilisation.[19] The respect and near veneration accorded to Kabiyesi were important ingredients of their civilisation. I know of no other Nigerian group that exhibits its respect for their ruler and indeed for all elders quite so demonstrably. The court was also the centre of the rituals and art of Yorubaland. As the Oba of Benin recently pointed out, the craftsmen who produced the famous Benin bronzes and other works of art did not see themselves as artists. They were serving their monarch; recording important events through brass casting, wood carving, and so on.[20] In other words, in an age when there was no writing, no photographing, sculptors and brass casters helped to record events and incidents. Today the Bini carry the photograph of the deceased and dance round the city as part of their funeral rites. In earlier days they probably carried a carved figure of the dead. What is true for Benin may well have been true for the Yoruba. To that extent, the traditional sculptor, etc., cannot be such a key figure unless deliberate efforts are made to keep the craftsmanship alive. Our history – and its attendant technological developments – thus continues to affect our cultural life.

Like other Nigerian groups, the Yoruba must also have borrowed various cultural traits. Ade Obayemi has drawn attention to the influence of the kingdoms of Igala and Nupe on the political and other cultures of surrounding peoples, especially the north-east Yoruba and the Igbira.[21] This would suggest that before these influence, the culture of the groups concerned was different in detail. The coming of Igala and Nupe influence resulted in changes in certain aspects of the culture of the peoples of north east Yorubaland. This is what I mean by culture being a dynamic entity. Even Oyo regarded by some as the greatest (whatever that means) of the forest kingdoms is said to have borrowed some of its masquerades from Nupe. Writes Obayemi, "Also, some Nupe masquerades were said to have been copied by the Yoruba of Oyo during the reign of the Alafin Ofinran – in the seventeenth century. The Alapini, one of the Oyo Mesi, echoes the Nupe title Lakpene.[22] This need not surprise anyone; for Oyo and Nupe land had centuries of commercial and social contact. Mutual culture borrowings would thus easily have been part of the history of both groups.

Within the Yoruba geographical area itself, the 19th century wars led to a great mixing of the Oyo Yoruba with other Yoruba groups, so much so that it has been argued that there are probably now no Yoruba group that can be described as "pure". Mixing of peoples would also have led to a mixing of cultural traits as between the different Yoruba groups.[23] The same century saw the coming of Christian missionaries and the beginning of Western European education, both of which factors have left a major mark on the Yoruba of the 20th century.[24] The main features of Yoruba culture have certainly survived, but there can be no doubt at all that a certain blending, a certain accommodation of old and new, have taken place. Thus both Muslims and Christians in Yorubaland have had to use certain traditional titles in their respective faiths. Anyone who has attended the naming ceremony of a Christians Yoruba family cannot but be impressed by the blend between the Yoruba and the Christian. Thus a Christian priest performs the naming ceremony. But the ingredients used – kola nuts, palm oil, and honey, salt etc. – are taken over from the pre-Christian Yoruba traditions. And at the end of the ceremony it is not palm wine that is served, not even *eko*, but bread and tea!

If we turn our attention now to the Igbo, we will find a similar development. First, the nature of their political and social organisation is clearly the product of their history. But what is more, that organisation has a marked effect on the socio-political culture of the Igbo. For the bulk of the Igbo, the most active and functional socio-political unit is the village. If one may be permitted to generalise, it can be said that the *Okpara-Uku*, the oldest man in the village or of a particular lineage within the village, is the head of the village. Although the *Okpara-Uku* is given due respect, he is not necessarily the most influential or active person in the social and political life of the village. The most influential are those, usually younger, who have proved themselves in different fields – war in the times of old, farming, smithing, divining, trade, oratory, combined with a deep knowledge of the law and customs of the people. Given a socio-political system in which all male adults theoretically have a say in government, those who command respect and attention are those who have achieved success in one field or the other. Hence competition that produces that success is an accepted way of life among the Igbo. For the Igbo it is a matter of pride to be able to say that he has made his mark in his village, as it is for the Yoruba, the Hausa-Fulani, the Bini, the Itsẹkiri or the Ijọ of the eastern delta to be able to claim that he is from the royal family or heir of a particular chieftaincy. The Igbo predilection for competition, his urge to achieve success is thus the product of the history of his people. Seen outside the cultural setting, however, we, non-Igbo, have tended to accuse the Igbo of vaulting ambition and a tendency to grab. In so judging the Igbo out of context, we commit a major injustice against a whole people.

But Igbo socio-political institutions have not been developed in isolation. What Professor A.E. Afigbo has described as presidential monarchies[25] among the Aboh, Asaba, Onitsha, etc, are the product of the historical contacts between these Igbo and the kingdoms of Benin and Igala. Similarly, the Igbo of the Nsukka area had rather close relations with the Igala kingdom, to which they gave some of their cultural traits and from which they borrowed certain titles, drums, masquerades and so on. The importance of the horse in these parts obviously also owes something to the ties with Igala.[26]

The Igbo title system is surely a product of its history. But there can be little doubt that the great increase in the number of "chiefs" – title holders – in Igboland today is partly owed to the larger history of Nigeria. Following the amalgamation of 1914, Lugard did attempt to "create chiefs' in those parts of Nigeria which had no emirs, obas, olu, obis etc. Igboland was easily the largest area with none of these monarchical structures. Unfortunately, the British and some Nigerians after them, tended to equate the presence of a "king" with civilisation and progress. So there was a tendency for groups to find or create chiefs. The Tiv who ar̩e just as fragmented as the Igbo ended in 1945 with a Tor Tiv, a paramount chief for all the Tiv, because it was believed that this would enhance their standing with the British. Igboland did not react in so radical a manner. But I believe they have reacted somewhat. The fact that in the early 1950s the North and West had each a House of Chiefs while the East did not, led to an agitation for such a House. When a House of Chiefs was granted to the East, there was a noticeable increase in the number of persons who became chiefs in their various communities. Since in origin, title-taking was linked with leadership and success in one field or the other, those who aspire to political leadership in our modern system now find the means to take a title. And so the number of chiefs sours year by year. Unfortunately, as happens when such prostitution takes place, it is not always that good character, an important consideration in yester years, is insisted upon. This in itself is another product of history! For how is the character of an Igbo of Awka who has spent most of his life in Kano to be assessed by those in Awka who decide that he can take a title? But, to return to my subject, the point being made is how history has continued over the years to affect culture and cultural adaptations.

Were I to bring this talk to a close at this point, I believe I would have made my point. But I would be guilty of focusing only on Nigeria's dominant and dominating groups. Being a minority person myself, that would be an unforgivable crime against the smaller groups. Besides, I am in Efikland which, in the inimitable words of your former Vice-Chancellor, is "an atomistic society." So I must, however briefly, touch on some of these smaller groups.

The work of Professor E.J. Alagoa[27] has shown how the history of the Ijọ of the eastern delta has affected the political culture. The transformation of the *Amaokosowei* (the village elder) of the central delta to the *Amayanabo* of the delta city state; the increased powers which the head of the Ijọ House had, as compared with the lineage head of the Ijọ of the central delta; the fact that the House of the eastern delta state like the lineage of the Efik came to include slaves, some of whom played a crucial role in the socio-political as well as the economic life of the states – all of these were the result of the history of the Ijọ after their migration to the eastern delta. The new culture required the head of a house to demonstrate his fitness for his role by feasting the *Amanyambo* and other house heads and by laying on certain dances and masquerades. The regattas for which the delta states have become famous were obviously affected by Ijọ contact with the Europeans from whom they obtained the decorations. The bilingualism of some of these states is traceable to their commercial contact with the Igbo hinterland as well as to the large numbers of Igbo slaves who became acculturated subjects of these states in the days of the slave trade and following the suppression of the overseas slave trade in the 19th century. Attention had earlier been drawn to dress and the kinds of houses the well-to-do put up. To that we may add the taste for Gin and Schnapps!

As for the Efik of Calabar, I fear to speak about them when there are so many persons here present better qualified than myself to do so. And yet not to speak would be worse. The debate about Efik origins and migration continues among scholars in that field. However, the link between the Efik and the Ibibio is now generally accepted. Although there are differences of detail, your own Dr. Monday Efiong Noah, agrees that Efik social and political institutions have been greatly influenced by Ibibio institutions.[28] Consequently, Efik culture has borrowed quite a bit from Ibibio culture, though of course, it has also built up part of that culture from its locale.

If the Efik began with institutions rather similar to these of the Ibibio, their history diverged from Ibibio history after they settled along the estuary of the Cross River. But let me not take coal to Newcastle by going into any prolonged discourse here. We know that the transformation of the position of the Obong from that of a *primus inter pares* almost like the Igbo village council head, to that of an effective ruler, and the other changes which went with that transformation were a product of Efik trade with the Europeans.[29] It has been claimed by Latham that the ndem Efik, the water goddess that was a major deity for the Efik, ceased to be that crucial as the slave trade made fishing a less major occupation, and that the priest enjoyed less regard as a consequence.[30]

We know about the impact of slave holding on the Efik lineage and on the rise of a number of splinter lineages which, while recognising their origins, acted rather independently in matters of trade. The Ekpe Society, one of the most distinctive institutions of the Efik, did not owe its origin to the challenge of the European trade, but its role in society, especially that of debt collecting and imposing general control on the people, was crucially affected by the problems arising from Efik trade with the Europeans. Efik society by the 19th century was thus different in important ways from what it had been earlier. Efik culture had to respond to changing times; to its history.

European commerce over some four centuries could not but leave its mark. Go to the centre of the town of Calabar and look at a memorial in honour of one of the obongs. His dress is clear testimony to the impact of European contact on Efik culture. That contact also explains the fact that certain Efik rulers and traders acquired some kind of English and actually kept dairies even before schools were formally established. Recall the coming of Hope Waddell and Mary Slessor and the eventual doing away with twin murder, Order of the Bloodmen, and the eventual stoppage of burying slaves alive with prominent men on the latter's death. Observe the Efik woman's preference for the frock whatever her vital statistics. In many ways, Efik culture has been responding to its history, changing in reaction to the needs of the time.

Mr Chariman, fellow students of History, Distinguished Ladies and Gentlemen, while I may have succeeded in boring you, I am fully aware I have said nothing new! Given my subject, I can perhaps say nothing new. So why did I choose it, and what is my message? My message is simple. That the culture of a people is a product of that people's history; that it is always changing and adapting itself to new circumstances brought about by the history of the people. That consequently a knowledge of the history of the people concerned is crucial to an understanding of their culture as it is today. That the absence of such knowledge can lead to what Professor Ifemesia described as "blatant misconceptions and alienating stereotypes," and that these stereotypes constitute a drag on national integration, and so retard national development. I am saying, in other words, that although when culture is being discussed, we seem to think of dances and masquerades, of drama and regattas, the term has a much broader meaning and this broader meaning cannot be fathomed in full except within the context of history. It thus becomes our duty as practitioners of history to ply our craft in such a manner that the relevance of history for the culture of our multifarious peoples becomes obvious. Not to do so would, in my judgement, constitute a major crime against our discipline of history and the state which funds education. In relating History to cultural development of our peoples, we help to deepen understanding, and hope that greater understanding would lead to less cultural arrogance and a greater readiness to live and work together, despite cultural differences, experiences and circumstances over the years.

NOTES

1. Chieka Ifemesia, "The Role of History in Nation Building. The Nigerian Experience" – Lecture delivered at Ahmadu Bello University, Zaria, at the Launching of the Students' Historical Society of Nigeria, Saturday 28, March, 1983, mimeographed, p. 29.
2. Obaro Ikime, "History for the Development of Nigeria" – Lecture delivered on 24 May, 1982 at the formal opening of the History week of the Students' Historical Society of Nigeria, University of Benin Branch.
3. See H.F.C. Smith, "The Early States of the Central Sudan", in J.F. Ade Ajayi and Michael Crowder (Editors) – *History of West Africa* Vol. 1, London, Longman Group, 1971.
4. See R.A. Adeleye, "Hausaland and Borno", in Ajayi and Crowder, *op. cit.*, and J.E. Lavers, "Kanem and Borno to 1880", in Obaro Ikime, (Editor), *Groundwork of Nigerian History,* Historical Society of Nigeria and Heinemann, 1980.
5. See footnote 3 above.
6. Mahdi Adamu, *The Hausa Factor in West African History*, Ahmadu Bello University Press, and O.U.P. Nigeria, 1978, p. 5.
7. Adamu, *op. cit,* p. 2.
8. Adamu, p. 3.
9. Adamu, p. 33.
10. Adamu *op. cit,* Chapter 2.
11. For details see Sa'ad Abubakar, "The Northern Provinces Under Colonial Rule", 1980 – 1959" in Obaro Ikime (Editor) Groundwork of Nigerian History.
12. Adamu, p. 9.
13. S.A. Balogun, "History of Islam up to 1800", in *Groundwork of Nigerian History*, and Peter B. Clarke, *West Africa and Islam*, Edward Arnold, London, 1982.
14. Clarke, *op. cit.*, p. 61.

15. See footnote 11 above for details about this aspect of British colonial rule.
16. Adamu, p. 8.
17. Adamu, p. 9.
18. Adu Boahen, *Topics in West African History*, Longman Group, London, 1966, p. 92.
19. See I.A. Akinjogbin and E.A. Ayandele, "Yorubaland up to 1800" in *Groundwork of Nigerian History.*
20. Address by His Highness Oba of Benin on the occasion of the formal opening of the Exhibition on Lost Treasures of Benin, 26 April, 1982, (Mimeograph).
21. See Ade Obayemi "States and Peoples of the Niger-Benue Confluence Area" in *Groundwork of Nigerian History.*
22. Ade Obayemi, loc. cit, p. 163.
23. See J.F. Ade Ajayi and S.A. Akintoye, Yorubaland in the Nineteenth Century" in *Groundwork of Nigerian History.*
24. For details see J.F. Ade Ajayi, *Christian Missions in Nigeria 1841-1891,* Longman, 1985.
25. A.E. Afigbo, "The Traditional Igbo System of Government" in *Tarikh* 1970.
26. P.A. Oguagha has just successfully completed a Ph.D. Thesis for the University of Ibadan on Igbo-Igala Relations.
27. E.J. Alagoa, "The Development of Institutions in the States of the Eastern Niger Delta" *Journal of African History*, Vol. 12, No. 2, 1971, and "Peoples of the Cross River Valley and the Eastern Niger Delta" in *Groundwork of Nigerian History.*
28. Monday Effiong Noah, *Old Calabar: The City States and the Europeans 1800-1885* Scholars Press, (Nig.) Ltd., Uyo, 1980.
29. See A.J. Latham, *Old Calabar 1600-1891: The Impact of International Economy Upon a Traditional Society*, Clarendon Press, 1973.
30. Latham *op. cit,* Chapter 2.

2

THROUGH CHANGING SCENES: NIGERIAN HISTORY YESTERDAY TODAY AND TOMORROW*

Given the Ibadan system of multiple chairs, in which one's professorship is not tied to any specialty within the broad discipline to which one belongs, it is not immediately obvious what the subject of one's inaugural lecture should be. Were I still the Head of the History Department, and therefore occupying the one established Chair of History in this university, I may well have felt obliged to engage in a detailed review of the work of the department, as well as the department's role in the promotion of historical scholarship in the country. Indeed, given the tendency on the part of certain other History Departments in the country, as well as some individuals outside the discipline, to run down and belittle what I consider major achievements by the Ibadan History Department, there is an urgent need for such a review. Even so, however, I have resisted the temptation to make that kind of review the main burden of this lecture. Instead, I have opted to speak on the subject: "*Through Changing Scenes: Nigerian History Yesterday, Today and Tomorrow.*" This subject may create the impression that I am about to deliver a lecture on the state of the discipline as this applies to Nigerian History. Let me hasten to confess that I do not feel competent, as of

* This was my inaugural lecture as Professor of History, University of Ibadan on 26 October, 1979.

this time, to engage in such a wide-ranging exercise. I intend to limit myself largely, though not exclusively, to the area of Nigeria's political history, the area in which I like to think I have made a little contribution to the emergent Nigerian historiography. Another limitation, which some will no doubt be able to pin-point in what follows, is that I base my discussion exclusively on the works of Nigerian historians, the bulk of whom are from the Ibadan History Department. I offer no apologies for this latter limitation, for my intention is to look at the work which Nigerian historians have done on the history of their own country, within the context of my chosen subject.

I have indicated that I intend, for the most part, to engage in an examination of the work that has been done on Nigeria's political history. To do this in 1979 is to expose myself to scathing criticism in an age in which the cry is for work on Nigeria's social and economic history. Admittedly, no one has said, "Enough of political history; over now to social and economic history". But it is clear that the feeling is that there is a surfeit of political history and a dearth of social and economic history. For too long, my friend and colleague, Professor Adiele Afigbo, said in a public lecture delivered here at Ibadan in 1976, the new African historiography remained a study of political history to the neglect of social history.[1] The current President of the Historical Society of Nigeria, Professor J. F. Ade Ajayi, has repeatedly reminded us of this negligence in his presidential addresses these last few years. No one would want to question the wisdom and intrinsic value of the call for work on our social and economic history, though I confess I am not always sure that the implied compartmentalisation always makes sense as between, for example, political and social history. Nor do I accept the impression sometimes created that work on social and economic history is of a higher order than work on political history, ancient or more recent. What I do intend to demonstrate, is that whatever work has been done in the area of the political history of Nigeria, the problems of today, and by implication, tomorrow, require that more work, albeit of a markedly different nature from what now exists, be urgently undertaken.

Nigerian History Yesterday

One should perhaps preface any discussion of Nigerian History Yesterday with a tribute to all who in different ways and in different scripts 'wrote' our history long before our academic historians came on the scene. The fact that their contributions are not treated in this lecture should not detract from their extremely valuable role in the development of Nigerian historiography.

The writing of Nigerian history by Nigerian academics began in 1950 with K. Onwuka Dike's Ph.D. thesis, *Trade and Politics in the Niger Delta*, published as a book in 1956. In 1957, S.O. Biobaku's *The Egba and Their Neighbours 1842-1872*, also the revised version of his 1951 Ph.D. thesis, was published. The late J.C. Anene; J. F. Ade Ajayi, A.B. Aderibigbe and C.C. Ifemesia followed with M.A. and Ph.D. theses in 1952, 1958 and 1959 respectively. These scholars, despite the variety of the subjects about which they wrote, constitute Nigeria's first generation of academic historians. All of them produced their first major works in the 1950s, at a time when Nigeria was struggling to regain her independence. Naturally, their work was influenced by the political and ideological ferment of the age in which they wrote. Yet it is interesting to note that not one of these scholars engaged in any markedly declamatory kind of history. The approach was more subtle.

As Professor Afigbo has reminded us, colonial rule in Africa was based, apart from straight military conquest, on an "ideological brainwashing [which denied] that the African, especially the Negro African, had a valid past and an autonomous culture."[2] Our first generation of scholar-historians took up the challenge of that denial. Dike and Biobaku, working on the history of different parts of Nigeria, began the process of reinterpreting Nigerian history by bringing Nigeria and Nigerians into their own history! Admittedly, latter day Nigerian scholars have pointed out various weaknesses in the work of these two pioneer scholars. Yet no one can deny that a distinguishing hallmark of their work is the quality of the internal history of the Nigerian peoples which constitute the subjects of these works. It is this internal history of Bonny or the Egba which provides the evidence of how the African in the Nigerian geographical area and, by extension, elsewhere on the continent, ordered his social and political life; what economic activities supported the socio-political edifice, and how the creative and adaptive genius of the African enabled him to find answers to the challenges of his environment and of his age. These works thus sought to demonstrate that the African had "a valid past, an autonomous culture".

You will forgive me if, for consideration of time, I do not dwell in detail on the achievements of these pioneer historians in terms of the role they played in identifying and using new sources for writing African history, or in terms of the establishment of archives and museums.[3] It was largely as a consequence of their work and that of the others listed that African history became accepted as a worthy branch of the discipline of history, fit to be taught to the human species, black, yellow, white or pink. That was no mean achievement.

If one is searching for more direct evidence of the commitment of this first generation of scholars to the promotion of the identity of the African and of his creative genius, one can find it in some of J. F. Ade Ajayi's work. In this regard, it is interesting, that it is in his seemingly insignificant pamphlet, *Milestones in Nigerian History* (I.U.P., 1962), rather than in his *Christian Missions in Nigeria* (Longman, 1966) that this commitment is best seen. This pamphlet, the published version of four talks broadcast on the eve of our independence, provides, to my mind, an excellent example of the historian's role in his society. I will comment on just two of the four milestones identified. In his conclusion to the section on the Fulani Jihad, Ajayi wrote, "The new empire must be reckoned as having done more than bring together a large area of Nigeria. In its conception, it had an important contribution to make to the future development of Nigeria in this idea of a cosmopolitan state demanding loyalty to something outside parochial loyalties."[4] Similarly, in his discussion of the age of Ajayi Crowther, Ajayi tells us of the returnee slaves turned missionaries, "consciously acquiring new arts and techniques in the knowledge that such arts and techniques were necessary for the building of a new state. More than that, they were men with new cosmopolitan views that went beyond kith, kin and locality."[5] The pre-occupation with the emerging Nigerian nation-state is unmistakable. The historian was properly plying his craft.

Or take another pamphlet arising also from a series of broadcasts also before independence – *Eminent Nigerians of the Nineteenth Century.*[6] Whether one agrees with the selection or not, it is patent that the aim was to demonstrate that we have our own heroes, our own leaders of thought and movement who, even in the century in which European activity in our country became triumphant, demonstrated a vision, courage, competence and commitment to their independence of which we can be justly proud. Today, scholars have begun to question whether it is right and proper that we should set up as national heroes men and women who built their economic or political empires on slavery and slave trade; or extol political systems that were allegedly tyrannical and undemocratic. Why, it is being asked, do Nigerian historians want to make us believe that such 'tyrants' were great men? Are the historians aware that such adulation of slave traders and 'tyrants' may well explain why we have so many dictatorial regimes on the African continent today?[7] My answer is simple. Let the historian of these 'tyrants' be faithful to his evidence. Let him have the courage to condemn aspects of his subject which he finds damnable. But let him do so in the context of the age in which his subject lived, for as Marc Bloch has warned; "How absurd it is," by elevating the entirely relative criteria of one individual, one party, or one generation to the absolute, to inflict standards upon the way in which Sulla governed Rome, or Richelieu the States of the Most Christian King!"[8]

One more caveat. There is a certain tendency on the part of African scholars to take their cue from Europe and America. We are anxious to be seen by our European and American colleagues as progressives who can identify the evils in our society and boldly condemn the same. How many of the older generation today did not learn about Sir Francis Drake at school? Is it not possible to see him as a common thief and pirate? Yet is he not a national hero in England? How were the empires of the world founded, if not on slave labour or related systems? The great pyramids of Egypt – who built them? Can we truly think of many really great names in history who achieved the heights they did without a streak of tyranny or some other form of exploitation of their fellowmen? How many nations of the world to which we belong have sought, or are seeking, to desecrate the almost sacred memory in which such men and women are held? Yet, here in Nigeria, in some mistaken concept of academic excellence, the call goes forth for the dishonouring of our national heroes. Our historians of the first generation, in setting before us some of these heroes, were properly performing their duty in the context of their age. Given our different circumstances, the historian of today may want to take another look at these heroes. By all means. Let us, however, ensure that our re-examination is not based on a false premise; let us beware lest we respond unconsciously to the new academic imperialism which seeks to use Africans to belittle African achievements.

I do not wish to create the impression that the works of our first generation historians are faultless. Dike's account of Bonny history, for example, reveals the changing patterns of alliances between the

Houses and various British interests as each group sought to promote its commercial interests. These alliances played an important role in weakening Bonny in the face of increasing British encroachments. Indeed they are reminiscent of the activities of today's business tycoons, bureaucrats, intermediaries, etc., who place their personal or group interests above Nigeria, and are prepared to ally with foreign business or diplomatic interests in sabotaging the political economy of their own country. Perhaps in 1956 when Dike's book was published, the parallel was not this obvious. Even so, now looking back, one may have expected Dike to consider the general principle regarding the danger to the state, the larger body politic, of alliances contracted for purely economic interests. Similarly, Biobaku's work on the Egba, while bringing out clearly the confederate nature of Egba political arrangements, does not engage in a general discussion of the political problems of a confederacy. There are, no doubt, other weaknesses.

Ajayi's *Christian Missions in Nigeria 1840-1891: The Making of a New Elite,* like E.A. Ayandele's *The Missionary Impact on Modern Nigeria 1842-1914*[10] are competent works in many regards. They provide us, for example, with the complexities of the background against which various Nigerian peoples decided to accept or reject Christian missionary activity in their midst. They reveal that usually the considerations were either political or economic (or both), not religious. They provide the details of intra-mission politics, details which reveal that the men and women of God were so human as to be racist and unashamedly ambitious. But perhaps even more important for the history of our country, these works give us the background to the development of Western European education in Nigeria. Ajayi's focus, as his sub-title clearly indicates, is the making of a new elite. Yet nowhere in the work does he pointedly discuss the uneven spread of this elite as it began to be made. Abeokuta received missionaries in 1846. Benin did not till after 1897, a whole half century later. The *Dayspring* brought its cargo of missionaries to Onitsha in 1857. The more hinterland parts of Igboland did not receive missionaries till after 1914. The first grammar school in Lagos was founded in 1859. There are parts of this country where there were no grammar schools till a whole century later. These inequalities clearly deserved comment in 1963-64 when Ajayi revised his thesis for publication.

Ajayi's work, focusing as it does on the elite, also discussed the aspirations and frustrations of the emergent elite in its search for meaningful employment in the colonial civil service, in the missions, and in the European-dominated commercial houses. Indeed, it is well known that their frustration in this regard was an important ingredient in the rise of Nigerian nationalism. Ajayi also makes the point that it was this same frustration that drove the elite into studying law and medicine, so they could be independent of the British ruling class. Because educational opportunities were unequal, only certain parts of Nigeria produced these lawyers and doctors during a certain period of our history. Yet the historian of the rise of our new elite did not then stop to ponder the significance of this fact for Nigerian politics and Nigerian History five years after the writing of the book, and three years after its publication, the Igbo and Yoruba elite, the second generation, as it were, of Ajayi's new elite, were engaged in a fierce competition for dominance here at the University of Ibadan, a competition which some insist, played an important role in the chain of events that ended in the civil war of 1967-70.

Similarly, Ayandele, another historian of missionary activity, whose focus was the social and political impact of this activity, fails to make good this weakness in Ajayi's work. In some ways, this oversight in Ayandele's work is the more remarkable because Ayandele pointedly draws attention to the difference in educational development between the north and south. He writes, "The consequences of the prohibition of Christian missions from the larger part of Northern Nigeria are not easy to ascertain. There is no evidence to show that outside the 'pagan' areas, the people would have been willing to receive western education, the aspect of missionary propaganda which hastened the political and social sophistication and 'enlightenment' of Southern Nigeria, and the lack of which accentuated the 'backwardness' of the Northern territory."[11] I wonder why a work revised for publication in 1965 should have failed to 'ascertain' the consequences of the disparity in education between the north and the south! It could not be that Ayandele was afraid to fish in troubled waters, for such fear is not one of his weaknesses. Be that as it may, one year after the publication of this book, Nigeria was engulfed in a civil war, a major remote cause of which was the inequality of political and other opportunities for the different groups which constituted the new nation, an inequality which we owed, for the most part, to unequal educational development. Whatever the original conception of their works, it is my judgement that both Ajayi and Ayandele failed to display sufficient sensitivity to the problems of the Nigeria in which they lived as they revised their theses for publication. Ayandele has since redeemed himself in his *The Educated Elite in the Nigerian Society* (Ibadan University Press, 1974) in which he analysed the role of the elite in Nigerian politics. Nobody would argue that he should have produced two books in one in 1966; but many of the issues which he took up in 1972[12] were apparent in 1965, and the historian's role demanded that he draw attention to them, however tentatively.

Before I move on to the successors of our first generation of historians, let me state that in some ways, my criticism of Dike, Biobaku and perhaps even Ajayi and Ayandele, may be unfair. In levelling criticisms of this sort, we need to remind ourselves about an important aspect of historical scholarship, to wit, the various influences which condition the historian's writing. Wrote Henri Pirenne, "Historians are not conditioned in various ways solely by inherited qualities; their milieu is also important. Their religion, nationality, and social class influence them more or less profoundly. And the same is true of the period in which they work. Each epoch has its needs and tendencies which demand the attention of students and lead them to concentrate on this or that probem."[13] In the works which they published before independence, Dike, Biobaku and Ajayi decidedly reflected the problems of the age. This reflection was sometimes put across in the turn of phrase; sometimes it was the total impact of the work that reflected this awareness of society's pre-occupations. The criticisms of aspects of the work of Ajayi and Ayandele which have just been made appertain to works published after 1960. We must now turn to the corpus of other published works in Nigeria's political history which belongs to the decade 1961-1970.

Time does not permit an examination of all of the works in the category referred to. For the purpose of this lecture, reference will only be made to the works of the late J. C. Anene, T.N. Tamuno, Obaro Ikime, A.E. Afigbo, J.A. Atanda, P.A. Igbafe, all of which works dwell on one aspect or another of British colonial rule in Nigeriaa, as well as the work of R.A. Adeleye entitled *Power and Diplomacy in Northern Nigeria 1804-1906* (Longman London, 1971). In examining these works, we need to bear in mind that they were all written in the 1960s. Nigeria was already independent and grappling with the challenge of nation-building. The perceptive Nigerian historian of Nigeria, working in a newly independent country, ridden with inter-party and inter-ethnic rivalries, as well as a medley of other socio-political problems, would be expected to demonstrate an awareness of these problems, as well as a sensitivity commensurate with the complexity of the situation. For if history is to serve any useful purpose at all, it must deepen man's understanding of why and how things have happened. If we may quote Marc Bloch again, "...a single word 'understanding' is the beacon light of our studies... We are never sufficiently understanding. Whoever differs from us – a foreigner or a political adversary – is almost inevitably considered evil. A little more understanding of people would be necessary... in the conflicts which are unavoidable."[14] It would be instructive to find out to what extent Nigerian historians of Nigeria in the first decade of independence saw their task as that of deepening understanding as between our multifarious peoples.

Let us begin with Adeleye's *Power and Diplomacy in Northern Nigeria*, an excellent work in many ways, on the Sokoto Caliphate. Adeleye provides an in-depth analysis of the background to the Sokoto jihad, its prosecution and the working of the religio-political edifice which it produced. The work is equally useful in its exposition of the relations between the caliphate and the non-Muslim areas of what became Northern Nigeria, as well as the nature and course of Caliphate-British relations from Clapperton's first visit to Sokoto in 1824 to the British conquest of Northern Nigeria in the period 1900-1906. Adeleye does not, however, attempt a discussion of the significance of the Sokoto jihad for the history of Nigeria as a whole. Though implied in some of what Adeleye says, nowhere is the point directly made that the very success of the jihad meant the triumph of Arab cultural and religious imperialism; that from that time on the Sokoto Caliphate adopted more intensively a foreign culture and a foreign religion. Today, because no historian of the Muslim areas of Nigeria cares to make the point, we have tended to treat this Arab religious and cultural imperialism as if it were indigenous to the former Northern Nigeria. The Muslims of the North see themselves as a people who have stuck to their traditions and their culture, while they look upon their southern brothers as having given up their culture and traditions when they accepted Christianity. Thus Sharia, a body of laws based on Islamic precepts, is a matter for pride; British or received law, based on the British legal system, is evidence of imperialistic enslavement! Conversely, the Southerner thinks that because he has accepted Western European education and culture, he is thereby superior to the Muslim Northerner who had to accept an Arab and Islamic culture. Both positions, it must be clear, are equally untenable. Both sides seem to forget that they really had no choice in the matter – it was all a matter of historical accident. They need to understand this if they are not to think of themselves more highly than they ought.

Adeleye tells us in his sub-title that the work is also concerned with a study of the Sokoto Caliphate and its enemies. Its most devastating enemy turned out to be the British who conquered it and imposed their rule on it. By seeking, as they did, to preserve the Arab and Islamic culture of the Muslim North, while at the same time insisting that government and commerce shall increasingly follow a Western European model, the British created a most fertile ground for the tensions, which later developed between the North and South. For as Muslim education was not seen as suitable for a career in the British civil service or the British-dominated mercantile houses, southerners with their Western European education were recruited to serve in these areas in the north. When the same British introduced regionalism into our politics, tension arose over whether or not the southerners were to continue in the Northern civil service. Many today will recall the acrimony that this matter generated in the 1950s. The historians of the jihad and of British imperialism must see these imperialisms in their true and full light including especially, their respective legacies.

It may be argued that Adeleye's terminal date is 1906 and that as of that date none of the issues here raised had arisen. We must grant that. However, Adeleye revised his thesis for publication in 1969 when the civil war was raging. The issues to which attention has been drawn were as of that time issues of contemporary politics. Yet not even in a postscript did he relate his work to these issues. And yet the jihad and its consequences were germane to the differences in attitude, differences in educational systems, and differences in political evolution, all of which were important ingredients in the remote, some would say immediate, causes of the civil war. Adeleye failed, like the rest of us did in our various ways, to pointedly draw attention to how historical accidents can threaten the very being of the body politic. To the extent to which we have failed in this and similar regards, to that extent have we failed to perform one of the major functions of the historian - to deepen understanding.

Let us now turn our attention to those works which concern themselves with Nigeria's colonial period. If we leave out the journal articles, the main works are J.C. Anene's *Southern Nigeria in Transition 1885 – 1906*, Cambridge University Press, (1996), my *Niger-Delta Rivalry* (1969), T.N. Tamuno's *The Evolution of the Nigeria State: The Southern Phase 1898-1914* (1972), A.E. Afigbo's *The Warrant Chiefs* (1972), J.A. *Atanda's The New Oyo Empire (Indirect Rule and Change in Western Nigeria 1894-1934* (1973) and P.A. Igbafe's recently published *Benin under the British* (1979). Two Ibadan Ph.D. theses study British rule in the Kano Emirate, and British rule in Sokoto, Gwandu and Argungu Emirates, respectively. A.I. Asiwaju's *Western Yorubaland under European Rule (1889-1945)* (1976)[15] provides a welcome comparative study of colonial rule, French and British style.

It will take too much time to examine each of these works in detail. I will therefore do no more than make a few comments of general and common applicability to all of the works listed. A cursory look at these works will reveal that each deals with some region, some province or provinces, each of which latter is broken up into divisions and districts. All of us are agreed that this was an innovation introduced by the British. Yet not a single one of us has bothered to discuss the concept of a region, a province, a division or a district. Indeed, it is illuminating that it is Anene, the pioneer historian of Nigeria's colonial period, who makes the most telling comment on the creation of divisions and districts. Wrote Anene with regard to the 1895 administrative arrangements of the Niger Coast Protectorate:

> It should be obvious that the new pattern of administrative control involved the elimination of the separate identity of the traditional coast states, and was in fact the beginning of the artificial division of the territory into administrative units which cut across the traditional groupings of the various communities. It was the first step towards the amalgamation of the many groups in the region to produce a politico-territorial unit called Southern Nigeria.[16]

Commenting on the 1900 arrangements, the same scholar drew attention to "fluctuations in the status of the coast city states" as a consequence of administrative rearrangements. Having drawn our attention to a crucial issue, Anene leaves it at that. No further discussion follows to relate that issue to the problems of the 1960s. Herein lies the weakness of the work in the context of this lecture.

Tamuno sets out to study the evolution of Southern Nigeria in the period 1894-1914. He touches on the amalgamation of 1914. He was, in fact, the first Nigerian scholar to work on this period of Nigerian history. Writing about the administrative arrangements of the period, he says, if "the 1898-1914 amalgamation arrangements ever made Nigeria an 'artificial' British creation, so were the various administrative districts, divisions and provinces which developed arbitrarily". He proceeds to state that these amalgamations "constituted important landmarks in Southern Nigeria's political developments"[17] and leaves it at that. We are not told what were the provinces that emerged in 1914, with a view to indicating their artificiality and the problems that could arise therefrom. Similarly, the importance of the 'landmark' is not discussed. Yet the book went to press in 1970 when these provinces, divisions, districts even regions had undergone major changes. Did these changes not raise fundamental questions of inter-group co-existence in a newly emerging nation? Should not present realities affect the vision of the past?

Still on this matter of administrative arrangements. Afigbo points out that "the town in which a (native) court was located generally tried to treat her neighbours who attended the court as inferior or subordinate to her".[18] What about the town in which the seat of the region or state, province, division or district was or is located? How many of us in this field have cared to study how this attitude of the capital or headquarters people has affected their relations with others, how it has affected politics, commerce, industries, etc?

Perhaps we should take an example from nearer us. Atanda's study of Oyo – Ibadan relations in his *New Oyo Empire* raises this same issue.[19] For most of his period, 1894-1934, Oyo was given an importance completely unrelated to its power even under the Old Oyo empire. As the headquarters of the new Oyo Province, even Ife was made subordinate to it. Ibadan was then of little consequence. The ruler was only a *baale*, upon whose head the Alafin had to place the traditional leaves. In 1934 the tide changed. Ibadan, an Oyo town, was removed from the overlordship of the Alafin by a colonial administrative fiat. Ibadan, a new city by Yoruba standards, grew to become the headquarters of the old Western Region, the former Western State and the present Oyo State. Why the name Oyo State? What has happened to Ife in all of this? Only recently, the Olubadan, already an Oba from being a baale, was given a beaded crown. Had the administrative status of Ibadan anything to do with this development? How have these developments affected the politics of Oyo State? Is the history of yesterday influencing the political decisions of today? Have we dwelt on these things, so we can cause others to dwell on them? Have we written our history in such a way as to deepen understanding of these and related issues?

Igbafe has studied Benin under British rule. What does he see as the significance of a Benin Province which included the Igbo of Agbor and Asaba? Has he or any of us, his colleagues in the field, studied Benin-Igbo relations in this context? Or take the Onitsha Province which constitutes part of Afigbo's area of interest in *The Warrant Chiefs*. What has been the relationship between Onitsha as a town and the other towns in the province? Was it mere co-incidence that not one of the governorship candidates for any of the political parties that contested the recently concluded elections in Anambra State is from Onitsha town? Has the history of yesterday anything to do with this and other decisions of today? Are we writing the kind of history that aids our peoples to better understand these things?

An even more fundamental defect in all of our works is our failure to see that although we are engaged in a study of British colonial rule, that phase is part of the larger history of the Nigerian nation. Preoccupied as we have been with examining British policies, we have failed to identify the larger issues, those issues which remain a major challenge to our nation-building effort. So Ikime, for example, has in his *Niger Delta Rivalry* sought to explain Itsekiri-Urhobo relations in terms of problems arising from British administrative decisions. In a sense this is true. But there are other equally important issues to do with the economic opportunities available to the two groups about which Ikime says nothing. There is the psychological problem of how people react to changing political fortunes. Perhaps even more importantly, Ikime fails to put his fingers on a really fundamental and nagging problem: how do groups so recently separate and independent cope with the administrative innovations and adjustments that must take place when a new nation is born? How does government get to the people and persuade them to give up part of their identity (the issue raised by Anene) in order to partake of the identity of the larger whole? The historian of the colonial period, writing in the post colonial period, when the problems of nation-building are exercising the minds of rulers and challenging the followership, must begin to see these larger issues. He may not be able to offer solutions. He could and should write in a manner that shows his awareness of these larger issues; a manner that can deepen understanding.

I may have created the impression from the foregoing that the works of the 1960s were either timid or short-sighted. Let me hasten to add that that is not my purpose, nor would it be a fair verdict. In many ways the works to which reference has been made are most worthy contributions to Nigeriana both in terms of subject matter and methodology. My point is that whereas the works of the 1950s to which reference has been made, had, and fulfilled, a purpose, our works in the 1960s have not had the same success in that regard. We may have flogged the departed British harder; we certainly did not provide enough food for thought for the succeeding Nigerians. It is as if in the first post-independence decade we ceased to ask ourselves what is the purpose of history. We may have produced good academic history, as indeed even the worst reviews of our works tell us we did. Perhaps because the majority of those of us whose works have been mentioned were still busy trying to establish ourselves as academics, we saw our duty as that of writing 'academic' history only. Therefore, although the works mentioned have sufficient data and evidence on which conclusions relevant to national social and political issues and problems could have been based; although they had the material to enable us point out the larger issues and the more general principles pertaining, for example, to our nation-building efforts, we failed to address ourselves to such larger issues. And so we failed in our calling.

Nigerian History Today and Tomorrow

What kind of Nigerian history is being written today, in a country which has been through the trauma of a civil war, a country still grappling with the problems of national integration? How is the changing scene affecting our historiography? One can discern two tendencies. There is a definite swing to economic and social history in quite a few of the Departments of History in the nation's universities, especially Ahmadu Bello University, the University of Lagos and the University of Calabar. Here at Ibadan, Dr Wale Oyemakinde's work on Labour on the Nigerian Railways and the History of Agriculture gives us hope that Ibadan will not be completely left out when the roll of the new history is called up yonder! I do not feel really competent to comment meaningfully on the quality and value of the work that has been done thus far. I must, however, make the same appeal to our economic historians. Just telling us how we grew, harvested and organised the sale of kolanuts in yester years is no longer enough. In addition to the commercial relations which developed between groups and the social contacts engendered as a consequence, the time has come for some identification of who the most successful kolanut traders were, what kind of surpluses they amassed, how they used these for the development of their families or villages, and what kind of offsprings they left behind – combining thereby economic and social history. It is clear that we cannot go back to the trading methods of the past. We may, however, yet learn a few things from what kinds of responsibilities leading traders in the communities assumed or were called upon by the society to assume.

With regard to social history, a call for the writing of which is a major feature of this half decade, no one would want to question the need for it. One would like to hope, however, that we shall not over-compartmentalize our history. The call must be for our history to be multi-dimensional in order that it may be more complete. Those of us whose chosen field is political history need to do more than add a chapter on "Social and Economic Developments" as has tended to be the case. We can weave quite a bit of social history into the political history we write. Let us take, for example, the era of colonial native courts. At least four of us have written on that subject. But we have been so concerned about how the courts were set up, what their powers were and how these were wielded, etc, that not one of us has given thought to studying what has happened to the families of the leading court members, the beneficiaries of the system. Is it a forturious accident that Mr Justice D. Onyeama is the son of the famous Warrant Chief Onyeama? What about the Obaseki family of Benin, descendants of Chief Agho Obaseki, whom the British made into a formidable paramount chief and then Iyase of Benin? Are there not many children of court clerks and court messengers who made it educationally and professionally, while their other age mates failed to pull themselves out of the circumstances into which they were born? Had we been so oriented, we could have made quite a major contribution to social history. So let us specialise by all means; but let us also seek to make our specialisation more meaningful by making whatever history we write just that much more complete.

Before I leave social history, I must join those who have been crying out for more biographical studies. As one of the few who have tried their hands at writing biographies (see my *Merchant Prince of the Niger Delta and The Member for Warri Province*),[20] I see biographies as a major contribution to social history. Take Bishop Ajayi Crowther - from slave boy to bishop. What a transmutation! J.F. Ade Ajayi owes us a duty to bring out that long-awaited biography, a foretaste of which is provided not only in his *Christian Missions* but also in his 1970 article in *Odu.* entitled, "Bishop Crowther: An Assessment." My understanding of delta society has been enriched by S.J.S. Cookey's *King Jaja of the Niger Delta*,[21] and those who have read Ayandele's *Holy Johnson*[22] must agree that it provides a much deeper insight into the society of missionaries and missions than the general works on missionary activity. If I may take another example on which I have just begun work – the late Chief Jereton Mariere, a John Holt clerk who grew to become a member of Nigeria's House of Representatives, was honoured with honorary degrees by three Nigerian Universities, Ibadan included, became Governor of the Bendel State and Chancellor of the University of Lagos! And Nigeria abounds in examples of this type, a study of which, in the form of biographies, cannot but constitute an important contribution to our social history.

During the Congress of the Historical Society in Calabar last April, our colleague, Professor E.A. Ayandele, Vice-Chancellor of the University of Calabar, in characteristic style lambasted Nigeria historians for their failure to produce biographies of our men and women in all walks of life who have made some contribution to the development of our nation or to the promotion of societal values.[23] Is it not a shame that thirteen years after their deaths there exist no biographies of Tafawa Balewa, the Sardauna of Sokoto, Chief Okotie Eboh, Chief S.L. Akintola? Is it not a shame that Mbonu Ojike, Eyo Ita, Chief Adegbenro and a host of others have been consigned to oblivion by our historians? Here let me say straight away that I disagree completely with colleagues who think that biographies do not constitute proper history. In a recent article R.S. Smith wrote, "It is now widely accepted that biography constitutes only an adjunct to history,"[24] and I bet there are Nigerian historians who agree with him. I don't. Writing biographies is decidedly not the sole preserve of historians. Journalists, political scientists, any interested observer, can and should be encouraged to produce biographies. But a biography by a historian should bear the stamp of his training. Besides, we must never forget that we Nigerian historians are operating in Nigeria where neither reading nor writing is a national habit. This fact imposes on us a responsibility which we dare not shirk. As an undergraduate I had to read loads of English and European history. In doing so I found the biographies of Cromwell, Pitt and Fox, George III, Richelieu, Frederick the Great of Prussia, Peter the Great of Russia, Napoleon – to select just a few – stimulating commentaries on the history of their respective countries and eras. We in Nigeria must wake up to our responsibilities in this regard.

Perhaps one reason why my colleagues shy away from biographies is that they do not want to be accused, by the declared socialists among us, of promoting the idea of the 'big man' in history. While I agree that we need urgently to bring the peasantry, the factory and office workers and so on into our history, I fail to see that we can wish away the so-called 'big men' in history. The entire world abounds in them. Every nation has its 'big men' of history, but none of these men and women is 'big' until his/her nation says so. The declared socialists frown at the idea of the 'big man' in history, but they teach their wards about Karl Marx and Lenin who, in the words of Ayandele, have been turned into 'secular divinities.'[25] Our failings in identifying and putting on record the men and women throughout the ages who have made significant contributions to their communities, their age, their country, is a veritable slur on our understanding of our functions as historians in a society which does not boast of novelists and journalists inclined to engage in the writing of biographies. Who knows, the writing of such biographies may well be the best why of pricking the bubble of the 'big man' in history. Here, let me again quote from Ayandele who said during that same address to us in Calabar, "For while, in my judgement, the history of Nigeria should not be seen primarily as that of oversized heroes or of the traditional and educated elites, the fact remains that rulers have in all ages quite often played a decisive role in the shaping of events. Political, cultural, military and religious leaders are veritable symbols of the national will whose ideas, thought-patterns and activities should be chronicled and projected for the education of the masses."[26] I would substitute for 'of the masses' the phrase 'of us all.'

But to return to the realm of political history. Today there is a definite trend to look backwards beyond the nineteenth century. This is a welcome development, for the history of what is now Nigeria did not begin in that century. In this connection, I wish to draw attention to the works of Professor E.J. Alagoa, now of the University of Portharcourt.[27] Professor Alagoa, whose interest is in the more ancient part of Nigeria, is probably the only colleague whose history is clearly informed by a deep understanding of the culture of the peoples who constitute his subject of study. While he is to be congratulated on this achievement, one would wish that he could more pointedly draw attention to this aspect of his work, in an effort at making an even more profound contribution to the nation's search for cultural re-awakening. Having paid tribute to whom tribute is due, one should, in the context of this lecture, pose the question – what kind of history of our more ancient past is to be written? Is there a justification for such history in other than purely academic terms?

One of the often repeated claims as to why newly independent African states are finding it difficult to forge really meaningful nation-states, is the fact that they are artificial creations of the colonial powers. Our study of Nigeria's more ancient past can furnish evidence of links of a social and economic nature which bound together many of the peoples who constitute what became Nigeria. Put crudely, the historians of our ancient past can demonstrate, and are demonstrating, that while there are many things in our past that are different for the various groups that now make up Nigeria, there are also a large number of facts which could be used to seek to unite. Indeed, during FESTAC '77, this latter possibility was seen almost as the only sensible role for history! Find the things that unite us. Professor Ayandele in the same address already quoted spoke to this aspect as well:

> Our patriotic obligations as historians should flower in many directions. Firstly, we should consciously select those elements of our cultural heritage and past that reveal in bold relief that, in a sense, there was a Nigeria before British Nigeria. In other words that before the colonial period, peoples in what became Nigeria coexisted, practised good neighbourliness, engaged in inter-ethnic trade and did cultural borrowing. We should ferret out the data about the cultural and linguistic links, apart from theories of origins, of our country.[28]

Yes indeed. There is a certain validity in this advocated role of the historian. However, it is my view that the expected role need not constitute the sole justification for studying our ancient past. Indeed one must warn against false unities as against false autonomies. In the Nigeria of today, we have seen many attempts to use history to build false empires. It is my view that the historian can remain faithful to his evidence and yet contribute to the nation-building effort. If, in his unearthing of the Nigerian past, the historian finds that the evidence points to divergencies rather than unities, he owes a duty to say so and yet make his contribution to the forging of a new nation. For I am persuaded that it is the function of the historian to demonstrate why things have happened the way they have happened, and to go on to examine the consequences. In doing so, he appeals to general principles: he demonstrates that given certain circumstances, man does tend to behave in certain ways; at the same time he also shows that particular groups behaved in particular ways for reasons peculiar to their respective situations. In this way the historian fulfills his purpose which, in the word of J.H. Plumb, "is to deepen understanding about men and society, not for its own sake, but in the hope that a profounder awareness will help to mould human attitudes and human action."[29]

In the Nigeria of today the historian can only hope that by unearthing the history of the past, ancient and recent, the leaders of today will have material with which to appeal to all concerned for a sympathetic understanding of the problems with which society has to contend. For not infrequently, the attitude of one group to another in this country derives from a certain insularity, the result of inadequate knowledge about that other group. This inadequacy of knowledge, and the attitude which it generates, are just as important for the nation-building effort as the decisions and policies of the ruling elites. There is thus a valid role, conceived of in these terms, for those who today seek to deepen our knowledge of Nigeria's ancient past. For such colleagues study the ancient past in a present beset with certain pre-occupations, of which nation-building is decidedly major. The present thus informs the past, as the knowledge of the past should illuminate the problems of the present. No doubt this is what E.H. Carr meant when he wrote, "Great History is written precisely when the historian's vision of the past is illuminated by insights into the problems of the present."[30]

Given the case made for the validity of the study of our ancient past, those of us involved in that study must no longer gloss over the harsher aspects of our history. While we laud the achievements of the Old Oyo and Benin empires and the Sokoto Caliphate, we must see them as systems of imperialism which imposed a political system over a wide area and over a large number of peoples by force of arms. Let us study in greater detail the relationships which developed in these imperialisms between the rulers and the ruled; let us apply to Benin, Oyo and Sokoto imperialisms the same yardsticks that we apply to British imperialism; let us draw up a careful balance sheet. We need also to draw attention to the many coups that took place within these systems and indicate the situations in which they occurred, lest we think that violent change of governments began in 1966. Where avarice, self-seeking and disregard of the greater good of the community generated civil disorder, the historian of the ancient past must sketch the details in clear and bold relief, for I am persuaded that the lessons of the past lie as much in our failures as in our successes.

I must draw this to a close by going back to my own field of interest, the political history of Nigeria's recent past from the colonial period to the present. From what I said earlier about existing works, it must be clear that my call is for the study of this recent past to be made more germane to the problems of today. For example, one of the major problems of today is inter-ethnic differences and tensions. Much of these differences and tensions is clearly the result of the fact that colonial rule brought people together in new ways and for new purposes as our colonial masters sought to forge a system of administration. The point about the constitution of provinces, divisions and districts has already been made. Today our rulers are up against the same task – creating new states, new provinces, new local government areas. Each such creation throws up its own problems, generates a new kind of inter-group relationship as some groups feel cheated and others seek to capitalise on their good fortune. In the colonial period, the fact that such arrangements were seen as good for administration was enough: the people did not have to be taken into confidence. Today, we dare not take the same attitude. The relationship between the governors and the governed today must be pointedly different from that between the governor and the governed in a colonial situation. These administrative re-arrangements may be necessary, and even ultimately beneficial. Government must, in this as in many other matters, enter into close and even prolonged dialogue with the peoples whose welfare it is its business to promote and protect. Our study of colonial boundary-making, and the on-going boundary-making efforts of our rulers of today, must thus bear in mind the problems that arise and offer suggestions as to how these may be tackled.

We need to remember that colonial rule introduced into this country all sorts of differentials and disharmonies. This indeed is the paradox of colonial rule. That rule is credited with having brought our peoples together into the new geographical unit known as Nigeria. Yet it not only underlined certain differences as already existed before the imposition of colonial rule but, in some instances, intensified these differences and introduced new ones. Thus, differences in socio-political institutions as between various groups were often used as an index of development or lack of it, resulting in different treatment being meted to such groups, and thereby creating new tensions. The consequence for us is that we have inherited the prejudices of our colonial masters and built stereotypes unto which we hold with stubborn persistence. Nearly twenty years after independence, one still comes across the student of history who writes that the Igbo had no government in the pre-colonial period. Government for such a student means an emir or an oba. So invidious can the colonial heritage become. Yet our study of that period devotes far less space and thought to crucial issues like this than to various legislations and theories of colonial rule.

Or take the issue of road building. There is not a single history of this important aspect of our nation's life. It is not the kind of history that we have been brought up to write. And there may well be some who will question whether writing about roads is the proper function of a historian. Yet anyone who has lived through the Nigeria of the last twenty years must see the impact of changing road patterns on the role and importance of various towns and groups. Thus Ọrẹ, a collection of motley huts, suddenly acquires a new importance, while some of the towns along the old Ibadan-Ife-Ilesha-Akure-Owo-Agbanikaka-Beni n road (to take just one example) have faded into the background. The quality of life of these towns now off the route is bound to be affected by the loss of traffic and trade. A fall in the quality of life may well affect the attitude of the people to the government of the day. Thus new and improved network of roads can create new inequalities, unless government takes steps to prevent these.

Or take the civil service. There is yet to emerge a book by a Nigerian historian which looks at this important body from the point of view of its changing structure and functions and the consequences of these for the nation. The colonial civil service was created for the successful exploitation of a colony. Has the structure of our civil services altered significantly with independence? Is that body which was designed to exploit (almost in a punitive sense) now able to ensure development? Perhaps even more crucial to the problems of today – has the attitude of the civil servant to the rest of the community changed now that he is part of that community, or does the civil servant still see himself as being outside that community? Will not a history of the civil service, which addresses itself to these and related questions, be making an important contribution to the understanding of national problems of today?

I could go on. But perhaps enough has been said to indicate my main thrust – a call for more imaginative histories that will see our problems in something of a holistic manner, the past being constantly "illuminated by insights into problems of the present," and the present drawing from the accumulated experiences of the past in a creative and innovative manner. Put differently, I am saying that our history must become more functional. We must break away from the fear that unless we say the kinds of things our European and American colleagues are saying or approve of, we have no chance of becoming accepted in the international community of scholars. There can be no international community without national communities. The kinds of subjects we select for study must be subjects which relate to our national needs and problems. And in studying our subjects let us be sturdily Nigerians first and world citizen only thereafter.

Let me illustrate. Two years ago, I published a book, entitled *The Fall of Nigeria*[31] which is a study of the British conquest. My colleagues in Britain have not ceased taking issues with me for using 'Nigeria' when, as they argue, there was no Nigeria. If that were all, I would not bother to mention it. But even my Nigerian colleagues raise the same issue. Nigeria, they tell, me, was created in 1914. My book covers the period just before. So I am wrong to entitle my book *The Fall of Nigeria*. Yet these same colleagues will happily talk about Italy before the unification of 1870. The fact that the geo-political entity known as Nigeria had acquired a meaning in 1975 when the book went to press is irrelevant to my colleagues. They demand that I must be correct by European standards, failing to see in the process that those standards are designed to serve a political end. Also the book has been deliberately written for the non-specialist. All my reviewers take issue with me for not being sufficiently academic. I discuss in the book twelve episodes from the British conquest, one from each of the twelve states that existed in the country when I wrote. In my preface, I state, "My aim here has been to demonstrate that to whichever part of the country one turns, there is some story worth telling within the context of this book."[32] By the time the book was published we had 19 states. My reviewers therefore draw my attention to the futility of my effort. A Nigerian reviewer goes further: he talks about the unwisdom of making history serve political ends. Again the same old problem – the canons of historical writing, even when such writing pertains to Africa, shall be spelt out in Europe and America. We here in Nigeria and Africa must be faithful to those canons. To venture outside those cannons is to place one's neck on the academic scaffold. This fear, that our academic necks will thus be chopped off, has hindered the full development of our historiography in directions that can best serve the needs of this country. When I raise these issues I get a wry smile and a request to stop preaching to the converted! I like to think I have said enough to make the point that the process of conversion needs to go on in more ways than one.

Before I end, let me join Professor Ayandele in appealing to my colleagues to break away from the tradition of writing only for the tiny university audience of the world and begin, additionally, to write for the ordinary citizen.[33] How many Nigerians, be they policy makers or just the interested reader, will want to plough through the Ibadan History Series, for example? We need to produce works of a different type based on the accumulated material in our academic publications. This also means that many more works of synthesis on much broader topics and broader areas are urgently called for, if we have the nation in mind. Micro studies are all very well in their proper place. We need many more macro studies in the years ahead. If history, conceived of and written to serve a social and political purpose, is to achieve the desired end, it must be made available to the wider community in an easily readable form. Perhaps when we begin to do this, we may be more constantly reminded about the purpose of history.

To conclude, let me own that what I have said may create the impression that I consider that all we have to do is to write our history with the kind of purpose I have tried to indicate and a blueprint for the political problems of our society will be provided. He is but a presumptuous historian who thinks his writings can, of themselves, create a revolution or even a major departure in policy. Nor do I consider that it is possible, or necessarily desirable, to straight-jacket history and the historian. For when the chips are down, what determines the kind of history a particular historian writes are his personality, his individual concept of history and how it should be written, far more than any generalised ideas or ideologies. Thus, the historian may even think that there is room for history for history's sake. Indeed, a former colleague here at Ibadan has claimed that history is history, and so there should be no difference between how history is written in Britain and how it is written in Africa. It is no surprise that that colleague is British.

For my part, I have always maintained that history must have a purpose. Our country is seeking to forge a true nation, that demands the instinctive loyalty of it citizenry. This is a worthy goal after which all nations of the world have striven. In the achievement of that goal, every nation has used history as one instrument. All that has varied is the way and the degree to which history has been used. The Nigerian historian need not be ashamed of playing a role that historians all over the world have unashamedly played and continue to play. It is my view that the historian can play this role by the kind of history he writes, his choice of words, his turn of phrase. I do not consider that, in the process, the historian should gloss over such aspects of our history as are unsavoury or problematic. Rather, he needs to analyse even those aspects with a view to informing present leadership and present followership. Increasingly, our researches must take into consideration national problems of political and social relations, of government and governmental systems and the ends which society seeks to attain. Only in this way can we ensure that the Nigerian History that we write will not be history for history sake, but history which makes some definite contribution to the national effort in its varying ramifications.

NOTES

1. A.E. Afigbo, "The Poverty of Contemporary African Historiography." Public lecture delivered under the auspices of the Institute of African Studies, Ibadan, 1976.
2. *Ibid.*
3. Afigbo dwells in more detail on these things in the lecture cited.
4. Ajayi, *Milestones*... pp. 15-16.
5. *Ibid.* p. 24.
6. K.O. Dike was editor of the pamphlet published by Cambridge University Press in 1960.
7. For some of these ideas, see Afigbo's lecture already cited: see also Peter

Ekeh, "Colonialism and State and Society in Africa," paper presented to History Department, Seminar, University of Ibadan, 20 January, 1977.

8. Marc Bloch. *The Historian's Craft*, Alfred Knopf, New York, 1953 (Peter Putnam's translation), p. 140.
9. Published by Longman, London 1965.
10. Published by Longman, London 1966.
11. Ayandele, *Missionary Impact...* p. 152.
12. Ayandele's *The Educated Elite...* was published in 1974. The University Lectures out of which the book grew were delivered in 1972.
13. Henri Pirenne, "What Are Historians Trying to Do?" in Leonard M. Marsak (Editor), *The Nature of Historical Enquiry*, Holt, Rinehart and Winston, New York, 1970, p. 32.
14. Marc Bloch, op. cit., pp. 143-144.
15. All the words listed, except Anene's are part of the *Ibadan History Series*, published by Longman, London. The two theses are: C.N. Ubah, *The Administration of Kano Emirate Under the British 1900-1930* and P. Tibendarana, *The Administration of Sokoto, Gwandu and Argungu Emirates Under British Rule 1905-1946*, both University of Ibadan Ph.D. theses.
16. Anene, *op. cit.,* p. 175. See p. 214 for the quotation that follows this.
17. Tamuno, *op. cit.,* pp. 244-245.
18. Afigbo, *Warrant Chiefs,* p. 261.
19. Atanda, *op. cit.*, See especially Chapters 3, 4 and 7.
20. Obaro Ikime, *Merchant Prince of the Niger Delta*, Heinemann, London, 1968 and *The Member for Warri Province (The Life and Times of Chief Mukoro Mowoe of Warri)*, Institute of African Studies, University of Ibadan, 1977.
21. S.J.S. Cookey, *King Jaja of the Niger Delta: Life and Times 1821-1891,* Nok Publishers, New York, 1974.
22. E.A. Ayandele, *Holy Johnson (Pioneer of African Nationalism 1936-1917),* Frank Cass, London, 1970.
23. E.A. Ayandele, "The Task Before Nigerian Historians Today" (Keynote Address at the 24th Annual Congress of the Historical Society of Nigeria, 5 April, 1979).
24. R.S. Smith, "Explanation in African History: How and Why?" *Tarikh*, Vol. 6, No.7, 1978, p. 5.
25. Ayandele, Keynote Address.
26. *Ibid.*
27. See for example, E.J. Alagoa, *The Small Brave City State*, Ibadan University

Press, 1964; *A History of the Niger Delta*, Ibadan University Press, 1972 and various articles.

28. Ayandele, Keynote Address.
29. J.H. Plumb, *The Death of the Past*, Houghton Mifflin Co., Boston, 1971, p. 106.
30. E.H. Carr, *What is History?* Penguin Books, Harmondsworth, 1971 edition, p. 30.
31. Obaro Ikime, *The Fall of Nigeria*, Heinemann, London, 1977.
32. Ikime, *The Fall of Nigeria*, p. ix.
33. Ayandele, Keynote Address.

3

BENIN IN NIGERIAN HISTORY*

On Thursday, 29 April, 1982, the National Commission for Museums and Monuments mounted an exhibition titled "The Lost Treasures of Ancient Benin" at the Museum in Benin City. The exhibition was formally opened by His Highness, the Oba of Benin. The timing of the exhibition was in my judgment particularly apt. This is because there has been in recent months a renewed interest in the history of Benin spearheaded by the Benin palace. The mounting of the exhibition could not but heighten this renewed interest in Benin: its art, its culture, its history, its place in the larger historical experience of what we now know as Nigeria. Hence my choice of subject, namely, Benin in Nigerian History.

History can be an emotive subject, when handled without due regard to the accepted canons of the discipline. This becomes particularly so when history is written for the purpose of scoring political or other

*As part of the celebration of the repatriation of "The Lost Treasures of Ancient Benin", The National Commission for Museums and Monuments mounted a number of lectures to commemorate the event. I was invited to deliver the lecture with this title on the 6th of May, 1982.

specific points. Also, it is easy for the unwary practitioner of history, whether professional or amateur, to do havoc to the discipline, simply by concentrating on his particular area of history to the exclusion of all else. I fear that some of us who have taken an interest in what may be described as micro-history have been guilty of this offence. The result of our guilt is that we reach conclusions which do not accord with all the known facts of history available even at the time of our particular study. Some of the new efforts at the re-telling and rewriting of Benin history, have, I fear, been made without due regard for the existing body of knowledge available in other areas of Nigerian history. This is an additional reason for my choice of subject.

The Issue of Origins

If there is any one aspect of Nigerian History about which it is impossible to make definitive statements, it is the issue of origin. We just do not know from which specific centres the various Nigerian peoples came. To say this is not to say that we do not know from where the peoples of Nigeria claim to have come. But a claim is no more than a claim; it is not necessarily a fact of history. True we must pay due regard to what the people say. But what the people say must be subjected to the full searchlight that the known corpus of historical knowledge constitutes. If what the people claim is in conflict with established historical developments, the trained historian must reflect this in his findings. Many complications arise when one is dealing with the issue of origins. In my survey of Isoko history I say that a number of Isoko clans trace their origins to Benin.[1] To say that is not to say much. For exactly what does the claim mean? What are we to understand by "Benin" in the context of the claim? The Benin kingdom? The Benin Empire? The Benin geographical area? And did those who claim to have migrated from Benin move into virgin territory or did they move into the area because they knew that it was already peopled? As Professor A.E. Afigbo has reminded us, the peopling of the Southern Nigerian area took place much earlier than the rise of the Benin Kingdom.[2] Indeed, the peopling of the Benin area itself had to be part of the larger process. Hence the chances are that parts of what is now Isokoland were peopled long before the migrations from Benin to which J. U. Egharevba refers in his now famous book.[3] If this be so, then the Benin migrants merely moved in to settle with earlier settlers.

So the claim to Benin origin becomes, in fact, a claim valid for only a section of the indigenes in each of the Isoko clans concerned. A general statement to the effect that the Isoko are of Benin origin thus becomes strictly unacceptable. So what appeared at first a straightforward and easy explanation of origins becomes in fact quite complex. What is true for the Isoko is true for virtually all other Nigerian peoples. And this underscores the point earlier made that it is extremely difficult to make definitive statements about the origins of Nigerian peoples.

In the light of what has been said above, let me now turn to the issue of origins as this concerns Benin history in the context of the larger Nigerian geographical area. Benin traditions of origin are varied. If we leave out the alleged role of Osanobua (God) sending messengers to the earth for the purpose of founding Benin, we are left with the traditions which speak of migrations from the 'east' through the Sudanic belt, into the forest region.[4] Some versions of this story claim that on arrival in the forest belt, the Bini occupied the site that became Ife (which the Bini call Uhe) at a time when the Ife Yoruba had not yet arrived there. Later, the story goes on, the Ife arrived, and they and the Bini co-sojourned for some time before the Bini moved to what I may here refer to as 'Beninland,' following reports by a scouting or hunting party that there was fertile land in the area that became 'Beninland.' There is in fact no way of knowing whether at any time in history the Ife and the Bini co-sojourned in Ife or Uhe. Nor is it clear what exactly we are to understand by Ife or Uhe. Is it the same Ife that we know today or an earlier Ife situated in a different locality? The tradition itself may have developed as the Bini sought some way of explaining what would appear to have been rather close relations with Ife at some period of their history. In other words, the traditions may not in fact be referring to origins at all, but to some association after the peopling of both Ife and Benin. In terms of Benin's relations with other Nigerian peoples, then, this particular tradition may thus constitute an important pointer to Benin-Ife relations.

Then there is the issue of the origin of the Benin dynasty. We are told that the Ogiso period of Benin history came to an end, following some dispute as to how the succession was to be arranged. It was out of the confusion created by this situation that the idea of sending to Ife for a prince to rule Benin arose. A request was accordingly made to the Ooni of Ife for a prince to be sent to Benin. The traditions say that this prince was Oranmiyan. There is, however, another school of thought which claims that in fact the prince sent from Ife was not Oranmiyan, but Ekaladerhan, an Ogiso prince, who, as a result of court intrigues, had earlier been banished from Benin by his father. According to this version, Ekaladerhan fled to Ughoton on leaving Benin and eventually found his way to Ife. When the Ooni of Ife received the request for a prince from Benin, he sent Ekalalerhan who was also apparently known as Omonoyan.[5] It was, according to the proponents of this view, Ekaladerhan, alias Omonoyan, who fathered Eweka I. We thus have an Oranmiyan tradition and an Ekaladerhan tradition. Let us now examine both a little more closely.

At the formal opening of the exhibition already referred to, the Oba of Benin in commenting about Benin art, found himself discussing 'the historical link between Ife and Benin'. Said the Oba, 'There is no doubt that both the Ife Royal House and the Benin royal House have a common ancestor. The point of disagreement is who that ancestor was and where he came from. To the Yoruba who call him Oduduwa, he came to Ife from the east. To us in Edo that person was no other than Ekaladerhan who was exiled by his father, the last Ogiso of Benin.' Later in the same address, the Oba said, 'Now, after Oranmiyan there were four Obas before Oguola, starting with Eweka I, the founder of the present dynasty.'[6] When we take the two statement together, we can only reach the conclusion that the Oba accepts that Oranmiyan was the prince sent from Ife to Benin. But, since, according to the Oba, Ekaladerhan was the ancestor of the Ife Royal House, Oranmiyan has to be seen as the descendant of a Benin ancestor, since Ekaladerhan was Bini. Yet, observe that the Oba does not accept that Oranmiyan was the founder of the present dynasty, for 'after Oranmiyan there were four Obas before Oguola, ***starting with Eweka I, the founder of the present dynasty'*** (My emphasis). Oranmiyan came before any other Oba; but the present dynasty was founded by Oranmiyan's son, Eweka, not Eweka's father! There is thus here a pointed rejection of a Yoruba ancestry for the Benin dynasty. Puzzling as this conclusion must be to the disinterested observer, other experts on Benin have in fact tended to reach the same conclusions. A.F.C. Ryder recounts the tradition of 'how a number of Benin chiefs, sought a sovereign from the Yoruba dynasty ruling in Ife. There is nothing inherently implausible in the story. If the Edo community had became deeply divided – as the traditions imply – one party might well have turned for protection to the magical powers of a distant potentate, while the other upheld the indigenous system against this intrusion'[7] Ryder warns, however, that the tradition could also be a piece of culture capture designed to relate the Benin dynasty to the prestigious Ife royal line.[8]

The late R.E. Bradbury states that Oranmiyan on arrival in Benin found that it was difficult for a foreigner to rule Benin, given his inability to speak the language. 'He therefore returned to Ife, having first impregnated the daughter of a village chief who, he said, would bear a son that would become king. The son was duly born and, fostered and instructed by the followers his father left behind for that purpose, eventually became the Oba Eweka I'. How did Oranmiyan know that the baby would be a son? In what language did the followers he left behind instruct the newborn child? Traditions don't answer such questions! Bradbury goes on to say: 'That this dynasty was derived from Ife is beyond reasonable doubt', and gives as the reason for this statement the fact that the insignia of office used to be sent from Ife only when the Ooni has approved the successor to the Benin throne; that the remains of a Benin Oba used to be sent to Ife for burial. 'Yet,' says Bradbury, 'the essential point of this foundation legend is that, while the kingship was from Ife, its first incumbent was a native-born Edo.'[9]

P. A. Igbafe puts the matter this way: 'Tradition has it that after the people rejected Ogiamwen's rule, two factions emerged in Benin – the Ogiamwen faction, uncompromising and turbulent, who struggled to restore hereditary rule, and the opposing faction who supported a prince from Ile-Ife. Benin traditions are not unanimous on whether Oranmiyan or Eweka, his son by a Benin woman, first ruled in Benin, as Oba of the new dynasty. The balance of evidence favours Eweka. The new dynasty therefore had Ife antecedents, though rooted on Benin soil.'[10]

All of our Benin experts thus pointedly or by implication accept the Oranmiyan connection. It seems to me, however, that consciously and unconsciously there is some preoccupation with ensuring that nothing is said in connection with the Oranmiyan episode (if it was a historical episode) that would create the impression that an Ife dynasty was established in Benin. Note that while the kingship was from Ife, the first incumbent was a native-born Edo! (Bradbury). Note also that the dynasty had Ife antecedents but that it was rooted on Benin soil! (Igbafe).

A close look at these traditions, and the way they have been used by various scholars and commentators, bears out the point I made at the beginning of this section of the talk, namely, that it is extremely difficult to make definitive statements about the origins of the peoples of Nigeria. All the scholars and commentators are clearly anxious to avoid saying that Benin was at any stage of its history, and for whatever reason, dependent on Ife for any aspect of its political survival or revival, however minimal the degree of dependence. The nature of the evidence – oral traditions – makes this anxiety and caution understandable. Yet there are worrying aspects of the matter. It seems to me that at one point in the history of Benin, there was something to be gained from some form of association with Ile-Ife. The tradition as recorded by Egharevba was then probably acceptable. Later that tradition would appear to have become unacceptable because of its political overtones. So Ekaladerhan replaced Oranmiyan as the prince from Ife. Now the Oba of Benin has pushed Ekaladerhan back into history – he has become the ancestor of the Ife royal house! There is evident in this new effort at re-telling and re-writing Benin history proof that oral traditions are a dynamic entity: they tend to change with prevailing conditions and the changing aspirations of the people or group to which they refer. The fact that certain traditions get written down and so become "orthodox" or "accepted" must not blind the serious historian to this essential fact. Yet these traditions are of historical value, for although the place of Ife in the traditions varies according to the narrator's vested interest, the fact of some relationship between Ife and Benin is undeniable. It is in the nature of the relations that there is disagreement. Such disagreement is understandable, given the genre of the evidence. We shall return to the nature of Ife-Benin relations presently. But before that some further comments.

My special field of interest is political history. The changing attitudes to Benin history interest me from the view point of political history. It is clear to me that the new and official version of the history of Benin has to do with giving Benin a new image in the context of Nigerian history. The motivation would thus appear to be political. For that reason, it is decidedly emotive. History can be used for all sorts of ends. In this particular case, I am constrained to raise a question: does origin from a particular source necessarily involve a dependence relationship? With reference to Benin history, for example, there are traditions (some of them questionable for reasons already adduced) of groups leaving Benin to escape the tyranny of an Oba or to flee from a state of constant warfare. Such migrations can be interpreted to mean a search for independence by the migrating groups. Unless such groups are compelled by force to relate to Benin, there is no logical reason to expect them, having settled elsewhere, to put themselves under the "tyranny" from which they escaped. Hence it can be argued that origin from a particular source does not necessarily imply a relationship of dependency. On the other hand, it could denote such a relationship, depending on the circumstances of the migration and the nature of relationships which developed thereafter. This being so, we must not present Nigerian history in a manner which creates the impression that dependence by one group on another for a period of time because of prevailing circumstances is a phenomenon that is not to be entertained. Such dependence is a fairly common phenomenon in the history of the rest of the world. We must not, on the basis of incomplete or one-sided evidence, deny it in our history simply because we are dealing with oral evidence, or because of pressure of present political sensitivities. I do not mean to imply by what has been said above that there was a dependence relationship as between Benin and Ife. My plea is that we leave all the options open as research continues to deepen our knowledge and open up new possibilities.

Let us now return to the nature of Ife-Benin relations. It is noteworthy that none of the experts and commentators quoted earlier asked what relation existed between Benin and Ife that led to the former (or elements within it) sending to Ife for a prince. Was Ife a random choice? I would doubt it. We must postulate certain pre-existing relations that disposed a Benin group of chiefs to send to the Ooni of Ife for a prince, if indeed such a request was ever made. What was the genesis of such pre-existing relations? I have suggested elsewhere that it is possible that the two kingdoms (Benin and Ife), having established themselves in the forest region, forged friendly relations for the sake of peaceful co-exitstence.[11] In present day parlance they may well have established what we call diplomatic relations. Close relations may have resulted in culture borrowing, which may explain the similarities in certain court ceremonials and chieftaincy titles as between Ife and Benin. The traditions may, in fact, be seeking to explain this kind of relationship now couched in terms of origins of the people or dynasty. Over-preoccupation with the issue of sovereign-vassal relationship, which relationship is seen as politically provocative in our present circumstances, can make us fail to see this possible interpretation of the traditions. I suggest that for the larger history of Nigeria, as distinct from the micro history of Nigeria's component parts, interpretations such as that being here suggested are probably far more important and rewarding than the issue of origins.

I said earlier that the new and official Benin history that is being peddled has a political purpose. Put bluntly and crudely, it is an effort at using history to build a new Benin empire. Thus while the official historians of Benin are anxious to deny any interpretation of the traditions which would suggest that Ife came to Benin's aid in a moment of crisis at some point in Benin history, the same historians seem quite able to claim in very categorical terms that the peoples of the Bendel State (as at 1982) are all of Benin origin. Let us for a moment grant that this claim is indeed historically correct. My next question will be, so what? How does the fact that, say, the Isoko people migrated from Benin in the 14th century affect their political alignment today? If the present effort at establishing historical links between the various peoples of Bendel State is designed to emphasise our historical homogeneity, what is its purpose in practical political terms? Is it to stress that Benin occupies a pre-eminent position in terms of the composition of the state? When it comes to appointment to top positions in the public service or in politics does our much-vaunted common origin influence decisions? We have enough evidence to answer that question in the negative. When it comes to such mundane matters, we disintegrate into Bini, Etsako, Esan, Urhobo, Ika, Isoko, Ijọ, and so on. In other words, it would appear that common origins do not necessarily lessen strife or competition. Indeed I fear that the issue of common origins is being whipped up almost in order to defend certain questionable attitudes in the politics and public life of the state.

But enough of what may be dismissed as polemics. Let us return to more serious history. Is there historical justification for the claim that the peoples of Bendel State have a common origin? It is difficult in the present state of our knowledge to answer that question in definitive forms. Egharevba has claimed that most of the peoples of the state migrated from Benin during the period of Benin's imperial expansion.[12] There may well have been such migrations, the result of the turbulence that must have accompanied that phase of Benin history. While such migrations may partially explain certain Benin-like features among the other Edoid groups as well as among the Igbo of the Bendel Sate, the point has already been made that such migratory groups probably moved into areas already peopled. The linguists tell us that the languages of the Edoid groups – Urhobo, Isoko etc. are of greater antiquity than the period of migration postulated by Egharevba.[13] This would further strengthen the argument that the areas into which Benin groups may have moved was already peopled before their arrival.

The point also needs to be made that the groups now referred to as Urhobo, Isoko, Etsako, etc. were not originally as homogenous as they now appear. An examination of Urhobo traditions of origin reveals that certain clans – Ughienvwe, Ughelle, Ewu, Uwherun – claim Ijọ origin; Evwreni is sad to be of Igbo origin; some clans like Agbọn and Uvbię are said to be connected with the Isoko in their origin.[14] Given such claims, one cannot accept the Benin claim without closer examination. Even among the Isoko, many of which clans claims to be of Benin origin, there are a few clans – Igbide and Umę for example – that are said to be of Igbo origin.[15] Professor E.J. Alagoa's work on the Ijọ has demonstrated convincingly that a general claim of Benin origin is not tenable for the Ijọ.[16] As for the Itsękiri who recently demonstrated their solidarity with the Benin monarchy as part of their preparation for the celebration of the quincentenary anniversary of their kingdom, it is accepted that their monarchy is a branch of Benin's. But that is not to say that the Itsękiri people as distinct from the monarchy are of Benin origin.[17] Observe the fact that the Itsękiri culture is on the whole markedly different from that of Benin despite the connections between the monarchies. Itsękiri songs and dances are, from the view point of a non-expert like me, markedly different from Benin's. So is their dress, their food and so on.

As for the Igbo groups within the Bendel State, I do not feel called upon to dwell at any length with them, as Professor Adiele Afigbo discusses the matter in his contribution to this series.[18] What I must say is that for them, like for the other Bendel peoples, a general claim to Benin origin cannot be made in the present state of knowledge. There is need for more painstaking research before firm conclusions can be reached.

Let me stress that nothing that has been said about origins should be read to mean absence of inter-group relations among the peoples of Bendel State. Rather, the point being made is that inter-group relations – be these cordial or hostile, social, commercial or political – are not necessarily a function of origins. The discussion of inter-group relations is taken up later. As for the issue of origins, my position is that given the nature of the traditions, we can make no definitive statement about the origins of Nigerian peoples. And that any effort to build up the greatness of any Nigerian group, Benin included, on the fact that this or the other group originated from there is bound to be an exercise in futility, for the very good reason that what happened five centuries ago does not necessarily determine relations today. Besides, the Bini must have come from some place too. I believe that in the context of Nigerian history, Benin has played certain significant roles. Her greatness in history rests on what she was able to achieve as a state, not on how many different groups she spawned. If there is to be a new interest in Benin history, I suggest that that new interest should focus on the actual history of the Benin kingdom and empire, and on its relations with other Nigerian groups and not just on the issue of origins, in the mistaken and misguided belief that issues of origin prove something or the other. Let us therefore proceed to other aspects of Benin history in the context of my subject.

Benin and The Europeans

It is now generally accepted that the European's first made contact with Benin in the last quarter of the 15th century. It is not relevant here for us to go into the details of why Portugal, the first European power to come to West Africa, undertook the venture. We know, however, that commerce was one reason for these journeys. Benin was not a coastal state. It was thus not the accident of geography that decided the Portuguese to visit Benin. Rather it was the fact that Benin had developed into a well organised state that led the Portuguese thereto: they had a guarantee there was a political authority that could ensure profitable trade. The period coincided with the reign of Ewuare the Great. If we are to go by Egharevba's testimony now supported by the work of scholars like Alan Ryder,[19] Benin under Ewuare launched out on a career of expansion and internal development. Egharevba speaks of Ewuare building roads and walls as well as laying the foundations of the empire by his wars in Yorubaland and parts of Western Igboland.[20] We will discuss the significance of the empire later. Here the important point to make is that the Europeans were attracted to Benin because of its political development as of that time. With what consequences?

One consequence was Benin's involvement in the overseas slave trade. Ryder has argued that at no time was Benin a great slave trading state, comparable to, say, the states of the eastern delta.[21] In the context of the wider history of Nigeria, therefore, Benin's participation in the overseas slave trade was not one of the most significant aspects of her history, though her involvement in the trade did affect her economy. There were, however, two areas in which Benin's contact with the Europeans was significant. The first had to do with the issue of missionary activity.[22] Benin was the first place in the entire Nigerian geographical area where the Portuguese made an attempt to convert the ruler and his people to Christianity. The first missionaries arrived in Benin in 1515. From that date until 1711 a total of seven missions were sent to Benin. No success attended these efforts. Not a single Oba was converted to Christianity, and only a handful of courtiers or their children were baptised into the Christian faith, and even they did not become proper Christians for the very good reason that there were no priests to teach them the mysteries of the faith. If the missions failed, why do I regard the effort as significant? The answer is to be found in the main reason for the failure. The Portuguese missionary venture had a political motive as well. Prince Henry the Navigator who began the West African venture was said to be seeking a Christian ally to use in his wars against Islam. Indeed, Ryder tells us that one reason why Benin was choosen as a missionary centre was the belief, wrong as it turned out, that the Oba may b a Christian ruler, because his headgear had something that resembled the cross. In welcoming the missionaries at first, the rulers of Benin also had political motives. Wars of conquest and expansion were being fought. Benin required arms and ammunition to strengthen her army. The Portuguese had arms and ammunition to supply. Oba Ozolua sent an embassy to Lisbon in 1514 to persuade the Portuguese king to supply Benin with arms and ammunition, in addition to requesting greater trading contact. The Portuguese King replied to the effect that no arms and ammunition would be supplied to Benin unless the Oba became Christian. From that time on, it became clear that the political aims of the two potentates diverged. Benin wanted arms and ammunitions more than she needed Christianity. Portugal failed to meet this need. The missionary effort became doomed to failure thereafter. Benin was thus the first Nigerian state to send a diplomatic mission to Europe; that mission did not mince words as to what Benin's priorities were. When those priorities were not met, Benin went her own way. Nevertheless, those early contacts enabled Benin to be known in Europe, and also resulted in some documentation of the state of the kingdom as of that time. It is true that the failure of the missions coloured the reports left behind by the priests. Even so, they do represent an important source of historical material.

Benin's contact with European powers other than Portugal, and the consequences of this contact, constitute the second area of significance.

If the Portuguese were the first Europeans to visit and trade with West Africa, they were soon supplanted by other European powers, especially as from the mid-17th century. Indeed it was partly the fact that Benin could trade with other European powers which had no qualms about selling arms to non-Christian potentates that enabled Benin to treat Portugal with increasing disregard. European visitors to Benin have left us accounts of the splendour that was the city of Benin up to the 17th and early 18th century. That splendour – wide and well kept streets, elaborate court ceremonials, craftsmanship that was to become world famous and other aspects of Benin life that came to adorn the pages of the accounts of these 17th century visitors – was a testimony to Benin's creative genius. Indeed it is clear from these accounts that Benin City was an extremely well planned city in terms of the laying out of the streets, a feature which still remains with the city even today. We owe this aspect of the city of Benin not so much to the city planners of today as to the great rulers of yesteryears. If Benin is anxious to establish her greatness in times past, it is in areas like this which reflect the genius of her rulers and people that such greatness is to be found, not in how many different groups of Nigerian peoples migrated from Benin. No other city within the Nigerian geographical area received the kind of encomiums lavished on Benin by European visitors in terms of the orderliness of the city and the excellence of the planning. In these regards, the creative genius of the black man, in the years before the influence of Europeans began to be felt, stood in very clear focus: a great credit to the Bini, the Nigerian of today and the negro.

On other point needs to be made. Benin's contact with Europe and her involvement with the overseas trade led to a strengthening of the economy which in turn led to a strengthening of the monarchy. The expansion of the kingdom into an empire was made possible partly by the improved economy of the central government and the acquisition of fire-arms. And, as we shall proceed to argue presently, the successful establishment of the Benin empire is significant for the wider history of Nigeria.

The Significance of The Benin Empire for Nigerian History

It is an accepted historical fact that Benin established an empire. The true extent of this empire has, however, not been empirically studied. There is in fact no detailed study of the Benin Empire. It has, even so, been fairly well established that the empire at its height included parts of Yorubaland – Owo, Akure, parts of Ekiti, Lagos. Professor A.B. Aderibigbe has given an account of the Benin conquest of Lagos and how Lagos became a vassal of Benin up to the 19th century (though there were periods when the tribute that was a recognition of this vassalage was temporarily withheld).[23] It is also believed that groups like the Esan, Afenmai, Etsako, Ora, some of the Urhobo groups which, with some others now described as the Edoid, were also part of the Benin Empire. The truth of this assertion has, however, not been established definitely, through empirical study. Traditions of payment of tribute to Benin by many of these groups would suggest that they did come under the influence of Benin during the latter's imperial phase. The detailed nature of relationships awaits its historian. Those normally described as western Igbo – the Igbo of Aboh, Ndokwa, Ukwuani, Asaba and its hinterland, Agbor – are also said to have been part of the Benin Empire, and the traditions of some of these groups give credence to the claim,[24] though it is possible that some of these traditions were created to serve a particular purpose in the past.

Like all empires, the establishment of the Benin Empire involved conquests. Existing accounts speak of the conquest of the Yoruba areas already indicated, of the "western Igbo" and some of the Edoid groups. Professor A.E. Afigbo has warned against any facile acceptance of the conquest theory as this applies to the Igbo groups.[25] Part of the problem here is the fact that the claim that Benin conquered the Igbo groups is a generalized one. There are many groups involved. While research may well confirm that some of the Igbo groups were conquered, others may have come under Benin influence through more peaceful means – trade, geographical proximity and close social relations and the like. It is also possible that some of the Edoid groups like the Esan did feel the heavy hands of Benin. The point has already been made that Benin's trade with the Europeans enabled her to acquire fire-arms and that in this regard she would have been at an advantage over many of those groups which came under the imperial influence.

However the Benin empire was established, whether through conquest or other form of incorporation, I consider the fact of the existence of the empire significant for Nigerian history. By incorporating different Nigerian peoples into an empire, an opportunity was created for groups that would otherwise have developed completely separately to share certain common institutions. Thus the western Igbo socio-political institutions were definitely affected by Benin institutions. Even if as Afigbo argues, this was not necessarily as a result of conquest, we cannot rule out the possibility that the fame of Benin played some part in making different groups want to have some kind of association with her. Sending title holders to Benin to be invested by the Oba may even have served as a kind of insurance against attacks by other groups, in addition to making such title holders acquire a greater importance among their people and thereby, presumably, ensuring greater stability. From Lagos we have evidence that the chieftaincy system has been affected by the period of Benin overlordship.

Writes Professor Aderibigbe, 'There was the nucleus of the *Akarigbere* made up of *Eletu Odibo* and the *Eletu Iwase* who originally came with the Oba of Lagos from Benin.[26] Indeed the same authority indicates that the present dynasty of Lagos is descended from Ashipa on whom the Oba of Benin conferred the title Olorogun of Lagos as a reward for having brought to Benin the corpse of a famous Benin general, Aseru. The Oba also gave to Ashipa 'a state sword and the loyal Gbedu drum' as symbols of his authority.[27] Admittedly, Ashipa was Yoruba not Bini. Those who eventually took various titles would increasingly have been Yoruba. But the Benin influence is not denied. And the point being emphasised here is that the functioning of the empire brought certain common influences to bear on otherwise separate groups and so led to greater awareness, thereby reducing the degree of separateness. This fact is clearly of importance for what became Nigeria. When in the heat of present day politics we argue that after all Nigeria was an artificial creation of the British, and that its component parts were separate until the coming of the British, we ignore the role of empires like Benin, Old Oyo, Kanem-Borno, and of kingdoms like Nupe and Igala in incorporating different groups of Nigerian peoples and so giving them certain common experiences. Our peoples were not quite as separate as we sometimes want to claim. Herein lies part of the significance of the empire of Benin for the wider history of Nigeria.

It is important to stress that the influences were not one way. It was not only Benin that influenced those who came into contact with her. Benin was also influenced by parts of her empire. Thus the practice of stationing Benin agents in Yorubaland for the purpose of ensuring the payment of tribute, as well as the settlement of Benin elements in parts of

Yorubaland for the purpose of trade led to considerable mixing. Children born to Benin agents were known to have been given Yoruba names, and a sizeable proportion of those Bini who had dealings, political or economic, with the Yoruba acquired the Yoruba language. Indeed the Bini language would appear (and here I speak as a layman) to have incorporated certain Yoruba words. Benin dress would also appear to have been influenced by the Yoruba. Among the Igbo of Aboh, Ndokwa and Ukwuani the Benin elements were certainly conquered linguistically, even though Bini political institutions were introduced.

Before I leave this aspect of my subject, it is important to say that I am fully aware that the concept of conquest in our situation was different from that which we experienced when the British conquered us. Conquered peoples were very often allowed to continue to run their own affairs very much as before, provided they paid annual tribute. Conquest thus did not involve close administration of the conquered by the conquerors, nor did it always involve imposing institutions of the conqueror on the conquered. But it cannot be denied that certain common influences were shared by those who found themselves having to operate within the ambit of an empire like Benin. My thesis is that that sharing of common influences was an important preparation for living together in what became Nigeria. The British may have brought us together in new ways. But, before the coming of the British, we were not as separate as is sometimes made out. What is said here for Benin applies to the other empires and large kingdoms which incorporated different ethnic groups within them. To say that is not to say that the monarchies and empires dictated what happened to those who remained fragmented in their political organisation. Far from it. It is merely to acknowledge a historical role played by Benin and these other empires and groups. To deny that role is, in my opinion, to do havoc to known historical facts.

Finally on this head, one must also point out that the Benin empire was sustained on what Ryder has described as far-flung commercial relations between Benin and other Nigerian peoples – the Yoruba, the Itsẹkiri, Nupe, Igala, the Igbo as well as the other Edoid groups.[28] Consideration of space does not allow us to go into the details of these commercial relations. I mention them here to underline my point as to how the functioning of the Benin kingdom and empire had the effect of deepening relations between different Nigerian peoples.

The Decline of Benin

If there be any doubts as to the importance of Benin relations with other Nigerian peoples in the heydays of that kingdom and empire, there can be none about the significance of developments among other Nigerian groups for the decline of Benin in the 19th century. Admittedly, Benin's decline had to do with certain internal developments such as succession disputes, revolt by outlying provinces of the empire and so on. These were worsened and sometimes made more easily possible by a decline in the Benin economy brought about by circumstances outside Benin's control. These circumstances can be briefly summarised. With the suppression of the overseas slave trade there were developments in the trade of the western delta which adversely affected the Benin economy. Ughọtọn, the port of Benin, ceased to be an important centre of trade, as European trade moved to the Benin River where the Itsẹkiri controlled the trade. This meant that the Oba lost revenue from customs duties and presents usually paid and given at Ughọtọn. Benin's external trade therefore suffered. The Sokoto jihad led to an unsettled state of affairs in the area north of Benin. This disrupted Benin's trade with Nupe and Igala. Then the Nupe carried the jihad into parts of the Benin Empire, especially the Etsako area which Benin, in fact, lost to the Nupe. Meanwhile the Yoruba wars of the 19th century had broken out. As part of the developments attendant on those wars, Ibadan grew into a major military power and began an imperialistic career of conquest. It was as part of this career of conquest that Ibadan overran Akure, Owo and parts of Ekiti territory, all of which were parts of the Benin Empire. Benin was unable to defend her territories against Ibadan aggression, and so lost those territories. The overall effect of the developments here summarised was the weakening of the economic base of the Benin empire and the shrinking of its territorial limits.[29] Nothing could better demonstrate the interrelatedness of the fortunes and fate of different Nigerian peoples.

The Sack of Benin

In the series of lectures of which mine is a part, the Director-General of the National Commission for Museums and Monuments will speak on the subject of the Sack of Benin. I do not wish to anticipate that discussion here. In the context of my subject, the sack of Benin by the British, which led to the looting of Benin's works of art, has a certain relevance. The works of art looted from Benin were sold to private individuals and museums in Europe. It is an exhibition of some of these works of art bought back from Europe by the Federal Government that has occasioned this series of lectures about Benin. As the Oba of Benin told us at the official opening of the exhibition, those who originally produced the various works did not see themselves as artists as such. They were merely carrying out certain functions for their ruler: they produced their carving or cast their bronze works to mark important events in the kingdom in the days before writing and photography. Yet the works produced were, by all accounts, intricate and sophisticated artistic creations. But it took the sack of Benin and the looting of those works to draw attention to the artistic excellence of the craftsmen who created them. The sack of Benin thus led, paradoxically, to international acclamation of the excellence of Benin craftsmanship. That acclamation has become a proud reference point not only for Benin but for Nigeria as a whole and indeed for the black man all over the world. Such is the place of Benin in Nigerian artistic history.

Conclusion

What has been attempted here is some discussion of Benin in the context of the history of the larger entity, Nigeria. In my judgment, Benin does occupy a worthy place in our history. That place is the result of concrete achievements in the areas of trade, politics and state craft, within the Nigerian geographical area as well as internationally; the result of her role in giving a certain socio-cultural unity or at least similarity to a sizeable sector of what became Nigeria; the result of the artistic excellence of her citizenry which has become internationally recognised and of which all Nigerians can be justly proud. In the face of such solid achievements, I consider it unnecessary for Benin to seek to establish her claim to greatness by claiming that other groups in the Bendel State of 1982 originated from her. For just as the new Benin history seeks to deny relations with Ife which may create the impression that Benin did have occasion to appeal to Ife for assistance during a crisis period in her history, so can the groups that Benin is so eager to claim as her 'children' develop their own new history which can deny any origins from Benin. We will never know the full story of our origins as peoples of Nigeria, even though all of our peoples are so eager to know their origins and to talk about it! What the traditions of origin of Nigerian peoples offer to the historian are certain possible relationships between our various peoples now couched in mysterious terms in the traditions. Those relationships properly studied and interpreted are, from my point of view, far more important for Nigerian History than the building up of new traditions calculated to score political points in our present circumstances. As for the place of Benin in Nigerian history, enough has been said to make it quite clear that I consider that Benin played an important role in our history, especially in the area of giving a heterogenous group of peoples certain common experiences and similar institutions. Preoccupation with the issue of origins is unlikely to make Benin's place in our history more worthy. Indeed it could produce the opposite effect and lead to a deliberate campaign of denigration against Benin. Such a development would be a great pity and could detract from our appreciation of Benin's role in our history, a development which should, in my judgment, be studiously prevented.

NOTES

1. See Obaro Ikime, *The Isoko People: A Historical Survey*, Ibadan University Press, 1972, Chapter I.
2. A.E. Afigbo, "The 'Bini Mirage' and the History of South-Central Nigeria", *Nigeria Magazine*, (Lagos) No. 137, 1981. Hereinafter referred to as Afigbo, 'Bini Mirage'.
3. J.U. Egharevba, *A Short History of Benin*, Ibadan University Press, 1960.
4. See Egharevba, *op. cit.,* for Benin traditions of origin. Dr S. Omorogie's forthcoming work on Benin history has elaborations of the version here summarised.
5. I am grateful to Professor P.A. Igbafe of the Department of History, University of Benin, for some of the details about the Ekaladerhan tradition.
6. A.F.C. Ryder, "The Benin Kingdom" in Obaro Ikime (Editor) *Groundwork of Nigerian History*, Heinemann Educational Books for the Historical Society of Nigeria, Ibadan, 1980, p. 110.
7. *Ibid.*
8. R.E. Bradbury, *Benin Studies*, edited by Peter Morton-Williams, O.U.P., 1973, p. 8.
9. P.A. Igbafe, "Benin in the Pre-colonial Era" in *Tarikh* Vol. 5, No.1, 1974, p. 7.
10. Obaro Ikime, "*History, The Historian and The Nation: The Voice of a*

Nigerian Historian", Ibadan, HEBN Publishers Plc., 2006, Chapter 2.

11. Egharevba, *op. cit.,* pp. 14ff.
12. See B. Elugbe's contribution to these series.
13. For a discussion of Urhobo traditions of origin, see Obaro Ikime, *Niger Delta Rivalry*, Longman, 1969, Chapter I.
14. Obaro Ikime, *The Isoko People*, Chapter I.
15. See E.J. Alagoa, *A History of the Niger Delta*, Ibadan University Press, 1972, for Ijọ traditions of origin.
16. For a discussion of Itsekiri traditions of origin, see Obaro Ikime, *Niger Delta Rivalry*, Longman, 1969, Chapter I. See also J.O. Sagay, *The Warri Kingdom.* Press Publishers, Sapele, Chapter I.
17. Adiele Afigbo, "Igbo-Benin Relations: Some Problems of Methodology and Perspectives".
18. A.F.C. Ryder, *Benin and the Europeans 1485-1897*, Longmans, 1969.
19. Egharevba, *op. cit.*
20. Ryder, "The Trans-Atlantic Slave Trade" Chapter 13 in *Groundwork of Nigerian History.*
21. A.F.C. Ryder, "The Benin Missions", *Journal of the Historical Society of Nigeria*, Vol. 11, No.2, 1961.
22. See A.B. Aderibigbe "Early History of Lagos to about 1850", in A.B. Aderibigbe, (Editor) T*he Development of an African City, Longman, Nigeria, 1975*, pp. 1-26.
23. See K.O. Ogedengbe, "The Aboh Kingdom of the Lower Niger C.1650-1900", Ph.D. Thesis, University of Wisconsin, 1971 and E.O. Okolugbo, "Ukwuani Religion and Christianity", Ph.D. Thesis, University of Ibadan, 1972, for some of these traditions.
24. Afigbo, "Bini Mirage".
25. Aderibigbe, *op. cit.,* p. 7.
26. *Ibid.*
27. *Ryder, Benin and the Europeans.*
28. *Ryder, Benin and the Europeans*, and Obaro Ikime, "The Western Niger Delta and the Hinterland in the Nineteenth Century" in Obaro Ikime (Editor) *Groundwork of Nigerian History,* Chapter 15.

4

INTER-GROUP RELATIONS IN NIGERIA UP TO 1800: THOUGHTS OF A POLITICAL HISTORIAN*

Introduction

"Inter-group relationship," wrote A.E. Efigbo, "is multi-faceted and dynamic. Among its more common facets are the political..., the economic and technological, the cultural... So far the tendency has been to concentrate on the military and political aspects of the relationship to the neglect of all the others."[1] It is not clear what Afigbo had in mind when he used the word 'political' in this context. In my judgment, merely stating that B migrated from A, or that C conquered D, or that E borrowed certain socio-political institutions from F does not constitute any real study of political relations between our diverse peoples. In fact, it is my contention that in the study of inter-group relations thus far, historians have been extremely wary about venturing into direct discussion of political relations between groups, in the period up to 1800.

* This paper was presented to the Department of History, University of Ibadan, Staff Seminar in January 1984, and represents a drastic revision of an earlier paper presented to the History Departmental Seminar, University of Benin, in 1982 when I spent my sabbatical leave at that University. The 1982 paper was published in Obaro Ikime, History, *The Historian and The Nation; the Voice of a Nigerian Historian*, Ibadan, HEBN Publisher PLC, 2006, reprinted 2008.

It can be stated with a measure of truth that in terms of Nigerian historiography, comments about inter-group relations were first made in the attempt to assail the concept that Nigeria is an artificial creation of the British. Thus we have been quick to point out that long before the British arrived on our shores, our peoples traded together, inter-married, and became aware of the presence of neighbours around them. Some empires did exist, but none of these brought the entire geographical area that became Nigeria under its aegis. The economic activities of these empires were, however, wide-ranging and so promotive of greater interactions.

Thus far and no farther have most of us been willing to go. Observe that as late as 1970 the planners of *Groundwork of Nigerian History* were only able to include a chapter entitled, "Nigeria Before 1800: Aspects of Economic Developments and Inter-group Relations," creating thereby the impression that it is in the economic sphere that inter-group relations can be most meaningfully studied. Yet a reading of that book does, in my view, provide material for a discussion, however tentative, of political relations among the peoples of Nigeria in the period up to 1800. It is the aim of this paper to attempt such a discussion, including, but also going beyond, the arguments about conquests, etc.

It is necessary to comment on the use of the word "group" in this paper. Writing in the 1980s it is tempting to use the word "group" to refer to Nigeria's many ethnic groups as we know them today. It is a fact of our history, however, that these ethnic groups (Igbo, Yoruba, Hausa, Fulani, Idoma, Ijo, Urhobo, Ibibio, etc) did not exist as such in the period covered by this paper. What did exist were many "groups" within each of today's ethnic groups, each of which was independent of the other, and had its own specific interests to protect. With the coming, first of the colonial quasi-state, and then the Nigerian nation-state, new challenges forced these pre-colonial "groups" to coalesce into today's ethnic groups for the purpose of meaningful participation in the politics of the new state. This fact of our history does create some problems for those engaged in a study of inter-group relations. While we know that, in the period covered by this paper for instance, it does not make historical sense to speak of Yoruba-Igala, Igbo-Igala or Edo–Yoruba relations, it is not yet possible to be always specific about which particular groups of Igbo, Yoruba or Edo were relating with which other specific groups. Where we can, we do specify the groups involved. Where we are compelled to use the groups as we know them today, this should always be read to mean that certain entities within one group related with certain other entities within the other group. This is bound to create some confusion for the reader. We apologise for this confusion which has arisen from the fact that the concept and identity of the various "groups" have changed over time in response to changing political realities. We do hope, however, that the context in which various groups are mentioned in what follows helps to make clear the intended meaning.

In deciding to engage in this discussion, I am fully aware that the subject is explosive, and that he who dares to throw out postulates on political relations among our peoples is likely to find himself assailed by historians and non-historians alike. This is because political relations in times past do touch on a most sensitive chord, and are capable of being exploited by various groups, as they seek the greatest advantage for themselves in the heat and differences of contemporary politics. So that the assault, when it begins, may have some focus, let me amplify what I am seeking to do in this paper.

First, let me state that I lay no claim to introducing any new materials on Nigerian history. Most of what I use in the discussion that follows are well known facts of Nigerian history. My aim is to raise certain questions to do with possible political interpretations of these well known facts. In the process some synthesis is also offered.

Secondly, I plan to have another look at the role of kingdoms and empires in inter-group relations in Nigeria. Some scholars have rightly drawn our attention to the fact that there is an over-concentration on these kingdoms and empires in our study of Nigerian history. Afigbo has drawn attention to the danger in "the myth that essential African history must be written around, and in terms of, the achievements and at times the equally grand failures of large political agglomerations usually known as empires and kingdoms."[3] In the same vein, Afigbo condemns the tendency to present the history of the smaller polities as mere footnotes to the history of the empires and kingdoms. These warnings are well taken, and there is a clear need to redress the balance. It would appear to me, however, that in dichotomising our history in terms of large and small-scale polities, certain misconceptions can arise. In my view, to see, for example, the history of the Isoko people in terms of the history of Benin must also be to see the history of Benin in terms of the history of the Isoko: the thrust must cut both ways. Certainly, in the context of inter-group relations, this is the only really acceptable interpretation, for the evidence abounds that the initiative in terms of relations did not always lie with the kingdoms and empires. The discussion which follows will, it is hoped, make it clear what the main thrust is in this regard, namely, a call for another look at certain aspects of our study of these kingdoms and empires in the context of the subject matter of this paper.

Thirdly, I am claiming that an attempt at a more penetrating analysis of political relations among our peoples in the period here covered constitutes a useful and important contribution to the search for a deeper understanding of how things have come to be, providing in the process answers to those who may wish to use past history for scoring cheap political points in today's setting. Such understanding, we historians believe, should be capable of influencing for the better, our peoples' attitudes to one another. By implication I am saying that the political history of Nigerian has not been so well and fully studied that the political historian must necessarily move into other areas of history in order to maintain a degree of respectability and acceptability. If anything, the undeniable link between trade and politics must call for more holistic historical studies which have to be the end products of our varying specialisations. Having thus barred my chest for the thrusts that must come, let us now proceed with the gamble.

On Origins of Dynasties*

One area where I consider it necessary to raise questions is that which deals with the origins of dynasties. In this regard, perhaps the most rewarding is that which deals with Benin –Ife dynastic links. The traditions which speak of Oranmiyan, an Ife prince, being sent to Benin at the request of the latter (or at least some group from the latter) are well known. We will, of course, never know exactly what transpired at the end of the Ogiso period of Benin history. But the Oranmiyan tradition appears to have gained acceptance, albeit in varied forms, in both Ife and Benin. However, there is argument as to the real founder of the Benin

*The reader would at this point notice that the issue discussed hereunder was also taken up in the last chapter (See pp. 48-51). I was tempted to just refer the reader to the previous chapter. I decided against such reference in order for this chapter to make sense to a reader who, for whatever reason, chooses to read this chapter without reading Chapter Three!

dynasty. A.F.C., Ryder, while recounting the tradition of how a number of Benin chiefs sent for "a sovereign from the Yoruba dynasty ruling in Ife", warms that this could be no more than a piece of culture capture designed to relate the Benin dynasty to the prestigious Ife royal line.[4]

The late R.E. Bradbury states that Oranmiyan on arrival in Benin found that it was difficult for a foreigner to rule Benin. "He therefore returned to Ife, having first impregnated the daughter of a village chief who, he said, would bear a son that would become king."[5] That son eventually become Eweka I. Goes on Bradbury, "That this dynasty was derived from Ife is beyond reasonable doubt", and proceeds to justify this claim in terms of Benin royal insignia being sent from Ife and the Ooni having to approve the succession. Then Bradbury concludes, "The essential point of this foundation legend is that, while the Kingship was from Ife, its first incumbent was a native-born Edo."[6]

P.A. Igbafe also comments on the Oranmiyan tradition. He recalls the division in Benin, following the rejection of Ogiamwen's rule,and how while a group sought to uphold the succession, another supported sending for a prince from Ife. "Benin traditions are not unanimous on whether Oranmiyan or Eweka, his son by a Benin woman, first ruled in Benin, as Oba of the new dynasty. The balance of evidence favours Eweka. The new dynasty therefore had Ife antecedents though rooted on Benin soil."[7]

There is, additionally, the Ekaladerhan tradition. A version of this tradition claims that Ekaladerhan was a Benin prince who was barred from the palace as a consequence of some palace turmoil. He eventually found his way to Ife and settled there. When the political crisis in Benin later led to a request for an Ife prince, this version goes on, Ekaladerhan was sent to his own people by the Ooni. The Ekaladerhan tradition has received a new twist from the immediate past Oba of Benin, Erediauwa II, who on a public occasion in 1982 claimed:

> There is no doubt that both the Ife Royal House and the Benin Royal House have a common ancestor. The point of disagreement is who that ancestor was and where he came from. To the Yoruba who call him Oduduwa, he came to Ife from the east. To us in Edo that person was no other than Ekaladerhan who was exiled by his father, the last Ogiso of Benin.[8]

Later in the same address, the Oba said, 'Now, after Oranmiyan there were four Obas before Oguola, starting with Eweka: the founder of the present dynasty."[9]

All of our Benin experts thus pointedly or by implication accept the Oranmiyan tradition. Yet there is, consciously or unconsciously, some preoccupation with ensuring that nothing is said that would create the impression that an Ife dynasty was established in Benin: the kingship was from Ife, but the first incumbent was a native-born Edo (Brandbury); the dynasty had Ife antecedents but it was rooted on Benin soil (Igbafe): Oranmiyan fathered Eweka but it is not Oranmiyan who founded the Benin dynasty but Eweka 1, Oranmiyan's son by a Benin woman.

What is the significance of the attitude of these experts? Because we are in the realm of oral tradition, it is understandable that the historians of Benin should be cautious. But I am not sure that their caution does not derive from a fear that they may be accused of saying that Benin was at some point in its history dependent on Ife, however minimal the degree of dependence. While the historian does not necessarily have to accept the traditions as history, he should not, by the way he presents our history, create the impression that dependence by one group on another for a period of time because of prevailing circumstances is a phenomenon that is not to be entertained in early Nigerian history. Such a phenomenon is a common-place of the history of the rest of the world. Are we to reject it for Nigeria just because we have no written documents to fall back on? Let us be cautious, certainly. But let us also leave all the options open.

Moreover, there is, in my judgment, an even more significant element to which attention should be drawn. It is noteworthy that none of the experts quoted saw fit to ask the question, what was the relationship between Benin and Ife that led to Ife being chosen as the place to send to for a prince. Was it a random choice? In seeking to answer this question, let me borrow the ideas of Afigbo who, in discussing the phenomenon of one group going elsewhere to be invested with particular offices, proffered this explanation:

> In the kind of environment that engendered the belief in the "brotherhood" of neighbouring monarchs, it would be nothing unusual for one crowned head to go to an elder or more powerful brother for the settlement of a dispute that seemed to threaten the integrity of the realm, or to procure from his court those of the symbols of his own office for which his "brother's" craftsmen were widely famed.

> Nor would it be anything unusual to obtain the "brother's" blessing during his accession and coronation.[10]

Afigbo's hypothesis, that of a "brotherhood" deliberately contrived as a charter for determining relations between neighbouring groups, is widespread in the Nigerian geographical area. How were these "brotherly" relations maintained? How was the relative age and influence of the "brothers" determined? Did the "brotherhood" become operative only in times of crisis? Did Benin send to Ife for a prince because Ife was the closest of the forest kingdoms? Was Ife indeed the closest kingdom? Would one send to a hostile neighbour for the kind of assistance Benin was seeking at this particular point in her history? In my judgment, we must postulate on-going relations between Benin and Ife prior to the Oranmiyan episode. Today, we would call those relations diplomatic. It seems to me that because we are over-preoccupied with the issue of sovereign-vassal relationship, which relationship is seem as being politically provocative in our present circumstances, we shy away from discussing other possible political relationships. To do so is clearly to limit the range of our analysis of inter-group relations.

From Benin let us move on to Igala which kingdom, it has been claimed, was firmly established in the 16th century or a little earlier. The emergence of this kingdom, Ade Obayemi has claimed, followed a "transfer of sovereignty form an aboriginal population – (the Okpoto of some accounts) to a foreigner, usually identified as Abutu Eje....or as a prince from Ado (Benin) or Apa (Wukari Jukun), or Yorubaland."[11]

Then there "was the emergence of Achadu, a foreigner from Igbo whose personal qualities led to his marriage to the female Atta and who became the patron (as ritual husband) of the Atta, and the leader of the traditional king-makers – the *Igala-Mella.*"[12] These traditions represent to my mind an expression of certain types of political relationship between the emerging Igala state and their neighbours. Obayemi tells us that at a later stage of development the Igala waged a war of independence against the Jukun and successfully rejected a tribute-paying status.[13] This presupposes a period of Jukun overlordship. The nature of this overlordship is unclear. It may well be that the 'foreigner' who is alleged to have played a role is the evolution of the Igala state was Jukun and that he had tied the Igala to the Jukun state system. Or it may be that the Jukun sought to maintain a continuing hold on one of themselves who had gone on to

Igala and so precipitated a crisis in Jukun-Igala relations. The Achadu tradition may well be seeking to explain a certain level of Igala-Igbo relations sufficiently crucial to have led to a degree of accommodation which made people of Igbo descent play an important part in the state system of Igala. The suggestion being made here is that the traditions which relate to the evolution of dynasties and state structures may well be encapsulating certain complex aspects of political relations between different Nigerian peoples, and that research must direct attention to this possibility and not just to the issue of sovereign-vassal relationship.

On the Issue of Socio-political Institutions, Titles and Investiture of Offices

A common phenomenon of Nigerian history is that certain groups have adopted or adapted the political institutions and/or titles systems of others. Also we have instances in which certain groups went outside their groups to take titles or to conduct investiture ceremonies. Thus those normally referred to as the western Igbo have adopted Benin-style political institutions and titles systems. The Urhobo and Isoko claim that certain aspects of their socio-political institutions were of Benin origin; some of their *ivie* used to go to Benin for investiture. The northern Igbo of the Nsukka area took Igala titles and also went there for investiture. S.A. Akintoye has shown that among the Ekiti, Akoko, and Owo, many chieftaincies have titles found in Benin.[14] The staff of office of the chief of Panda used to be given to him by the Atta of Idah.[15] For quite a while, the *Ohimigi* of Igu had to be recognised by the Atta of Idah before he could exercise the powers of his office.[16] The Idoma used to obtain titles first from Wukari, then from Idah.[17]

The above phenomenon has given rise to certain arguments in Nigerian historiography. What was the significance of the phenomenon in term of inter-group relations? Afigbo and P.A. Oguagha as well as a number of other scholars who have worked on the Igbo have been quick to point out that adoption of the socio-political institutions of Benin or Igala by the Igbo must not be seen as evidence of conquest or political domination of the Igbo by the Bini or Igala.[18] The point is well taken. Geographical proximity, migrations, social and commercial intercourse on a regular basis could and did lead to mutual borrowings. But so could conquest and political domination over a period of time. Akintoye's study of relations between Benin and the north-eastern Yoruba, already referred to, makes it quite clear that in the case of Owo, Akoko and Ekiti, Benin military and political dominance did play a part in determining the nature of the political institutions and chieftaincy titles which developed in those areas.[19] And in this instance, the issue was not between an empire or kingdom and a non-centralised political system; it was a matter of relations between one kingdom and other kingdoms. Indeed, the dichotomy between kingdoms and segmetary societies particularly explicit in Afigbo's handling of Igbo-Benin relations[20] may well be a false dichotomy.

Or let us take the issue of Benin-Lagos relations. Professor A.B. Aderibigbe's study of early Lagos history reveals that Lagos, then under the Olofin, was conquered by Benin probably in the 16th century.[21] The traditions speak of a heroic resistance by the soldiers of the Olofin, led by the ruler himself. In the upshot the Olofin was captured and taken to Benin. He returned to Lagos a vassal of the Oba of Benin. In fact Aderibigbe suggests that the present line of Lagos Obas descended from a Yoruba man by the name of Ashipa who conveyed to Benin the corpse of a Benin warrior-chief, Aseru. In gratitude for this noble act, the Oba of Benin, according to Aderibigbe, conferred the title of Olorogun of Lagos on him and also gave to him "a state sword and the royal Gbedu drum."[22] Ashipa, so the story goes, returned to Lagos with other persons sent by the Oba to assist him in the governance of Lagos. From the time of Ahipa's return, tribute was paid by Lagos to Benin with some breaks, till the British occupation.

If the above account represents anything like what actually happened, it is easy to see that the new ruling class would have contained Benin elements; but also that with time the Benin elements would have been assimilated into Lagos society and the descendants would increasingly become Yoruba till little of Benin blood remained. Even so, however, as Aderibigbe has pointed out, the Lagos chieftaincy system has been affected by the Benin period. Writes Aderibigbe, "there was the nucleus of the *Akarigbere* made up of *Eletu Odibo* and the *Eletu Iwase* who originally came with Oba from Benin."[23] Note the distinctly Edo sound of *Eletu Odibo*. Clearly, the Lagos political system was affected by the Benin conquest and here again we are concerned with political relations between two kingdoms.

Let us then return to the problem of Igbo – Benin and Igbo-Igala relations, and the preoccupation with excluding conquest as a determinant of these relations. In a sense, the issue is not that important. That presence of Benin and Igala titles is evidence of relations between some of the Igbo groups and these kingdoms. Admittedly, these titles, etc., could have been adopted as a consequence of prolonged contact of a social and economic nature. But why are we anxious to rule out the possibility of conquest? That Benin entered into an expansionist period in the 16th and 17th centuries is not doubted. If Benin could, and did conquer, certain parts of Yorubaland, including Lagos, why should we be unwilling to accept the possibility of conquest for some of the Igbo? Clearly the problem of logistics would be less than in the case of Lagos. The argument by Afigbo that Benin did not, as of the time, have a superiority in arms or a larger population to provide the manpower needed for the conquest[24] is untenable once we remind ourselves that speaking of Igbo-Benin relations makes no real sense unless we mean Aboh-Benin relations, Ogwashi-Uku-Benin relations, Agbor-Benin relations and so on. The Igbo groups were not acting as one large ethnic group; they were acting as so many sub-ethnic groups. It is therefore unlikely that the population of any of these sub-ethnic groups would have been so much more than that of Benin in its expansionist period as to rule out the possibility of Benin conquest. No one is saying that all the claim to conquest are to be accepted. What I do say is that it is just as objectionable to reject the conquest theory off hand on the ground, among others, that to accept it is to present "the history, of the West Niger Igbo….(as) a kind of footnote, to the history of the Benin empire."[25] I agree completely with both Afigbo and Oguagha when they argue that a great deal more research is needed in this area of Igbo-Benin relations. But to say that is to say that we must keep all the options open.

Finally, on this head, let us address ourselves to the basic issue. For me the basic issue is, what do groups seek to gain when they seek investiture from other groups or go to other groups for titles? Part of the answer is obvious: prestige and legitimisation. Benin, Igala, Nri, Wukari – all of these were important ritual centres as they were strong political entities. To be linked with them was to partake of their glory and prestige. And there is evidence that decline in glory resulted in a fall in the number of groups that maintained the association. I suggest, additionally, that there may well have been another consideration – that of security. Some of the smaller groups may well have sought to be linked, however tenuously, with some of the kingdoms and empires in the hope that knowledge of such a link would preempt attacks by their other neighbours. Such a consideration would be part of realpolitik. We also need to remind ourselves that groups that deliberately took titles or sought investiture from others would seek to maintain friendly relations with same. Would it be too farfetched to argue that here again we are considering aspects of diplomatic relations, deliberately cultivated for the purpose of satisfying certain needs of state?

On the Role of Kingdoms and Empires in the Nigerian Geographical Area

In what has been said above, reference has been made to works which claim that Nigerian history has been written by some in a manner which creates the impression that the larger political entities, the kingdoms and empires, dominated the history of smaller, non-centralised groups. Evidence of this trait, Afigbo claims, can be found in the traditions of origin of groups like the Isoko, Urhobo, some of the Igbo groups – those traditions which link these groups to Benin.[26] Further evidence has to do with the conquest theory already discussed. Some of the criticism is fully justified. On the issue of origins, as this affects Benin, the state of knowledge, and the evidence from linguistics, are such that many of the claims need revision. Often what the claim to Benin origin means really is no more than that at some stage in Benin history groups moved out and settled among other 'Nigerian' groups already settled elsewhere.[27] The reference to Benin as a place of origin in such circumstances may be due to the fact that the migration from Benin was the last of the migrations and so the most remembered. Or the tradition may have been deliberately built up for the selfish reason of the particular group itself, not in glorification of Benin but in self-glorification. More fundamentally, how does a claim to origin from a centralised political system Benin, Idah, Ife or whatever, provide evidence of the dominance of our history by certain groups who themselves must have migrated or received migrants from other groups? Admittedly in the Yoruba country, the alleged role of Ile-Ife as a centre of dispersal for the Yoruba people (a theory that has, I believe, been exploded by Obayemi and others) has in recent times led to all sorts of complications in relations between the Obas of Yorubaland. But observe that that alleged role did not stop the rise of the Old Oyo Empire which, in terms of over-all impact on Nigerian history, can be said to have dwarfed Ife. Note that in the changed circumstances of the

19th century, the alleged place of Ife in Yoruba history did not stop Ife falling before the onslaught of Modakeke or becoming a tributary state to Ibadan for a period.[28] Clearly, it would be wrong to claim that because certain traditions of origin say that certain Yoruba groups migrated from Ife, therefore the history of former is but a footnote to the history of the latter. To make that kind of claim is clearly to over-react. Our conclusions must be based on the totality of the evidence, not on chosen strands thereof. With that comment, permit me to leave that aspect of the matter and proceed to some re-interpretation of the role of kingdoms and empires in our history in the context of inter-group relations.

Perhaps the first point that should be made is that which has to do with the state formation and empire building process. Wherever one looks, that process necessarily involved the widening of the area of activity. If we take Old Oyo, for example, and assume that Oranmiyan and his followers went on one long trek from Benin to Ife and then on to their new home, the very wanderings would have resulted in a thorough mixing of peoples. Then would come the actual settling down process in an area in which both Nupe and Borgu elements already had or were soon to have interests. The accompanying struggle for supremacy (and land?) in the area accounts for the Oyo-Nupe and Oyo-Borgu wars with which we are all familiar. These wars, while they lasted, were admittedly disruptive of economic and other peaceful pursuits. But, as has been argued by Akinjogbin and Ayandele, they undoubtedly had the result of forcing all parties concerned to strengthen their fighting forces and to become more cohesive in the process.[29] A strengthening of fighting forces was a major prerequisite for the expansionist phase of Old Oyo which ended with the establishment of her power and influence over the Egba, Egbado, Dahomey, etc, a definite widening of Old Oyo's area of activity and of influence.

Or let us take the situation in Hausaland.[30] The state formation process in the area can be said to have involved the migration of groups from surrounding areas. Thus, whether we take the example of the Bagauda dynasty or of 'the stranger from Turunku' in the case of Zazzau, we are dealing with a process of social and political accommodation of various groups. But perhaps even more important for our purpose is the inconclusiveness of empire building efforts in Hausaland in the period up to 1800. The many wars which feature in the history of Hausaland in this period represent the effort by the various states (each of which in the context of this paper represents a separate, independent, distinct unit) to expand their economic, political and military might at the expense of the neighbouring peoples. Sometimes, the rise of new states like Kebbi or the consolidation of others like Gobir, was only possible at the expense of already established ones. The 'empires' of Queen Amina of Zaria and Kebbi about which Adeleye speaks must have represented wide-ranging contacts and influence involving the reduction of certain other states to tribute paying status for varying lengths of time. The struggle for economic and political supremacy between Kano and Katsina is well known. That struggle was only brought to an end by the menace of the Kwararafa which forced Kano and Katishina into a treaty of amity, the better to be able to withstand the Kwararafa threat. The Gobir-Zamfaara conflicts were marked by shifting loyalties and varying fortunes which had a marked effort on the geo-politics of the area. Taken together, these wars of the period from the 16th to the 18 century, including the wars between the Kwararafa and Hausaland and Borno, as well as those between Borno and Hausaland, would have involved considerable population shifts in the form of war captives. Such captives were forced to make new homes, for themselves; some became important members of the *masu sarauta* in their new homes. Indeed, one can claim that the wars would have played an important role in the emergence of a common Hausa culture.

Nor was that all. The Hausa states also waged wars in the Middle Belt area. Not all the soldiers and the traders' who accompanied them to minister to their needs returned to Hausaland. Some stayed back and fused with peoples of the area into which they had moved. Mahdi Adamu tells us that this kind of fusion was responsible for the emergence of certain new ethnic groups like the Gwandara, Dakarawa, Dukawa and Muryam.[31] In other instances, Hausa settlers succeeded in establishing new dynasties in the areas into which they had moved. Adamu gives the examples of Yawuri, Kumbashi, Gwari and Kanam.[32] In other words, the state formation process and the struggle for survival and mastery which followed that process in Hausaland produced important and lasting geo-political results in the area, involving a delicate balancing of interests among quite a number of groups, as well as producing a permanent impact on the demography of the entire area north of the Niger-Benue confluence.

There is perhaps no need to take the case of Borno at any length in this paper, for that is one of the better known cases of our history. Even within what one might describe as metropolitan Borno, the emergence first of the kingdom and then of the empire represented not just an on-going process of fusion and accommodation, it also saw series of migrations from the Borno area which migration are reflected in the traditions of many groups in the 'Middle Belt.'[33] It also saw various Hausa states becoming tributary for varying lengths of time to Borno. The stalemate between Borno and Kwararafa was testimony to a balance of military might between them. In fact, Adamu has argued that the military might of the Kwararafa was one of the factors that checkmated Hausa and Borno empire building efforts in the 'Middle Belt'[34] in this period – a fact of lasting political significance for Nigerian politics.

The activities which have been summarised in the immediately preceding pages, to which one must add similar activities involving the Delta States, Benin, Igala, etc, were clearly wide-ranging. To them we must add the trading activities of these states and empires which, necessarily, were just as wide-ranging. Robin Horton has argued that one phenomenon of the non-centralised polities was the absence of a class, the full time business of which was to govern.[35] Conversely, in every kingdom and empire there did exist a class that needed to be provided for because it was concerned with the business of governing. Providing for this class called forth additional economic activity. Also, once an empire gets under way, new demands arise – including the maintenance of the military machine – which necessitates greater economic activity. In sheer volume, complexity and range, therefore, the economic activities of a kingdom or empire are likely to outstrip those of a smaller polity. In this context it is not, I consider, necessary to detail the trading activities of Borno, the Hausa states, Nupe, Igala, Benin, Old Oyo, the delta states, etc. These are well known in terms of their extent, range and many-sidedness. In terms of what I regard as the needless dichotomy between kingdoms and empires and non-kingdoms, it must be clear that the initiative in terms of trade was dictated not by the size of the polity but by the needs of such polity. Therefore there can be no question of one group constantly dictating how the economy shall be ordered, except where one is vassal to the other. A good example of a small polity taking a leading initiative in trade is that of the Aro. Aro commercial activities are well known. Those activities have given the Aro a predominant position in the history of South-eastern Nigeria in the period up to 1800, and even in the 19th century. The point which has been made that the Aro did not establish a "political empire" over Igboland can, in my judgment, detract nothing from that predominance. In terms of inter-group relations, Aro trading activities were an important determinant of inter-group relations even in political terms, in certain areas of South-eastern Nigeria. It is, for example, difficult to argue that a group that provided a final court of appeal for others had no political impact on these others. But that is a debate that can be taken up elsewhere.

On Conquests and Payment of Tribute

Before we conclude, it is perhaps necessary to say a few words about conquests and the payment of tribute. First, we need to remind ourselves that in the African setting, before the coming of Shaka, conquests were hardly ever total, nor was the payment of tribute always permanent. Perhaps the best example of the latter fact can be found in relations between Borno and Hausaland and between the different Hausa states. The evidence from these places is that payment of tribute was an acceptance of temporary defeat or incapacitation. Thus Kano, or Katsina paid tribute to Borno as a means of securing a lull in hostilities. Whenever either state felt internally strong enough, it withheld the payment of tribute. If Borno felt strong enough, war was resumed; if not, things were allowed to lie. In other words, the payment of tribute was quite often an instrument of diplomacy. What is true for Borno and Hausaland is true for other areas. References to Igala refusing to pay tribute to the Jukun, or of some Edoid groups falling off in the payment of tribute to Benin, or of Nupe and Oyo each seeking to throw off tribute paying status at different time in their history, are clear indications that conquests were not always permanent; that no one state was dominant for all or even most of its history over all surrounding peoples. There was something of a cycle in the history of these states. The size of empires kept altering all the time in line with the balance of power between the metropolitan power and the outlying provinces. That balance of power was in turn determined by a variety of other factors. It is also important to remind ourselves that sometimes payment of tribute must have been embarked upon to pre-empt war and conflict, another instance of diplomatic manourve. Thus it is more than likely that some of the Edoid and western Igbo groups which claim to have paid tribute to Benin fall into this category. Seen in this light, I believe that inter-group relations among our multifarious peoples fall into greater historical perspective.

By Way of Conclusion

In concluding, it is important for me to state that nothing said in this paper is designed to justify an over-concentration on the history of empires and kingdoms. I certainly don't take the view that the history of the non-centralised polities was dictated by the kingdoms and empires. That history had its own dynamics, which included relations with other groups, be those centralised or non-centralised polities. Indeed in the realm of inter-group relations, there were ways in which non-centralised polilties played crucial roles in the history of centralised polities. Perhaps an excellent example is that given by E.J. Alagoa in his examination of relations between Benin and the Ijọ groups of Olodiama, Furupagha and Egbema. These groups, according to Alagoa, controlled the site of Ughoton, the port of Benin. The Oba of Benin had to enter into formal agreement with these Ijọ groups to secure hitch-free use of the port.[36] Clearly, in this instance, a non-centralised polity was important enough in the affairs of a centralised polity to demand adequate attention. As earlier indicated, the thrust of relations was not and could not have been always one way.

Secondly, I find it unacceptable that historians of early Nigeria should seek to debunk the idea of conquests in the relations between certain groups. Certainly not all such claims are to be entertained. We need to examine the evidence closely, to continue our researches in the bid to establish what in fact did happen. But we cannot reject the idea of conquests even before our researches are concluded. History is full of groups gaining temporary ascendancy in war as in other fields over their neighbours. We do not have to deny that possibility for our history. What we need to do is to seek to understand exactly how the conquests which took place took place; to seek an understanding of their significance and impact; what they meant to the two groups concerned; what relations subsisted after the hostilities.

Thirdly, it is my view that our examination of political relations between Nigerian groups has been too simplistic. Political relations do not consist just of an examination of sovereign-vassal relationship; they consisted of a number of other forms of association. I am making a call for a closer examination of these other possibilities.

Finally, it is my contention that as historians, we have not sufficiently drawn attention to the role of the kingdoms and empires which did flourish in the Nigerian geographical area in the shaping of what we may refer to as modern Nigeria. It is not enough to say that peoples traded together and that they intermarried. They did more. The kingdoms and empires through conquest, assimilation and other processes brought many Nigerian peoples together, albeit in different geographical locations. The Benin Empire had within it not only those who may be described as Edoid, but also Yoruba and Igbo. It had relations with the Igala and Nupe kingdoms. It clearly also had relations with Igbo and Ijọ groups which may never have come within its political umbrella as such. The Old Oyo empire had within it a number of the Yoruba groups which would otherwise have been independent. It had fairly close dealings with the Nupe and Borgu. The Igala kingdom, as has been shown, had relations of a political nature with many groups of the Middle Belt. So had Nupe. In the farther north, the Hausa states, in their effort to see whether any of them could become the master of the region, must have come to know each other very closely indeed. Nor was that all. Warfare between the Hausa states and Borno and the Middle Belt led not only to a great mixing of peoples, but to permanent settlement of Hausa in the Middle Belt and the emergence of new ethnic groups, the result of fusion between the hosts and the newcomers. Some of these Hausa migrants succeeded in establishing dynasties in some of the Middle Belt centres. The over-all consequence of these developments was that those who became Nigerians were not nearly so strange to one another as is so often proclaimed when we are faced with political difficulties in modern Nigeria. Our history before the coming of the British had witnessed 'overlapping imperialisms' which must have left their mark on the thinking of our peoples; on their estimation of various neighbours and on their attitude to the coming of the British. Besides, the remembrance of the events of pre-British days must continue to linger in certain areas and under certain circumstances of our present day politics. The more we understand the politics of the past, the more we are likely to present a fuller interpretation of the politics of today.

NOTES

1. A.E Afigbo, "Igbo-Benin Relations: Some Problems of Methodology and Perspective" – Lecture delivered under the auspices of the National Commission for Museums and Monuments, 1982, (mimeograph), Hereinafter this paper is cited as Afigbo, "Igbo-Benin Relations".
2. See, for example, Afigbo in the lecture cited above and Ade Obayemi, "Some Observations on the History of the Nigerian Middle Belt" – mimeograph.
3. A.E. Afigbo, "The Bini Mirage and the History of South Central Nigeria" *Nigeria Magazine* (Lagos), No. 137, 1981.
4. A.F.C Ryder, "The Benin Kingdom" in Obaro Ikime (Editor), *Groundwork of Nigerian History*, Heinemann Educational Books for the Historical Society of Nigeria, Ibadan, 1980, p. 110.
5. R.E. Bradbury, *Benin Studies*, edited by Peter Morton-Williams, O.U.P 1973, p. 8.
6. Ibid.
7. P.A. Igbafe, "Benin in the Pre-Colonial Era", in *Tarikh*, Vol. 5, No. 1, 1974, p. 7.
8. Address by His Highness the Oba of Benin at the Formal Opening of the Exhibition of "The Lost Treasures of Ancient Benin" by the National Commission for Museums and Monuments on 29 April, 1982, (Mimeograph).
9. *Ibid.*
10. Afigbo, "The Benin Mirage".
11. Ade Obayemi "States and Peoples of the Niger Benue Confluence Area" in *Groundwork*, p. 150.
12. *Ibid.*
13. *Ibid.*
14. S.A. Akintoye, "The North-Eastern Yoruba Districts and the Benin Kingdom", *Journal of the Historical Society of Nigeria*, Vol. IV, No. 4. 1969, pp 539-553.
15. Paula Brown, "The Igbira" in Daryll Forde (Editor), *Peoples of the Niger Benue Confluence*, London, International African Institute, 1970 p. 57.
16. *Ibid.*
17. P.A. Oguagha, "The Igbo and their Neighbours: An overview" – paper presented at the University of Benin during the National symposium on Igbo Origins and Culture, May 21, 1983. Mimeograph) p. 19.
18. Oguagha as cited above; Afigbo, "Benin Mirage".
19. Akintoye, *op.cit.*
20. Afigbo, "Benin Mirage" and "*Igbo-Benin Relations*".

21. A.B. Aderibigbe, "Early History of Lagos to about 1850" in A.B. Aderibigbe (Editor) *Lagos; The Development of an African a City* Longman, Nigeria, 1975, p. 5.
22. Aderibigbe, p. 7.
23. Aderibigbe, p. 9.
24. Afigbo, "Benin Mirage".
25. Afigbo, "Igbo-Benin Relations".
26. Afigbo, "Benin Mirage".
27. Dr. Ben Elugbe's work on the languages of the Edoid peoples reaches this conclusion.
28. See J.F. Ade Ajayi and S.A. Akintoye, "Yorubaland in the 19th Century" in *Groundwork*, p. 285.
29. I.A. Akinjogbin and E.A. Ayandele, "Yorubaland up to 1800" in *Groundwork*, p. 129.
30. The discussion of Hausaland in this paper is, except otherwise indicated, based on Abdullahi Smith, "The Early stages of the Central Sudan"; John Hunwick, "Songhay, Borno and Hausaland"; and R.A. Adeleye, "Hausaland and Borno". in J.F. Ade Ajayi and Michael Crowder (Editors), 1976. *History of West Africa*, Vol. I, Longman (Second Editor), 1976.
31. Mahdi Adamu, *The Hausa Factor in West African History*, Ahmadu Bello University Press, Zaria, and O.U.P., Ibadan, 1978, pp 27-32.
32. Adamu, pp 32-37.
33. See for example, Sa'ad Abubakar, "Peoples of the Upper Benue Basin and Bauchi Plateau before 1800" in *Groundwork of Nigerian History.*
34. Adamu, p. 26.
35. Robin Horton, "Stateless Societies in the History of West Africa" in Ajayi and Crowder, *op.cit.* p. 72.
36. E.J. Alagoa, "Neighbours of Benin" (mimeograph).

5

THE HISTORICAL BASIS OF NIGERIAN UNITY*

The formulation of the title of this lecture is such that lends itself to at least two interpretations. It could, for example, imply that Nigerian unity already exists, and that what we are about to do is to explain the historical basis of that already existing unity. Or it could be raising the question whether there is a historical basis on which Nigerian unity can be forged, implying thereby that that unity is yet to materialise. It is, of course, the latter interpretation that I adopt in what follows. I will naturally be tackling my subject as a historian; but I will also be doing so as an informed citizen of Nigeria.

Getting Rid of Certain Misconceptions

Whenever the issue of Nigerian unity comes up for discussion, there is a tendency for many a Nigerian to be apologetic, to find excuses which are deftly paraded as reasons why we have, almost necessarily, to remain disunited! We all know the usual arguments. Nigeria is a multi-ethnic

*This lecture was delivered at the Ogun State University, Ago-Iwoye, on the occasion of the launch of the Students Historical Society of Ogun State University on 29 May, 1985.

nation – a commonwealth of separate nations almost. It is difficult, given this intractable problem, for us to achieve true national unity because of the many differences that exist amongst our multifarious peoples. Or Nigeria is an artificial creation of the British. Not only does the artificiality of our creation continue to militate against efforts at achieving national unity, the very colonial experience which followed on the artificial creation has left a heritage of ethnocentricity and divisiveness which constitute veritable obstacles in our search for national unity. On the surface, these arguments appear plausible, and it is easy to point to specific episodes in our history to justify same. I wonder, however, whether, when we make these arguments, we bother to put Nigeria into the wider context of world history. How many mono-ethnic nations are there in the world? How many nations which now have a *lingua franca* began with only *one* language? Even Great Britain, the country that colonised us, is it a mono-ethnic nation? How many ethnic groups are to be found in the United States of America? Does the fact that the term "ethnic group" or "tribe" etc is not used to describe the Irish, the English, the Poles, the Germans, the Jews, the Africans, etc. who constitute the citizenry of the United States make that country a mono-ethnic state? Take France, Germany, Italy, Russia or whatever nation you will, the story is the same. If these other nations have managed to achieve national unity, we too can do the same.

As for the artificiality of Nigeria, which nation of the world is not artificial in that sense? Which nation is the Garden of Eden – created by God Almighty? And with regard to our colonial experiences, few peoples of the world have escaped being colonised by one power or the other over varying periods of time. Our colonisers were themselves once a colony of the Roman Empire. The United States grew out of a collection of British colonies. Even Japan, today a threat in the industrial field to the world's super-powers, had her share of colonial experience. Clearly, then, sixty years of colonialism cannot, must not, constitute for us an eternal excuse for our inability to forge a united Nigeria. National unity, wherever it has been successfully established, has not always been a child of natural growth. Quite often, deliberate and painful steps had to be taken to force the concept of unity on the people and then to evolve a philosophy or ideology that has sustained and nurtured the idea of national unity. A few examples come readily to mind! Germany, Italy, the United States, France. Bismarck's blood and iron policy may have been objectionable to some; yet German unity owes a great deal to the vision of Bismarck. Garibaldi and Carvour had to shed blood to transform Italy from a geographical expression to a meaningful geo-political entity. America's civil war may have been fought over conflicting perspectives on slavery and slave holding; it was also fought to keep the emergent state one. Even the English civil war of the 17th century had elements of ethnicity in it: Scots versus English. Why is Britain sinking funds in Ireland? One can go on, but there's hardly any need to. What emerges is clear: the unity of any nation is invariably a product of its history.

Unity is an attribute that once achieved requires to be deliberately cultivated and delicately nurtured. That nurturing is manifested in developmental and other programmes consciously undertaken in the interest of that hard won unity. I shall come back to this idea later in this talk. For now the point I wish to make and stress is simply this: that there is nothing in our history that is so different from the history of the rest of the world, that national unity should elude us for all time. Other nations of the world sought after and achieved national unity. We must do likewise. Away then with all of those misconceptions, all of those facile arguments which create the impression that ours is a very special, almost rare, problem. It is not. What we lack is the will to realise an end which we all agree is desirable. If we are to acquire that will, I suggest that our past history has certain lessons to teach us. We must proceed to examine those lessons soon; but before that there's one more aspect of our mental make up that must be jettisoned. Just what is that?

Ignorance and Stereotypes as Factors Militating Against National Unity

If national unity means anything, it must, among others, mean that the component parts of the united nation know about themselves and respect their varying cultures and susceptibilities. In Nigeria, it is precisely in this sphere that we are at our worst. Far too many Nigerians, including many in high places of policy-making and execution, know painfully little about the peoples for whom they make policy. I am sure there are ministers who have never read any history of the country over whose affairs they now preside. University teachers are no better. There may well be many here at the Ogun State University who have never visited the Cross River State, and the Efik, the Ibibio, the Anang, etc. of that state. I have met people at the University of Ibadan who think that Bonny in Rivers State is the same as Borno. Yet these ignoramuses aspire to high office and make pronouncements about Nigeria from their high pedestals, sometimes in a manner which makes national unity more difficult to achieve. Because of our massive ignorance about the culture and history of the various peoples who constitute Nigeria, we are content to make do with stereotypes. Here in the South, the Hausa-Fulani (and by this is meant virtually all the peoples who inhabit the area north of the Niger-Benue waterway!) is *gambari* – an ignorant fool; the Yoruba is tricky and utterly untrustworthy, a specie to be constantly watched; the Igbo is grabbing and fiercely and incurably ethnic: the Bini, wicked and dangerous; "Sobo wayo".

These "blatant misconceptions and alienating stereotypes" not only prevent us from knowing the real peoples with whom we must live and work, they make inter-personal and inter-group relations difficult and so retard national unity. If we are to grow beyond these stereotypes, we must diligently seek knowledge about Nigeria's multifarious peoples. Historians, sociologists, ethnographers, etc., must provide the material that will furnish this knowledge. Our educational system must insist that this kind of knowledge be acquired, certainly before our young people get into tertiary institutions. Permit me, in this regard, to quote what Professor C. C. Ifemesia has said about this same matter:

> Self-knowledge, diligently acquired, enables one to appreciate one's likes and dislikes, strengths and weaknesses, excellencies and imperfections, and everything else that goes to promote one's emotional poise and spiritual stability, and so to foster inter-personal relations. As with individual and inter-personal relations so with the culture group and Inter-group relations. These would be advanced if culture groups knew enough about the backgrounds and antecedents of their neighbours; for that would enable the one to know the merits and defects of the other and so they can tolerate one another and interact with the minimum of friction and conflict.

In other words, national unity requires a deepening of knowledge and understanding as between our various culture groups and peoples, the promotion of a spirit of tolerance, the development of empathy. These are all attributes that require conscious effort and cultivation. The search for knowledge about our fellow Nigerians must be accompanied by a humbling awareness about the factors which shape a people's culture. There is in this country a certain cultural arrogance about our different peoples which can be off-putting. Since I am in Ogun State, let me start with the Yoruba. The Yoruba, like all other peoples, are extremely proud of their language and culture. Often, again quite naturally, they break into their language even when in mixed company. I, as a non-Yoruba, understand that this is not done with intent to hurt the non-Yoruba present on the scene. However, the same Yoruba that feel free to break into their language in mixed company are quick to react when I, for instance, speak Isoko to a fellow Isoko. It is as if while they are free to speak their language, I must not speak mine. And quite often, they react with derision in their voices. Mahdi Adamu, writing on the Hausa in West African History, says that the Hausa language is a colonising language. The implication is that there is something special about the Hausa language.

Mahdi Adamu must know that if the Hausa language has spread as widely as it has, that is a factor of history, not result of anything special about the Hausa language itself. In North-South relations in the country, the Hausa-Fulani (used in the broadest sense) tend to believe that they have retained their culture while we in the South have jettisoned ours and become Europeanised. Culture is a dynamic entity. It is changing all the time, however imperceptibly. It changes in reaction to its environment, contact with other cultures, the prevailing economic situation, and so on. Not to be aware of this is to be massively ignorant. Thus the culture of which the Hausa-Fulani are so justly proud is the product of the local environment, and centuries of contact with North Africa, the Arab world and Islam. If the Hausa-Fulani and the Kanuri have reacted culturally to contact with other peoples and cultures, they must grant those in the South the same right to react culturally to their contacts. To behave and speak as if our own particular culture is something special and is inherently superior to those of others is avoidable cultural arrogance. And cultural arrogance can militate against harmonious inter-personal and inter-group relations. Let us, therefore, seek knowledge about one another - consciously, continuously. And I submit that the key to the kind of knowledge that we must seek lies in the history of our different peoples. Let us now look at aspects of this history.

The Issue of the Separateness of Nigeria's Ethnic Groups

Origins: As already indicated, one of the arguments usually advanced for why national unity tends to elude us is that our peoples lived separate and independent lives before the British forcefully brought us together. That claim is a fact of history. Yet, I wonder just what we mean by our peoples in this context. I wonder, also, when these peoples about whom we speak emerged. Who in the 14th century were the Kanuri? Who were the Hausa? Who were the Fulani? Who were the Igbo? Who were the Yoruba? Who were the Tivi? Who were the Bini? Who were the Ijọ, the Efik, the Ebira, the Kakanda, the Igala and so on? Any historian who has cared to study the traditions of origins of our peoples must be struck by the fact that all of our peoples eventually emerged as a result of a fusion of many strands of migrants. I don't know when the Yoruba could be said to have finally emerged as an identifiable cultural and linguistic group. Whenever that was, the group that emerged was an amalgam of different earlier groups. What is true for the Yoruba is true for all of Nigeria's ethnic groups. In other words, the ethnic and/or cultural group, which today have hardened into such blocks as to threaten the very fabric of our nation, are all a product of the coming together of formerly different peoples, brought together by forces of geography and history and ultimately evolving into what we know today.

Clearly, the same or similar forces of geography and history, now strengthened by the legal, ethical and physical sanctions of a nation-state, Nigeria, are still at work and, properly harnessed, can create the much sought-after citizen of Nigeria. When I make this point to my students, they laugh at me: they think I am a dreamer. Some even accuse me of falsifying history. Really? Permit me to illustrate my point with just one example. The founding father of the Old Oyo Empire is said to be Oranmiyan, the same Ife prince who is said to have founded the present Benin dynasty. The story is that after fathering the child who was to become Eweka I of Benin, Oranmiyan left Benin, convinced that as a stranger his rule would not be acceptable to the Bini. It is not clear whether he returned to Ife before setting off on the journey that led to the founding of what became Old Oyo. Be that as it may, let us imagine how long it must have taken to wander from Benin to Ife and then on to the outskirts of Nupe and Borgu territory. Who were those who finally arrived at this new area? The same small group that left Benin or Ife? Hardly. Clearly, the years of wandering must also have meant years of admixture of population. Those who settled near Borgu and Nupe territory must have been a thoroughly mixed group – who became known as Oyo. The mixing continued after settlement as inter-marriage between the new comers and the Nupe and Borgawa became a regular feature of relations in that area. So, who were the Old Oyo Yoruba? Yet the hybrid nature of their origins did not stop them becoming identified as Oyo Yoruba. It was as Oyo Yoruba that they fought the Nupe and Borgawa. So, what is so inherently impossible about today's hybrid peoples of Nigeria developing into real Nigerians, united in certain common goals and philosophies? Our peoples were and are separate, but not quite as separate as is sometimes imagined and/or even propagated in the heat and differences of today's politics.

While still on the matter of the origins of our peoples, which student of history has not come across the inevitable sons of a common father, each of whom founded the settlements that constitute a clan, chiefdom or even a kingdom? Is that not what lies behind the ebi system propounded by Professor I.A. Akinjogbin in his treatment of the origins of the Yoruba kingdoms? Is that not what the Bayajida legend represents in Hausa history? And yet, do we not know, or at least strongly believe, that what these stories represent is probably different? Some have argued that what these stories really mean is that various groups settled in different areas. Over time expansion brought them in contact with one another. Conflicts ensued over claims to territory; wars were fought. But conflicts and wars militated against peaceful and gainful pursuits. So the groups concerned entered into a covenant by which they agreed to regard themselves as brothers. As brothers they were, by the same covenant, forbidden to make war on one another. Thereafter, closer contacts developed; more fusion took place; a people emerged. In other words, the challenges and realities of history produced some of the groups we now identify as this or that ethnic group. If it happened before, it can happen again: our multifarious peoples can, with the right leadership, be made to work towards a more united Nigeria. But, there has to be the will; compelling reasons and reasoning that can nurture the will. Above all, there has to be equal rights and justice.

I am only too aware that the points made about origins of our peoples and deliberately forged covenants may, for many in this audience, sound rather farfetched. At any rate, it may be argued, I am talking about activities which took place in the dim and remote past. Clearly, today's

Nigerians cannot be expected to be guided by such remote antecedents! For those who are inclined to argue that way, let me hasten to say that the issue of origins is not the only one on which I hang my argument that our peoples were not nearly as separate, as distinct, as we often prefer to think. Let us look at the sphere of trade.

Inter-Group Trade: Perhaps this is one sphere about which there cannot be too much argument. It is a well known fact that pre-colonial Nigerian peoples traded among themselves. The very geographical configuration of our nation – a coastal, mangrove zone, an evergreen forest zone and a savannah zone – was one which made interchange of the commodities of these various zones a major determinant of inter-group relations. The varying endowments of different parts of the country in terms of relative fertility of the soil, the presence or absence of particular minerals like salt, iron, tin, etc, also determined the nature of the exchange of commodities. It is not intended here to go into the details of inter-group trade in pre-colonial times. It is assumed that these details are, on the whole, well known by the majority of my listeners. What must be done is to draw attention to certain issues related to, or arising from, inter-group trade which I consider relevant to our subject.

One, is the intensity of commercial relations between geographically proximate peoples – Borno and the neighbouring states; Benin and the Yoruba of Owo and the Akure region: the northern Igbo and the Igala; the Ijọ of the eastern delta and their Igbo neighbours to the hinterland; the Efik and the Igbo and Ibibio; Oyo and Nupe; Itsẹkiri and the Urhobo; Benin and the western Igbo, to list only a few selected examples. Successful and intense trade of the type that existed between these various peoples had important consequences for other forms of relationships. Thus inter-marriages were a common feature between the peoples listed above. Given our socio-cultural milieu, these inter-marriages were a major cementing factor in inter-personal as in inter-group relations. Then there was the bilingualism that commercial activity engendered. Taken together, these two factors must have reduced considerably that feeling of separateness that politicians like to stress when it suits their purposes. Our peoples were not as separate in their living and their activities as is sometimes imagined. If we thus have a history of considerable interaction in these spheres, we can use that as part of the basis for forging national unity in our changed circumstances of the 20th [now 21st] century.

Two, commercial relations also often led to cultural borrowings as well as voluntary migrations and settlements. Let us take a few examples. It is well known that some of the northern Igbo moved into the Igala kingdom for purposes of farming and trading. These Igbo settled in southern Igala, creating thereby a zone of mixed population and becoming heavily Igalarised as a consequence. Later on in the history of the two peoples, the Igala, responding to the southern pull of the Atlantic slave trade, moved into Igboland via the Niger and Anambra rivers and established settlements or quarters in Igboland and Igbo towns, reversing the earlier direction of movement and acculturation. Is it any wonder that Igala titles are found among the northern Igbo or that some of these northern Igbo went to Igala for title-taking ceremonies? Or take relations between Benin and the western Igbo. While some scholars have questioned the thesis that Benin conquered western Igboland and imposed political dominion over it, none has denied the presence of Benin type socio-political institutions in this area. Indeed, the scholars who question or deny the conquest theory explain the similarities in socio-political culture in terms of the close social and commercial relations between these western Igbo communities and Benin. So, just how separate, how strange, were these two groups, one to the other? Or take Old Oyo and Nupe. Today, the *Egungun* festival is, with most people, more associated with the Yoruba than with the Nupe. Yet we know, don't we, that the *Egungun*, was borrowed by Old Oyo from Nupe as a consequence of geographical proximity and intense commercial relations. Although we recognise that the area north of the Niger-Benue is made up of a large number of ethnic groups, is it not also true that there are certain common cultural traits, especially in the mode of dress and the use of the Hausa language as a *lingua franca* in this area? Is it not true that these common cultural traits are largely a function of centuries of commercial relations (including movements of peoples as earlier pointed out) and other social contacts? And can anyone doubt that these common cultural traits (even if for now we don't add Islam, itself a veritable conveyor of culture) have made it easier for these groups to relate? What has been said for the groups here mentioned can be said for many other Nigerian groups. I submit that cultural affinities and a heritage of common sojourning can be harnessed for the building of national unity, just as some unpatriotic Nigerians have sought to use cultural dissimilarities to drive us farther apart.

The Role of Kingdoms and Empires in Widening the Scope of Activities and Operations among Nigerian Peoples

When people argue that before the coming of the British the various Nigerian peoples each had a separate existence, they pay little regard to the role of kingdoms and empires in widening the scope of activities of various Nigerian peoples. This role was political, economic, social and ritual, if we may take a few examples, beginning with the kingdoms. The emergence of the Igala kingdom has been dated to the 16th century, and possibly earlier. Ade Obayemi tells us that the emergence of the kingdom followed a "transfer of sovereignity from an aboriginal population...to a foreigner, usually identified as Abute Eje... or as a prince from Ado [Benin] or Apa [Wukari Jukun], or Yorubaland or Agenapoje from heaven. The next phase thus expressed in myth is the emergence of Achadu, a foreigner from Igbo whose personal qualities led to his marriage to the female Atta and who became the patron (as ritual husband) of the Atta, and the leader of the traditional kingmakers – the Igala Mella". Obayemi also talks of a period when the Igala rejected a tribute-paying status and waged a successful war of independence against the Jukun. Obayemi further draws attention to the linguistic affinity between the Igala and Yoruba; and suggests that the territories of the Igala and Yoruba were, at some time in the past, geographically contiguous, pointing out that Ajaokuta and Geregu on the west bank of the Niger are Igala-speaking, reminders of the period of geographical contiguity. Closely examined, what Obayemi is saying is that the emergence of the Igala kingdom involved relations of different types with quite a number of Nigerian peoples – the Idoma whom the Igala pushed out of their original habitat, the Jukun against whom a war of independence war fought; the Yoruba who were neighbours of the Igala kingdom; the Bini with whom the Igala claim ritual connections and against whom they fought at least one major war. Then there were the contacts made through military conquest in the heydays of the kingdom. Thus Paul's Brown claims that "all Igbira [Ebira] groups" experienced Igala colonisation, and goes on to give specific examples. Consideration of time does not allow us to discuss these specific examples. Obayemi stresses the wide-ranging influence of the Igala kingdom when he writes, "So extensive was the Igala prestige that up to the middle of the 19th century the Kakanda as well as the Kupe around Eggan on the right bank of the Niger were still paying tribute to the Atta of Igala".

Attention has already been drawn to relations between the Igala and Igbo arising both from migrations and settlements, as well as trade between Igbo and Igala groups. The result of these contacts was mutual borrowing of ideas and cultural traits, a greater understanding of the way of life and values of one another. So when we talk about the separateness of our peoples in pre-colonial times, just how separate were they, judging by the experience of Igala relations and contracts with other Nigeria peoples?

Or take the Hausa states. The very emergence of each Hausa state involved a fusion of different peoples. The development of each *birni* invariably involved the accommodation of foreigners. Some of the most famous dynasties, as in Kano and Zazzau, were founded by foreigners who fought their way to eventual acceptance. Once established, the history of the Hausa states is dotted with inter-state wars as each state sought to gain particular advantages. Admittedly, these wars – and there were rather many – were destructive of peaceful pursuits. But there can be no doubting the fact that the movement of fighting forces, the taking of slaves at the end of wars, the lessons learnt from defeat, etc., all had their effect on the eventual emergence of what we know today as Hausa culture, which culture, as already pointed out, eventually spread to non-Hausa areas. Indeed as Mahdi Adamu has pointed out, the very existence of Hausa groups settled in the middle Belt – the Gwandara, Dukawa, Muryam, etc., – as well as the emergence of Hausa dynasties in places like Yawuri, Gwari and Kumbashi is traceable to these wars as well, of course, as to commercial relations. Admittedly, no Hausa Empire, embracing all the Hausa states, emerged before the 19th century. But they were not so separate as to make living together an impossible task in the changed circumstances in which we find ourselves as a new nation.

When we move from the kingdoms to the empires of Borno, Old Oyo and Benin, we find interactions on an even wider plane. Although these empires did not have the same operative frontiers throughout their existence; although the political control they exerted over areas brought under their sway was often not uniformly intense, and certainly of a very different order from the European imperial systems which we later experienced; there can hardly be any doubt that each of those empires brought various Nigerian peoples together under a common influence for varying periods of time. Every year at festival time, the component parts of the empires gathered together at the metropolis to re-affirm their loyalty to the centre. The need to maintain the ruling group led to economic activities of a wide-ranging nature. Thus Borno's trading activities involved relations not only with the Hausa states, but with Nupe and Old Oyo, the Bauchi Plateau and Wase areas and through these areas with other Nigerian groups.

There was also the fame of these empires. As centres of power and wealth, they attracted people who were not necessarily under their imperial control. Thus, for example, not all the Urhobo, Isoko, other Edoid groups and the western Igbo who linked themselves to the Benin title system were necessarily conquered peoples. The desire to be associated with a famous centre of political, economic and ritual power explains some of this kind of association. Today, many of these groups have built up traditions of Benin origin. These traditions have been found to be sometimes historically untenable and so unacceptable. But they do represent some evidence of the pervading fame of Benin as a centre of power. So, when one takes into consideration that Benin influence, even if not its political power, spread to virtually all of today's (1984) Bendel State, to Owo, Akure, parts of Ekiti and to Lagos, one sees just how widespread this influence was; just how many different Nigerians peoples operated within a certain common orbit, however informal. Our history is thus not necessarily devoid of reference points that can be used for demonstrating that our degree of separateness in pre-colonial times was not as great as is sometimes imagined.

Or take the Sokoto Caliphate and the large number of polities that came under the umbrella of Sokoto. Admittedly, each emirate had a large degree of autonomy. Yet there can be no doubting the unifying role which a common commitment to Islam and the Caliph in Sokoto had among the many emirates that constituted the caliphate. Nor can we deny that that unifying role has remained an important factor in the later history and politics of our nation, even if its influence has not always conduced to greater unity. The point being made here is that long before the British imposed their rule on us, there had been, through the instrumentality of large polities, the coming together of many groups under common influences and control, a certain sharing of common ideas and experiences which can be exploited in our desire to achieve national unity.

The Colonial Experience

The British conquest of Nigeria and the imposition of British colonial rule which attended that conquest brought the diverse peoples who inhabited the Nigeria geographical area together for the first time under a single political authority, namely, the colonial state of Nigeria. Admittedly, what became Nigeria was owed to the vagaries of international diplomacy – the outcome of various bilateral agreements between Britain and other European powers, especially France, as Professor J.C. Anene has pointed out in his work on Nigeria's international boundaries. To say this is to say that Nigeria could well have been differently composed, in terms of the peoples that constitute it. Perhaps this is the justification for the oft repeated statement that Nigeria was the artificial creation of the British. Differently put, that statement means no more than that Nigeria, as we have come to know it, is the product of historical accident. Which nation of the world is not a product of historical accident? Indeed, the burden of what I have been trying to say thus far is that by the time the British brought our multifarious peoples together in the colonial state, those peoples had come to know themselves far better than is sometimes conceded, and so could be expected, under proper guidance, to operate as a meaningful geo-political entity.

I do not intend, given the constraint of time, to bore you with a treatise on the colonial history of Nigeria. You must, however, permit me to draw attention to certain selected features of that period of our history which, in my judgment, could conduce to the emergence of a united Nigeria. In doing so, I would be the first to admit that the British did not necessarily embark on their administration of Nigeria for the purpose of preparing the way for a united Nigeria. Yet certain aspects of British policies proved to be irreversible and, as will be presently demonstrated, could be used as part of the basis for creating a truly united Nigeria – another historical accident, if you like so to call it.

In order to administer the colonial state, the British created new administrative units – districts, divisions, provinces, regions, the concept of which was new to our peoples. Over time, however, we became not only used to these concepts, but attached to them. Can anyone today fail to acknowledge the crucially important role which attachment to these new units has played in our history? When we speak of relations between the North and South, are we not speaking of relations between two of these new concepts? When before independence, no agreement could be reached about the creation of more regions or states, was it not because strong loyalties had been built up around the three existing regions of the North, West and East? Did not those who belonged to the old provinces come to regard themselves as belonging together in a unit distinct from others? Since independence have we not continued to create new provinces, new local government areas, new states? And have there not emerged strong loyalties to whatever new units of administration have been created? Was Biafra not based on the concept of the Old Eastern Region? And did Biafra not evoke strong emotions and loyalties? So then, British administrative arrangements, as indeed our own similar arrangements since independence, have had the result of creating units to which our people have become attached. In each such situation this loyalty has been supra-clan, supra-kingdom, supra-emirate and/or supra-ethnic. I submit that if Nigerians have been able to develop a loyalty to their local government area, their region or their state, they can also be made, given the right leadership and ideological orientation, to develop a strong loyalty to the larger entity known as Nigeria. It is when that kind of loyalty is developed, that true unity can be achieved. Let me admit straight away, that the loyalty of our peoples to these units about which I speak has been one of the obstacles to the forging of true national unity. But that is because successive leaders have manipulated that loyalty for their selfish political ends rather than harnessing it for the achievement of a higher purpose, namely, national unity.

Colonial rule also linked different parts of Nigeria with roads and railways, with a postal service, etc. Colonial rule led to the rise of new urban centres which became the meeting place of Nigerians from different parts. Colonial rule drastically reduced inter-group warfare and, by instituting a police force charged with the maintenance of law and order across the country, created an atmosphere of greater peace and security. Taken together, these developments gave Nigerians the opportunity of greater mobility across the length and breadth of the country, greater exchange of ideas and services and commodities, a greater opportunity of knowing about other Nigerian groups, etc. I submit that in the days when there was a unified civil service – when a civil servant could serve in Kaduna, Kano, Ibadan, Warri, Enugu, Calabar, Portharcourt, etc., in the course of his career, the opportunities for making lasting friends across the country were more than has become the case since the regionalisation of the civil service. I cannot pretend to be unaware that greater mobility and greater urbanisation have had their unpleasant effects on inter-group relations. That notwithstanding, it is my contention here that colonial rule made it possible for many a Nigerian to reach out beyond his immediate environment in safer and a more conducive atmosphere, and so to learn more about Nigeria. Today our educational policy at all levels must provide for that travel and exposure which alone can eliminate ignorance and deepen understanding about Nigeria's various peoples and cultures.

Colonial rule gave us a common factor against which to fight. One of the most observable features of our politics of decolonisation was the readiness of our political leaders to agree on certain compromises in order not to prolong colonial rule. Over revenue allocation, boundary adjustments, control of the police, the status of Lagos or Ilorin, creation of states and a number of other issues, the aspirations and wishes of the leadership of the three regions were different and conflicting. Yet those leaders were able to reach agreement in the national interest. I agree that those compromises created problems for independent Nigeria. Even so, however, I submit that the spirit of give and take which marked the negotiations for independence is crucial for the forging of true national unity, especially in a multi-ethnic state like Nigeria.

Independent Nigeria and the Search for National Unity

Few will fail to agree that true national unity has eluded Nigeria since independence. Yet I have been arguing throughout this lecture that there is enough in our past history to provide a basis for national unity. So what has gone wrong? Each person will no doubt have his or her own answer to that question. Let me share my views with you.

One, as a nation we have failed to promote the study of our multifarious peoples with a view to understanding them. Our educational system is yet to grapple with this all important fact. Statism can be potent factor for disunity if not countered by nationalism, here defined as the deliberate cultivation of national goals and aspirations. Our younger ones need greater exposure to Nigeria than they are getting. The Federal Government Colleges with their motto of "Pro Unitate" are not enough. Nigerians – all Nigerians – must know more of the history of their country, more about the way of life of the nation's diverse peoples. Travel must be made cheap and attractive. The educational system must make excursions to different parts of the country an important aspect of the learning process. Our Festivals of Art and Culture must take on new dimensions. Let the Yoruba boys and girls learn Efik songs and dances and vice versa as part of learning to appreciate each other's way of life. Even when all of this has been done, our differences will never disappear. It is not even desirable that they should, for those differences enrich our national culture. I as an Isoko may never fully appreciate Hausa music and dance, Hausa cooking or the Hausa concept of beauty. But also, let me not condemn same, realising that if Hausa music is strange to me, so is Isoko music strange to the Hausa. So we must seek knowledge that we may deepen understanding, and banish fear and ignorance and those "blatant misconceptions and alienating stereotypes" which can cause rancour amongst our peoples and hinder our march to true national unity.

Two, we need to evolve a philosophy of even and equitable development for the nation. It is my contention that nothing promotes centrigugal forces – ethnicism, statism or what you will – more than a feeling of injustice. Since independence no government, civilian or military, federal, state, or local, has worked out a philosophy of even development. At all levels, the winner-takes-all syndrome of our political life has led to lopsided development, whatever the blueprint for national development may contain. Even under our various military regimes, personal, group, ethnic and all sorts of other pressures have led to the over-development of certain areas to the neglect of others. We cannot have national unity when sections of our people feel that they do not belong. Only even and equitable development can create a commitment to that agency of development, which is ultimately the nation, for in the final analysis it is the state of the nation that can generate circumstances favourable for even private enterprise.

Three, as a multi-ethnic nation whose peoples have not all developed at the same pace and to the same level, we have a great problem of how to accommodate our varying levels of development. Since I am addressing a university audience, let me take the issue of educational imbalance. If we are honest with ourselves, we have to admit that the difference between the educationally advantaged and educationally disadvantaged areas of our land is explicable in terms of a historical accident. The Christian missionaries landed in Abeokuta and Lagos before anywhere else in Nigeria. Later, another lot landed in Onitsha. In the 1860s missionaries began their labours in the eastern delta. By contrast, real missionary effort did not begin in what used to be called Northern Nigeria till the beginning of this century, a whole century after the Jihad

had consolidated the hold of Islam in the Muslim areas, and just after Lugard had promised he would not tamper with the Islamic religion. If then the Egba and the Lagosians produced the first crop of highly trained Nigerians; if among the Igbo the Onitsha threw up the first educated elite, it is clearly not because either group was mentally superior to the other Nigerians. It was merely because they had the opportunity, thanks to an accident of history. While we must not deride their achievements, they for their part must not think of themselves more highly than they ought. As I often tell my students, were Nigeria colonised by an Arab country and not by Britain, the Northerners would have been the educated groups and the Southerners the educationally disadvantaged – so potent can a historical accident be.

Be that as it may, we have the reality of educational imbalance to live with, at least for some while to come. How do we cope with it in the Federal civil service, in Federal universities and other arms of the federal public service? Each time the expression quota or catchment area is used, emotions and tensions rise. Need they? If as a nation we would seek understanding of our problems, we could keep these tensions and tempers down. But if, as we tend to do, we play the numbers games in such a manner as to create the impression that some groups must be compelled to remain static so that other parts can catch up with them, there is no way we can generate harmony. We must seek understanding through honest dialogue. At university level, for example, we do in fact have a situation in which relatively junior and inexperienced academics from educationally backward areas of the country have been appointed Vice-Chancellors for some of the nation's universities in the interest of the federal character of Nigeria. I accept and understand this situation. So when I say "Sir", to a Vice-Chancellor who took his Ph.D. two years after I became Professor of History, that is a genuine token of my commitment to a united nation, for national unity will always demand its sacrifice.

However, the beneficiaries of this kind of arrangement must not, as some of them have tended to do, see themselves as a special breed either, for clearly they are not. The nation must not, and cannot afford to, promote the interests of a particular group to the neglect or at the expense of the interests of other groups, if in our multi-ethnic situation we seek meaningful unity. Indeed, such a policy is contrary to that philosophy of even development which I advocate. If Nigeria is to become a truly united nation, we cannot afford the luxury of first class and second class citizens, the distinction being based not on merit or achievement, but on place, state or region of birth and/or religion. Nobody, no group, owns the nation more than others. The challenge of our multi-ethnic nature requires that we seek accommodation. I submit that we can only achieve meaningful accommodation in the context of equal rights and justice across the board.

Four, and this is my last point, Nigeria needs to develop a leadership that can act in line with the views expressed above, a leadership that is truly dedicated to the idea of national unity in deeds as in words. When I say leadership, I am not restricting myself to political leadership. By leaders I mean all who are in a position to take decisions that affect the lives of Nigerians as a corporate entity at different levels. Are you a university teacher? Is your attitude to your students based on fairness and a commitment to merit? Are you a Head of Department? Is your relationship with your staff based on fair play and justice, or are you inclined to let parochial, ethnic and other considerations sway you? Are you a Vice-Chancellor? And have you politicised and polarised your institution so that you can perpetrate all sorts of injustices and abuse your office? Are you the President of the Students Union? How did you win your elections – through fanning ethnic loyalties? If leadership at these and other levels would rise above sectional interests and seek deliberately to promote justice and fair play, the political leadership may well be forced to toe the line. Alas, however, we know, don't we, that it is the tone of the political leadership that often dictates how these other cadres of leaders act and react. This means that we need to be extra careful in how we choose the men and women who lead this nation. Personal friendships and relations which would appear often to dictate who becomes a minister even under the military cannot be enough. Ethnic considerations can never be eliminated, but I believe that among every ethnic group are people of probity, persons with a commitment to Nigeria and its continued existence as a united entity. We must search for these persons and use them. I do not pretend to know how we can achieve this desired end; but I am persuaded that only the right kind of leadership at all levels can work towards the much desired goal of national unity.

Conclusion

I have tried to demonstrate that there is nothing in our history which makes unity impossible. I have made the point that as a geo-political unit we are not as artificial as is sometimes made out; that there were contacts of an intense nature among our peoples which enabled them to know something of the ways of life of their various neighbours. Let me stress that I have not sought to build false unities. National unity depends as much on understanding the things which unite us as those which divide us. My plea has been that we seek that knowledge which alone enables us to understand and so tolerate our differences. I have called for a philosophy of even and equitable development as a necessary basis for asking for our peoples' commitment to the nation. Let no group or groups regard national leadership and the spoils of office as God's gift to them. Rather let us aim for equal rights and justice for all of our peoples. If we are to achieve these and other goals not specifically listed here, we must have a leadership that accepts the goal of national unity; that can reach into our history and deliberately identify aspects of that history which can be used in the task of forging that unity; a leadership which can, above all, by example, promote true national unity.

At a time in our national development when there is sceptism as to the value of historical studies, I hope that this lecture has demonstrated, in a little way, just how vital history can be in the task of nation-building in which we are all engaged. Those of you who have decided either by accident or design to study history need to remember at all times that your study of history is not just for the purpose of passing examinations and securing jobs. We teach you history in the hope that as a result of what you learn and the method with which you learn it, you will be better prepared to play a meaningful and responsible role in the affairs of our nation. May you indeed be agents of tolerance and understanding; may you develop that humility of spirit and empathy which true knowledge confers; may you, in the context of our nation-building effort, be advocates of social and economic justice, of even development, of the philosophy of Nigeria for all Nigerians.

It now gives me great pleasure, as President of the Historical Society of Nigeria, to formally launch the Students Historical Society of Ogun State University, on this 29th day of May, in the year of our Lord, 1985.

6

TEACHING NIGERIAN HISTORY FROM A NATIONAL PERSPECTIVE*

We are gathered to witness the formal opening of a one-week Workshop on the Teaching of Nigerian History from a National Perspective. The teaching of Nigerian History as a distinct branch of the larger discipline began at the University of Ibadan, when the old University College of London was transformed into an independent University, with the coming of political independence. Those of us who took the degree of the University of London, via the University College, Ibadan, did not take a single paper in Nigerian History. Indeed there was only one paper in African History in our time. Today, at Ibadan and in all other universities of our land, no student can obtain the B.A. degree in History without offering and passing at least one, often two to three papers, in Nigerian History. What this means, clearly, is that the universities realise the crucial importance of the teaching of Nigerian History within the larger framework of their respective History curricula. The question which arises, and to which I will presently be addressing myself, is whether the nation has any national policy on the teaching

*An opening address presented as president, Historical Society of Nigeria, to the Society's Workshop on the Teaching of Nigerian History from a National Perspective, 02 - 08 February, 1986, at the University of Lagos.

of Nigerian History, and on the role of national history in our on-going efforts at nation-building.

At the lower levels of our educational system, especially at the secondary school level, the teaching of Nigerian History – as a subject on its own – is only some five odd years old. For most of our history since independence, such Nigerian History as has been taught was taught as part of West African or African History. Only in the last few years have our secondary school pupils begun to offer Nigerian History at "O" level. Under the new 6-3-3-4 education system, Nigerian History is one of the options available at the senior secondary school level. I had the privilege of serving as the Chairman of the National Panel that drew up a new Nigerian History curriculum for the senior secondary schools in the early 1980s. The school teachers who worked with us at different levels of that exercise had, on more than one occasion, to remind us that the number of candidates offering History at "O" level was falling as compared, for instance, with the number offering Government. Asked to explain the phenomenon, the answer came readily: there was more work to do in History than in Government; the History syllabus was more loaded than the Government syllabus; results in Government are better than results in History, largely because Government was examined through objective-type questions, while History was largely examined through essay-type questions. What we were being told was clear enough: do not load the Nigerian History syllabus too much if you want our pupils to offer it. No one can blame the school teachers for taking that position. They want to have students to teach. And they want their students to do well at the "O" level examination, especially in a situation where the teachers' careers may well depend on the performance of their wards.

Yet the position taken by the teachers is unsatisfactory, and represents a rather limited insight into the value of History, especially National History, in the school curriculum. So long as we see History as just another subject, taught for the main purpose of passing particular examinations, so long will we be unable to give due place to a subject which, even in an age of science and technology, ought to be at the very core of our educational system. I will come back to this point later.

At the lower levels of the educational system – junior secondary school and primary school – History as a subject is not taught. We are told that elements of our history are woven into the Social Studies Curricula taught at those levels. One of our missions at this Workshop will be devoted to just how much history there is in the Social Studies Curricula, and I do not want to pre-empt the discussions that will take place then. I must, however, warn against a certain tendency for us to import into Nigeria ideas and concepts developed for systems very different from ours.

So, then, at the present moment, Nigerian History is taught at senior secondary schools, colleges of education and universities. The evidence from the senior secondary schools is that the number offering History is dwindling. At university level, History has continued to attract a good number of students. At that level, however, the enrolment for History will inevitably fall as the nation seeks to attain a 3:2 ratio as between science-based and humanities-based disciplines. That apart, the direct linkage between a degree and a job has allegedly led the Director of the National Youth Service Corps to advise Nigerians seeking university education not to offer History. If indeed Nigerians were to listen to that advice, then perhaps by the end of the next decade History would disappear at university level! Nigeria would thus set a world record in that regard. Thank goodness that the realities of our situation will continue to defy the wisdom of the N.Y.S.C's director. Yet, when all that has been said, the fact remains that our educational system is such that only a tiny proportion of our citizenry ever has the opportunity of being formally taught Nigerian History. The bulk of those who pass through our educational system never have to learn the history of their country. This means that they never really get to know how we have come to be as we are; what are the antecedents of the various groups that make up Nigeria; what were those historical accidents that have determined the roles certain persons and certain groups play in the affairs of our nation. Yet this majority of the educated elite occupy top positions in our public life, offer vital advice and take crucial decisions about the affairs of a country about whose peoples and whose history they are so staggeringly ignorant. Is it any wonder that we make so many avoidable mistakes in national planning? Is it any wonder that Nigeria has been unable to evolve any meaningful strategies for even and equitable development? Is it any wonder that national integration continues to founder on the rock of sectional and class interests?

Why the Workshop?

We are gathered here today at the beginning of a Workshop on the teaching of Nigerian History from a National Perspective. Why is such a workshop considered necessary? What is the end in view? As already indicated, the teaching of Nigerian History is some twenty-five years old. At the beginning, there were few works available to the teacher of Nigerian History, and most of such works as did exist were written by foreigners. The first and subsequent generations of professional Nigerian historians took up the challenge that this situation represented, and began to produce works on different parts of the country and different aspects of our history. Although there are still many Nigerians in high places who remain largely ignorant of the kind of work Nigerian historians have produced in our first quarter century of endeavour, it is a fact beyond questioning that substantial work has been done and published both in the form of books and in the form of journal articles. Today's university undergraduate cannot justifiably complain of lack of reading material for his Nigerian History courses. However, only a few of the works that exist cover the entire country. We have, for the most part, tended to remain within our narrow specialisations. Thus there are many books and articles about different parts of Nigeria, but only few books about Nigeria as a whole. This situation arises out of the training of the professional historian. Most of our Ph.Ds. deal with specific areas and topics, not Nigeria as a whole. There is nothing wrong with this at the Ph.D. level. The professional historian must, however, in the course of his career, break out of the narrow specialisation and attempt to wield his brush over a much wider canvass. After the first quarter century of research into, and writing of, Nigerian History, the time has come to combine specialised research into different parts with more general surveys and synthesis based on available material. Indeed that is partly what this Workshop will be seeking to do.

Because of the nature of the bulk of the existing materials in Nigerian History, the teaching at university level has tended to be based on team work, with each teacher handling areas in which he feels most at home. Consequently, few of our university teachers have, in fact, been challenged to look at the history of all of the country in detail, and few would agree to teach Nigerian History all by themselves. It was largely in response to this situation that our Society, after a Workshop like this, published *Groundwork of Nigerian History* in 1980. That book sought to cover all of Nigeria's history in a single volume, albeit on a regional, sectional basis. Unfortunately, there are important gaps in that work which the Society hopes to fill in subsequent editions. But even with the publication of *Groundwork*, there are still many in our ranks who cannot cope with teaching Nigerian History all on their own. What is even more galling is the fact that there are universities in the country where the teaching of Nigerian History is noticeably deficient, because staff in such universities do not make the extra effort needed to teach areas outside their specialisations. At the lower levels of the educational system, where one teacher has, per force, to teach all of Nigerian History, what he puts across to his students is a reflection of what he or she knows. It follows that the inadequacies of teaching at university level are replicated at the lower levels. Additionally, there is the fact that at the lower levels, the syllabuses are such that students can get away with good passes without having to pay attention to all parts of the country. So, even those who have a chance to learn Nigerian history, end up learning it rather imperfectly.

It is the situation depicted above that the Historical Society of Nigeria is seeking to remedy through this Workshop. Secondary school and even university syllabuses may continue to be regional, sectional or topical. Indeed at certain levels this is inevitable. But the teacher who teaches Borno history needs to be aware of the History of Old Oyo, and be able to identify similarities, and indicate and explain differences between the two imperial systems, as he goes along. In other words, there is a need to provide a general framework of our nation's history; a need to indicate broad influences and operative factors in our history; a need to identify the nature and impact of contacts between our peoples; a need to identify factors that make for the differences discernible among our peoples; and so on. The teacher needs to be familiar with these factors at the level of the nation and to fit his teaching of component parts of the country into this larger framework, and this larger perspective. Hence all the papers to be discussed at this workshop look at issues across the nation rather than parts of the nation. The teacher will then be expected to use the Handbook that will be ultimately published alongside the regional and other sectional studies which exist. It is the teachers' responsibility to translate the end in view into reality as he handles his subject. This is a responsibility which must not be taken lightly. It is a responsibility which imposes on the teacher a challenge of consistent and conscientious self-application.

Later on in this morning's proceedings, we will be listening to the Keynote Address which will be discussing the concept of national history. I do not wish to anticipate the details of that address now. It must be clear, however, that it is impossible to write national history unless there exist micro histories out of which that macro national history can be written. Hence although I may have created the impression, in what has gone before, that we have concentrated too much on micro histories, the need for such histories will always remain. Indeed there are many parts of this country still waiting for their historians. This is particularly true of many of the communities of Benue, Plateau, Gongola and Niger States, some groups in Bendel (today's Edo and Delta States), and quite a few in Anambra and Imo States. Not even all of Yorubaland, the area with the largest number of trained historians, has been adequately covered. The histories of these peoples and communities will never be written so long as Government persists in its present policy of granting few or no scholarships for postgraduate work in History. And if these peoples do not have their histories scientifically studied, our national history will be deficient to the extent to which it does not benefit from the known experiences of these groups. We must thus urge on State and Federal Governments not to persist in their mistaken belief that we already have a surfeit of historians in Nigeria. We are only just beginning our task, and need many more labourers in History's vineyard.

I said earlier on that as a nation we really have no policy on the teaching of our nation's history, nor are there any nationally set goals that we seek to achieve through teaching Nigerian History. Perhaps this is why it was possible for so high a public officer as the Director of the National Youth Service Corps to urge aspiring undergraduates not to take a degree in History. I realise that everywhere the passing of examinations and the acquisition of jobs are necessarily tied in with education. However, we must also accept the fact that there is more to education than passing examinations and acquiring jobs. There is the issue of the preparation of the individual for meaningful and positive participation in the affairs of the nation other than through doing a job. I refer here to preparation for full and positive citizenship. It was this preparation for full citizenship that was the goal of our pre-colonial systems of education. It is that preparation that, we must insist, should remain an important goal of our educational system. And I hasten to submit that in the preparation of the individual for full, meaningful and positive citizenship, National

History, properly taught, has an important, if not a more important, role to play as any other subject in our school, college or university curricula. For it must be fairly obvious that he is but an ignorant citizen who does not know how the diverse peoples of Nigeria became what they are; how their societies and their political institutions evolved over time in response to varying challenges and circumstances; how their societies and their political institutions evolved over time in response to varying challenges and circumstances; how they interacted and sorted out their conflicting aspirations and claims on dwindling resources; what forces brought formerly separate groups together, and how such coming together was lived out; what are the factors that explain the differentials in educational and other developments of our different groups, and the impact of such differentials on our national life.

Time prevents us from launching forth on a full blown lecture on the role of History in nation building. That is a lecture that has been given by many a lecturer on many a platform. No nation can live and hope to progress on the basis of ignorance of its own self; no nation can afford, whatever its level of scientific and technological advancement, to ignore its own history, for as someone has said, "without history we have no knowledge of who we are nor how we came to be, like victims of collectives amnesia groping in the dark for our identity. History is the memory of human group experience. If it is forgotten or ignored, we cease in that measure to be human." Our nation must demonstrate active awareness of this all important truism, and evolve a policy for the teaching of Nigerian History that will provide a stable pad for launching the Nigerian into meaningful citizenship. This Workshop is being organised because we, for our part, are conscious of the place of History in our national life and wish to see Nigerian History taught in a manner that will maximize the benefits derivable from teaching it. We invite our educational policy makers at Federal and State levels to join hands with us as we seek to make history, Nigerian History, serve the nation.

Making History Come Alive

It is the view of the Historical Society of Nigeria that our educational system should be such that makes the study of Nigerian History compulsory for all who pass through it. Past and present governments have evinced a desire for cultural revival, a going back to the search for those things which identify us as Nigerians. Too often, however, such a call for cultural revival has not encompassed a call for an intensified study and teaching of Nigerian History, because our history is not seen by policy makers as part of our culture. So the nation spends millions every year on the promotion of indigenous dance, song, drama, languages and the like, but hardly makes any allocation for systematic research into our history. Yet even those aspects of culture that the nation is ever so prepared to invest in are a product of our history. There is thus, I submit, an urgent need for a national policy on the teaching of Nigerian History at all levels of our educational system. The present administration has indicated its willingness to consider whatever ideas the citizenry may have on different aspects of national policy. The Historical Society of Nigeria calls on the governments of the land to take a hard look at their lack of policy on national history and the teaching thereof. We, for our part, are prepared to put ourselves at the service of our governments in the process of forging such a policy.

Two, even if a national policy were to be evolved and everyone who passes through the educational system was made to study Nigerian History, there would still be a need to bring different aspects of our history to those of our peoples – and they are the majority at the moment, and will remain so for a long time to come – who remain outside our formal educational system. What this means is that the nation must find some way of making our history come alive to our peoples, young and old. As a nation we have so far failed to erect any memorials to the men and women who have shaped our destiny. Not even to those who fought for and regained our independence, but are now departed, have we erected any memorials. Where are the memorials for men like Nnamdi Azikiwe, Tafawa Balewa, Ahmadu Bello, Obafemi Awolowo, Okotie-Eboh, Michael Okpara, Eyo Ita, S.L. Akintola? What memorial have we erected to Adekunle Fajuyi, who paid the supreme sacrifice playing host to Aguiyi-Ironsi? What marks the spot where Murtala Muhammad was gunned down in 1976? How many of our young children can identify that spot today? Yet have we not declared Murtala Muhammad a national hero? Why are we so busy honouring the disreputable living that we dishonour and forget the memory of the men and women who have laboured to help make us what we are? The issue is not that those past leaders were blameless. No. The issue rather is that they represented a phase of our national endeavour and we need to make today's Nigerian remember that these men and women lived and toiled for us, admittedly with varying degrees of failures and successes. We can make aspects of our history come alive to our peoples, even without sending them to school – and I submit that we all join hands and begin this process NOW. We of the Historical Society of Nigeria offer our services to our nation – if the nation cares to take up the offer. Other institutions must do likewise. The National Commission for Museums and Monuments must not content itself with declaring this or that a national monument. It must take one step beyond – it must begin to create national monuments. I pledge the collective wisdom and co-operation of the Historical Society of Nigeria in any such task.

Finally, permit me to touch on the issue of the keeping of the nation's records, the raw materials for our nation's history. The National Archives is one of those institutions, the value of which far too few Nigerians appreciate. Our National Archives deserves the full and urgent attention of the Federal Government. We are hopelessly out of date in terms of the system of storing, preserving and retrieving our national records. Substantial investment will be required if we are to build a really modern archives. Even in our present situation, the nation's general attitude to records and record-keeping is shocking. Ministries, parastatals, universities, treat their records with criminal negligence. Little wonder we are a nation without basic statistics for planning. Government does not even seem to know where the Archives ought to be in the scheme of things. At one point it was under the Ministry of Education; at another it was moved to the Ministry of Information; now (that is 1986) it is part of a Department called Culture and Archives. We submit that the National Archives are too crucial an institution to be tossed about like that. The Historical Society of Nigeria has made its views on this matter known on many an occasion. We call once again for a new Archives Law, for the resuscitation of the National Archives Committee which has not met for over a decade (as at 1986). We call for a national drive aimed at awakening in the Nigerian an awareness of the value of records and record-keeping. As historians, we have a major stake in the nation's records, and are prepared to join hands with Government and other agencies in the tasks to which we have drawn attention.

7

THE COLONIAL EXPERIENCE IN NIGERIA: ADMINISTRATIVE AND POLITICAL CHANGES*

In 1862 the British declared Lagos their colony. In 1885 the British informed the rest of the world that they had declared a protectorate over the Oil Rivers. According to the declaration, the protectorate encompassed the "territories on the line of coast between the British protectorate of Lagos and the right or western bank of the Rio del Rey, and the territories on both banks of the Niger, from its confluence with the Benue at Lokoja to the sea, as well as the territories on both banks of the River Benue, from the confluence up to and including Ibi." The next year the British granted a charter to Taubman Goldie's Royal Niger Company, thereby conferring on it powers of administration over a stretch of territory defined in the charter. In the same year, 1886, the British intervened in the stalemates between Ibadan and the Ekitiparapo and helped negotiate the peace treaty that brought the Yoruba wars to a gradual end. Thereafter, the British pushed their influence and power into Yorubaland, creating ultimately the Colony and Protectorate of Lagos, the protectorate being the rest of Yorubaland outside Lagos. In 1893 the

*This was the paper I presented at the Historical Society of Nigeria's workshop on the Teaching of Nigerian History from a National Perspective held in February 1986. Each of the papers presented at that Workshop addressed topics that covered all of Nigeria.

Oil Rivers Protectorate became known as the Niger Coast Protectorate which nomenclature was in turn changed to the Protectorate of Southern Nigeria in 1900, the same year as the Protectorate of Northern Nigeria was declared by the British over the bulk of the territories formerly claimed by the Royal Niger Company. As at 1900 then there were three separate British administered territories in what was to become Nigeria – the colony and Protectorate of Lagos, the Protectorate of Southern Nigeria and the Protectorate of Northern Nigeria. In 1906 the first two were amalgamated to form the Colony and Protectorate of Southern Nigeria. In 1914 Northern and Southern Nigeria were amalgamated and a single geo-political entity known a Nigeria was born. From 1914 -1938 Nigeria was administered virtually like a federation of two groups of provinces – Northern and Southern. In 1939 Southern Nigeria was broken into two – Western and Eastern Regions. The tripartite division of Nigeria was to remain until 1965 when the Midwestern Region was created.[1] This paper is concerned with a discussion of the administrative and political changes that the developments listed above represented. The emphasis is on the nature, impact and significance of these changes for the Nigerian peoples.

On Administrative Units

Clearly the most obvious point to make under this head is the fact that the various colonial territorial arrangements indicated above represented, ultimately, a major revolution in the political life of the Nigerian peoples. None of the protectorates created by the British coincided with any pre-colonial state, kingdom or empire. The British-created protectorates each represented the beginning of that process of bringing Nigerian peoples together in new ways and for new purposes which was to end in the creation of the Nigerian nation-state.

For purpose of administration each protectorate was divided into administrative units. In 1900 the Protectorate of Southern Nigeria was broken into four divisions: Eastern Division, with Calabar as headquarters, included Opobo, the Ibo, Bonny and Degema; the Cross River Division had Ediba as headquarters and encompassed a large but rather unspecified territory; the Central Division had Onitsha as its headquarters and included Akassa, Brass, Agberi, Oguta and Asaba; the Western Division with Warri as headquarters included the Urhobo and Isoko, Itsẹkiri, Western Ijọ, the Ndiosimili and Ndokwa peoples countries as well as what were loosely referred to as the Benin-City districts.[2]

As of the same date, the Lagos Protectorate was similarly divided. The Western District, roughly the area of present day Egbado Local Government area, had its headquarters in different places – Badagry, Imeko, Ilaro – at different times; Ibadan was the headquarters of a Central District which encompassed all of what may be described as the Oyo-Yoruba as well as Ife and its satellite settlements; the Ekiti and Ijesa countries made up the Northeast District with headquarters first at Ilesa, then at Ado-Ekiti; the Eastern District comprised Owo, Idanre, Ondo, Akure, Okitipupa and Ilaje, with Ode Odo as its headquarters.[3]

When Lugard imposed British rule on what became styled the Protectorate of Northern Nigeria, he broke the protectorate into provinces. In its final form there were some fourteen provinces in that protectorate in Bassa, Kabba, Ilorin, Borgu, Nupe, Kontagora, Zaria, Nassarawa, Muri, Yola, Bauchi, Sokoto, Kano, Borno.[4]

When in 1906 the Protectorate of Southern Nigeria was amalgamated with the Colony and Protectorate of Lagos, it became necessary to re-structure the administrative units. The amalgamated Colony and Protectorate of Southern Nigeria was broken into three provinces – the Western Province with headquarters at Lagos encompassed most but not all of Yorubaland; the Central Province which had Warri as headquarters encompassed all of what was Bendel State in addition to Ifon, Owo, Onitsha, Awka, Udi, Nsukka, Idah; the Eastern Province had its base in Calabar and included territories that made up the former Rivers and Cross River States as well as the rest of Igboland.[5]

In 1914 came the amalgamation of Northern and Southern Nigeria. As part of that process, Lugard split up the three large provinces of the south. In the end twelve such provinces emerged – Abeokuta, Colony, Ijebu, Oyo, Ondo, Benin, Warri, Owerri, Onitsha, Ogoja and Calabar. The provinces of the north remained largely untouched. Each province was sub-divided into divisions.

As of 1914 each province was headed by a British political officer styled a Resident. Under the Resident were District Officers (D.O.) in charge of the various divisions. The District Officers were assisted at divisional headquarters by assistant district officers (A.D.O.). Sometimes A.D.O.s were posted to take charge of districts or sub-districts where such units were created out of existing divisions.

From the viewpoint of the British, the creation of these administrative units was a *sine qua non* for the effective governance of the areas they had acquired as colonies or protectorates. For our peoples these new arrangements represented radical departures from their previous political practices and relations. If we take the delta states and Calabar, for example, the 19th century had been a century of acute competition between them. Each state had not only sought to maintain its identity but had attempted to wrest the markets of its neighbours. Then came the British and lumped Calabar, Bonny, Opobo and Degema into a single administrative unit, with Calabar as headquarters. How did Ife, the spiritual metropolis of Yorubaland, feel to be placed in a district with Ibadan as headquarters? Kano and Katsina had been the leading states of Hausaland before the Sokoto jihad. Under the British arrangement, Katsina became part of Kano Province, as did Hadeija and Katagun, the two previously part of the Borno empire which had on occasion reduced Kano to a tribute-paying status. In Lugard's Upper Benue Province there were dozens of separate and autonomous ethnic groups. But as Sa'ad Abubakar has shown, many of these were arbitrarily brought under Ibi by the new British arrangements.

Provinces, divisions and districts were new phenomena in the political experience of our peoples brought about by colonial rule. Looking back on what has happened since independence and in human history, it must be clear that these arrangements were necessary steps in the gradual integration of peoples into the nascent Nigerian state. This, no doubt, is what the late J.C. Anene meant when, commenting on this phenomenon of creating administrative units in his area of study, he wrote, "the new pattern of administrative control involved the elimination of the separate identity of the traditional...state, and was in fact the beginning of the artificial division of the territory into administrative units which cut across the traditional groupings of the various communities."[6] Anene, of course, over-stated the case when he spoke of the elimination of the separate identity of the traditional states. That identity can never be really eliminated. Indeed it was in the effort to fight the subversion of that identity that conflict developed among component parts of the new units, as we shall show presently. This new phenomenon, then, may have been necessary and has, in fact, had the long term effect of forging new and larger unities, but it also introduced new inequalities into relations between our peoples, as the new arrangements favoured some groups more than others.

It has been argued in the literature that in fixing these administrative units, especially in delimiting boundaries between units, a number of considerations influenced the colonial actors. These considerations are usually given as the principle of established local jurisdiction, 'the principle of ethnicity' and 'administrative convenience.'[7] The evidence hardly supports the first two. British conception of "established local jurisdiction" was often as faulty as its knowledge of the ethnic composition of the areas being brought under its jurisdiction was inadequate. Surely the example of Kano and Upper Benue Provinces already given can hardly support the principle of established local jurisdiction. Both Ogoja and Calabar Provinces were made up of myriads of ethnic groups: Ilorin Province had five ethnic groups within it and Benin Province several. In the majority of cases, the conclusion is inescapable that the main consideration was administrative convenience.

The point should also be made that the desire on the part of colonial administrators to be seen to be administering a large territory also influenced some of the boundary-making. In such situations, it became convenient to invoke one or two of the so-called principles. Thus, in keeping Ilorin and Kabba as part of Northern Nigeria even after 1914, it would have been easy to argue the case of established local jurisdiction: Ilorin was part of the Sokoto Caliphate (a Caliphate which the British dismantled!); Kabba had been overrun by the Nupe in the 19th century. It suited the interests of Lugard to use such arguments to maintain the size of the protectorate he established in the period 1900-06. Even after this, and right up to independence, no Governor listened to the often repeated plea of the Yoruba that their kith and kin in Ilorin and Kabba be re-united with them in Southern Nigeria. This enforced union became a sore point in relations between the old Western and the old Northern Nigeria. In the upshot the continuous association of Ilorin and Kabba with the other groups in the old "North" has had a marked effect not only on the culture of those areas, but also on the nature of its politics from the period of decolonisation till now. Thus Kwara State which encompasses both Ilorin and Kabba is, even in our time (1986), regarded as one of the "Northern states", and has been torn in its politics between allegiance to the political party usually associated with the "North," and the dominant political party in Yorubaland, whatever its name. So permanent can the impact of administrative arrangements be.

There were, of course, other communities affected by British boundary-making. The Afenmai of the former Bendel State were for a long time divided between North and South. The same applied to parts of Owo territories. In Ekiti, Otun which was in fact regarded as the leader of the Ekitiparapo was consigned to the North in 1900. When the ruler of Otun dared to protest, he was arrested and exiled. It was not till 1936 that Otun was allowed to rejoin the other Ekiti kingdoms. There was also the case of the Tiv whom Walter Egerton wanted to be placed in the Southern Protectorate on the grounds that Southern Nigeria was more used to handling non-Muslim communities![8] Other examples can be found. The communities which found themselves thus removed from their kith and kin naturally felt ill-used and often agitated against their enforced union to groups they regarded as strangers. The other point to stress is that in the bargaining that went on either between protectorates or within protectorate provinces and divisions, the Nigerian peoples concerned were not consulted nor were their feelings, or even their economic welfare (in terms of farmlands, for example) a major consideration. One aspect of the impact of colonial rule on our peoples which has not received due attention is how such neglect of the peoples' feelings conditioned their general attitude to what they saw as "Government" and what problem that attitude constitutes even today.

Perhaps the best example of administrative arrangements being made without consideration for the feelings of our peoples was the amalgamation of Northern and Southern Nigeria. That event has left a most permanent impact on the nature and character of Nigerian politics since then. It has now been definitely established that the compelling reason for amalgamation was economic. The South had attained self-sufficiency in revenue, thanks largely to import duties. The North was running a deficit and depending on the British treasury for some 300,000 pounds sterling a year. Amalgamation would enable some of the revenue of the South to be used in servicing the North and so save the British tax payers' money, in keeping with the established British colonial policy that each colony must be self-sufficient. Secondly, there was the need to have a uniform railway policy. Each of the two protectorates had built its own railway. Since the aim of railway building was the same, namely, to evacuate produce from the hinterland to the coast for export, it made sense to unify the two railway systems. Unification of the railway system would be easier if the two protectorates were merged. Then there was the fact that given two British protectorates, one with a long coastline and the other landlocked and depending on the other's ports for its external trade, amalgamation was a sensible thing. So amalgamation took place.[9] What began as three separate British protectorates thus became one Nigeria in 1914, because it suited the British not because of any consideration of the wishes of the Nigerian peoples.

Proof that amalgamation was seen largely as an economic rather than a political phenomenon can be found in the fact that Lugard treated the amalgamated entity as a federation of two virtually separate groups of provinces. Those arms of government which were vital for the maintenance of law and order and for attaining the economic ends in view were duly amalgamated: the Military, Judiciary, Treasury, Audit, Railways, Survey, Post and Telegraphs. For the rest the Lieutenant Governors of the North and South continued to operate as before. Until the Richards' Constitution of 1946, there was no common legislative body for the Nigeria that had come into existence in 1914. This is to say that the two bodies had different laws even though a common Supreme Court served them. There was no common educational policy. Northern and Southern Nigeria though now parts of a colonial state were, in many regards, treated as separate entities. Lugard had rejected the advice of those who had suggested that the country be divided into four or five groups of provinces in order to create a more balanced edifice. That was how we came to have a Northern Nigeria that was in area much larger than the South, with problems that will be discussed later. British interests were served by the arrangements they made. What did it matter if those arrangements created problems for a future Nigerian nation-state, even if such a state had been envisaged in 1914?

Before leaving the issue of amalgamation, the point needs to be made that amalgamation, as carried out by Lugard, gave permanence to the concept of South and North in Nigeria. The reason the two regions were treated as near-separate entities in the years 1914-1946 was that the British saw them as being different. The South had had exposure to Christianity and Western European education; the North had an Islamic tradition which the British had promised to respect. Consequently Christian missionary activity was not allowed in the Muslim parts of the North. This meant that western European education was kept away from the Muslim areas even though that kind of education was needed for entry into the colonial civil service and for service in the European-controlled commercial houses. The differences between North and South were a function of history – both pre-colonial and colonial. Having amalgamated the two entities, the British, rather than initiate policies that would reduce existing differences, pursued policies that tended to solidify these differences. To the extent to which this is true, to that extent must the conclusion be reached that British colonial policies laid the foundation for that North-South dichotomy which constituted a major obstacle in Nigeria's search for true national unity as at 1986, and which still constitutes a problem in North-South relations even today (2018).

Having said the above, it is also necessary to add that it was the 1914 amalgamation which made the Nigeria of 1986 emerge in its form and size. Admittedly, the process of transferring the colonial state into a well integrated truly united nation-state is far from complete. Yet certain loyalties and vested interests have been built around the political entity known as Nigeria. We sufficiently desired to preserve it as a single entity to the point of fighting a civil war in the years 1967-70. Our role in Africa and the wider world has not been unconnected with our size and our resources as a nation. This is clearly an unintended result of the 1914 amalgamation. But then in history, unintended results are sometimes even more crucial than the results intended by planners.

In 1939 Governor Bourdillon split the South into two, creating Western and Eastern Nigeria in the process. His argument for taking this action was one, that Enugu, the capital of the Southern Provinces was not central and so created communication problems, and two, that the peoples east of the Niger were culturally different from those west of it. By contrast, Bourdillon argued that Kaduna, the capital of the North, was centrally located and the peoples of the North were culturally more homogenous than those of the south. Consequently, the north was left undivided.[10] Bourdillon's act created the tripartite division of Nigeria which was to survive till 1963. That act also made the Nigeria federation that was based on these regions as from 1952 extremely lopsided. That lopsidedness explains part of the instability in Nigerian politics right up to the civil war. It is true that the three regions were, like Nigeria itself, artificial creations. But over time, loyalties and vested interests developed around these regions, just as they have developed around states created since 1967.

On British Indirect Rule and its Impact

British colonial administration operated at two levels – central and local. At central level, power lay largely in the hands of the white officials, especially in the period up to about 1952. At the local level, the Residents, D.Os and A.D.Os (or officers with equivalent titles) worked with Nigerian "Chiefs" and others. It is British colonial administration at the local government level that is usually known as Indirect Rule. A main feature of indirect rule was that, because the British did not have the means to hire as many hands as they would have needed to run local government, they fell back on Nigerian personnel to carry out the duties of this tier of government along lines directed by the British political officers. In the sphere of justice, the British reorganised an already existing corpus of laws which they called "native laws and customs" and appointed Nigerian personnel to administer these laws shorn of whatever aspects were objectionable to them. In order to raise revenue for the local government system, the British imposed court fees, prescribed various levels of fines for various offences and at various times, imposed taxation. Conceived of in these terms, indirect rule was in operation in the different protectorates that were in existence before 1914. At amalgamation, Lugard attempted to introduce to the southern part of the country the system of indirect rule he had earlier established in the North. In the South there had earlier been set up bodies called Native Councils or Native Courts which performed the functions of local government. Lugard's northern model was based on three instruments – native authorities, native courts and native treasuries. We shall, for convenience, use these terms in the discussion which follows.

Indirect Rule and Traditional Authorities: A major misconception about British indirect rule is that it recognised, respected and used the pre-colonial rulers of Nigeria's various peoples for the purposes of local government. Indeed the British are often credited with having preserved the indigenous political system through the use they made of it. In reality the pre-colonial ruling elite suffered a major diminution of authority with the establishment of colonial rule, as they were transformed from rulers to agents of the British. From being rulers who owed their positions to the established laws and customs of their peoples, and who had the right to raise revenue, make war and peace and generally conduct the internal and external affairs of their peoples, this class became "chiefs" who had to be appointed by the British, who also now assumed the power to remove them from office as indeed they did on a number of occasions. This change in the status of the pre-colonial rulers was not lost on the people. On the other hand, some of these former rulers now called "chiefs" did become extremely powerful so long as they remained in the good books of the British, as exemplified in the careers of Emir Muhammadu Abbas of Kano, Alaafin Ladigbolu, Chief Dọghọ Numa and Chief Onyeama. Indeed the use which the British made of these "chiefs" was such that undermined the pre-colonial systems of government among our peoples, in so far as many of the other office holders in these systems were ignored by the British. Additionally, as we shall see, although the British recognised customary law, the legal system set up was such that the British-type courts were superior to the native courts. Appeals lay from the latter to the former, and there were spheres in which people did not have to go to the native courts at all. This was clearly diminution of the status of pre-colonial rulers. Then there was the fact that in parts of the country where Christianity took root, the religious and spiritual sanctions of the rulers were gradually undermined, thereby weakening the indigenous socio-political system. Thus, contrary to the popular view that British indirect rule was designed to preserve our traditional institutions, a close look at its operation reveals that it actually undermined those institutions. In a sense this was inevitable, in so far as the traditional authorities could only operate at local government level. The functionaries of central government were necessarily superior to those of local government, since the powers of the latter derived from the former. Indeed it is the same situation that persists today in terms of relations between state and federal governments on the one hand and traditional rulers on the other. That situation lies in the logic of the fusion of formerly independent kingdoms and communities into first the colonial state and then the new Nigerian nation-state.

The Native Court System: While it is true that the recognition by the British of customary law and Muslim law has resulted in the survival of those types of law in Nigeria, it is important to draw attention to certain changes that the working of the British-created Native court system brought about. Under colonial rule, native courts could not be established in every village. Just as the British arbitrarily created districts, divisions, provinces and regions, so they arbitrarily created native court areas. The main consideration in the creation of these areas was the convenience of the D.Os who were supposed to supervise the courts that were set up, in order to ensure that they functioned along lines acceptable to the British. Especially in the southern part of the country, the arbitrary creation of native court areas meant that those away from the centres where the courts were located had to travel (usually on foot) what were regarded as considerable distances. This created discontent and new inequalities, as the discontented groups felt they were being unfairly subjected to groups that had no traditional authority over them. Also it was not always possible to appoint court members from all the villages that were required to attend some of the courts. Villages that had no court members could hardly regard the courts they were compelled to attend as their courts. While from the point of view of administration the situation which thus arose was understandable, it nevertheless resulted in tensions and dislocations which necessarily took time to sort out.[11]

In some parts of Nigeria Lugard introduced the concept of a Native Court of Appeal. In the North, the Emir's court, the highest of the Muslim courts, served as a court of appeal for other alkali courts. Lugard, enamoured of a hierarchical system, sought to set up a similar system in Yorubaland and in the old Warri Province. In the Eastern Province the idea was quickly abandoned. J. A. Atanda's study reveals that the court of the Alaafin of Ọyọ was made a court of appeal for cases heard in the Ọyọ Province, including cases from the Ooni of Ife's court! That not a single appeal came from outside Ọyọ settlements to that court of appeal shows the people's utter rejection of the experiment.[12] In the then Warri Province, however, a Native Court of Appeal did function under the permanent presidency of Chief Dọghọ Numa, whom Lugard appointed as a paramount chief, even though he had no traditional claim to any such office. All the native courts in the province – Urhobo, Isoko, Ijọ and Ukwuani courts – were expected to take their appeals to Warri. Yet none of these other ethnic groups had a single member on the court of appeal. The upshot was a noticeable intensification of Itsẹkiri-Urhobo tension as well as persistent complaints and petitions which ultimately resulted in the dismantling of the court of appeal in the early 1930s.[13]

There was another aspect of the working of the native court system which created tensions between groups in the period before the reorganisation of the 1930s. This was the need to have court clerks keep records of court proceedings. In the early years of the system, certain parts of the country did not have educated men to serve as court clerks. In Igboland, for example, the early court clerks were Ijọ or Efik. In Urhoboland they were Itsẹkiri. These clerks became extremely powerful in a situation where court members were all illiterate in English. All instructions to the courts from the D.O.s were passed down through them. Any litigant wanting copies of a judgment had to go to the court clerk. The court members could not even check the accuracy of the records the court clerk kept. Little wonder that the clerks quickly became not just corrupt, but effective masters, rather than servants of the courts to which they were posted. The situation thus created an artificial domination of the hinterland by these coastal persons in the first three decades of this century. When, following reorganisation, this situation ceased to exist, those who had enjoyed that artificial dominance nursed a sense of grievance.[14] Thus did changing colonial policies produce varying reactions among our peoples, depending on the impact of such policies on different groups.

Although the native courts were expected to administer customary law, over time the process adopted by these courts was deeply influenced by British legal proceedings. One area where this became marked was the taking of evidence and the role of witnesses. Litigants quickly learnt that the British based their law on evidence as adduced by witnesses. A clever litigant who succeeded in drumming up enough witnesses to testify in a particular way could win his case even if he was really guilty. In pre-colonial days religious and other sanctions influenced the manner in which certain cases were settled. The British gradually destroyed these sanctions and with them an important part of our people's commitment to the truth. The sense of justice, which was usually in evidence at trials in traditional systems, was gradually destroyed. It has never been replaced. Then there were the punishments prescribed for various offences. The British abolished such offences as they found objectionable like maiming and so on. But they also lifted law out of the realm of the religious. For example, in most of our societies, adultery was an offence against both man and the gods. The prescribed punishment for it took this fact into account. The British merely prescribed refund of dowry and a fine. Cases of adultery flooded many a native court. Men who made money from the new economic situation took other people's wives, then went to court and paid their fines! The situation is still with us today. Additionally, the authority of the "chiefs" and elders linked with their being custodians of the laws (including procedures and punishments) as laid down by ancestors were permanently impaired.

Indirect Rule and Inter-Group Relations: From what has been said, it must be obvious that the working of indirect rule created problems for inter-group relations in different localities. One source of such problems was the grouping of peoples into provinces, divisions and/or districts and the appointment of chiefs over them. We have a growing number of studies that have concerned themselves with this phenomenon. Atanda's *The New Oyo Empire* is, partly, an examination of Ibadan–Oyo relations in the period up to 1934. Initial British policy favoured Ibadan which was made the centre of British colonial rule. Many Ọyọ towns as well as Ife settlements were brought under Ibadan. In doing this, the British were no doubt acting on the basis of Ibadan's military successes in Yorubaland. Then came a change in British attitude when the Alaafin of Ọyọ began to be regarded as having been ruler of Yorubaland before the disturbances of the 19th century. Ultimately Atanda's New Oyo Empire was built around this mistaken and exaggerated concept of the place of Ọyọ in Yorubaland. Ibadan felt deprived and cheated when Ọyọ became the capital of Lugard's Oyo Province which included Ibadan. Oyo-Ibadan relations remained unsatisfactory even after 1934 when Ibadan was made independent of Ọyọ, for that represented a new victory for Ibadan and a measure of defeat for Ọyọ.

My own study of Itsẹkiri-Urhobo relations is a good example of how changing British attitude favoured first one group and then another, creating unintended tensions and hostility. The creation of an Itsẹkiri-Urhobo Division based on the premise that those that constituted it had a long tradition of inter-relationship became a source of veritable tensions because by that time Itsekiri-Urhobo relations were already severely frayed. [15]

C. C. Akomolafe's analysis of Ọwọ-Akoko relations reveals how British acceptance of the false claims of overlordship over the Akoko led to extremely tense relations between the two groups in the Owo Division that was created in 1918. What is more, efforts by the British to correct what they saw as errors merely threw up fresh tensions.[16]

John Agi's study of British administration in Lowland Division is an interesting study of the impact of British local government arrangements on inter-ethnic relations in the region inhabited by the Maun, Dimmuk, Bwel, Kwalla, Jukun, Mentol, Yergan, Mirrian and others. It is a tale of fluctuating relations brought about by changing British administrative arrangements at the local government level.[17]

The problem which colonial local government arrangements posed for different Nigerian peoples was a measure of our people's reaction to the new realities of the colonial state. The issue was not that of sinner or saint. It was one of how best to secure group interests in a new and rapidly changing political and economic setting. Viewed from a long term perspective, it can be argued that it was a reaction to the challenge of the first stages of political integration.

While on the issue of political integration, it is necessary to state that because it was in the sphere of local government that Nigerian peoples participated in any meaningful measure in the governance of themselves, indirect rule did not promote inter-group contact on a national scale. The tensions and conflicts about which we have spoken were acted out within districts and divisions for the most part. Few of the "chiefs" involved in local government knew what was happening in other, distant parts of Nigeria. The up and coming educated elite were excluded from participation at this level until the late 1940s, just as they were excluded from participation in the central government. So although the British had created a new geo-political entity known as Nigeria, and created various administrative units within it, their administrative arrangements were not, until the early 1950s, such that promoted a great deal of contact among those who ultimately took over from them. The personnel of local government were in no position to take over from the British, because of the level at which they operated, as well as their level of education and political awareness. Therefore the claims often made that British indirect rule prepared Nigerians for eventual self-rule is hardly borne out by the available evidence.

On Nigerian Participation in Central Government

Until the 1950s, only a handful of Nigerians participated in central government institutions. Central government was regarded as the monopoly of the British. This was partly a function of racial pride; partly, it resulted from the fact that Western European education, a necessary prerequisite for effective participation in central government, took time to develop and to throw up the crop of educated elite that was ultimately to take over power from the British. There were two areas in which Nigerian participation was possible. One was in the Legislative and Executive Councils that constituted part of the British crown colony system. The other was the colonial civil service.

Nigerians first got into the Lagos Legislative Council in 1872 when James Labulo Davies was nominated into that body. From that date till 1922 a number of Nigerians served on that body: C. J. George, James Johnson, C. A. Sapara Williams, Dr. Obadiah Johnson. When, following the introduction of the Clifford's Constitution, the elective principle was conceded, those elected into the Council in the days before Herbert Macaulay organised his Nigerian National Democratic Party were J. Egerton-Shyngle, E. O. Moore and Dr C. C. Adeniyi-Jones. As their names clearly indicate, those men all belonged to the families of repatriates from Sierra Leone where they had received some education. Anyone who has read the contributions of these men to the debates of the Legislative Councils would be impressed by their efforts to promote the interests of the Nigerians and by their bold criticism of colonial government policies. Their effectiveness, as Tekena Tamuno has pointed out, was however limited by the fact that they were always in the minority, as well as by the veto power which the Governor had, not to mention the superior authority of the British Parliament and the Secretary of State for the Colonies. Besides, for most of the period before 1946, the Legislative Council was concerned only with the affairs of Lagos colony. Nigerian participation was thus clearly limited both in terms of numbers and in terms of power.[18]

With regard to the civil service, racial intolerance ensured that the senior positions were reserved for whites well into the late forties. Even when Nigerians had comparable, sometimes better, qualifications than whites, they were paid lower salaries. By the thirties and forties a sizeable number of educated Nigerians were already available for employment in the civil service, the instrument for the execution of government policies. These Nigerians did not get appointed into the senior grades of the civil service. These were the men – lawyers, medical doctors, engineers, journalists, teachers, etc – who began to agitate for more effective Nigerian participation in central government institutions. Their agitations did not bear much fruit before the late 1940s. Indeed Nigerian nationalism was partly born out of the frustrations of the educated elite. This frustration was double edged, as the educated elites were excluded from both central and local government spheres. The lawyers, for example, were angry at their exclusion from appearing for litigants under the native court system. One important consequence of this situation for the evolution of Nigeria's political culture, which has not been sufficiently stressed, is the fact that it tended to force these educated elite back on their primordial communities and loyalties. James O'Connell may have put it rather strongly, but there is a great deal of truth in his assertion:

> ...there was little in the political scene to inspire social attitudes that were incipiently universalist and that at least reached out to the boundaries of the colonial quasi-state. By and large educated Nigerians, deeply imbued with loyalties that had their roots in the relatively closed cosmologies of the traditional religions and the kinship systems, carried out their professional or commercial activities in new towns but took their social identities from their communities of origin.[19]

Herein lies part of the explanation for the emergence of ethnic-based and region-based political parties in the 1950s.

Consideration of space and my own as yet limited study of the subject make it impossible for me to dwell at length on the colonial civil service. Even so, I feel called upon to make two points. One is that it lay in the logic of the colonial situation for the civil service to be the instrument for attaining the end of colonialism, namely, the exploitation of the colony for the benefit of the metropolitan power. The colonial civil service was thus an instrument of exploitation. That was the instrument which Nigerians began to take over in the 1950s and have now completely taken over. Twenty-five years after independence there is still the debate about whether we have, as a nation, succeeded in transforming the civil service from an instrument of exploitation to one for the development of the nation. It looks as if we are finding it extremely difficult to lay the ghost of the colonial civil service.

Secondly, it was to the lower ranks of the civil service that Nigerians were usually appointed. These Nigerians saw themselves as working for an alien authority to which they hardly had any loyalty. Indeed government was a distant, almost irrelevant, body so far as they were concerned. There was no compelling reason why they should put in a good day's work for a good day's pay. Indeed in certain circumstances, it would be an act of nationalism to sabotage the programmes of the colonial government. Unfortunately, that attitude is still with us; the Nigerian's attitude to work remains one of our major drawbacks as we seek to develop as a nation. Also the continuing attitude to Government as something foreign to us partially explains the staggering level of economic and other forms of sabotage that have afflicted us as a nation.

Constitutional Development, Decolonisation and the Evolution of Nigeria's Political Culture[20]

Until 1922 Nigeria was ruled as a typical crown colony. The Legislative and Executive Councils were dominated by the British officials. Nigerians who served on these bodies were nominated by the Governor. The first major change occurred in 1922 when Governor Hugh Clifford introduced a new constitution. Although Clifford's Legislative Council still had an official majority – 27 officials to 19 unofficials, the principle of elective representation granted by the constitution was significant. Admittedly only 4 of the 27 unofficials were to be elected (3 from Lagos and 1 from Calabar). Admittedly the suffrage was qualified – adult male, one year residential qualification and an annual income of £100. Yet the principle of elective representation was significant. Nigeria led the rest of colonial West Africa in this regard. Let it be noted, though, that educated Africans had been agitating for this concession since the late 19th century, and the National Congress of British West Africa had pointedly demanded it in 1920. Clifford may thus be said to have been reacting guardedly to the demands of the emerging nationalists.

One other aspect of the constitution warrants comments: Clifford's Legislative Council had jurisdiction only over Southern Nigeria. The Governor was to continue to issue proclamations for the governance of the North, eight years after amalgamation. Clifford argued that the emirs would resent being represented in the Legislative Council; that the North was made up of "self contained Native states" ruled by their Native Administrations; that there were communication problems and that the large number of ethnic of groups in the country made it necessary to limit the jurisdiction of the Council to the South. Seventeen years later, another British Governor was to split the south into two while leaving the North intact on the grounds that there were diverse ethnic groups in the south while the North was culturally homogenous. Actions like Clifford's and later Bourdillon's make it look like the British had certain vested interests in the North which they were eager to protect. Be that as it may, the point that can and must be made is that keeping the North and South apart in this manner was little calculated to facilitate that degree of contacts and understanding that the future Nigeria would require.

The Clifford's constitution also triggered off the formation of political parties that would contest the elections. Of these the most important was the Nigerian National Democratic Party (N.N.D.P.) formed by Herbert Macaulay. That party dominated the politics of Lagos till the arrival of the Nigerian Youth Movement (N.Y.M.) in 1934.

The Second World War and the Quickening of Constitutional Advance: It is now common knowledge that various developments associated with the 1939-45 World War helped to quicken the rate of political concessions made to colonies. These can be briefly summarised: war propaganda about democracy and the rights of all peoples to choose the kind of government under which they would live; a feeling of gratitude to colonial peoples for their roles in the war; a general world opinion in favour of decolonisation; the pricking of the bubble of white supremacy brought about by the participation of black soldiers alongside white soldiers in many sectors of the war. Against this background, continued discrimination against Nigerians in the civil service while demobilized white soldiers were being recruited; the failure to find jobs for Nigerian ex-servicemen and the continued economic exploitation of the colony, intensified by the requirements of war and post-war reconstruction – all these heightened political agitation in Nigeria. Indeed, it was in this ferment that the National Council of Nigeria and the Cameroons (N.C.N.C.) was formed in 1944. Herbert Macaulay became its President while Nnamdi Azikiwe became Secretary. The N.C.N.C. was to dominate the nationalist agitation till the introduction of the Macpherson Constitution.

It was as a concession to the growing nationalist feeling that the Richards' Constitution was promulgated in 1946. For the first time since 1914 the constitution provided for a Legislative Council that would have jurisdiction over the entire country. Also there was to be an unofficial majority in the Legislative Council – 28 to 16 officials. Regional Councils were to be established in each of the three regions. The Native Authorities were to send delegates to the Regional Councils which in turn were to send delegates to the Legislative Council in Lagos. The elective principle remained as in 1922 – three to be elected in Lagos and one in Calabar. The North was to have a House of Chiefs in addition to its Regional Council.

The Richards' Constitution occupies an important place in Nigeria's evolution. Its architect argued that it was designed to promote the unity of Nigeria, while at the same time recognizing the diversity of peoples and cultures within the country. Definitely the legislative union that was provided for in the constitution was a major step forward in the promotion of greater union between North and South. Critics of the constitution accused Richards of balkanizing the country. In a sense this is unfair, in so far as the three regions already existed since 1939. Besides, because the Regional Councils did not have legislative powers, the regions remained as yet administrative rather than political entities. But perhaps what made the constitution most unpopular was that it was imposed without consultation with the Nigerian nationalists, despite a promise by Bourdillon that there would be consultation. Consequently, the nationalists, led by the N.C.N.C., mounted a nation-wide campaign against the constitution and petitioned London against it. The N.C.N.C. campaign did not lead to the withdrawal of the constitution which came into effect in 1944, but it did result in its not lasting the nine years originally envisaged, for as from 1949 the colonial administration began to prepare the ground for a new constitution which ultimately came into effect in 1952.

From the Macpherson to the Independence Constitution: Whatever the deficiencies of the Richard's Constitution, it represented an advance in the process of increasing involvement of Nigerians in the decision-making process that was to culminate in independence. The agitation mounted against it by the nationalists ensured that future constitutions would not be promulgated without involving our people. Sir John Macpherson, who replaced Arthur Richards as Governor, therefore set up a machinery for consulting Nigerians before the constitution which bears his name was drawn up. These consultations began at local government levels, moved up to provincial and regional levels and ended with a national conference.

The nature of the Macpherson Constitution and the differences between regions which influenced that nature cannot be fully understood without some discussion of the rise of ethnic and regional nationalism. It was earlier stated that until the Richards'Constitution, the nature of politics was such that offered limited opportunities for the growing number of educated elite. Most of the political action took place in Lagos. Because the repatriates were among the very first to receive western education, and because Christian missionary activity began in Yorubaland before anywhere else in Nigeria, it was the Yoruba who dominated the politics of Lagos in these years. But increasingly Lagos was becoming a city of mixed population, as were other urban centres. Because of land shortage and population increase, the Igbo were among the Nigerians who took advantage of the greater opportunities offered by the colonial state to move out of their homes and settle in the towns and cities of the West and North. With time also, they produced a substantial number of different levels of educated elite. Although other ethnic groups also migrated to different centres in Nigeria, the Igbo stand out because of their numbers. Since his return from America (after a brief sojourn in Ghana) in 1937, Nnamdi Azikiwe (Zik), who founded a chain of newspapers, had become the leading figure among the Igbo in Lagos, as well as a major force in the nationalist movement.

Migration to urban centres forced different Nigerian groups, in search of some identity in their new homes, to form mutual Benefit Societies or Improvement Unions. In addition to providing a 'home away from home', these unions, usually led by the educated elite, played a useful and constructive role in promoting education and other developments in their original home communities. However, they also became easy recruits into the ethnic political parties that were to dominate Nigerian politics from the 1950s. By 1944 we had both an Ibibio State Union, and a Pan-Igbo Federal Union of which Azikiwe became President in 1948. In 1945 Yoruba students in London formed a cultural organisation known as the Egbe Omo Oduduwa. Obafemi Awolowo was one of the founding members. When the Egbe Omo Oduduwa held its inaugural conference at Ife in 1949, Adeyemo Alakija, its President, declared, the "Yoruba will not be relegated to the background in the future". This statement may have been in partial response to Zik's assertion that "it would appear that the God of Africa has created the Igbo nation to lead the children of Africa from the bondage of the ages..." Earlier in 1943 Tafawa Balewa, Sa'ad Zungur, Aminu Kano and others had formed the Bauchi Improvement Union. Balewa and Aminu Kano were also among the founders in 1949 of the Northern Peoples' Congress, a cultural organisation which was soon to be transformed into a political party. Similar unions were formed by other ethnic groups. Few of these other unions, however, were to have the same impact on national politics as those formed by the Hausa-Fulani, the Yoruba and the Igbo, the three giant ethnic groups in Nigeria. The point of this narrative is to demonstrate that the period of rapid constitutional development in Nigeria coincided with that of increased ethnic and regional affiliations which helps to explain why ethnicity and regionalism became such features of our political culture as we prepared ourselves for independence. The Macpherson constitution was thus fashioned in an atmosphere of ethnic and regional jingoism.

The Macpherson Constitution provided for a federal system of government with a fairly strong centre though considerable powers were to be delegated to the Regions. The central Legislative Council was to be 148 strong, made up as follows: 136 elected – 68 from the North and 34 each from the East and West; 6 were to be nominated by the Governor to represent interests not adequately represented by the elected members and 6 were to be officials. There was to be an Executive Council of 18-6 officials and 12 Nigerian ministers, 4 each nominated by the regional assemblies. Revenue allocation was to be on the basis of need rather than derivation. In the regions there were to be Houses of Assembly and Executive Councils with a majority of Nigerians over officials. Additionally Houses of Chiefs were provided for the North and West. Elections to the regional assemblies were to be direct. But these assemblies were then to constitute electoral colleges for electing delegates to the central legislature. The central legislature was to have no powers over bills to do with public revenue and the public service. Regional bills had to be sent to the Governor who was given powers to disallow such bills if they clashed with the general interests of Nigeria.

The Macpherson Constitution was a compromise document. The East had wanted more states created; but the North had insisted on maintaining existing boundaries. The West also advocated more states, wanted Ilorin returned to the West and wanted Lagos to remain part of the West. Also while the West would have liked revenue allocation to be based on derivation in the days when cocoa fetched good money, the North advocated allocation on a per capita basis, hoping that its larger population would give it a definite advantage in this regard. The original draft recognised the larger size of the North and suggested 30 for it and 22 each for West and East. The North insisted on getting half the seats in the central legislature and eventually had its way in that regard.

The Macpherson constitution may have failed to completely satisfy any of the regions. Yet it was a significant advance on the Richards' constitution. Having said that, it must be conceded that the Nigerian politicians who had accused Arthur Richards of balkanizing the country did not do any better. There can be no mistaking the clear regional emphasis in the arrangements. Central ministers were to be nominated by the regions. Such ministers could hardly see themselves as representing national interests. It was the Regional Houses which were to elect members of the central legislature. Such members would see themselves as representing their regions. A federal system was set up; yet the distribution of seats was such that one region clearly dominated the centre. All the seeds of future political instability were thus present in the new constitution.

In preparing for the formal coming into effect of the new constitution, political parties were formed. The Action Group (A.G.) formed in 1950 was formally launched in April 1951. It was clearly a West regional party. The Northern People's Congress (N.P.C.) was also formed in 1951. Its motto of "One North, one People irrespective of religion rank or tribe" openly acknowledged its regional allegiance. Indeed throughout its existence, the N.P.C. never sought any vote outside the North, though it did enter into alliance with southern parties. The N.C.N.C. retained a semblance of a national party, though events were soon to make it an Igbo-dominated party.

The elections which were held towards the end of 1951 confirmed that our political parties were all essentially region-based. The N.C.N.C. won in the East; the N.P.C. won in the North. In the West the N.C.N.C. gave the A.G. a hard fight, since there were parts of the region that preferred the N.C.N.C. and there was a number of leading Yoruba elements in it. In the end it was only as a result of carpet crossing that the A.G. managed to acquire a majority of 49 out of the 80 seats. Nnamdi Azikiwe was the only party leader who contested the elections outside his region of origin. He led four other N.C.N.C. stalwarts in capturing the five Lagos seats and so took his seat in the Western House of Assembly. The constitution provided 2 seats for Lagos in the central legislature. Zik was anxious to go to the centre. But the Western House of Assembly, which was to elect members to the centre, was now A.G. and Yoruba dominated. To ensure Zik's election, his N.C.N.C. colleagues who were Yoruba agreed that they would not contest against him. Unfortunately, these colleagues reneged due, no doubt, to ethnic preserve. In the upshot, Zik was defeated and so could not go to the centre. In many ways this brazen manifestation of ethnic politics was unfortunate for the emerging Nigeria, for since then most Nigerians irrespective of where they live and work, have had to go to their original homes to contest elections.

Zik's reaction deepened ethnic tensions. He resigned his seat and went home to the East. He then sought to fight the constitution, the provisions of which he saw as responsible for his fate. As leader of the N.C.N.C., he requested N.C.N.C. ministers in the East and the Centre to resign. When these refused they were expelled from the party. He then fomented a crisis in the Eastern House which ultimately led to its dissolution. In the ensuing election, Zik contested in Onitsha and won convincingly as did the N.C.N.C. overall. He then, like Awolowo of the A.G. and Ahamdu Bello of the North, led his parliamentary party in the East. At the time Zik moved East, Eyo-Ita, Vice-President of the N.C.N.C., headed the cabinet. He was a non-Igbo. He was one of these expelled from the N.C.N.C. He became the leader of a new party, the United National Independence Party (U.N.I.P.). Although at the beginning the party had some Igbo members, it rapidly became associated with the non-Igbo parts of the East and was to seek close association with the A.G. later. As Nigerians took their first opportunity of playing any meaningful role in policy-making at regional and central level, they did so essentially on an ethnic and regional basis. As it turned out, they had only eight years before independence and other events during that period accentuated rather than diminished ethnic and regional antagonisms.

Meanwhile at the centre, a crisis also developed. In March 1953 Chief Anthony Enahoro, an A.G. member of the House of Representative, moved a motion calling for self-government for Nigeria in 1956. The Northern members strongly opposed the date 1956, convinced as they were that they did not have the manpower they would need and therefore were, afraid of southern domination of the public service. They therefore proposed an amendment which called for self-government as soon as practicable. The fears of the North were justified in many ways. But the Southern members were not prepared to accept the amendment. They walked out of the House and the four A.G. members of the cabinet resigned. The constitution could hardly be worked in the circumstances.

The disagreement over the self-government motion was but symptomatic of the different levels of political development of the South and North. Two other factors worsened North-South tensions. The Southern press launched a virulent attack on the Northern members of the House of Representatives, calling them rude names. The A.G. decided to undertake a tour of the North to educate the people about the self-government motion. And they chose to start their tour in Kano, a cosmopolitan centre with substantial southern population. Riots broke out in which some 50 persons died and over 250 were injured. North-South tensions worsened.

The events described above virtually killed the Macpherson Constitution. The Colonial Secretary, Lyttleton, decided that a new constitution should be worked out. In view of the events already indicated, it was little surprise that the Lyttleton Constitution ended up creating strong regions and a comparatively weak centre. At the same time, some of the outrageously regional emphasis of the Macpherson constitution was eliminated. Thus elections to the House of Representatives were to be direct, and no one could be a member of both that House and any of the Regional Houses. Ministers were not to be nominated by the regions but appointed from among members of the House on the recommendation of the party leader having a majority in the House; but there had to be three from each region. The three-regions structure remained. The North had 92 seats out of 184, maintaining its dominance in that regard. The police were to be under the Governor-General. Each region was to have its own civil service. Residual powers were to be vested in the Region. Lagos was declared federal territory despite a spirited fight by the A.G. that it should remain with the West.

The 1954 Constitution was to be further revised in 1958 and 1959. But in terms of structure of the Federation no further major change took place after 1954. The vexed issue of creation of more states remained unresolved, because in the face of the determination of the North to keep its territory intact, the other two states were unwilling to reduce their own territories. Thus a situation in which there were three regions each easily dominated by a majority ethnic group was preserved into independence and was to influence Nigerian polities right up to the civil war and beyond. The events of the first few years of independence showed quite clearly that minority interests could, in no way, be adequately safeguard by the entrenchment of Fundamental Human Rights in our constitution. The issue of self-government was resolved in1957 by the decision that these regions that wanted it could go ahead. The West and East therefore became self-governing in that year while the North opted for 1959. As a result of various other compromises, it was ultimately possible for all parties to agree to the date of 1 October, 1960, for national independence.

Although we have not, in this discussion, provided all the details of constitutional developments, nor have we presented all the details about political events in different parts of the country, it is hoped that enough has been said to demonstrate that the period of decolonisation was one in which the political leadership that was to take over from the British at independence was concerned essentially with serving the best advantages of their particular regions. The fact that all our political parties were largely regional parties meant that at independence, there were really no national leaders. In the circumstances national leadership was only possible on a compromise basis. This fact made it difficult for our leaders at the centre to evolve truly national policies, with strategies that would ensure equitable development and distribution of amenities. A great deal of Nigeria's post-independence problems derives from this fact.

Conclusion

Clearly the most significant change that British administrative and political arrangements brought about was the fusing of a large number of hitherto disparate and autonomous villages, clans, kingdoms and empires into what we now know as Nigeria. This revolutionary change was brought about without the consent of the various peoples concerned. The process was often painful. It involved the imposition of Nigeria's international boundaries, as well as various internal boundaries – regional, provincial, divisional and district. These boundaries have rightly been described as artificial. At national level this artificiality which involved breaking up ethnic groups (of our northern, western and eastern borders) has had the effect of creating problem for those ethnic groups who live around the borders. It has also been a major factor in the phenomenon of smuggling at such borders. Equally significant are border disputes between us and our neighbours, especially the Cameroons but also Chad and Niger. It is necessary in this regard, however, to make the point that the existence of more "natural" frontiers between peoples (nationalities?) in pre-colonial times did not constitute a guarantee of peaceful relations between neighbours.

As for the internal boundaries, they constituted a major problem for our peoples who had to adjust to the new units. If at first these units meant little, over time they acquired an importance in their lives. What in effect was happening was the creation of new identities and new loyalties as well as new vested interests around the new units. At the level of local governments (divisions, districts, native court areas, etc.) the delimitation of these units often caused tensions, conflicts and disharmonies. But, if I may use the words of U.D. Anyanwu, to stress a point already made, what was happening was "part of the political education of the people. For the issues which arose were those of the co-existence of hitherto separate groups within a new political order such that all concerned could feel a genuine sense of belonging… Having to face the problems [which arose] was and is an important aspect of the political evolution of a colonial state [that ultimately had to] transform itself into a sovereign nation-state."[21] No such nation-state can come into being without radical alteration of primordial socio-political arrangements. The methods may vary but the need for a rearrangement of the pre-existing setting will always be there.

The coming of the British meant the replacement of our rulers by a new set of rulers. British administrative policies at central and local levels permanently weakened the indigenous systems of government. Ironically, these policies also turned some of these rulers into petty despots as Adamu Fika demonstrates for Kano. A longer term effect of the change which took place was that our political systems having been permanently weakened, the new Nigeria had perforce to adopt the political system of our colonial masters. Our experience since independence can leave no one in any doubt that our forced acceptance of an alien political system and culture has failed to serve the best interests of our new nation-state. There is thus a challenge of developing a political system that will be vested in the essential ethos of our various peoples.

It was out of the large-scale monopoly of the powers of government by British officials that Nigerian nationalism grew. On the one hand, that large-scale monopoly denied the would-be Nigerian political leaders adequate apprenticeship in handling the affairs of the new state. Inadequate apprenticeship resulted in inadequate performance at independence and after. On the other hand, the background to Nigerian nationalism made it declamatory and negative. Our leaders were agreed on what they did not want; they found it difficult to agree on what they wanted. After independence was regained, these leaders were unable to develop a nationalism that would foster stability and orderly and equitable development. The challenge of today (1986) is how to develop this new nationalism and patriotism.

BIBLIOGRAPHY

- Because of the nature and subject matter of this chapter, we have provided below a Bibliography of some of the works available on the subject of British rule in Nigeria, on which the chapter is largely based. We have also provided such footnotes as we consider necessary.
- Abubakar, Sa'ad (1980) "The Northern Provinces under Colonial Rule 1900-1959" in Obaro Ikime (ed.) *Groundwork of Nigerian History*, Heinemann, Ibadan.
- Afigbo, A. E. (1972) *The Warrant Chiefs*, Longman, London.
- .... (1966) "The Warrant Chief System:Direct or Indirect Rule" JHSN, III, 4
- .... (1980) "The Eastern Provinces under Colonial Rule" in *Groundwork.*
- Ajayi, J.F. Ade and Crowder, M. (Eds.), (1971), *History of West Africa*, Vol. II, Longman, London.
- Anene, J.C.A. (1966) *Southern Nigeria in Transition 1885-1906*, C.U.P. London.
- Asiwaju, A.I. (1976) *Western Yorubaland Under European Rule 1889-1945,* Longman, London.
- .... (1980) "The Western Province under Colonial Rule" in *Groundwork*
- Atanda, J. A. (1973) *The New Oyo Empire*, Longman, London.
- Crowder, M. (1973) *The Story of Nigeria,* Faber and Faber, London.
- Crowder, M. and Ikime, Obaro (Editors), 1972, *West African Chiefs,* Ife University Press, Ife.
- Ezera, Kalu (1960) *Constitutional Developments in Nigeria,* C.U.P. London.
- Fika, Adamu (1978) *The Kano Civil War and British Over-rule 1884-1940*, C.U.P., Ibadan.
- Igbafe, P. A. (1979) *Benn Under British Administration,* Longman, London.
- Ikime, Obaro (1969) *Niger-Delta Rivalry*, Longmans, London.
- .... (1968) "Reconsidering Indirect Rule: The Nigerian Example" JHSN, IV, 2
- .... (Ed) (1980) *Groundwork of Nigerian History*, Heinemann, Ibadan.
- Nicolson, I. F. (1969) *The Administration of Nigeria 1900-1960,* O.U.P. Oxford.
- Olusanya, G. O. (1980) "Constitutional Developments in Nigeria 1861-1960" and "The Nationalist Movement in Nigeria" both in *Groundwork of Nigerian History.*
- Perham, Margery (1960) *Lugard: The Years of Authority,* Collins, London.

- Tamuno, T.N. (1966) *Nigeria and Elective Representation 1928-1947*, Heinemann London.
- .... (1972) *The Evolution of the Nigerian State: The Southern Phase, 1898-1914,* Longman, London.
- .... (1980) "British Colonial Administration in Nigeria in the Twentieth Century" in *Groundwork.*
- White, Jeremy (1982) *Central Administration in Nigeria 1914-1948*, Frank Cass, Inst. Academic Press.

NOTES

1. Chief Obafemi Awolowo, Premier of the Western Region, believed in the creation of more states, but insisted that such state-creation should be nationwide. The creation of the Mid-West Region in 1965 was made possible by the Federal Government which was an alliance between the N.P.C. and the N.C.N.C. That these two parties did not support the creation of the Middle Belt Region and a Calabar – Ogoja – Rivers Region in their respective regions, reveals the bad faith in which they acted. The aim was to reduce the area over which Awolowo could exercise authority.
2. See Anene (1966) and Afigbo (1980).
3. Asiwaju (1980).
4. See Sa'ad Abubakar (1980) and Perham (1980).
5. Anene and Afigbo.
6. Anene, p. 175.
7. See Tamuno (1972) and Asiwaju (1976).
8. Tamuno (1972).
9. Tamuno (1972) and Crowder (1976) for detailed discussions of amalgamation.
10. For some comment on Bourdillion's act, see Obaro Ikime, *History, The Historian and The Nation: Voice of a Nigerian Historian*, Ibadan, 2006, HEBN Publishers Plc., Chapter 5.
11. See Afigbo (1972), Ikime (1969) and U.D. Anyanwu, *Local Government Its Changing Nature and Role in a Nigerian Setting: A Case Study of the Imo State Area, 1930-1966*, University of Ibadan Ph.D. Thesis, 1984, for detailed discussions of the issues raised here.
12. Atanda (1973) Chapter 4.
13. Ikime (1969) Chapter 5.
14. Afigbo (1972) and Ikime (1969) discuss this phenomenon in greater detail.
15. Ikime (1969), especially Chapters 5 & 6.

16. For details see C. O. Akomolafe, *Akoko under British Rule 1900-1935,* University of Ife, M.Ph. thesis 1976 and his "The Establishment of British Administration and its impact on Owo-Akoko Relations, 1990-1935" in J.H.S.N., X, 1.
17. J.O. Agi, *British Administration in Lowland Division 1898-1959: A Study of the Impact of Colonial Rule on Inter-Ethnic Relations*, Ahmadu Bello Master's thesis, 1978.
18. See Tamuno (1966), 1972 & 1900) and Olusanya (1980).
19. James O'Cornell, "Political Integration: The Nigerian Case" in Arthur Herslewood (Ed.) (1967) *African Integration and Disintegration* O.U.P. London, p. 138.
20. For more details of the issues discussed in the remaining part of this chapter, see Tamuno (1980), Olusanya (1980), Crowder (1978) and Kalu Ezera (1960).
21. Ayanwu, *op. cit.*, p. 405.

and

8

LEADERSHIP AND THE NIGERIAN POLITY: PROSPECTS FOR THE THIRD REPUBLIC*

Introduction

I am delighted by the opportunity afforded me by the Common Cause Club to share some thoughts on leadership and the Nigerian Polity as we progress in the transition to our next interlude of civil rule – for civil rule is now the interlude and military rule the norm in the system of governance in Nigeria. In doing so, I want to draw attention to the fact that the organisers are conscious of the fact that the nature of the Nigerian polity is a, perhaps the, crucial factor in determining the nature and kind of leadership that we can hope to get in the Third Republic. I also want to remind you that this lecture is being delivered under the auspices of the Common Cause Club. I wish to state that the name of the club is significant. If Nigeria has thus far failed to evolve a leadership pattern that is (i) national (ii) effective (iii) responsive to the commonweal, I submit that it is largely because, we have not, thus far, been committed to a common cause. Before I proceed much further, let me confess that I am not about to present much that is new in what follows. In the last

*A lecture delivered under the auspices of the Common Cause Club, Ibadan, on 23 November, 1988.

few years, I have had to speak so often on topics related to that given me by the organisers of this lecture, that I would have a really hard task presenting completely new materials and arguments. Even so, I can only hope that I do not bore you to death.

The Nature of the Nigerian Polity

Nigeria, we often tell ourselves, is an artificial creation of the British. The different groups which make it up were never under the same political umbrella before the coming of the British. This being so, the argument usually proceeds, it is not surprising that we are not yet a united polity. Not being a united polity invariably influences the kind of leadership we get. It is almost as if the fact of our colonial experience not only excuses our failings thus far, but also justifies it. I have argued many times before and I must re-state that argument here, given the subject of this lecture, that all nations of the world are artificial, in the sense that few are made up of just one nationality, what we in Nigeria continue to refer to as ethnic group. The welding together of diverse nationalities into a nation-state and the investment of the nation-state, with a distinct individuality with identifiable national goals are, clearly, invariably the challenges which national leaders must face. It is a challenge which whoever will be leader in the Third Republic must be prepared to face. Put differently, what I am saying is that the very fact of our colonial experience – with all the problems of inter-ethnic and inter-regional relations which that experience left behind – ought to challenge whoever would lead into greater effort, not for ever excuse the failure of national leadership.

The Factor of Ethnic Plurality

However one looks at Nigeria and its leadership, there can be no escaping the fact that ethnicity has become an important factor in determining political action. Who and what are Nigeria's ethnic groups? Here again I can only repeat myself. The very groups that today vie for political leadership, the very groups loyalty to which vitiates genuine effort at nation-building – Hausa, Fulani, Kanuri, Yoruba, Efik, Igbo, Ijọ, Tivi, Ebira, Bini, Urhobo, Isoko, Itsẹkiri, Ibibio, etc – did not exist in their present forms till the British brought all of them together under colonial rule, by force or show of force.

It was competition for resources and office within the colonial state that forced hitherto separate socio-political groupings to begin to see themselves as having certain common interests which they began to come together to defend. It was the identification and defence of certain common interests that gave rise to today's ethnic groups. It is the identification and spirited promotion of national interests that can produce true and acceptable national leadership.

When a Yoruba says he is Yoruba, he says so only in the national setting. When he says so, he thereby, whether he thinks about it or not, plays down his real roots – his Oyo-ness, Ijebu-ness, Ijesa-ness, Ekiti-ness, etc, in order to take advantage of a larger identity. He would not play down his roots if he sees no advantage in doing so. This is both the lesson and the challenge for the would-be Third Republic leader. As an Isoko man, I can have no real interest in saying I am Nigerian in a Nigeria in which I am a second or third class citizen, a Nigeria in which I am denied full citizenship and recognition commensurate with my abilities and proven merit. What is true for me is true for every other person. We will never legislate ethnic groups out of existence, nor is it desirable that we should, for all nations have their ethnic groups. What we must seek to do is to create an atmosphere at national level which, while allowing for a certain degree of self-determination, also promotes equitable distribution of national resources as well as equitable development. Constitutional provisions alone will not, cannot, bring about the desired goal. Only a political leadership that is dedicated to the realisation of the spirit as distinct from the letter of the constitution can lead us to true nationhood. Our ethnic groups will and must remain. After all, we owe our size and therefore our potentially strong economy to the multitude of our ethnic groups. But Nigeria must arise and tower over these ethnic groups. Nigeria cannot, however, arise and so tower unless all, emphasis on all, who lead within Nigeria rise above ethnic and sectional interests and commitments; unless our citizenry is sensitised to realising that ethnicity is really only a weapon used by the political elite to promote their selfish class interests, while leaving the bulk of the ethnic groups they exploit among the wretched of the earth. Observe, for example, how long political power at the centre has been in the hands of persons from North of the Niger-Benue waterway. But also observe the continued poverty of the rural poor in that region, whose population is used as the justification for why political power must reside in that region. Wherever you look, the story is the same. What is the lesson? This, that political leadership will remain selfish and jaundiced until the led begin to demand – and demand vociferously – a just ordering of society. Herein comes the dilemma. The citizenry cannot demand their just rights unless they are organised and led. Who leads them? How? With what ends in view? Forgive my pessimism, but I do not yet see on the horizon too many possible leaders who would encourage the citizenry to demand their rights.

The Absence of a National Political Culture

Nigeria has not, thus far, evolved a national political culture. There really is nothing which the holder of political office is forbidden to do! A minister forced to resign from office for corruption can win a landslide victory at a subsequent election. He can, when he dies, receive a state funeral! A military officer found to have abused his office as a governor and consequently stripped of his rank, can contest and win elections as a civilian governor and subsequently becomes an appointee of a Federal Military Government. An executive President can be removed from office by the military because of the corruption of his regime; and yet be absolved of all blame for the corruption of that regime. Hail Nigeria, Africa's giant!

Why do we not have a national political culture? Because we do not yet have a nation. Because the British did not bequeath such a culture to us. Colonial regimes do not promote the evolution of a political culture. This is because the colonial administrators are not responsible to the people or peoples they govern. They are responsible to the metropolitan authority. Their business is simple: to achieve the end for which they are appointed, namely, the exploitation of the colonised peoples for the economic benefit of their home country. Since to do this, they must necessarily trample on the rights of the colonised, they cannot afford to bring into play the political culture from which they come. Britain, the country that colonised us, has a well developed political culture. Even a mere suspicion of unbecoming relations between a minister and a company seeking to do business with the British Government is enough to force such a minister to resign. By contrast, here in Nigeria, the wife of a Head of State can incorporate a company in the name of a relation and win massive contracts from her husband's Government. British political culture is a factor of the totality of their historical experiences. At independence we took on aspects of British political institutions without the ground rules which inform the operation of those institutions.

All we were able to take over was the non-culture of our colonial civil servants, from the Governor downwards. The colonial civil service was set up to exploit us. So our civil services proceed to exploit us – with one significant difference. Where the colonial civil servant exploited us for the benefit of Great Britain, and was in that sense patriotic, the Nigerian civil servant exploits us for the benefit of his personal pocket and is consequently both unpatriotic and criminal! The exploitation of Nigeria and Nigerians by the civil servant would have been less successful and thorough had they had to cope with a political elite that was committed to the development of the nation. As it turned out, our political elite, like the civil servants, saw themselves as inheritors of the rights and privileges of the colonial administrators. An unholy alliance thus developed between the political elite and the civil service. That unholy alliance has been partially responsible for the continued absence of a national political culture in Nigeria.

Undisguised political corruption, the consequence of the unholy alliance already identified, has been fed on a winner take-all syndrome in national and regional politics. A winner-take-all syndrome denies the fact that Government exists to promote the welfare of all. For most of our history since independence, Governments – Federal and Regional/ State – have tended to deny basic amenities to groups identified as politically hostile. Discrimination of this type has, naturally, resulted in the alienation of those who are its victims. Alienation in turn produces a rugged we-want-our-own-man syndrome in national politics. Electoral corruption for which Nigeria has become notorious, is partly a product of this we-want-our-own-man syndrome. How does this affect the evolution of a political culture? Our ethnic groups are quite prepared to regard as heroes persons from their groups who rifle the national treasury! Indeed our people expect that if their son is a minister, he should steal enough to distribute to them!. If he is caught, they know that nothing will happen to him any way – so are they all, all thieves! Even if anything were to happen to him – even if he were tried and jailed – the day he leaves jail his people will carry him shoulder high; the guns will boom. For what? For being a thief. Those who will call for the head of him who steals from the treasury of a town union are quite ready to glorify him who steals from a State or Federal treasury. So long as this attitude persists, so long will it be difficult to really curb official corruption in high places. Unless we can begin, in the Third Republic, to consciously evolve a political culture – to lay down and, above all, enforce rules that must govern political behaviour, I can see no radically new leadership emerging. Both the Constituent Assembly and the Armed Forces Ruling Council must see the laying down of such ground rules as a major aspect of their responsibility.

Acceptance of the Rule of Law

Closely related to the absence of a national political culture is Nigeria's penchant for abusing the rule of law. Again, this is a product of our colonial heritage as well as since independence. Although the rule of law is well established in Britain, it was denied British colonies, for the very good reason that you do not make omelettes without breaking eggs. Colonial conquest necessarily involves the use of force, which is the very antithesis of the rule of law. Colonial rule itself often involved abuse of the rule of law in so far as laws were passed which were in themselves a denial of fundamental human rights or abuse of due process. Thus the laws which provided the forced labour that built the roads and bridges and cleared the waterways; those which denied a free press; the practice which denied employment to qualified Nigerians, especially in the senior segment of the colonial civil service – all of these were a negation of the rule of law. Similarly, in a colonial setting, the executive and the judiciary have a common aim: the maintenance of that "Law and Order" needed for effective economic exploitation. Given this undeniable fact, the executive expected the judiciary to uphold its authority even at the expense of substantial justice. In other words, in a colonial setting there cannot be a really independent judiciary. Is it then any wonder, that since independence, there have been regimes in Nigeria which have expected the judiciary to support their authority even when this authority is exercised at the expense of the legal rights of the citizenry? While it is true that we have had judges of impeccable integrity who have administered the law without fear or favour, there have also been those – and quite a number too – who have allowed their perceived or informed wishes of the executive to influence their judgements. Additionally, there has been the phenomenon of objectionable laws passed by the legislatures and by decrees and edicts under military regimes which the judiciary has had no option but to enforce. Notable in this class of laws are those enactments which have retrospective effects: laws which make an action which was not criminal at the time it was committed a crime years or months afterwards. Virtually every regime since independence has been guilty of this abuse of the rule of law, the military regimes much more than the civilian. When the rule of law is abused or even denied in detail as it has been in Nigeria, the result is an increasingly irresponsible leadership which inevitably deepens the alienation of the citizenry from the ruling class.

In connection with this issue of the rule of law, there is a fact that military regimes are themselves necessarily a negation of the rule of law. Every military regime is, by definition illegitimate, since it comes to power as a result of a coup and not the expressed wishes of the people. Usually, military regimes also suspend certain aspects of the nation's organic law – the constitution. Even such sections as are not suspended may be abused or rendered non-effective by specific decrees. For us in Nigeria, then, the fact that we have had more years of military rule than of civilian rule means that we have had even less an opportunity of enthroning the rule of law in our land. Leadership in the Third Republic is not likely to be different in any real measure if there is no abiding commitment to the rule of law.

On the Fragility of our Constitutional Arrangements

It is hardly possible to breed effective leadership in an atmosphere of political instability. Yet political instability has been our lot since independence. Part explanation for that instability has been the fragility of our constitutional arrangements. In thirty six years since 1952 when the Macpherson Constitution came into effect, we have had seven constitutional arrangements in addition to two major military interventions, each of which also saw constitutional adjustments, making a total of nine. That gives us an average of four years per constitutional adjustment. What this means is that just as we have not been able to enthrone the rule of law in our nation, so have we failed to build up a tradition of constitutionalism. Needless to say, our political life and the leadership which goes with it have been as fragile as the constitutions themselves. Earlier on we spoke about the importance of a political culture. We cannot evolve a stable political culture when the basic law of the land is being constantly reviewed. Here is a problem which demands our serious attention. It is true that we have felt let down by our political leaders since independence. We must, however, honestly ask ourselves whether we have given those leaders time to really settle down to learning from their mistakes. In politics and governance as in other areas of life, we will make mistakes. Of that, let there be no doubt. If each time mistakes are made we kick out the leaders and change the constitution, it is doubtful if we will ever enjoy political stability. And without political stability, stable, mature leadership will hardly develop. It is something of a vicious cycle, a vicious cycle made more vicious by military coups d'état, since each coup entails not only a suspension of aspects of the constitution but the enforcement of a de facto unitary system of government, even though we pretend to be a federation. Nigeria must learn to abhor military coups as part of her search for a stable political culture and the enthronement of constitutionalism.

On the meaning of Nigerian Citizenship

Both the Buhari and Babangida regimes have harped a great deal on patriotism. Nigeria, as I have argued elsewhere, has failed thus far to produce Nigerians. There is hardly any Nigerian; what we have are Isoko, Yoruba, Igbo, etc, not Nigerians. Indeed Nigerians only exist when the Isoko, the Yoruba, the Igbo, the Idzon, etc. find themselves abroad! Without Nigerians there can be no patriotism. No amount of radio and television jingles will make Nigerians out of the non-Nigerians who now occupy the Nigerian territory! Why are there no Nigerians? A number of reasons may be adduced. I have already spoken of the ethnic factor. At Abuja two years ago, I spoke about the distribution of political offices and the abuse of political patronage; I spoke about the danger of a part of this country being made to feel that supreme political office is its birthright. Despite the Abuja Seminar on the National Question, nothing much has changed. It is not yet clear whether the recommendations of that seminar will ever inform Government action.

I will dwell briefly only on the issue of Nigerian citizenship. I submit that as of today, there really is no meaning to Nigerian citizenship. When it comes to admission policy in the Federal Government Colleges, we, especially those of us south of the Niger-Benue waterway, are quick to cry out against differentials in cut-off points. In a country such as Nigeria with our diverse peoples, differing historical experiences, differing levels of educational development, I have no doubt at all in my mind that we must devise ways and means of making all of our peoples feel that they belong. One way of doing this, is to work out some quota system. We need some quota system, given our situation. I submit, however, that the quota system we are operating in our educational system is unacceptable and unlikely to generate true patriotism among our young ones.

In my view, every system must encourage merit and hard work. Within the broad policy which lays it down that every Federal Government College must have children from all the states, we must recognise and promote merit. If 10% or whatever proportion of places must be filled on merit, let us proceed to fill that proportion on merit without reference to state of origin. Conversely, we can decide that x% of places should be filled on the basis of equal representation and go on to pick the best from each state to fill those places. It kills the spirit of a child who was born in Lagos and is schooling in Lagos to be told that because his or her father or sometimes her grandfather was born in Bendel State she must score higher marks than another child also born in Lagos and in her school for her to be admitted into a Federal Government College. Such contradictions are difficult to explain to children. And a child who feels cheated at that tender age cannot grow up into a patriot. Citizenship must cease to be determined by the birthplace of parents and grandparents.

The tragedy of Nigeria is that while we cry out against the kind of example I have just cited, we commit the same error in our little corners. I have spent all my working life at the University of Ibadan. All my children were born at U.C.H. All my tax has been paid here in Ibadan. But I am not an indigene. My children are said to be Bendelites. They can enjoy no scholarships from Oyo State. They are expected to get scholarships from Bendel State where I have never worked nor paid tax! What I suffer here in Oyo State, Yoruba and other non-"Bendelites" in my own state – Bendel – suffer. Is it any wonder that we have Nigeria without Nigerians?

I suggest that one reason why there is, as of now, no real meaning to Nigerian citizenship is that we have never really sat down to fashion out an Act of Union. The British brought us together as one colony. We attained independence as one nation. We fought a civil war to keep that nation together. But we have not deliberately forged an Act of Union. Wanted urgently is an Act of Union which will lay down the rights of all Nigerians who subscribe to that Act directly or through their chosen representatives. Such rights, duly enshrined in the Constitution, must be justiceable. Too often the rights of citizens are overthrown on the basis of *locus standi*. An Act of Union must confer the right to sue in defence of one's rights. The Constituent Assembly as well as the Armed Forces

Ruling Council will do well to pay attention to this matter.

Some in the audience may wonder what all of this is got to do with leadership. Let me remind such persons that my subject is "Leadership in the Nigerian Polity", and that what I have been doing is analysing the nature of that Nigerian Polity. Besides, the success or failure of leadership is inextricably bound up with the nature and behaviour patterns of the followership. Any "citizen" who feels cheated becomes alienated and therefore is unwilling to yield any instinctive loyalty to his nation. It is this that leads to a lack of patriotism. No leadership can succeed if the followership is unwilling to grant it instinctive loyalty. He who aspires to lead in the Third Republic must grapple effectively with the issue of the meaning of, and the rights which accrue to, Nigerian citizenship.

On Leadership

Whenever we talk about leadership, we immediately assume political leadership. We also almost invariably think of leadership at state and federal level. Although we may not always be aware of it, when we make the above assumption, it is because we are unwilling to turn the searchlight on ourselves. As we plan for the Third Republic, I would like us to remind ourselves that all tiers of leadership are important. Take, for example, Nigeria's university system. The problems we face today are partly created by the leadership of our universities. Inefficiency and, sometimes, criminal negligence, go unpunished even when detected because the leaders are either lily-livered or because there are sacred cows to protect. Some lecturers turn themselves into tin-gods and victimize their students, male and female. Faced with new challenges, our university system often lacks the imagination to seek effective answers because the leadership – from vice-chancellor to heads of departments – is content to follow routine. Too often the perquisites of office become far more important than the duties of office.

Or take the various parastatals – Airways, Railways, Ports Authority, NITEL, NEPA. A numbing apathy has destroyed efficiency and service. Is your telephone faulty? It is not enough to report it. You must hire a truck that will carry the ladder and the men needed to fix the fault. If you protest against such a system, your telephone may remain permanently dead! Complain to the Oga, he will sympathize with you and tell you they are ill-equipped, but may do nothing about it. As for NEPA, your bills may not reach you for months on end, though you may suffer disconnection for not paying bills that have not been served on you for payment. If you complain, you are advised to always pay something in advance of the bills coming in. One can multiply the examples. The consequences? A nation in which inefficiency and indolence are the norm. If the Third Republic is to be different from the past, whoever finds himself, herself in a leadership position at whatever level – in the schools and colleges, polytechnics and universities, churches, local governments, parastatals, etc. must realise that the same standards which he/she expects from the State Governor and Head of State are also expected from him or her.

What Prospects for the Third Republic?

To all the problems of the Nigerian polity to which attention has been drawn thus far, we must, as we look forward to the Third Republic, add that of religion. Whether we like it or not, religion has become a major factor in our national life. This is largely because a particular religion has been so favoured in terms of political and economic patronage since the last two decades in particular that a reaction against that patronage has set in. Given the factor of religion, I can foresee a situation in which persons on whom Islam and Christianity sit only very lightly, seek to ride to political office at different levels. Let us all pray that God will save us from such hypocrites, for their regimes could well be even more corrupt, more disastrous, than anything we have experienced thus far. Yet religion can be a major factor for good. Nigeria is crying out for men and women who will refuse to touch the unclean thing while in office. There are such men and women in our land. It is just that the system is so weighted against them that they may never surface, except by the grace of God. Only men and women with the fear of God in their hearts can genuinely lead by example. And I believe – firmly – that in His own time God will raise up such leaders for us. Whether this will be in the Third Republic I know not.

It is often said that a people get the kind of leaders they deserve. To say this is to emphasise the importance of the nature of the followership. Declamations against our leadership are negative so long as they are not backed by self-reformation. In our little corners we re-enact all the evils of the nation. We acclaim the merits and virtues of persons when we want them to labour for us. When there is an office to be filled, we say they come from the wrong ethnic group and cannot get the job for which they are eminently qualified. If this attitude persists in our Third

Republic, I can see no tangible change in the leadership pattern.

The present economic hardships have hardened the class line in our society. While some of the hideous crimes about which we read in the newspapers are the result of interpersonal strife leading on to the hiring of assassins, quite a number of these crimes smack of class war. He who would succeed as a leader in the Third Republic is he who is genuinely prepared to pay attention to the common man. For too long the common man has been exploited for the benefit of the political, bureaucratic, intellectual elite. A few nairas from various candidates at election time have produced monstrous leaders who not only milk the nation but, in that same process, force the common man to lead a beggarly life. The Third Republic would, I predict, be extremely short-lived if those who emerge as leaders fail to realise that the common man has become increasingly sensitive and has been so pushed around that he is virtually ready to bounce back from the wall to which he has been pushed. God help those on his path when the re-bound takes off!

Is there no silver lining in the cloud of the Third Republic? I confess that I see none. The underground politicking that is going on points to the fact that big money is at work once again. Big money breeds big thefts from the national treasury. As a people, we have installed money as our god. The gospel according to Saint Naira is abroad. I do not see enough renegades who would stand against that gospel. Our young men and women are money-crazy. They will do anything for money – that is the legacy we have bequeathed to them. This means that the next generation of politicians and businessmen are already frighteningly contaminated with the bug of corruption. Unless God raises for us men and women after His own heart, the Third Republic could well multiply our woes. So what? So let us wake up to the fact that each one of us is important in the scheme of things. If we, especially those of us with the benefit of education, refuse to be bought; if we refuse to worship at the altar of ethnic gods; if we insist on standing up for our rights; if we would speak out against evil and wrong-doing whenever we see same – we will be contributing to a new start that could, in time, produce a different Republic even if that Republic is not the Third.

I have no doubt, that many are by now heartily disappointed in me. What? No prescriptions to offer? I am afraid that I can offer no false hopes of radical changes, come 1992. Our socio-political system is the key to any change that can take place. My reading of that socio-political system does not fill me with any sanguine expectations. Thus far we have failed to learn from history. I have no reason to think we will learn so effectively in the next four years that the Third Republic will be radically different. There are only two possibilities. Either our peoples, hungry and frustrated, will break out in revolution and so forcefully change the social system, or God will raise a leader with a vision and a mission – a leader who will have the courage to do those things that must be done if we are to take any meaningful step forward. Such a leader, however, would have to be prepared to lead by example.

It would have become clear, I hope, that the main burden of my submission is that the nature of the polity and its leadership pattern are inextricably intertwined. If the Westminster Parliamentary system is seen as having failed in Nigeria, the explanation lies in our concept of politics, in that winner-take-all syndrome which makes our politics so vicious. An opposition which feels called upon to condemn every Government action, a Government which punishes areas regarded as strongholds of the opposition party/parties – these are some of the manifestations of that political immaturity which produces inept leadership.

Then we tried the presidential system. See what a mess we made of it. The party took over from the President as the Chief Executive. Appointments to office followed even more rigidly party lines than before. Merit and proven ability which abound in our land could not be tapped because the President had neither the strength of character nor the inclination to put the interests of the nation above the interests of his party. We failed to play politics of consensus. To get bills passed the Executive had to bribe the legislators! Legislators who had corrupted the electorates at election time corrupted themselves in office by receiving bribes from Mr. President. Provision made for maintaining offices and staff in the constituencies of our legislators was converted into private use, including maintenance of a long line of girl friends. When law makers become liars, having first been guilty of bribing the electorates, what moral leadership can they offer? Those whom they bribed, those from whom they received bribes, even the women of easy virtue and fearful vice on whom they lavished the nation's resources – all of these knew them for what they were, namely, glorified rogues. Who made these rogues? We did – you and I. We did by the way we reacted to our leaders, by our anxiety to be seen as part of the system, our refusal to question their sudden affluence.

What about military rulers? Four military regimes should, by now have convinced us that the corrective aspect of these regimes only lasts until the perquisites of office begin to corrupt the military rulers. As I have said again and again, a corrupt military regime is always a worse affliction than a corrupt civilian regime – for the military apply more force, more easily, than politicians. But here too we – the people – must share the blame, as we are ever so eager to share the loot of the soldier-ruler.

Yes, leadership and the nature of the polity are indeed inextricably intertwined. Yet, I have no doubt that the future of this land belongs to the people. Ultimately, it is the kind of people we are that will determine the kind of leadership we get. Let us therefore not concentrate on the issue of leadership to the neglect of the kind of people we are, for it is us who have thrown up the leadership that has landed us where we are. If, in terms of leadership, the future looks dismal, that is most certainly because we as a people have not yet learnt to demand high standards from our leaders. If anything, we encourage the irresponsible leadership that has been our lot by our enthusiasm to partake of its filthy lucre, our shameless hero-worship of corrupt, decadent leaders. If the leadership is to change, we too have to change.

9

HISTORY AND THE NATION: A MATTER OF NECESSITY OR ONE OF UTILITY?*

Introduction

I am delighted at the privilege afforded me to participate in the life and work of the Ogun State University by being invited to deliver this lecture. Because it is a faculty activity, it would have been ideal to pick a subject that spans the Humanities as a whole. However, I had the privilege only in March last year, to deliver the University of Benin Faculty of Arts Lecture. My subject was Quo Vadis Humanitas? That subject enabled me to take a hard look at our practice of the Humanities in Nigeria and the attitude of the nation to the Humanities and its practitioners. I cannot traverse the same ground here at Ago-Iwoye without a great deal of self-repetition. Having decided, in the circumstances, to talk about my own discipline within the Humanities, namely, History, I immediately ran into another difficulty. In the period 1984-88 when I was President of the Historical Society of Nigeria, I had cause to speak about history on a number of occasions. I had doubts in my mind whether it was wise for me to hold forth once again on the subject of History and the Nation.

*This was the Ogun State University Faculty of Arts Open Lecture delivered at Ago-Iwoye, Nigeria, on Wednesday, 12 April, 1989.

Then something happened that made up my mind for me. I had to chair the team that moderates the History questions for the Joint Admissions Matriculation Examination (JAMB). In the process, I discovered that in 1987 only just over 8,000 candidates offered History at the JAMB examination throughout the country. History was the second lowest chosen by candidates, the lowest being Geography which had less than 5,000 entrees nation-wide. It struck me forcefully, that given present trends, in another decade or so no Nigerian child may be offering history at senior secondary school. When that happens, our departments of history in the universities will have to fold up, since there will be no students to teach. And as I warned in an address in 1986, Nigeria would then have set a world record. We would have become the only nation in the world which does not teach its own history to its citizens – thanks to our penchant for always relegating national interests to the background; our failure, nay refusal, to see that there are certain subjects which must be taught to our people because without such subjects we can have no true identity.

Today history is not taught as a subject at primary school; it is not taught as a subject in junior secondary school. But it is listed as one of the optional subjects at senior secondary school. How children who have never been taught History are expected to wake up to it in Senior Secondary School only the experts who formulated our educational policy know. As a nation we have, as a matter of policy, deliberately marginalised history. As a nation, we are telling our young people that their antecedents are irrelevant to their understanding of their present realities. We are saying, as a nation, that we can press forward meaningfully without a thorough appreciation of those forces, the product of history, which consciously or unconsciously influence the thinking and actions of our various peoples; those factors which determine their perception of their group interests. Needless to say, I have nothing but condemnation for the nation's official policy towards the teaching of History in our schools. I take my position not out of self-interest, for I can retire today and feel that I have done my bit for history and for my nation. Rather, I take my position out of genuine concern for my nation, a nation that seems not to be aware of what history is. Here I am forced to quote a passage from Robert V. Daniels which I have quoted endless times without its losing its freshness and impact:

> History is the memory of human group experience. Without history we have no knowledge of who we are or how we came to be, like victims of collective amnesia groping in the dark for their identity. It is the events recorded in history that have generated all the emotions, all the values, the ideals, that make life meaningful, that have given men something to live for, struggle over, die for. Historical events have created all the basic human groupings – countries, religions, classes – and all the loyalties that attach to these.

It is against the background sketched above that I have decided to speak on the subject, "History and the Nation: A Matter of Necessity or One of Utility? "

The Past in the Present

History is the memory of human group experience. In that sense, it is concerned with the study of the past. The passage just quoted, however, reinforces J. H. Plumb's dictum that the past which the historian studies is not a dead past. It is past that is constantly impinging on the present. Says P. J. Lee in *Learning History*, "There is no escape from the past. It is built into the concepts we employ to cope with the everyday physical and social world." P. J. Rogers, in the same work, extends Lee's argument. "Like the poor," says Rogers, "the past is always with us, not because we choose to tolerate it (as we do poverty) but because we cannot escape it. *Experientia docet* [experience teaches, i.e, we learn from experience] because, as beings endowed with memory, we cannot have a perception of the present that is not strongly influenced by the version of the past- some sort of version – which we have internalised in the course of growing up, and articulated in our adult lives." Simply put, our present is, in varying degrees, a function of our understanding of the past. Let me illustrate what I mean by a simple example. Let us take four Yoruba public figures: Awolowo, Akintola, Ajasin, Omoboriowo.* We can meaningfully speak of these persons today only in terms of our understanding and assessment of the roles we know - or think we know – them to have played in the past.[1]

*The full names are Obafemi Awolowo, S. L. Akintola, M. A. Ajasin and Akin Omoboriowo – all active politicians in Yorubaland in the First and/or Second Republic.

Without such understanding and knowledge, however biased, we simply cannot speak of these persons. What is true for individuals is true for ethnic groups; for nations; concepts of government like democracy, communism, socialism, dictatorship, etc; for race and everything else. There simply is no present without the past. History is supremely concerned with the study of that past that is inexorably linked with the present. History therefore holds the key to our understanding of the present. If only for that reason, we cannot but teach history to our peoples. History may not prepare the individual for a specific profession. It is, nevertheless, a human necessity.

Let us now proceed to apply the concept of the past in the present to a few aspects of Nigerian History, beginning with Yorubaland where this lecture is being delivered. In the 19th century, as is well known, Yorubaland witnessed a series of wars resulting from the collapse and disintegration of the Old Oyo Empire. The disintegration of the Oyo empire led to a migration of Oyo elements southwards. One of the places that received Oyo migrants was Ile-Ife. One of the earliest of the series of wars that ravaged Yorubaland in the 19th century is that referred to as the Owu War. In its final stages the Owu found themselves fighting against a combination of Ife, Ijebu and Oyo elements already displaced from their homes. These allies, having levelled Owu, turned their aggression on the Egba, many of whom they expelled from their settlements. In the process, the allies set up war camps in a number of Egba villages. Ibadan, because of its defensible position, became the best known of these war camps. Such was the origin of what we might describe as the new Ibadan.

The new Ibadan was, in the circumstances, cosmopolitan, though leadership was, to begin with, in the hands of the Ife group, since it was Ife that originally put the alliance together. After a while, quarrels developed. Okunade, the Ife chieftain who was the leader of the new Ibadan, was expelled from Ibadan and the Oyo elements took over control of Ibadan.

Meanwhile, many other Oyo refugees had settled at Ile-Ife. These refugees were welcomed by Ife as a source of cheap labour and also as valuable tenants. Indeed there are authorities who argue that Ile-Ife began to adopt a martial attitude towards its neighbours, including the Ijesa, because she suddenly acquired a much larger population, the consequences of the influx of Oyo refugees. As the number of Oyo refugees grew, and following the developments in Ibadan which resulted in the expulsion of Okunade, tensions developed between the Ife hosts and the Oyo refugees. Additionally, Ife began to fear that the refugees might, thanks to sheer numbers, swamp them. This was why the Oyo refugees had to move out of Ile-Ife proper, and founded a new town, Modakeke, outside the Ife town walls. The founding of Modakeke did not, however, eliminate tensions between Ife and Modakeke. We will not go into all the details here. Tensions developed into acute hostility which eventually blossomed into war. Twice in the century – 1850 and 1881 – Modakeke sacked Ile-Ife and drove the Ooni and his people into exile. In the 1850 episode the Ooni only regained his throne as a consequence of the intervention of Ibadan, already a leading military power and still led by Oyo elements. But the Ooni and Ife paid a price for Ibadan intervention: they became vassals of Ibadan!

I have just given you a slice of 19th century Yoruba history. In recent years, Ife-Modakeke conflicts and hostility have been a disturbing feature of the politics of Oyo state. At least twice, open hostilities have flared up, and lives have been lost. It is impossible to understand the Ife-Modakeke debacle outside the context of 19th century Yoruba history. Ife can claim that the Modakeke are "tenants" on their land; strangers. That this being so, Modakeke must be subject to her. Modakeke can reply that after over one century, the "tenants" have become owners and cannot be dispossessed. Moreover, there is the memory of victory in war – two victories in war- against those who claim to be their overlords! The extreme elements in Modakeke can, in fact, argue that they are entitled to whatever land they have by right of conquest – conquest of Ife! This is the explanation of the strong antipathy between Ife and Modakeke. This explains why at the 1983 elections, Ife was solidly U. P. N. while Modakeke was N. P. N. to the core. I served on the Judicial Commission of Inquiry into the 1983 elections and had the opportunity of listening to persons from Ife and Modakeke testify. There was no mistaking the mutual hostility and derision. Come another election, and Ife and Modakeke are most likely to be in opposing camps. Successive governments of Oyo State have sought to find a permanent solution to the Ife-Modakeke conflict, with only limited and transient success thus far.

What I have just narrated is part of Nigerian history. Of what value is it to you? What does knowing what you have just learnt do to and for you? Admittedly, it does not provide an avenue for you to acquire naira and kobo like knowledge of Medicine, Law, Accounts, Architecture and other professions may do. But, without any doubt, the knowledge you have just acquired gives you a better understanding of the Ife-Modakeke affair. All who have a role to play in seeking a solution to that affair need to have that understanding. The Ife and the Modakeke need to have that understanding. Without understanding no really permanent solution can be proferred. History, above all else, seeks to deepen understanding. Because understanding the problem is the first step towards seeking a solution. I submit that for any nation, and much more so a developing nation, teaching and learning history, especially national history, becomes a national **desideratum**. It is a necessity imposed on us by our human condition.

In the 19th century, there occurred a movement known as the Sokoto Jihad. It was a movement which sought to make Islam the basis of government in the Hausa states. Islam had been introduced into Borno in the 10th century or thereabouts and into Hausaland, some would say, in the 11th century. After some seven centuries of existence in the Hausa states, Islam was still no more than the religion of part of the population, not of all of the population. Indeed, as the experts tell us, on the eve of the Jihad, i.e. in the dying years of the 18th century, what we had were scattered jama'a in the various Hausa states – pockets of Muslims under various learned and not-so-learned mallams. Because, wherever they existed, these Muslims were not governed by the Muslim law; because the Fulani who led the various jama'sa were, as migrants who came into Hausaland long after the Hausa states had crystallised their political systems, excluded from government, they (the Fulani) began to agitate for the islamisation of the Hausa states. In Uthman dan Fodio they found a leader with the right combination of piety, learning and charisma to head what turned out to be a major revolution. At the end of the movement, virtually all the Sarakuna (rulers) of the Hausa states had been dispossessed of their thrones and replaced by Fulani emirs. The various Hausa states that had enjoyed a fully independent status now found themselves as emirates within the Sokoto Caliphate, the largest geo-religio-political edifice ever to arise in the Nigerian geographical area before the coming of British colonial rule.

The Sokoto caliphate was a theocracy: Muslim law, the sharia, governed the lives of the believers. There was no distinction between religion and government; between mosque and state, for it was the caliph's religious standing that made him also head of the caliphate. This was the state of affairs for all of the 19th century. Between 1900 and 1903, the British invaders conquered and dismantled the Sokoto Caliphate and imposed their rule. With the British as imperial rulers, there was no question of sharia being the law that governed the British protectorate of Northern Nigeria. Sharia was down-graded to the level of "native Law," law which operated only at local government level. British-made law governed trade, administration, inter-personal and inter-group relations where these were at higher than local government level. The Muslims of Northern Nigeria thus found themselves living certain aspects of their lives under non-Muslim law, the very condition which, among others, had produced the jihad in the first instance! Since, after the jihad, the British imperial authorities had a monopoly of the means of coercion, the Muslims of northern Nigeria had no option but to live under non-Muslim law, contrary to the declared dictates of their religion.

In 1914 Northern and Southern Nigeria were amalgamated, and a new country – Nigeria – was born. The new country was a colony of Britain, and remained so till 1960. At independence, Nigeria inherited the British system of government and of law. The independent nation of Nigeria was not a theocracy. While in Northern Nigeria Muslim law governed certain aspects of the peoples' lives, the supreme law of the land was what is described as received law and the product of Nigerian legislation. Differently put, as a consequence of our colonial experience, what we may describe as Nigerian law (albeit heavily laced with a great deal of the British species) emerged. In 1979, Nigeria adopted a constitution which proclaimed the state to be a secular state, thereby ruling out the concept of the theocracy of the type that was the Sokoto Caliphate; thereby also confirming the practice whereby sharia law was limited in its application.

One of the greatest threats to unity and peace in Nigeria today is religious tension as between Christians and Muslims. The clear majority of persons in the former Southern Nigeria are Christians. They are Christians as a consequence of a historical accident, namely, that while dan Fodio was busy waging his jihad up in the northern parts, Christian missions from Europe who came by sea were busy spreading their faith in the coastal areas, from where the new faith moved into the hinterland. By contrast, it used to be the case that the majority of persons in the former Northern Nigeria were Muslims, the consequence of the jihad. A religious dichotomy as between North and South was thus introduced into our country as a product of our history. It now appears that the neatness of this dichotomy has been challenged. While in the former South, the Christians are still in a definite majority, it is not now so certain that in the former North there is still a clear Muslim majority, for Christianity has spread far more into certain parts of that former North than Islam has spread into the former South taken as a whole. The Muslims thus consider themselves threatened and insecure. That insecurity is the explanation for the attack on churches in certain states of the country during 1986. That same insecurity explains the OIC time bomb. Recently, Muslims in Gongola State protested over the N. T. A. in that State screening the popular soap opera, "Another Life". At the University of Ibadan in 1987, Muslims demanded that the Cross on what is usually referred to at the University as "holy ground," a cross which had been there for thirty years, be pulled down because it offended against their religion. Physical combat between Muslims and Christians was averted only thanks to good sense on both sides. Now, however, the Muslims have also put up a star and crescent, the symbol of their faith, and have ensured that the inscription against the white background of the symbol is in green to give the emblem a national significance, the national colours being green, white, green!

As Nigeria seeks to put in place a new (or at least revised) constitution for 1990, the Muslims would rather that the provision of the 1979 constitution which provides that Nigeria shall be a secular state be expunged. They would be happier if Nigeria were to become a theocracy in which the sharia would be the official law – if not absolutely, then at least as a parallel set of laws alongside Nigerian law. The Christians for their part are dead set on retaining the concept of Nigeria as a secular state, for their faith draws a definite line between church and state, the product of the experience of that faith in the history of Western Europe. Nigeria thus sits on a time bomb as Christians and Muslims are increasingly sensitive to the demands of their respective faiths.

With regard to the sharia issue, let me make a point which may not have occurred to most people who have commented on it, especially the Christians. The British imposed on the Muslims of the old North a foreign set of laws, just as Islam had done on the Hausa states in the

19th century. At independence, it was natural for the Muslim population to expect to get rid of this imposition. But this proved impossible because Nigeria inherited the British legal system. The jihad had been fought to enshrine the sharia. British colonial rule partially dismantled the sharia, The Muslims are now waging a jihad of a different type to reinstate the sharia under which, Muslims claim, every Muslim must live. From the standpoint of Muslims, there is logic in this position. There is, however, a rub. Nigeria is not the Sokoto Caliphate. Part of the price of being Nigerian – and the Muslims must agree that both economically and politically they have done very well for themselves by being part of Nigeria – is to reconcile themselves to the fact that the sharia can only be local law, not national law. The top echelons of the Muslims are not prepared to pay this price any more. They want Nigeria to become a Muslim country. To achieve this end, they seek to exploit that control of the political system of the nation which the British assured the former North when they handed over power in 1960. Hence the OIC; hence Muslim banks *et al.* The Muslims are seeking to make their independence meaningful by reinstating one of the major pillars of their faith pulled down by the same British who ensured that these Muslims were politically favoured at independence. In this desire, which is understandable from the Muslim standpoint, they (the Muslims) have to contend with the feelings and sensitivities of the Christian population of Nigeria, itself a product of our history. Nigeria thus faces something of a major dilemma.

What is the point of all this narrative and comment? The future of Nigeria is threatened by a religious dichotomy that is a product of history. How many Nigerians – what percentage of the population – thoroughly understand the forces that are at work? How can we stem the tide of religious intolerance without understanding the whys and hows of our present state? A thorough grounding in the history of these two religions, and how they have fared in the country since independence, is crucial for both policy makers and the generality of the citizenry. That grounding cannot be acquired except within the nation's school system. Our nation must thus be persuaded that all its citizens be taught its history, as a matter of necessity at school, irrespective of whether history as a subject assures them of a job or a profession. Learning history – national history at least - at school must not be predicated on job opportunities. It is a training for living. In terms of the capacity of our nation's citizenry to truly understand the problems – political problems among others - which confront them, learning the history that has produced these problems is a national necessity.

As of today's date (April 1989), political activities in the country remain banned. But there have been political or pseudo-political statements, and there are subterranean political movements. An interesting aspect of the emerging scenario is the attitude of that part of the country that we usually refer to as the Middle Belt. This was part of the old Northern Nigeria. In the context of the Sokoto jihad about which I have been speaking, this was one area in which the hilly nature of the terrain successfully frustrated the conquering thrusts of the jihad. Yet this area suffered doubly from the success of the jihad. Once set up, the Sokoto Caliphate demanded and received annual tributes from the emirates. Slaves were part of the annual tribute. Since Muslims were forbidden to enslave fellow Muslims, it was the non-Muslim parts that became the raiding ground of the emirates, leaving behind a legacy of hatred. When the British overthrew the Caliphate and imposed their rule, they not only adopted the existing emirate system for local government, they sought to extend this system to the non-emirate areas, notably the Middle Belt. In the process, Hausa-Fulani hegemony was imposed on the people of this region. This is why Professor Eme Awa argues that "in the Middle Belt areas of the country indirect rule meant a doubly alien rule.... This double alienation generated considerable resentment from the people of these areas, culminating in the Tiv Riots of 1964 and [the] brutalising [of the Tiv] by the Nigerian army at the request of the politicians". The jihad thus left behind a double legacy of hatred and resentment. When we add to that the fact that in this same area there are a large number of Christians, it becomes clear that there can be no understanding the politics of this region of Nigeria outside the context of its history. Knowledge of that history becomes for the Nigerian a matter of necessity.

I have chosen only three examples on how the past continues to impinge on the present. There are other examples. Take, for instance, Itsekiri-Urhobo relations, the subject of my Ph.D. thesis. There we have a fine example of historical accidents leading to what is fast becoming permanent tension between two peoples who are socially so mixed that one would expect cordiality to reign supreme among them. Those relations cannot be permanently assuaged until the leaders and people are taught to understand that the issue is not one of saints versus sinners. Rather such tensions that arise are explicable in terms of both groups seeking to react and adjust as profitably as they can to changing historical circumstances in a young nation that is subject to many and sometimes unduly frequent changes.

Or take the issue of the chairmanship of the Oyo State Council of Obas. Without doubt, the Ooni must feel that as the most revered Oba in Yorubaland in yesteryears, he has a right to the chairmanship. On the other hand, the Alaafin must be proud of the fact that the Old Oyo empire was the largest political edifice in Yorubaland for upwards of one and a half centuries. Both of these rulers are thus, whether they say so or not, falling back on previous history to bolster their claim to leadership. But then past history is often so different from present realities. In the days of yore, it was seldom the case that all the crowned heads in the area now called Oyo State met in a conclave requiring a chairman! Nor did the Oyo Empire ever include all of what is now Oyo State. Past history does not have a satisfactory answer to the tussle; and this for the very good reason that the political arrangements of today are vastly different from those of yesteryears. But history does teach a very humbling lesson: no condition is permanent! The Oyo Empire did collapse. Modakeke did defeat the Ooni in war and force him into exile. Ibadan did make both Ile-Ife and Modakeke vassal states. History is thus replete with claims and counter-claims which can be used to create situations of tension and unrest. However, that truth, properly identified and harnessed, can be used as the basis for a policy of live and let live, a policy which at the same time seeks to pursue fairness, justice and equitable distribution of available resources. The past thus continues to impinge on the present. Successful governance must thus necessarily take full cognisance of this reality, and seek, through knowledge of the past, to manage the present satisfactorily. History holds the key to that knowledge of the past. History thus becomes a national necessity.

Who Are The Nigerians?

I wonder what answer I would elicit from my audience were I to ask 'who are the Nigerians?'! Those who inhabit Nigeria? Who are these, pray? The Yoruba, the Igbo, the Efik, the Bini, the Hausa, the Tivi? Have you ever stopped to ponder over the fact that until this century these names had no political meaning? Has it struck you that it made no sense to speak of the Yoruba in the 19th century, as a socio-political group? Even when you go down to the level of the clan or the nascent kingdom – have you given serious thought to how these groups came to be? Since I am in today's Yorubaland, let us take those we now call the Yoruba. The Oduduwa legend; Akinjogbin's ebi theory, what does it amount to? Are they not the historians' attempt at presenting as neatly as he can an extremely complicated development which took time to unfold? All the Yoruba groups that now say they were founded by sons of Oduduwa, were they really so founded? I suspect not, though I am the first to admit that we will never know for sure. Even the Yoruba sub-groupings – the Ife, Ijesa, Ijebu, Oyo, Egba and so on – they could not have begun as such. Today's legends of origin may seek to rationalise the rise of these groups. It is nearer the truth to state that these legends have been developed as groups that found themselves close linguistically, culturally or even geographically decided to deliberately create a relationship designed to ensure harmonious living, a relationship often expressed in blood ties. It was such deliberate contriving of relationships that first produced the clan, the nascent kingdom and today's ethnic groups, the perceived interest of which groups so often vitiate our efforts at nation-building.

The point being made is that even at the lower levels, the sub-ethnic groups, the clans were not created as sub-ethnic groups and clans by God. They were all "the product of deliberate acts of statesmanship; the results of negotiated unions and amalgamations now clothed in legends of common origins." Those of us who teach Nigerian history must teach it with a full and constant awareness of what that history has to teach our peoples. We must teach our history not as some purely theoretical, classroom-based discipline that has little or no relevance for today's realities, but teach it in a manner which enables our students and our peoples to see that history, especially our national history, has practical lessons to teach. In my inaugural lecture as president of the Historical Society of Nigeria nearly six years ago, in May 1985 I sought to draw out what lessons there are in this matter of origins. I said "Our ancestors, when they found themselves thrown together by historical circumstances, found a way out of their differences by deliberately forging new alliances and amalgamations. The process was not always necessarily peaceful. The undeniable fact is that ultimately statesmanship triumphed and a meaningful and acceptable relationship was established. Those who parade themselves as leaders of Nigeria's multifarious peoples today need to go to the ancestors, learn their ways and be wise: to call into play such statesmanship as can help forge a truly united Nigeria, in spite of the differences that will always exist between Nigeria's component parts." History, seen from this kind of perspective, ceases to be just another subject in the school curriculum, taught for the purpose of passing examinations. It becomes practical, a national necessity as vital as science and technology for, as I have always argued, science and technology do not, cannot, **create** a nation; they can only **serve** a nation already in existence. In the process of creating a nation – forging a meaningful whole out of our diverse peoples – history, properly conceptualised and taught, can play a much more significant role than many another subject. However, this is not common knowledge. It is not common knowledge because we, who profess history, have not always been sufficiently sensitized as to the nature and the role History can play in the context of the problems with which our nation has to contend. The historians of Nigeria must rise as one man to a full and proper awareness of the value and place of history in the nation. Until we do so, we will never be able to establish the truth that history is a national necessity.

In the same lecture from which I have just quoted, I also made the point that for an Ijebu man to say he is Yoruba necessarily involves giving up some of his Ijebu-ness. He does that because he perceives a self-interest which, in the context of national politics, can be better served by his being Yoruba. I went on, "This instinctive giving up a small identity in order to take advantage of a larger identity is what we need to promote if we are ever to produce true Nigerians. Just as the Kanawa is prepared to give up some of his Kanawa-ness in order to be Hausa, so must the Hausa be prepared to give up some of his Hausa-ness in order to be a true Nigerian. However, it must be self-evident that there is a major pre-condition for this partial self-denial." Whoever "subdues part of his smaller identity in favour of the larger," does so "because he believes that his interests in all their ramifications can truly be served by the larger group. The search for Nigerians would continue to be unproductive so long as Nigeria fails to guarantee the genuine protection of the interests of **all** of its components peoples." That is the lesson of history waiting to be learnt and put into practice by the leaders of our nation, be they military or civilian. That is the lesson of history that teachers of history must pointedly draw out if history is to be seen for what it must be – a national necessity.

History and the Search for Nigeria

My 1985 lecture from which I have just quoted was entitled *In Search of Nigerians*. In it I was concerned about those aspects of our history which explain why we have not yet been able to produce truly Nigerian citizens. There is, however, a related search, namely, the search for Nigeria. Such truly Nigerian citizens as there may be – and we must admit there is a small proportion of our peoples committed to Nigeria - must feel frustrated that there is no Nigeria in which they can act out their commitment and faith. Why is there no Nigeria? History holds the key to that poser. Nigeria as a single political entity is only seventy five years old. Until the British arrived on the scene as from the late 19th century, our multifarious peoples were, for the most part, each politically independent of the other. Even when empires arose, as in Benin, Old Oyo or Sokoto (i.e. the caliphate) – there was never as close political control as there was when Britain ruled us as a colony. It is true that even in pre-British days, there was much greater contact between our various peoples than is often imagined, as many a Nigerian historian has pointed out. A crucially important aspect of such relations, however, was the fact that, for the most part, the groups concerned decided in what aspects and for what purposes they interacted – the autonomy of the relating groups was intact most of the time. Colonial rule changed all that and imposed a supra-ethnic superstructure called Nigeria, introducing what Peter Ekeh has christened the concept of "two publics". The first of these publics may be said to consist of that society that is still largely based on the primordial groups, albeit modified by the colonial experience itself – Ekeh's "transformed indigenous structures." The second public is society as it operates at the level of the supra-ethnic entity called Nigeria, typified by Eke's "migrated social structures."

The significance of our having two publics is that different moral values operate in these publics. Thus while the Treasurer of the Ago-Iwoye Improvement Union may never dream of embezzling his union's funds for fear of the repercussions, the same person, as Federal Minister of Finance, will have no qualms in rifling the nation's treasury and even using part of the filthy lucre as huge donations to the Ago-Iwoye Improvement Union. Not only will his people not condemn him for stealing his nation's money, they will in fact cheer him along and heap on him endless chieftaincy titles! How do we explain this seeming contradiction? The answer lies in the fact that the second public does not yet have the meaning and the hold it should have on the first public. And that it does not yet have that meaning and that hold is a function of our history: our peoples do not yet identify with Nigeria, the same way they identify with their sub-ethnic and ethnic groups in that order. Despite colonial rule and despite twenty-eight years of independence, the two publics have not merged. What is more, the distinction in moral attitude as between the two publics stands in danger of being eliminated, as the amoral values and attitudes of the second public are now gradually but surely being transferred to the first public, especially in the face of current economic hardships.

A proper awareness and understanding of the situation here described ought to call forth deliberate policies to counter the dichotomy highlighted and arrest the enshrining of amoral attitudes and values in our two publics. This is a challenge to which the leadership of the two publics must face up. They can hardly face up to that challenge if they are insensitive to the historical backdrop against which our peoples relate to the second public. Our leaders need to be schooled in our history, so that they may know how things have come to be and begin to seek long term solutions to the problems of the nation, including that of national integration. History holds the key to the understanding of this as of many other problems of our nation. Understanding is a necessary first step in the search for meaningful solutions. In our setting, and given the problems with which we have to contend, history is a national necessity. Part of the tragedy of Nigeria is that as a nation we have little or no sense of history, even though at local level our peoples are ever so conscious of their group history all the way down to the family level. Yet national education planners have virtually succeeded in eliminating history from the school curriculum. I dare to suggest that the huge sums being expended on Mass Mobilisation for Social Justice, Self Reliance and Economic Recovery – MAMSER – will and can avail nothing when those being allegedly mobilised are ignorant of their fellow Nigerians. History, properly taught and invested with the mission of promoting greater understanding of our multifarious peoples, can achieve more than the white elephant that is MAMSER. History is a national necessity and the sooner our educational planners realise this, the better for the nation.

Another consequence of our colonial experience is the absence of a national political culture. As I have argued elsewhere, basic to the abuse of the political system that has characterised our history since independence is the absence of a national political culture which lays down the rules of the political game and compels the dramatis personae in the political arena to operate in accordance with these rules. The working of a Westminster system of government or of an American-type presidential system is not the function of the institutions of government alone. It is even more a function of accepted norms and standards of behaviour in public life – norms of a political culture evolved over time.

In Nigeria we have taken on political systems divested of the political culture which informed the working of such systems. Thus far we have failed to anchor our borrowed political systems in any indigenous political culture. This is the way Peter Ekeh has put it "...the European organisational pieces that came to us were virtually disembodied of their moral contents, of their sub-stratum of implicating ethics. And yet the imported models were never grafted into any existing indigenous morality." It is important, in this regard, to draw attention to the fact that colonial rule did not, could not, impose any meaningful colonial culture on Nigeria. Colonialism was in itself a negation of the rule of law, a denial of the right to self-determination, a mentally brutalising experience and an economically crippling system. In the Nigerian setting, colonial rule was quickly followed by long terms of military rule, which rule has necessarily denied the rule of law and prevented the evolution of a national political culture. Our history over the last one century, then, has been one in which those values which ordered the working of our respective societies have been constantly eroded without being replaced by new values other than those of force and reckless exploitation and vandalization of the nation's resources. Once again, we are planning for a return to a hopefully "new" political order. I fear, however, that there will be nothing new, come 1990 or 1992. If Nigeria is to evolve a political culture that would begin to impose rules of the political game on our politicians and rulers, we must be fully aware of the factors in our history that have affected our development thus far. If our political culture is to be rooted in the varying political cultures of our many peoples, we must become more familiar with the essentials of these political cultures and distil from them those wholesome elements that we can meaningfully inject into the new nation, the second public that is Nigeria.

We are, in this country, in a situation in which the search is still very much on both for Nigerians and for a Nigeria in which the Nigerians can operate as citizens of one country. In the search both for Nigerians and

Nigeria, it is posited here that our history is a factor of major and crucial importance. This being so, the marginalisation of history that is now a feature of our national life must be arrested, for without a grounding in our history, that understanding which should inform the formulation of integrative national policies as well as many other policy options, will be absent. Hence I take the position that history is, in fact, a national necessity.

Explaining the Fate of History in Today's Nigeria

It is, I believe, fairly easy to explain the marginalisation of history in our educational system. History does not, like Law, Medicine, Engineering, Architecture, Pharmacy, Agriculture, Accountancy, etc, teach a profession. It is even assumed that history has no skills to impart to those who learn it. Given this assumption and given the fact of today's economic realities which, in turn, dictate the state of the Nigerian labour market, it is not surprising that Government, parents, the could-be student and, so, the vast majority of Nigeria's public take the position that history is a useless discipline. In a University of Ibadan Alumni Lecture delivered on June 24, 1988, Dr. Amadu Ali spoke, among other things, on the mission of the universities in Nigeria. Not unexpectedly, he asserted: "There is a need to restructure the curriculum in our universities, so that the products can tackle society's problems." He went on: "There is for example, a great need to produce psychologists who are [versed] in the mechanics and effects of poverty and hunger, sociologists who could tackle problems of religious extremism and thereby advice government on the perennial problems created by religious rioters." Admittedly, Amadu Ali merely chose two examples. That, clearly, is not to say that other disciplines not mentioned are useless. Observe, however, that he sees the sociologists as those who can provide Government with advice on religious extremism. I submit that those sociologists cannot even begin work without knowledge of the history of religious developments in Nigeria. History is necessary for the sociologist as for the political scientist. Without history, these other disciplines cannot, repeat cannot, engage in any meaningful analysis. As Daniels puts it, "History must be drawn upon by all fields. It offers the raw record of what has happened, and it sets the context of unique situations in the stream of time within which the other forms of specialised inquiry must operate." I am sure that the sociologist and the political scientist will be the first to admit the truth of this assertion made, not to glorify history, but to state an essential truth. Yet sociology and political science are regarded as relevant and necessary in the scheme of things in Nigeria but not history. The tragedy of history is that its value, its need, its undeniable contribution to the establishment of an identity for any nation are not always obvious and certainly not usually dramatic. This fact cannot, however, rob History of its intrinsic value.

Paul Gagnon, in a recent article on a related subject, says that when students ask the question "why history?", "the best answer is that one word: judgement." He goes on to argue that we demand judgement of all professions. He then makes what I regard as a very significant statement. "We need [judgement] most in the profession of citizen, which, like it or not, exercise it or not, we all are born into." What Gagnon is saying is, simply, that History provides a training for living.

Only last year (1988) a Committee on History in Schools was set up in the United States of America. In defending the need for the study of History, the committee argued that by its nature and its demands on the student, History helps to develop the mind and trains the student in how to make proper judgements. It is instructive to list, for the attention of the non-historian, the claims made for the subject by that committee:

1. History helps the students develop a sense of shared humanity;
2. History helps the students to understand themselves and others, by learning how they resemble and how they differ from other people over time and space;
3. History compels the students to question stereotypes. (And as we know in Nigeria, stereotypes can be extremely vexatious and constitute a real stumbling block to a proper appreciation of the values and cultures of other people.)
4. History enables the students to grasp the complexity of causation in human affairs, and to distrust the simple, mono-causal explanation;
5. History teaches the student to recognise particularity and avoid false analogy even while recognising general principles;
6. History enables the student to realise that not all problems have solutions;
7. History prepares the student to appreciate that in human affairs there is room for the irrational, the accidental;

8. History is full of situations which are influenced by ideas as well as by character or leadership. The student who properly grasps the role of ideas and forces as well as character and leadership should be able to better appreciate the problems of his nation and better play his role within that nation.

Admittedly, all of these claims are in the realm of ideas, which is probably why most people have difficulty in grasping their value. That value, nevertheless, remains unquestionable; these ideas remain crucial for every human society. Marc Bloch, in his *The Historian's Craft* says, "When all is said and done, a single word, "understanding" is the beacon light of our studies [i.e. historical studies].... It is so easy to denounce. We are never sufficiently understanding. Whoever differs from us – a foreigner or political adversary – is almost inevitably considered evil. A little more understanding of people would be necessary... in the conflicts which are unavoidable." It is as if Marc Bloch was writing with specific reference to Nigeria!

Let me move on to another explanation for the state in which History finds itself in our country today. There is a sense in which the fault is not in the Nigerian society or in the discipline of history *per se* as in us, the practitioners of history, that history has been marginalised in our country. For one thing, the historian does not get as involved in the issues of practical politics and government as he is intellectually equipped to do. By our criminal silence on burning national issues, we help to create the impression that the historian merely studies the past for its own sake. Yet, as has already been argued, the past which the historian studies is not a dead past, but one which is constantly impinging on the present. We, the historians of Nigeria, must see it as it is: a pressing and urgent task to make this feature of our discipline palpably clear to the Nigerian public and to makers of national policy at all levels. One way, perhaps the most effective way, of making the point is to bring to bear on contemporary Nigerian problems the insights which history provides. On a visit to Kano in April last year, I met a gentleman who said to me that until he read my paper, ***Towards Understanding the National Question***, delivered at the Abuja Seminar on the National Question in August 1986, he did not see any value in history. It was when past history was brought to bear on present realities, that history came alive for this gentleman. We, especially those of us who may be said to be leading the discipline at this time, need to remind ourselves of the essential logic of this gentleman's position. We must make the past live in the present.

Thirdly, there is the issue of what Professor A. E. Afigbo has described as the conceptualisation of history by our historians, which conceptualisation ought to influence the way we structure and teach history both at university and the lower levels of our education system. We must conceive of history as a discipline with practical lessons to teach man. We must teach it as such. Thus the Sokoto jihad, about which I spoke earlier, is a fine example of how a leader with a vision of how society should be ordered harnessed the ideology of Islam to carry through a revolution, thereby creating the superstructure that was the Sokoto Caliphate. One consequence of that was a super reduction of the inter-state wars that had punctuated the history of the Hausa states for centuries. Another was the promotion of a common allegiance. In a similar way a leader, with a vision in our national setting, can evolve an ideology or formulate some national integrative policy that can reduce inter-group, inter-ethnic suspicions and hostility and gradually get Nigerians to develop that proper allegiance to Nigeria that is the hallmark of patriotism.

The history of Yorubaland in the 19th century, to which reference has also been made in this lecture, is an excellent example of how a people adjusted to sudden and far reaching dislocations of their socio-political arrangements and institutions. The issue of host-refugee relations, the experimentation with republicanism and confederalism are testimonies to the adaptive genius of the Yoruba groups of the 19th century. Properly handled, the Yoruba wars of the 19th century hold out many a lesson which can turn studying them into instructive lessons in realpolitik. A similar case can be made for the politico-economic adjustments which the Niger Delta states had to make in the wake of the suppression of the overseas trade. Nigerian history can and should be conceptualised and taught in a manner which makes our past relevant to the national issues of today. We have not done enough of that thus far and have, to that extent, contributed to the marginalisation of history. Let me state, additionally, that it would be useless teaching Nigerian history the way here suggested if our examination questions are not set along the same pattern. And this raises yet another issue. Most of the existing books on Nigerian history have not been written from the kind of perspective here advocated. There is thus an urgent need for the revision of many of our books such that our concluding chapters, if not the entire body of the books, can draw out in clear terms the relevance of the past we study to today's problems. Finally, on this head, practising historians need to bear in mind the point being advocated here in their researches and writing – be these journal articles or books. History for history sake has its place just as there are scientists who are concerned with pure science. But, as we all know, it is when science is applied to tackling problems with which mankind has to contend that it becomes tangibly beneficial to man. Just as it is technology or applied science which gives science its most commonly acknowledged value, so it is with history. It is when we present history in a manner which makes its value apparent in nation-building, policy formulation, nature of government and politics, etc., that our peoples will recognise that history is not the useless discipline most people think it is.

There is yet another reason why history has become marginalised. This is that most people do not see history as a specialised branch of learning. It is as if everybody regards himself as a historian, and therefore history has become commonised. On another occasion when I had to address myself to the issue of the challenge before history, I drew attention to the perfectly understandable preoccupation of our nation with science and technology. I went on:

> Once must, however, ask the question science and technology for what? The answer can only be for the development of man. What man? Certainly, not man universal, but man in Nigeria. What is Nigeria? Who are the Nigerians? How has Nigeria fared? How come Nigeria is at this level of technological development? Can science and technology answer these questions? By no means. To answer these questions we must have history.

The key to any meaningful understanding of our present lies in knowledge of our past. Some may argue that even scientists can answer the questions I posed earlier. Of course, they can. But not out of a knowledge of science and technology. They can only answer those questions through a knowledge of history, Nigerian History inclusive. Herein lies one of the dangers to history. Those who think they know about the nation have never bothered to ask themselves whence the knowledge has come. Clearly, it has not come from Biology, Physics, Chemistry, Mathematics.

It has not come from applied science or technology. It has come from history. But because some scientists who have some of that knowledge have not formally studied history, they are tempted to think, wrongly, that we don't need history. Yet unless that body of knowledge were available, they could not tap it consciously or unconsciously. If I may trivialize what I am saying, it is that because any one who cares can pick up some history, there is a tendency to conclude that history itself is unnecessary. Yet, unless it is there, it cannot be picked up. And it cannot be there unless the historian brings it into being. So, then, the pursuit of science, legitimate as it is and always will be, has led policy makers to devise an educational system which relegates subjects like Geography and History to the background. I have no doubt at all that in virtually every circumstance this is mistaken policy. In our own particular circumstance, in which we are still very much preoccupied with seeking to bring a nation into being, it is particularly bad policy. Nigerians need history – the history of their country at least – if they are to identify with Nigeria. There need be no dichotomy between the sciences and the humanities, for we need both in the service of humanity.

Conclusion: History and the Nation – A Matter of Necessity or One of Utility?

To conclude, I must go back to the question which constitutes the subject of this lecture. Is learning history a matter of necessity in the context of the role of history in the nation, or should the place and role of history in the nation be determined by its utility, conceived of purely in terms of what job it can fetch? I believe that my answer must be obvious from all that I have said thus far. I concede that it is not as easy to grasp the value of History as it is, for example, to grasp the value of, say, Medicine or Law. The market value of Medicine or Law is obvious. That of history is not. But that most certainly does not render History valueless or even only of little value. Admittedly, in a Nigeria that pays regard only to material wealth and power, the value of history is bound to be marginalised as it has become in our country. Yet, whether Nigeria realises it or not, material things, like naira power, for example, are not necessarily permanent as our present economic situation should clearly warn us. There are values, concepts and ideas that are more lasting, more edifying, more permanent. The idea of a nation is one such idea, and part of what I have been trying to demonstrate in this lecture is that in terms of the making of a nation, the formulation of nationally integrative policies, the evolution of a political culture, the closing of the gap in attitudes to the two publics earlier on identified, the evolution of wholesome relationships between the various groups that constitute Nigeria, history has a role and a value that cannot be computed in terms of naira power. Nigeria must sensitize itself to this fact.

That Nigeria may be enabled to do so, we the professional historians, must deliberately lead a crusade for the popularization of history – what it is, and what it can do for the nation. We must do more. We must provide the right kind of material and teach our subject in the context of the claims we make for it. Perhaps when we begin to do this actively, we may succeed in persuading Government that its decision to set a world record by gradually taking history out of the education system is extremely bad policy; policy which no other nation known to me has ever adopted. I look forward to the return of History as a distinct subject taught to all Nigerian children who pass through secondary school; to a major increase in the History content of the Social Studies taught in primary schools; to a system of adult education which insists on the teaching of History to those who had no opportunity of attending secondary school in their earlier years. I make this call because I am persuaded that the nation can only gain by elevating History to its rightful place in the scheme of things.

In essence, then, my position is that History is a necessity for any nation, and even more of a necessity for a new nation seeking meaningful integration. It is a necessity because, especially in the realm of ideas, and in the promotion of understanding and empathy, History, properly taught and harnessed, does have a high utility value as the history of the rest of the world has shown. The problem with history is that its utility, being in the realm of ideas, is not easily grasped. And because it is not easily grasped, there is the tendency to deny it any utility at all. What I have sought to demonstrate in this lecture is that History does, in fact, have a high utility value of its own. No nation ignores its history except at its own ultimate cost. This is because History is one of those few subjects that can be used to fire the imagination and inspire the patriotic zeal of the citizenry. Hence I have argued consistently in this lecture that History is a national necessity. It is precisely because it is a national necessity that it has a high utility value. However, this value will never be grasped by our peoples unless and until we, the practitioners of History, shout it from the roof tops so that he who runs may hear.

REFERENCES

- Afigbo, A. E. Nigerian History and Unity (Paper presented to Seminar on Culture and Personality in Nigeria Organised By Kaduna State Council for Arts and Culture 13-16 September, 1982.)
- Ajayi, J. F. A."The aftermath of the fall of Old Oyo" in Ajayi J. F. A. and Crowder, Michael, *History of West Africa*, London, Longman, 1974, Chapter 5.
- --- *The Problem of National Integration in Nigeria: A Historical Perspective*, NISER Distinguished Lecture Series, No. 11, 1984.
- Ali, Amadu "University Development in Black Africa with particular reference to Nigeria" 1988 University of Ibadan Alumni Lecture, 24 June, 1988 (unpublished).
- Awa, Eme O. *National Integration in Nigeria: Problems and Prospects*, NISER Distinguished Lecture Series, No. 5, 1983.
- Bloch, Marc *The Historian's Craft,* New York, Alfred A. Knopf Inc., 1953.
- Daniels, R. V. *Studying History: How and Why*, New Jersey, Prentice – Hall, Inc. 1972.
- Dickson, A. K., Lee, P.J., Rogers, P. J. (Editors) *Learning History*, London, Heinemann Educational Books, 1984.
- Ekeh, Peter P. *Colonialism and Social Structure*, University of Ibadan, Inaugural Lecture, 1980, University of Ibadan Press, 1983.
- Gagnon, Paul "Why Study History" – *The Atlantic Monthly*, November, 1988.
- Ikime, Obaro *Through Changing Scenes: Nigerian History Yesterday, Today and Tomorrow*, University of Ibadan Inaugural Lecture, 1979. Chapter Two of this book.
- ----- "In Search of Nigerians: Changing Patterns of Inter-Group Relations in an Evolving Nation State", Chapter Five in Obaro Ikime, *History, The Historian and the Nation: The Voice of the Nigerian Historian*, Ibadan, HEBN Publishers Plc, 2006, reprinted 2008.
- -----"The Challenge Before History" Lecture delivered under the auspices of the Students Historical Society of Nigeria, Lagos State University Branch, 25 April, 1988, (unpublished).
- -----"Why Teach History" Lecture delivered under the auspices of the Students Historical Society of Nigeria, Adeyemi College of Education, Ondo, 23 February, 1989 (unpublished).
- Plumb, J. H. *The Death of the Past*, Boston, Houghton Mifflin Co., 1971.

10

THE IMAGBON WAR: THE IJEBU EXPEDITION OF 1892 RE-VISITED*

Preface

A keynote address delivered by me at a seminar in Abuja on the national question in 1986 has earned for me certain bitter consequences. Yet one must ply one's craft. The historian owes a duty to humanity to study the past. That past, however, is not a dead past, for the past constantly affects the present. It is the failure of our nation to see that history has a role to play in our development that has led our policy makers to commit what I regard as a crime against the nation, namely, the killing of history as a subject at primary and secondary school levels. A nation, the bulk of whose population is never exposed to its history, deprives itself of that corpus of knowledge that should inform our collective behaviour, as well as relations between one group and another in our multi-ethnic-group situation.

You may begin to wonder what the relevance of what I have said is to this conference. This conference has been called to celebrate 100 years of Ijebu history, from the Imagbọn War of 1892 to this year, 1992. Why should the Ijebu want to celebrate an event like the Imagbọn War?

*This was a keynote address delivered at a conference in 1992 to mark the Centenary of the Ijebu Expedition of 1892.

Why should a people celebrate their defeat, for the Ijebu were defeated at the Imagbọn War! I do not know what answer the organisers of this conference would give. I do not know what answer the Ijebu themselves would want to give. Whatever answers are proffered, permit me to suggest that we situate them in the context of what history is. For this purpose, I would like here to refer the reader to the last paragraph of page 188 which ends on page 189: Nigerians need to pay more. It is an answer which I have given many heed to what they can learn from their history.

We are gathered to prod human memory. We are gathered, one hundred years after the Imagbọn War, to ask ourselves a series of questions about that war. Why did it take place when it did? Why did the war go the way it went? What have been the consequences of the war for the Ijebu? What lessons has 100 years of history since 1892 taught the Ijebu and taught us who study and write history? In a country whose most thriving industry is conferences, seminars and symposia, let this not be just another conference, called for the purpose of providing academics with one more line on their curriculum vitae. Let us, among other things, look at the history of Ijebuland and the larger Nigeria these 100 years and draw out lessons that can positively affect our understanding of the place of History in the life of a people, a nation.

The Imagbọn War in the Nigerian Context

There exist a number of accounts of the Imagbọn War, usually referred to as the Ijebu Expedition of 1892. Of these, perhaps the most detailed in technical terms is that of Robert Smith in Michael Crowder's *West African Resistance* (1971). In all of the accounts, the Imagbọn War is situated in the context of Yoruba power politics in the 19th century. Two reasons are usually advanced for the decision of the British to break the Ijebu. One, Ijebu refusal to allow Christian missionaries free play in Ijebuland. Two, Ijebu refusal to allow "free trade" through her territory.

Ijebu aversion to Christian missionary activity was predicated on observable consequences of such activities in Egbaland. True, Egba enthusiasm for missionaries had paid off in terms of securing arms and ammunition and British support in her wars with other Yoruba groups and with Dahomey. Those activities had also, however, begun to undermine Egba sovereignty. The Ijebu observed this and were anxious to safeguard their independence. Additionally, as Ayandele points out in his recent book, the Ijebu were shocked at the idea of former slaves seeking to set themselves up as rulers! Ayandele would argue that for the Ijebu this amounted to desecration of the land.

Perhaps if the Ijebu had limited their opposition to missionaries, the British authorities in Lagos would have found it more difficult to cook up a *casus belli*. As it was, the Ijebu were even more determined to keep the white man and other Yoruba groups out of trade in Ijebuland. In this matter, the Ijebu were pursuing their enlightened self-interest in the war situation in Yorubland in the 19th century, as were all other Yoruba groups. Geographical proximity to Lagos enabled the Ijebu to obtain arms and ammunition and other goods with which to do roaring trade with the more hinterland Yoruba groups, from which they obtained slaves in quantum, slaves thrown up by the inter-state wars among the Yoruba. The result was great commercial prosperity for the Ijebu.

The Ijebu were not, at the time, part of the British colony or protectorate of Lagos. Why should their economic policy become a matter of interest to the British in Lagos? The British had established a colony in Lagos since 1851. Once established in Lagos, the British had an interest in promoting the external trade of the Yoruba hinterland which had to pass through the port of Lagos. This prosperity was hampered by the inter-state wars in Yorubaland in the 19th century. Hence the British took a major interest in bringing those wars to an end. That end having been achieved through the Peace Treaty of 1886, it irked the British that the Ijebu should persist in refusing to allow all and sundry access to their territory for trade purposes.

British assessment of the situation was, of course, a function of their colonial interests. Ijebu assessment had, logically, to be equally a function of Ijebu interests. The Ijebu knew that their prosperity was the consequence of a jealously guarded middleman position. Ijebu aversion to "free trade" through their land was, in this context, exactly at par with the aversion of the delta states of Nigeria to direct trade between the Europeans at the coast and the Nigerian peoples to the hinterland of the delta. Just as the British chafed at what they regarded as the obstructionist commercial policies of the delta states, so they chafed at the trade policy of the Ijebu, the 'delta state' of Yorubaland! The conflicting interests of the British and the Ijebu ended in armed confrontation, as was the case in a number of other instances in the country.

The point which existing accounts have failed to make, and which we must make as we mark the centenary of the Imagbọn War, is that

that war was the beginning of the new British putsch that was to result in the effective occupation of Nigeria by the British. That geographical proximity to Lagos, which had resulted in the Ijebu dominating the trade of Yorubaland in the 19th century, now became a disadvantage. The Ijebu, after Lagos, became the first victims of the new aggressive imperialism of the 1890s. The dismantling of the sovereignty of our peoples gained great momentum after the Imagbọn War: the Itsẹkiri (1894); the Ijọ of Brass (1895); Ọyọ (1895); Benin (1897); the Igbo of Aro (1900-01); the Sokoto Caliphate (1900-03); the Tiv and other groups of the Middle Belt (1900-1911); Asaba (1902-1909) – see Obaro Ikime, *The Fall of Nigeria*, 1977. All who have worked on the history of Yorubaland are agreed that the attitude of other Yoruba groups to the British was radically affected by the British defeat of the Ijebu, probably the best armed group in the Yorubaland of the time, though certainly not the best in the martial arts. Anyone familiar with the records would know that the charges against the Ijebu were the same as those against Nana of Ebrohimi, the Brass people, Oba Ovonramwen of Benin, the Igbo of Aro and the Tiv: obstructing free trade! The British had made up their mind to occupy what became Nigeria. They had the force to back up their determination. It was only for the sake of international public opinion that they felt called upon to make the various cases they made against different Nigerian groups. You do not make omelettes without breaking eggs. The Ijebu omelette could be no exception. The age of the new imperialism was, logically, the age of might is right. The Ijebu bowed to that might. Enough has been said, I believe, to establish that the Imagbọn War has significance far beyond Ijebuland. It is, in fact, a major milestone in the history of Nigeria.

Some Comments on the Imagbọn War

While it is not intended in this address to go into the details of the actual military encounters between the British and the Ijebu, it is necessary to draw attention to certain features of the Imagbọn War. First, the evidence indicates that the Ijebu army of about 7,000-10,000 (I don't know how the number was arrived at!) was drawn largely from Ijebu-Ode and its immediate environs. Smith indicates that there were detachments from Ijebu Ife and Ijebu Imusin. It does not appear as if the Awujale asked for contingents from all of Ijebuland. It is pertinent to raise the question why this was so, having regard to the fact that the Awujale must have realised that the encounter with the British was bound to be much tougher than other wars fought by his people.

Secondly, the entire Ijebu army moved out of the capital, Ijebu-Ode. It is clear that the war aim was to prevent the British from getting into Ijebu-Ode. Although Ijebu-Ode had the usual defensive walls and moat of the typical Yoruba city, no forces were posted to defend it, in the event of the British overpowering the Ijebu forces that sallied forth to drive them back. This may appear to be a major defect in Ijebu war plans. I have argued elsewhere that the Ijebu were probably acting on the basis of previous experience. They have never had to defend Ijebu-Ode from behind the city walls, and they did not now think they would. When therefore the Ijebu forces were compelled by superior fire power to withdraw, they did not retreat to take a last-ditch stand in Ijebu-Ode. The Ijebu defeat at Imagbọn was the end of the war.

Thirdly, the accounts of the war reveal that on each occasion that fighting broke out as between the British and the Ijebu, it was the latter (the Ijebu) who opened fire first. This was so on 16, 17 and 19 May, 1892. This fact is a credit to Ijebu war readiness. This is the more noteworthy when we remember that the Ijebu were forced to change their war plans when the British decided to march from Epe rather than Itoiki. Ijebu forces which had been deployed to defend the Itoiki-Ijebu-Ode route had to be redeployed. This re-deployment was sufficiently quickly and well done to enable the Ijebu take the initiative when the first clash of arms occurred on 16 May, 1892.

Fourthly, one should draw attention to the doggedness of the Ijebu. On the 16th of May, 1892, they opened fire on the British first, using the forest as cover. British counter-fire forced them to withdraw. They re-grouped to oppose the British advance on the 17th, again opening fire from their forest cover. The evidence suggests that on this occasion they suffered heavier causalities than on the first day. Also by now, the Ijebu must have known that the British had artillery which they (the Ijebu) did not have. Yet they did not give up the defence of their independence. They took a third and, as it turned out, a final stand against the British at Imagbọn on 19 May, 1892. Imagbọn was chosen for its advantages for an army fighting a defensive war. To get to Imagbọn the British had to cross the Yemoji river. The Ijebu made crossing difficult by throwing boulders and other obstacles into the river. Then they took their positions in the forest on the Imagbọn bank of the river. It was as early as 7.15 a.m. when the Ijebu took on the advancing British in a hard battle that lasted some three hours. The British commanding officer, Colonel Scott, saw clearly that unless his men were able to cross the Yemoji, the Ijebu would not be beaten. Despite the devastation caused by a maxim gun, the Ijebu fought on. Indeed one of the officers who led the British in crossing the river was hit by the Ijebu. The men were badly affected by this fact and began to waver. It was at this point in the proceedings that Colonel Scott himself jumped into the river and urged his men on. The crossing was successfully effected only because the 7-pounder guns and rockets mounted on the opposite bank of the river continued to wreak havoc among the Ijebu forces as the British crossed. Once the British accomplished the crossing, superior fire power decided the day. The Ijebu were defeated but certainly not routed.

Earlier on we quoted Daniels: "It is the events recorded in history that have generated all the emotions, the values, the ideals, that make life meaningful, that have given men something to live for, struggle over, die for". It is sad that some seventeen war lords and 1,000 men laid their lives down in defence of their fatherland in the Imagbọn war. Can we mark this centenary of that sacrifice without saluting the courage of these men? Although we know that British commanding officers often gave an exaggerated report of the resistance of our peoples in order to justify their recommendations for war medals, we must, nevertheless, give some credence to Colonel Scott's claim there "there was no such severe fighting during the whole of the Ashanti campaign as that of Imagbọn" – clear testimony to the dogged courage of the Ijebu. Admittedly, the British force that opposed the Ijebu was made up of only 463 combatants and 536 non-combatants. Nevertheless the casualty of some 11% represents one of the highest figures in the wars of colonial conquest in Nigeria, another testimony to the fighting spirit and effectiveness of the Ijebu.

To conclude this aspect of this address I would like to repeat here a point I have made before. The Ijebu fell in 1892. Other Nigerian groups were to follow. Did the Ijebu think they would win the war against the British? Or did they fight to safeguard their honour? I am reminded of the story of Esther in the Bible. A favourite of her husband, King Xerxes of Persia, had got the king to issue a decree that would lead to the destruction of all the Israelites in the kingdom. She was Israelite. Her people appealed to her to go to the king to plead for them. But the law of the kingdom laid it down that if any of the king's wives went in to see the king without being sent for, such a woman would die, unless the king showed her favour. Esther was not sent for. After three days of fasting, she went in to see the king to plead for her people. And as she took that decision she said, "If I perish, I perish." The men who fought the British despite the imbalance of armaments against them were like Esther – if I perish, I perish. By deciding to fight rather than give up their independence tamely, they gave us, their descendants, a proud reference point. Yes, we lost to the British, but we showed that we were peoples endowed with pride and a fighting spirit. The men who died at Imagbọn gave the Ijebu something to live for. They gave all of us, Nigerians of today, something to live for. It is their spirit and their courage that we celebrate today. Let us, therefore live lives worthy of the sacrifices they made.

Aftermath of the Imagbọn War

"Historical events have created all the basic human groupings – countries, religions, classes – and all the loyalties that attach to these". The historical event of the Imagbọn War has left an indelible mark on the Ijebu. In my review of Ayandele's *The Ijebu of Yorubaland 1850-1950* yesterday (21 May, 1992), I said that the story unfolded in that book is one of new challenges, new ideas, bewildering innovations and how the Ijebu reacted to them. It is impossible in this address to take us through all the changes that were ushered in by the Ijebu defeat at the Imagbọn War. There is a great deal of truth in Robert Smith's assertion that for the Ijebu, May 1892 was the beginning of a new world. Yet there was also quite a bit of the old in the new.

Centre-District Relations: Ayandele brings out quite clearly in his recent book that in the aftermath of the Imagbọn War, and following the imposition of British rule, many of the outlying districts began to want to be independent of Ijebu-Ode. Of these districts, Ijebu Remo was the one that led the way. It is not intended here to take us through the history of Remo-Ijebu-Ode relations, however fascinating such a history may be. I prefer to draw attention to the lesson that history teaches, namely, that no condition is permanent! Trite, but very true.

In a lecture delivered in 1985, I made the point that the ethnic and sub-ethnic groups as we know them now are products of history. Those we call Ijebu today were not, *ab initio*, created Ijebu by God. The groups collectively known as the Ijebu only became so as conflicting interests were resolved and merged. No group, however small, would want to be associated with another, unless its interests would be served by such an association. It is for this reason that the 19th century inter-state wars in Yorubaland threw Yorubaland into a state of flux. New towns emerged with political systems designed to meet the challenges of the time. Ibadan, Abeokuta are well known examples. So is Sagamu which became the seat of the Akarigbo. Sagamu was made possible by the coming together of a number of Remo settlements that sought greater security in numbers. The settlements that fused to produce Sagamu were satisfied that fusion would serve their interest in the situational reality of the 19th century. It is remarkable that during the Ijaiye war, Ijebu-Ode allied with Ijaiye and the Egba against Ibadan. The Remo towns did not join the war against Ibadan. In fact they kept open their trade routes and did business with Ibadan. Why? Their economic interests so dictated, just as Ijebu-Ode economic interests determined her anti-Ibadan stance. Relations between the various Ijebu groups and Ijebu-Ode, I plead, should not be seen in terms of loyalists and rebels. Such tags obscure the historical realities that determined group interests. Ijebu defeat at Imagbọn immediately raised the issue as to the continued ability of Ijebu-Ode to serve as rallying point for the other groups. As all the experts agree, that defeat was not just a defeat of Ijebu arms. It was also a defeat of the Ijebu gods and the religio-political system that Ijebu-Ode represented. A supra-Ijebu authority emerged on the scene, and the outlying groups sought to take advantage of this development. The "independence movements" were thus a reaction to changing historical circumstances far more than they were rebellions qua rebellions. The purpose of history is to deepen understanding, in the hope that deeper understanding would influence man's actions for the better. In no other area is this deeper understanding as crucial as in the area of inter-group relations. As we celebrate the centenary of the Imagbọn War, let us be honest with ourselves. Let us admit the truth that in inter-group relations, as in international relations, the take off point is enlightened self-interest. And let us remember that no condition is permanent. The super power of today can become the beggar of tomorrow. In the specific case of the Ijebu groups in the years after the Imagbọn War, they reacted according to their understanding of the new British policies and their reading of the attitude of British political officers to specific Awujales. The entry of the British introduced new rules and brought in a new referee. The ball game changed accordingly.

Of Religions and of Classes: "Historical events have created....all the religions, all the classes...and the loyalties which attach to these". Ijebu society proves that this is true. For most of the 19th century, the Ijebu resisted Christian missionary activity. Those who died at the Imagbọn war died defending Ijebu policy in this regard. As is now well-known, defeat at Imagbọn cleared the way for the entry of Christian missionaries. And in the years immediately after Imagbọn, Christian missionaries took Ijebuland by storm. Ayandele details how this was done. In Ijebuland as elsewhere, the attraction was not just Christianity *per se* but Western European education of which Christian missions were purveyors. We do not know for sure what proportion of the Ijebu society became Christians. Some say about 32%. As for Western education, even non-Christians went for it. Within a quarter of a century Ijebuland had outstripped all other parts of Yorubaland except Egbaland in the area of education. There thus arose an educated class which sought to play new roles in the new situation created by British Colonial rule. We shall return to this presently.

As it turned out, as Christianity grew in Ijebuland, so did Islam. In fact the experts tell us that in Ijebuland there were (and may be there still are) more Muslims than Christians. As elsewhere the attraction of Islam may well have been the fact that it did not appear as foreign as Christianity. Be that as it may, the presence of these two world religions in Ijebuland claiming that their God and their Allah were superior to the Ijebu gods was bound to have its impact on Ijebu society. In the first two decades or so after the Imagbọn War, traditional religion and traditional festivals were subjected to severe badgering by the Christians in particular. They could do this more than the Muslims because British colonial authority backed them up. So deep did this badgering go that a number of Awujale were actually crowned in Church! For the diehard traditionalists, this must have been an abomination, that he who represented the soul of Ijebudom should be established in office by votaries of what such diehards would regard as a foreign God. Here was proof of my earlier contention that no condition is permanent! Those Awujale who were crowned in the church were no less Ijebu than those who were not. Is it not said that politics is the art of the possible? There were new rules, and a new referee. These Awujale found it necessary to play the game differently. Survival in the new setting was the name of the game.

The Ijebu may, however, congratulate themselves and claim that he laughs best who laughs last. Although the figures of the adherents of Christianity, Islam and Ijebu traditional religion show that those of the last named are the least, Ijebu religion has a mighty hold even on those Ijebu who profess the other two faiths. The Ijebu have a reputation nation-wide as medicine men (or *juju* men as the not so polite might say). Ijebu medicine is rooted in traditional religion. And patrons of Ijebu medicine cut across the three faiths! In this regard the old order has not changed as much as the presence of beautifully adorned churches and mosques in Ijebuland may suggest.

That Ijebu religion continues to thrive despite Islam and Christianity is evidenced by what may appear to be a mere accident. Only some twenty four hours ago, there was launched a book on the Ijebu. Adorning the covers of the book are emblems of *Obanta* and *Agemo*. Those who decided that these emblems should adorn the cover of the book are either Muslim or Christian! For them, the important thing is not their faiths, but Ijebudom or Ijebu-ness. At Imagbọn, Ijebu arms suffered a major defeat. But the spirit of the Ijebu marches on, one hundred years after the event. A triumph of Ijebu resilience?

At the risk of giving offence, though that is not my intention, let me in an aside here say what I have said in another setting. What is African about African traditional religion except the names we call the gods, goddesses, festivals? Has man all over the world not worshipped rocks, rivers, lakes, trees, idols and what have you? Those who brought us Christianity and Islam, did not their ancestors have their *Obanta*s and *Agemo*s? Yes, they did. The truth is that those who brought us these new faiths have moved on to higher grounds. Faced with a crisis of identity we in Africa seem to have decided that the only way we can have an identity is to keep going backwards – to what our ancestors did! For us culture is a going backwards, not a dynamic grappling with the realities of God's creation. One of my colleagues at the University of Ibadan created laughter during his inaugural lecture when he told us that the developed part of the world has an ordered dance pattern; but that in Nigeria all our dances involve a few steps forward and many backwards! He concluded that there must be something in our makeup that prefers to move backwards – little wonder we are so undeveloped. Jeremiah conveyed to Israel of old God's anger because they (the Israelites) used to say to a tree: "thou art my father; and to a stone, Thou has brought me forth". That was thousands of years ago. How do we stand in this matter today? And will God not judge us?

Enough of the aside. Let us return to our main subject. We drew attention earlier on to the avidity of the Ijebu for Western European education. That avidity introduced into Ijebu society a new class, the class of the educated elite. In the colonial period, and indeed even in our time, we saw and have seen titanic struggles between the traditional elite and the new elite. Thus Ayandele tells us of the conflict between the literate and Christian Joseph Odumosu and the illiterate Awujale Adeleke who found himself publicly humiliated by Odumosu and his followers. T. A. Odutola who began humbly as a Native Court Clerk, thanks to his education, rose to become a business guru and an *Ogbeni Oja.* His education and his wealth enabled him to hold his own against those Awujale who opposed him. In the post-Imagbọn War period the Ijebu had to come to grips with the fact that birth alone was not sufficient to guarantee a respected position in society. True the old elite with all the traditional societies and titles have survived. The travails of society in the first quarter of a century from 1892 convinced the Ijebu that the future lay in the hands of those who had excellent connections by birth as well as a good education. That has been the touch stone of Ijebu society. Today the profusion of well-educated Otunbas is a reminder that the marriage of the old and the new remains a major factor in Ijebuland. The Ijebu have learnt and are learning from the challenges posed to them by post Imagbọn War developments.

Operating on a Larger Canvas: The point has been made that the Imagbọn War was but the opening shot in a series of wars between the British and the Nigerian peoples that ended with the establishment of effective British colonial rule over Nigeria. The emergence of the colonial state of Nigeria, followed by that of the Nigerian nation state created a larger canvas of operation for the Ijebu. The products of that Western education, which the Ijebu so enthusiastically embraced, found employment far afield outside Ijebuland. Ijebu entrepreneurs achieved success as they operated in the new Nigeria as transport magnates, textiles traders, cocoa farmers and traders, gold smiths, etc. Those who have become industrialists in more recent times have had to operate within the Nigerian nation state. In banking, in the multi-nationals, in the new area of oil prospecting and mining, sons of Ijebuland are making a most impressive mark. In some ways one may be justified in saying that the loss of 1892 has been made up for in the gains of these past one hundred years. There have been changes, some of them unpleasant. But the Ijebu have weathered these changes well and have proved themselves a major force in all spheres of endeavour in Nigeria.

Ijebu defeat in the Imagbọn War brought an end to Ijebu independence. It did not destroy the Ijebu-ness of the Ijebu. The reaction of the different Ijebu sub-groups (especially Ijebu-Remo, Ijebu-Igbo and Ijebu-Ife) to the British presence and their policies gave Ijebu-Ode cause for alarm as the rulers of these sub-groups began to question the authority of the Awujale over them. Ironically, however, as Ijebu cohesion was being threatened by the self-interests of the Ijebu-sub groups, the Ijebu found themselves having to operate in a larger canvas – southern Nigeria up to 1939, and Western Nigeria from that time till the 1960s. The emergence of these new entities ensured that Ijebu cohesiveness was not allowed to disintegrate. In the politics of region and nation, it was more meaningful to seek to promote pan-Ijebu interests than the interests of the sub-groups. Also, within these larger entities – region and nation – it was not the Obas in whose hands real power lay; it was the new elite. These new elite – like Obafemi Awolowo and Adesanya, lawyers from Ikenne and Sagamu; J.A. Adesola and J. J. Odufuwa, journalists and proprietors from Iperu and Ijebu-Igbo; Canon S.A. Banjo and Stephen O. Awokoya from Ijebu-Igbo and Awa – found that they could hold their own against their counterparts from Ijebu-Ode. Through various organisations which cut across sub-Ijebu groupings, these persons and many others not here named began to work together at different levels to promote Ijebu interests within the region and the nation. In this way Ijebudom was kept alive, despite the tensions and differences which surfaced from time to time, as is not uncommon in human relations.

By Way of Conclusion

As I draw this to a close, I am the first to admit that I may not have set the best tone to mark the centenary of the British conquest of Ijebu-Ode, otherwise known as the Imagbọn War. What I have sought to do, with what success I know not, is to discuss a few selected topics related to the war and its aftermath. I have presented the facts and arguments in a manner which, I hope, makes it possible for us to learn certain lessons.

While Ijebu trade and politics were played out in the 19th century in the context of the power politics of Yorubaland, I have asked that we situate the Imagbọn War in the larger Nigerian context. When we do so we find that there were many others who took a position similar to the Ijebu, and who consequently had to face the fury of British maxims. The Imagbọn War was not just an aspect of Ijebu history. It was an important facet of Nigerian history.

With regard to the war itself, there is no need to recapitulate here all that was said earlier. Once the decision to go to war was taken by the British, they did everything to win the war. It is instructive that 100 Ibadan war boys were among the British forces. The Ijebu were particular about Ibadan not obtaining firearms through Ijebu territory, for fear that Ibadan would become dangerously powerful. In the circumstances, it was perfectly logical that Ibadan should seek the downfall of Ijebu. Little did Ibadan realise that once Ijebu fell, and the British were released from that quarter, they would turn their attention to Ibadan itself. In 1893, the year after the Imagbọn War, the British sent Captain Bower, one of those who had fought the Ijebu, with troops to occupy Ibadan and bring the Ibadan under British rule. The fact that Ibadan had sent a contingent to help the British against the Ijebu did not save Ibadan from British occupation. All those described as collaborators by some scholars in this period of British conquest found that collaboration was no antidote to British occupation. As for the term "collaborators," I take the view that the term obscures the hard realities that various peoples faced as they squared up to changing British attitudes. The truth was that the bulk of our people did not realise that the British had decided for effective occupation, and so sought to deal with them as they had done earlier on.

Before the war itself, Governor Carter of Lagos had told his employers at the British Colonial Office that he did not anticipate "any difficulty from a military point of view" in dealing with the Ijebu. The Ijebu proved him wrong. They (the Ijebu) may not have engaged in regular drill like the British forces did; they may not have handled their weapons as competently as the trained soldiers of the British. Still, they gave an excellent account of themselves and so gave us cause to be proud to be their descendants. As I said earlier on, we are this week celebrating the courage and the sacrifice of those who went before us. There is something about the spirit of man everywhere that prefers to go down fighting than to yield tamely to external aggression of the type typified by the British.

One more point needs to be made. In some of the existing accounts of this war, there is a tendency to see the war as the outcome of Carter's personal prefence for armed confrontation. This is the same kind of arguments that some scholars have raised with regard to events in the Niger Coast Protectorate, namely that Ralph Moor was inclined to go to war while Major Claude Macdonald was more pacific in his attitude. I have argued elsewhere that this argument ignores the circumstances in which the various wars were fought. The list of wars as indicated earlier in this address convinces me that we are not just dealing here with war-loving consuls, High Commissioner or Governors; we are dealing with policy. The British had decided that the time had come to dismantle the sovereignty of our peoples in order that they could more effectively exploit our economic resources. Herein lies added justification for putting the Imagbọn War in a Nigeria-wide perspective.

As for the aftermath of the Imagbọn War, enough has been said, I believe, to establish the fact that the Ijebu found that they had to adjust and adapt to changing circumstances. It speaks volumes for the genius of the Ijebu that they have adjusted and adapted so well. In doing so, there have been inter-personal and inter-group tensions and animosities, as there would nearly always be. It can be said, having regard to the achievements of the Ijebu within their homeland and the larger Nigerian nation, that they have put the defeat of Imagbọn behind them, and have carved out an enviable place for themselves within the Nigerian nation-state. The Imagbọn War may have been a disaster for the Ijebu in 1892. The Awujales who reigned in those early years of British rule may have been bewildered by the changes which British rule ushered in. The disaster of 1892 and the bewilderment of the Awujales of the first two or three decades gave way to a calculated reassessment of the new environment created by the colonial and Nigerian nation-state. Within that new environment the Ijebu have performed most creditably, despite internal squabbles and problems in the homelands.

11

CURRENT STRUGGLE FOR DEMOCRACY IN NIGERIA – THE PEACE OPTION: A LESSON FOR NIGERIAN YOUTHS*

Run to and fro through the streets of
Jerusalem, look and take note: Search her squares,
to see if you can find a man, one who does justice
and seeks truth; that I may pardon her.
–Jeremiah 5:1 (RSV):

You wicked, unholy ruler of Israel, your day, the day of
your final punishment, is coming. I, the Sovereign Lord,
have spoken. Take off your crown, and
your turban. Nothing will be the same again. Raise the
Poor to power! Bring down those who are ruling!
Ruin, ruin: yes, I will make the city a ruin.
But this will not happen until the one whom
I have chosen to punish the city has come.
Then I will give it to him.
–Ezekiel 21:25-27 (Good News Bible)

*This was a lecture in honour of Tunde Oshobi under the auspices of the Junior Chamber of Commerce, Ibadan, in 1993.

> .....know that the Most High rules the kingdom of men, and gives it to whom he pleases.
> .... Your kingdom shall be sure for you from the time that you know that Heaven rules. Therefore, o king....break off your sins by practicing righteousness, and your iniquities by showing mercy to the oppressed..... – Daniel 4:26-28

After I read this piece, I was tempted to exclude it from this volume. I changed my mind. While I agreed that what is contained in this chapter is different from all the other chapters, I dare to suggest that what is contained here is part of human group experience in the Nigerian context. Therefore, it is part of History!

Introduction

My circumstances at the time I was originally invited to deliver this lecture on 2 December, 1993, were such that I could have declined the invitation. I had ten days notice, six of which were already committed. In the remaining four days, I was billed to travel out of Ibadan twice, spending two nights away. I could, therefore, with a clear conscience, have made my excuses. I decided not to do so for two reasons.

One, nearly thirty years ago, Tunde Oshobi, in whose honour this lecture is being held, and I (among others) were involved in a students' demonstration to Lagos. I believe Oshobi was then Secretary of the Students Union. I had just put in my Ph.D. thesis and was waiting for my examination. The issue, if I remember correctly, was the census of 1964 which we believed had been shamelessly manipulated for political reasons. We went on this demonstration to protest against the manipulated figures. As was to be expected, the Police were waiting for us, and we had the usual "confrontation". I remember that Tunde Oshobi and I were among those arrested and made to sit on the ground at a petrol station in Lagos. Press photographers took our pictures which appeared in the papers the next day. Eventually, we were escorted back to Ibadan by the Police and again made to sit on the field at Iyanganku Police station until the then Vice-Chancellor, Professor Kenneth Onwuka Dike, secured our release. Question: what were we fighting for? Democracy? Justice? You can decide for yourselves. The point that has to be made is that nowhere in the world has democracy been installed as a way of life and a system of government without some people, some groups, paying a price for it. Ask Beko Ransome-Kuti. Ask Gani Fawehinmi. Ask the members of the Committee for Democracy (CD). Democracy will not become a way of life in Nigeria until more and more people are ready to pay a price. So, recalling Tunde Oshobi's role in the struggle in the 1960s, I felt compelled to accept to deliver this lecture despite a near-impossible schedule. I must beg you, therefore, to kindly forgive the inadequacies in what follows.

Two, the invitation came at a time when our march to democracy had, once again, been aborted with, "Fellow Nigerians". Isn't it ironical that again and again you and I are described as "Fellow Nigerians" and yet again and again you and I are told that though we are "Fellow Nigerians", we have no business trying to decide how our nation is to be governed! Yet, Harold Laski asserts that "the essence of democracy is full consultation before decisions are taken, and that the discovery of the organs which will make that consultation effective is of paramount importance". As I speak, a new Government is in place – without the mandate of the people. And you and I – Fellow Nigerians – are waiting to be told how long this new Government plans to stay in power. Just before this crowd now strutting about as our Government, we had another crowd headed by someone who described himself first as Head of the Interim Government and then as Head of State and Commander in Chief of the Armed Forces – on the mandate of one man who on many occasions referred to you and I as "Fellow Nigerians," and proceeded to act as if you and I do not exist! So, "Fellow Nigerians", I found the temptation to say a few things at this point in our nation's life too difficult to resist. As a minority of minorities in this country, I realise that all I can ever do is to talk. I thank God that I am even allowed to talk. And to labour – for it is when there is work to do that some of us are remembered. When it is time for reward, the cry is "away with them"; at such times, it is *ti wan, ti wan.** Let me hurry to say that *ti wan, ti wan* must always have its proper place. Abused as it has been at every level of our national life, it becomes a major instrument of injustice. I

**Ti wan Ti wan* means: "It is ours, it is ours"

worked for twenty-six years in a federal institution called the University of Ibadan and I know what I am talking about. Yes, so I decided to accept the invitation to speak here today, so I can have my own little say, even if I never have my way. Thank God for small mercies.

So, Fellow Nigerians, here we are. The subject as handed to me is "[The] Current Struggle for Democracy in Nigeria – The Peace Option: A Lesson for Nigerian Youths". I confess that I find the formulation of the subject a little unclear. I believe, however, that it is possible to make some sense out of it, and I will proceed so to do. Given my subject, and given the sponsors of this lecture, some in the audience must have wondered why I began by reading from *The Holy Bible*. Let me read those passages again. All three passages point to one conclusion. God insists on justice and frowns at injustice. The condition for peace in any land is justice. Wicked and unholy rulers will most certainly be brought down and brought to book – the day of punishment must most certainly come, unless there is repentance and restitution, repeat, restitution.

God is God. Let man strut about as much as he pleases. The day comes when God will give the government of our land into the hands of him whom He has chosen. In the meantime, God warns that the Government of Nigeria Will not be "sure" (i.e. stable and acceptable to Him and even to men) until those who rule, as well as you and I, acknowledge that there is God who rules over the affairs of men. Remember King Nebuchadnezzar? He is a historical figure, you know. He actually lived and reigned. Read Daniel 4. King Nebuchadnezzar was a successful warrior-king. One evening he climbed onto the flat roof of his palace and surveyed his capital city. Impressed by what he saw, he said, "is not this great Babylon, which I have built by my mighty power as a royal residence and for the glory of my majesty?" The Bible says, "While the words were still in the king's mouth, there fell a voice from heaven, 'O King Nebuchadnezzar, to you is this spoken: The kingdom has departed from you, and you shall be driven from among men, and your dwelling shall be with the beasts of the field, and you shall be made to eat grass like the ox [for seven years] until you have learnt that the Most High rules the kingdom of men and gives it to whom he will'" (Daniel 4:30-32). As God spoke, so it was. Yes. Let those who govern build palaces for themselves. Let them steal all the nation's wealth and stock-pile it in Swiss banks. Let them marry themselves wives and more wives.

God is God. Nebuchadnezzar ate grass for seven years. Some of those who have ruled us; some of those who are ruling us, will not eat grass for seven years; they will roast in fire for all eternity. Why? Because God is not mocked. Whatsoever a man sows that also shall he reap. It is not Obaro Ikime who says it. God Himself has spoken it. And it will most certainly come to pass. Enough of the preaching. Let us link all of this with the subject of our lecture.

The Current Struggle for Democracy

We have just emerged from eight years of the worst dictatorship that Nigeria has experienced thus far. And we have just begun another regime that we are in no position yet to judge, except that it is headed by one who may have learnt from the last regime, of which he was a high ranking member, how to dance a little to the right and a little to the left. In-between we had the Sonekan interlude. It has all been very depressing. And it is all still most depressing. What is the current struggle against? Is it not against military rule? So, how come, all who have been crying for democracy, and urging that the people have a right to choose who should govern them, have now taken up jobs with the Abacha regime? I am opposed to military rule and will always be. Why? I cannot accept that any professional class has any right to rule this nation. I am as opposed to military rule as I will be to rule by university lecturers or rule by nurses! And from all that I had heard and read, I thought we had had enough of military rule until "Fellow Nigerians" was intoned once more, a carrot was held out to the civilian population and we went scampering after it. What a shame. What better way is there to convince the Military that we are tired of being ruled by them than to refuse to take office under them? Let them hold every available office in the land, and let the rest of us be solid in our refusal to be ruled by soldiers. Oh, that we could be so united in our resolve as to be willing to suffer for that in which we believe. Democracy is never won without a struggle. Struggle entails suffering. Part of that struggle must entail refusing to participate in any Government that negates all that democracy stands for. And that is what military rule does.

Don't get me wrong. Any group in the nation has a right to aspire to rule – the Military included. But no group has the right to arrogate to itself a monopoly of wisdom and knowledge as to what is wrong with the nation and how to right the wrong. The Military have no basis whatsoever to lay claims to a higher degree of rectitude than the rest of us. I am therefore amazed that Nigerians have been so eager to welcome one military regime after another, expecting the leopard to change its spots! It used to be said that man learns from experience. Alas, it looks like Nigerians have gone past learning from experience – or any other thing for that matter! For the bulk of our people it is enough to breathe God's free air – the only thing that the Military have not taken over.

As I said earlier on, I thought we were agreed in our opposition to military rule. But judging from the response of our political big wigs to the present military regime, it is clear that we are not so agreed. If we are not agreed even on that, I doubt if we are agreed on what democracy is, and exactly what it is we are struggling for! I am not about to hold forth an academic discourse on democracy. For that you can go to Professor Omoruyi, Babangida's Director-General of the Centre for Democratic Studies, that taught members of the National Assembly how to run democratic institutions! They ran these institutions so well that they were quite prepared, having been elected by the people, to allow a dictator to stay in power. For them democracy acquired a new meaning: Government of an ogre by an ogre for the National Assembly! No, I am not about to engage in any academic definitions. What I do feel called upon to say is that democracy is not just about what form governance should take. The fact that we are allowed to vote for those who should govern us does not, of itself, guarantee democracy. If we are ever going to practise democracy in Nigeria, we must see democracy as a way of life. We must accept certain basic principles without which we may have elected legislators and an elected executive and yet not live under a democratic government. Time will not permit any full discussion of all of these principles. I will only be able to identify a few of these and speak briefly on them. But before that a few words about peace, in view of the formulation of the subject of this lecture.

The Peace Option

What is peace? The ordinary dictionary meaning includes the following: a state of quiet; freedom from disturbance; freedom from war; freedom from contention. As between political units, peace has been defined as the more or less lasting suspension of violent modes of rivalry between political units. It was Pope John XIII who said that peace and justice must go hand in hand. Asked the late Pontiff, "what are kingdoms without justice but large bands of robbers?" "In the long run," declared the late J.F. Kennedy, "peace is basically a matter of human rights," because, as he put it, "peace and freedom walk together." In the context of our subject, then, what do we mean by a peace option? Democracy, whether as a form of government or as a way of life, can really only function in a state of peace defined as a more or less lasting suspension of violent modes of rivalry between political units. Here, I would like to enter a caveat. Peace so defined must walk hand in hand with justice for it to be true peace. When, as in the case of Nigeria, governance is dominated by a particular group that insists that no matter what the people say it must rule, that is hegemony, and whatever peace there is, is necessarily an unjust peace. A peace option must thus necessarily make provision for the avoidance of such hegemony.

Harold Laski lists as part of the essence of the democratic way of life the absence of wide economic differences between citizens and the refusal to recognise privileges built on birth or wealth or race or creed. If ever Nigeria is to have anything like democracy with peace, we must fight resolutely against privileges built on birth, wealth, ethnic group or creed. The mistakes of history, the result of our colonial period, must cease to dominate our political thought. When Alhaji Maitama Sule addressed the Forum of Northern leaders not too long ago, he was reported in the media to have said: The northerners are endowed by God with leadership qualities. The Yorubaman knows how to earn a living and has diplomatic qualities. The Igbo is gifted in commerce and technological innovation…

Here was WAZOBIA* in full manifestation. For me as an Isoko, there is hardly a time I am made to feel that I am also a Nigerian. Maitama Sule, a man of varied and long experience, one for whom I have had high regard, is content to talk about "Northerners," the Yorubaman and the Igbo. As for the rest of us, we really do not exist in Nigeria's political arithmetic. Yet it is from among the geographical area where quite a few of the rest of us live that the oil wealth comes.

*WAZOBIA is formed form three words: *Wa* (Yoruba), *Zo* (Hausa) and *Bia* (Igbo). Each of these words has the same meaning – "Come" in the three respective languages. In the early 1980s and into the 1990s "WAZOBIA" became an acronym for Nigeria's three largest ethnic groups. It was as if once these three groups are "settled"; all is well – part of Nigerian's political immaturity.

Observe the wily Maitama Sule. He speaks of "the Northerner" but not the "Easterner." Why? A new Sokoto Caliphate is being built:: How many Tivs have exercised rulership in "Northern Nigeria"? Are Tivs among Maitama Sule's "Northerners" who are endowed with leadership qualities or are they not? Are the various qualities listed by Maitama Sule mutually exclusive? Who providd the leadership of the Benin empire and the Old Oyo empire long before the Fulani came to oppress and suppress the Hausa kingdoms in the form of the Sokoto jihad? Was leadership in those polities provided by Maitama Sule's "Northerners?" What about the rulers of the states of the Niger Delta who held their own against the Europeans for centuries? Did they have no leadership qualities? What about the nicely balanced village democracy of the Igbo? Was there no leadership there? Maitama Sule is concerned to find some justification for the continued hegemony of the Hausa-Fulani in Nigerian politics by appealing to some supra-human endowments. For most of our thirty three years of independence these God-gifted "Northerners" have been at the apex of rulership in Nigeria. Behold where we are as a result! We must come to the conclusion that the gift of leadership has been exercised to mislead and misgovern. The most recent coup must be seen by Maitama Sule as part of the vindication of the wisdom of the northern elders. Babangida has stepped aside and perhaps down. Abacha has stepped on top!! The northern hegemony continues. But it does not necessarily conduce to peace. Why not?

The answer to that question is found in the fact that in a democracy men assay to affirm their own essence. All barriers to such affirmation must be removed if there is to be peace. What am I saying? This. To claim, as Maitama Sule does, that certain groups have been ordained by God to exercise rulership, and to proceed, as has been our experience thus far, to manipulate the political system so as to ensure that rulership is in the hands of these groups, is to negate vital ingredients of the democratic way of life. These ingredients are the right of any person or persons to offer himself/themselves for leadership positions in the body politic, and the right of the people, through the exercise of their voting right, to choose the person or persons who shall exercise rule over them. The Caliph in Sokoto may be the agent of Allah and so supra-humanly ordained to rule. That is perfectly acceptable in an Islamic theocracy. If the Maitama Sules of this world still believe in the existence of Nigeria as one geo-political entity, they must forget about those who are born to rule and begin to worry about how so to live as to be found worthy to exercise rulership – as per the verdict of the people of the Federal Republic of Nigeria. Nigeria is not an Islamic theocracy – and can never be. Part of the right of a people to affirm their essence consists of the right to choose who shall lead them.

Related to the issue touched upon above is that of the rights of Nigerian citizenship. These rights have been so denied and violated that the time has come to clearly define them. Not only must the rights of Nigerian citizenship be clearly defined, their violation must be made justiceable. Let me illustrate my meaning. I am an Isoko who has spent all his adult life in Ibadan. All my children were born in University College Hospital, Ibadan, and registered in Mapo Hall, Ibadan. All my tax has been paid to the government with its headquarters in Ibadan. Yet my children are not qualified for scholarships or bursaries from that government with headquarters at Ibadan. If I want that kind of service I am expected to go to Delta State to which I have never paid tax! When I sought a passport for my son born in Ibadan, I was asked to go to Oleh, headquarters of Isoko South Local Government, to get a letter of identity. Am I a Nigerian citizen or not? Can I have true peace in such circumstances? Can I affirm my own essence in circumstances such as this? Is there a way out?

There has to be a way out. I am a historian. I know how Nigeria came to be. I spent twenty six years teaching that though there are observable differences among the multifarious peoples of Nigeria, these peoples did not live in isolation one from the other in the pre-colonial period. The demands and challenges of daily living led to diverse forms of relations between neighbouring peoples. I introduced the teaching of a course entitled "Inter-group Relations in Nigeria" into the Department of History at Ibadan – as part of my effort to contribute something positive to the nation-building effort. Now forced into retirement by the Babangida regime, I am beginning to think that perhaps I was mistaken to have taken that attitude. Perhaps there is sense in speaking about the mistake of 1914. Perhaps the promised Constitutional Conference should address that mistake and correct it!

I fear, however, that such an attitude is simplistic. From my experience at the University of Ibadan and elsewhere, I know that all Nigerian groups are desirous of exercising hegemony over other groups. How grieved I have been when those who joined me in complaining about injustice based on ethnicity at Ibadan have gone on to perpetrate similar injustice in State universities. And as was earlier indicated, there can be no true peace without justice. So, separation will not necessarily ensure peace with justice. Here I want to make a call I had made before and for which I have suffered. I call for a Bill of Union. The conditions under which we can remain a single political unit must now be carefully spelt out. We were forced together in 1914. We proclaim that Nigeria is an indivisible political entity. But at no time have Nigerians agreed the terms for union. The time has come for us to agree such terms, and to make provision for enforcing those terms as part of state policy. Those who will be handpicked to the Constitutional Conference will do well to address this issue. **For us to have democracy with peace, we must have a Bill of Union to which all ethnic groups in this nation must subscribe.**

I would like to end this aspect of the lecture with a quotation from Pope John XXIII. For "states" in the quotation, read "ethnic groups."

> .....all states are by nature equal in dignity. Each of them accordingly is vested with the right to existence, to self-development, to the means fitting to its attainment, and to be the one primarily responsible for this self-development. Add to that the right of each to its good name and the respect which is its due.

Hear, Nigeria, hear.

Some Basic Principles of the Democratic Way of Life and Government

Let me now return, briefly, to those basic principles I said we need to cultivate.

(i) Evolution of a Political Culture: Political culture has been defined as "the set of attitudes, beliefs and sentiments which give order and meaning to a political process and which provide the underlying assumption and rules that govern behaviour in the political system. It encompasses both the political ideals and the operating norms of a polity." Part of our problem as we mouth democracy is that we have still not developed a political culture. We have not evolved a political culture because we have not given ourselves the opportunity to do so. Political culture is like a plant. It must be given time to grow to maturity. That is precisely what we have not been given – time to evolve and nurture our political culture. Only six years into independence, our politicians created a situation in which the Military took over governance of the nation. From 1966 January until now, November 1993, the Military have been in power but for four brief years. All here gathered will agree that the Military have not proved able to follow any rules in the business of governance. After all the resources spent on the 1989 Constitution, we are told that we are back to the 1979 Constitution. This kind of "forwarding and backwarding" does not allow for the growth of political culture.

Some may not agree, but I make bold to declare that the stability observable in the established democracies of the world is the consequence of the acceptance of the ground rules of the political game by all who decide to participate in it. Conversely, the political instability that has characterised our national life has been due to the complete absence of any agreed rules of the political game. The absence of these rules is explicable by the fact that we have not been given time by the Military to make our mistakes and learn from them. We, the peoples of Nigeria, have been constantly denied by the Army the opportunity of changing our government. True, our politicians have nearly always let us down. But so has the Army. Yet, the Army has constantly used its monopoly of the weapons of war to cower us into believing that military rule can be corrective. Corrosive, yes; corrective, hardly. What am I saying? This, that we will never evolve a political culture in Nigeria as long as we are cowards enough to permit military rule; so long as we allow the soldiers to see themselves as the only umpires in the political arena. The struggle for democracy must thus necessarily involve a rejection of military rule.

(ii) The Doctrine of Popular Sovereignty: On this matter Professor Ladipo Adamolekun has written as follows:

> ...sovereignty belongs to the mass of the population who may delegate its exercise either to its representatives, elected in free and fair election at fixed intervals or to both elected representatives and an elected president. There are two critical tests of the doctrine of popular sovereignty: **that the delegation of sovereign power to a president and/or representatives be freely determined by the citizens and that the free choice be made at periodic intervals.** (emphasis mine).

Time and time again since the elections of 1960, we in Nigeria have refused to accept these basic tenets of popular sovereignty. Consequently, we have failed to develop the related principle of accountability. The people's way of rejecting a government that has not performed satisfactorily is to reject it at the polls. If the polls are manipulated such that the people's expressed wishes are undermined; or if the polls are cancelled for whatever reason other than the people's wishes freely expressed, the principle of accountability is destroyed. So has it been in Nigeria. Once again military rule which does not depend on the popular wish, freely expressed, has undermined the principle of popular sovereignty. The struggle for democracy must strive to restore popular sovereignty.

(iii)The Separation of Powers: In a democracy there is usually a separation of powers as between the executive, the legislature and judiciary. Part of the tragedy of our political system is that for over twenty three years of our thirty three years of independence, we have run a system in which the Head of the Executive arm of government has also been the Head of the Legislative organ of government. Also during these years, the judiciary has tended, through various ways, to be subjected to severe pressure by the Executive. While I must salute the courage of some of our judges, one must decry the seeming helplessness of many others under civilian and military rule. I do not have to say more. The consequence is that we are yet to practise this principle of the separation of powers. The disgraceful behaviour of the National Assembly in the dying months of the Babangida regime provides ample evidence of the atrophy of that arm of government under executive pressure.

(iv) The Rule of Law: In Nigeria, the rule of law, a key principle in all democratic systems, does not exist. Some will accuse me of exaggeration. How can there be rule of law in a political system as unstable as ours has been? How many different constitutions have we operated in a mere thirty-three years? And now we are told there is to be yet another constitutional conference. If the organic law of the land is changed so frequently, that in itself could contribute to a major problem, especially under military rule under which the decision to change the constitution is not the expressed will of the people.

One could go on, but time is against us. What I have sought to do, in drawing attention to a few of these principles, is to establish the fact that democracy is a complex system. It is not just a matter of elections, important as elections are. It is a matter of attitude to one another; attitude to life itself, life that is lived in a community; attitude to Government; attitude to one's nation. The main burden of my submission is that we have not, thus far, cultivated a democratic attitude to life. We have not cultivated that attitude because we have not been allowed to cultivate it by all those who have exercised rulership over us. Top on the list of those who have made sure democracy does not thrive is the Army. Yet, we are told that the reason for the most recent intonement of "Fellow Nigerians" is so that democracy can be installed! The leopard is about to give birth to a kid!

I have just said that we have not been allowed to cultivate the democratic way of life. Our situation has been made worse by the fact that we have not inherited the democratic attitudes either. To this we must add that in our pre-colonial political systems, there were aspects of rulership that were not "democratic" as we understand democracy in our day. A village head was head for life. So were Obas, Emirs, etc. Let us here state, however, that there were built into many of our pre-colonial systems control against abuse of power. We know that in the Old Oyo Empire, a number of Alafins were made to commit suicide because they fell foul of the unwritten code of conduct and performance expected from them. Even at village level, the fact that virtually anyone who cared to could hang around the meeting place, had a way of keeping in check the elders-in-council, because the people could reject a decision reached by the village council of elders by expressing their disapproval on the spot. Running the affairs of a village, clan, or even the kind of kingdoms we had in pre-colonial Nigeria was not adequate preparation for functioning in a modern democracy. Then came colonial rule which, because it was imposed and sustained by force, could not be democratic. All that the British did was to export into Nigeria certain institutions which conveyed the impression that democracy was being installed. In reality those institutions could not work as they do in the established democracies, because they were not backed by that political culture which makes democracy work, by setting rules of the game which even the most highly placed must obey.

Remember, President Nixon? He had to bow to the political culture of the United States. In Nigeria a man can break all the rules observed in civilised societies and remain in power. In fact, has it not been the case that persons known to have directly looted, or to have aided in the looting of, the national Treasury have used their ill-gotten gains to corrupt the electorate? Do we not usually acclaim such persons as great Nigerians and heap chieftaincy titles and other honours on them? Do not even universities cultivate such people and award them honorary degrees in anticipation of fat donations? In our system cannot such person become President or Head of Government? Of course, yes. Reason? No rules of the game; no political culture. And no such culture will evolve so long as the guns rule the waves. Members of the political class who have agreed to serve in yet another military regime may argue, as they have done, that they are being patriotic; that they are seeking to influence the Military for good. They are entitled to their opinion – being prepared to grant others their opinion is part of the democratic culture. As for me, I am persuaded that by our failure – all of us civilians – to refuse to participate in any way whatsoever in military rule, we are contributing actively to a delay in the evolution of that political culture without which democracy cannot thrive. We will not win democracy for our nation without paying a price. That price could include resisting the lure and attractions of office under a system that, by definition, negates democracy. Let our youths, to whom tomorrow belongs, mark my words in this regard.

By Way of Conclusion

I have no intention of summarising what I have said in the body of the lecture. Rather, I must end by addressing the issue of: what lesson for the Nigerian youths? Just over two weeks ago, I spent some eight hours queuing for petrol. Just before it was my turn, a young man came with his jerrycan and sought to fill it before I was served. Another man, aged about 60 years, walked up to this young man, not as old as my first child, and told him that what he was seeking to do was wrong. Another young man roundly abused the sixty year old. He said, among other things, that the elders of the land had failed them, the youths. Why was petrol scarce? Was it the doing of the youths or of the elders? Who cancelled the elections – was it the elders of the youths? Thank God, he was prevailed upon to keep quiet and to respect age.

I presume that the young man had a point. We have, in a manner of speaking, failed the youths of our land. We have bastardised politics. We have set up money as the god to be worshipped. The end justifies the means. Elections are won more with money than with programmes and established rectitude. Our youths of today (i.e. 1993) have known only four years of civilian rule. The rest of their lives they have been under military rule – rule by force and by draconian decrees. How can we, in fact, talk about democracy to our youths? Where have they seen it practised? Is there a culture of democracy in the land?

We all know the answer to these questions. We do not have a culture of democracy. Our youths join various demonstrations in favour of democracy. But do they really know what it is they are fighting for? Of course, they have some ideas, some ideals. They want an elected government. They want the results of elections to be respected. They want military rule out, and civilian rule in. In a sense, a struggle for these ends is a struggle for democracy. However, as I have tried to show earlier, democracy is more than these outward and visible trappings. Democracy is about attitudes to the state and to one another; it is about relations between groups; it is about respecting the rights and aspirations of others and creating an environment for free and fair competition for office in the state. Seen in this wider perspective, what lessons can the youth learn from our current struggle for democracy?

As we seek to answer that question, it is pertinent to ask, "Why has it been so difficult to accept the democratic way of life in the area of governance"? Why do rulers want office? Why is it that once in office they do not want to relinquish power? I believe that we all know the answer, namely, love of filthy lucre. Put differently, covetousness. We all must flee covetousness. The reason our rulers want to remain in power, never mind what they tell us, is that they are covetous. They desire to steal more and more and more from the national Treasury. In Nigeria, that is all most of our rulers really are interested in. Steal and build 150 bedroom mansions at home and acquire all sorts of businesses and properties abroad, while thousands die of starvation and diseases caused by malnutrition. Covetousness is a killer. Once it possesses a man or woman he or she abandons reason, hardens his or her heart and pursues wealth till wealth destroys him or her.

I began by reading from The Holy Bible. Permit me to take you back to the greatest library in the world. In the book, 1 Kings 21, we have the story of Ahab and Naboth. Ahab was king of Israel. He desired to have Naboth's vineyard. Naboth was an ordinary citizen. The king offered to buy Naboth's vineyard or to give him another in exchange for it. Reason? Naboth's vineyard was close to his palace! The king who had servants and laourers in plenty who could go to his many other vineyards and bring unto him whatever he wanted, decided to ask Naboth for his only vineyard. Naboth refused for good reason: the vineyard was an inheritance from his father. He would not part with it. The king was sorely disappointed. He went home and refused to eat. When his wife, Jezebel, asked what was the matter, the king told her. Her reaction? "Are you not king of Israel?" Jezebel said to her husband: "get up and eat. I will give you the vineyard." She, the First Lady, was going to give the king a vineyard which was not hers! And so she contrived to have Naboth killed, and gave the vineyard to the husband. This is not meant to be a sermon. If it were, I could spend the next one hour on this story. Were you to go and read that chapter carefully, you would discover that the sin of covetousness led to ten other sins as follows: (1) Arrogance and pride on the part of Jezebel (2) Dishonesty and deceit (3) Malice (4) Treachery (5) Conspiracy (6) Slander (7) False witness (8) Connivance (9) Injustice (10) Murder. That is how vicious the sin of covetousness can be. And I am suggesting that covetousness is a major factor in our rejection of democracy. If our youths aspire to be democratic, they must flee covetousness. In the Students Union, in their Clubs and Societies, in their private lives, in their offices and businesses – they must flee covetousness. Otherwise, covetousness, when it is fully conceived gives birth to death. Make no mistakes about it. Those who have made covetousness their god have no choice in the matter, they will pay the full price – they will die what the Bible calls the second death. The love of money which the Bible says is the root of all evils is at the bottom of our refusal to seek and adopt a democratic system of government and of living. Those in office do not want to leave office. They do not want to give an account of their stewardship. Covetousness consumes them. Therefore, youths, flee covetousness.

I once, in a public lecture, said that some of the inscriptions we read on our lorries and buses and laugh at often convey fundamental truths. On that occasion I said that the inscription "No Condition is Permanent" may sound trite; nevertheless, it sums up the lesson of History. In the context of today's lecture, I do want to urge that we take to heart another seemingly trite inscription, "Live and let Live." If the democratic way of life is to become part of our system, we must accept to "live and let live." I referred earlier to Maitama Sule's address to his brothers of the North. "Live and let live" did not inform his position. If it did, he would not have sought to persuade his brothers that they have a divine calling to rule. Tolerance is of the essence of the democratic way of life. Today it may be me. Tomorrow it could be someone else – live and let live. I understand that the young man who was buried on 1 December, 1993, was a member of the Unibadan Jaycees. Why did he die? Because the principle of "live and let live" was jettisoned by the students of the University of Ibadan and those of the Ibadan Polytechnic. If a group of students would not join you in a demonstration for whatever reasons, is it democratic to seek to coerce them or malign them? Can you be democratic and yet refuse contrary opinion? Can you be democratic and not accept the right to disagree? Two weeks ago, I read in one of the dailies how members of cults at the University of Calabar attacked Christian students who were holding a crusade at the Abraham Ordia Stadium, knifed the male Christians and raped the female ones. The papers reported that torn female dresses and underpants littered the field! Yet those same students would quite unashamedly join a pro-democracy, anti-military rule demonstration! Live and let live is the name of the game of democracy. Our youths must learn to accept differences of views, of opinions, of strategies.

Tolerance as an ingredient of democracy goes further than that. In Canada, the French-speaking Canadians constitute a small minority. Every product made and marketed in Canada is inscribed both in English and French, even though the French speakers are a minority. Reason? So that the French-speaking Canadians can feel a sense of belonging. What happens in Nigeria? WAZOBIA rules the waves. In 1979 and again in 1983, not one of the political parties chose a presidential running mate from the minority ethnic groups. In 1993 the story was the same. Can it really be argued that there is no one fit to be Vice-President from among the so-called minority ethnic groups? I challenge any one to say Yes. So, why has this been the attitude? Because we have not yet learnt that it is impossible to "arise compatriots, Nigeria's call obey" when in fact our system does not believe that we are "compatriots." I have said it before, and I say it again at this point in our nation's history, that no one who feels that he is regarded as a second or third class citizen will Nigeria's call obey. We can only be true compatriots if we accept the principle of "live and let live."

When was the last time that a minority person was president of the Students Union of the University of Ibadan? Do we want to be democratic? Yes? We must learn to recognise merit and proven ability.

And reward the same via the ballot box. I served at the University of Ibadan for twenty six years. I know how elections are won even among the academics. The truth is that what we accuse others of doing at national level that is precisely what we do at the University of Ibadan level and at other levels, including the Delta State University level. The majority takes all. Inevitably, mediocrity is installed in high places. Democracy is a game of numbers, yes. The democratic culture – and this is what really makes democracy what it is in other places – must, however, also seek justice. A culture of democracy must make provision for all citizens to feel part of the nation. Our youths must learn this lesson. If they don't, the Nigeria of tomorrow will be no better than the Nigeria of today. Nigerians must learn to "live and let live."

As I draw this lecture to a close, I like to remind our youths of some of the happenings of recent months. In the final analysis money cannot buy life. There have been certain deaths that have stunned us. Some have died and taken other people's money to the grave with them. The ill-gotten wealth is now being used to develop already developed countries. Yet democracy was frustrated because certain key players in the political arena were hell-bent on staying in office to make money for themselves. Such persons forget that there is God who says "I am that I am."

In all of my experience, I have never seen the mass media of our country abuse any individual as certain key figures have been abused in the last ten months. Any lesson? I think so. To stay in office when a leader has lost the respect of the citizenry is worse than death. The democratic culture calls on such a leader to bow out of office. In Nigeria that is one thing we have not learnt to do. Nigerians have a knack for holding on to office even when it is clear that the entire nation is saying, "get out". I call on our youths to learn that the path of honour is to bow out of office when it becomes clear that the people one is serving have lost confidence in one's leadership. Refusal to quit often paves the way to developments which militate against the march to democracy.

I may have disappointed many who came expecting a learned disquisition on democracy. My apologies to all such persons. I have preferred to be ordinary and down to earth. In so deciding, I realise that I may be thoroughly misunderstood. That is a risk I must take. The bottom line, is the truth that, there is a God-lessness in the land that will destroy us as a nation, unless we repent and seek justice. Permit me therefore to end as I began by reading from the word of God, as found at the top of the opening page of this lecture.

12

NIGER DELTA: YESTERDAY, TODAY AND TOMORROW: (THE EMERGENCE OF THE PEOPLES AND POLITICS OF THE NIGER DELTA)*

The formulation of this topic is such that is bound to attract the attention of a historian, whose concern is to identify and analyse the occurrences of yesterday, in order to provide understanding of the developments of today and influence our planning for tomorrow. I therefore confess that my acceptance of the invitation to speak at this event was heavily influenced by the formulation of the subject of our discourse. I was, additionally, fascinated by the decision of the organisers to focus on the Niger Delta. I who stand before you am a Deltan, born and raised in that region of what is now Nigeria. My Ph.D thesis was on an aspect of Niger Delta history. And as of the time of this Discourse, I am teaching Niger Delta and Nigerian History at the Niger Delta University, Wilberforce Island, in the heart of the Niger Delta.

As we proceed to look at "The Niger Delta: Yesterday, Today and Tomorrow", it must be obvious that we can only do so in the context of the history of that region and of the Nigerian nation-state. We gave a

*This paper was originally a presentation at a Discourse on the Niger Delta: Yesterday, Today and Tomorrow organised by Lead City University, Ibadan, on the occasion of the University's Third Foundation Day, Saturday, 01 March, 2008.

definition of History on page 169. The reader is advised, at this point to read that definition again. Without History we do not know "who we are or how we came to be". Whether we acknowledge it or not, it is History that has given us our identity. It is History that has created Nigeria's ethnic groups; that made Nigeria a colony of Great Britain; that brought into being the Nigerian nation state. History produced the states that today constitute Nigeria. It is History that explains the phenomenon of "geo-political zones" that one of our political parties has adopted. It is History that has shaped the nature of Nigerian's politics. Boko Haram is a factor of our history.

The Niger Delta peoples occupied the territories where they are now found for centuries before the first Europeans came into that region in the late 15th century. The accounts of the early European traders do not refer to the region as a single entity called "the Niger Delta". Rather they reveal contact with Bonny, Kalabari, Okrika, Brass [Nembe], the Jakri [Itsẹkiri]. I dare to suggest that the expression "Niger Delta" came into popular usage following the publication of the late K.O. Dike's book, *Trade and Politics in the Niger Delta* published in 1956. Herein we find proof of the point made earlier on that it is History that give us our identity. Until the historian, lay or professional, chronicles the history of a particular group, the identity of that group does not become common knowledge.

What has been said above leads me to another: Why is it that the Lead City University located in Ibadan, Oyo State, is so interested in the Niger Delta that it chose to organise what it has daubed a Discourse on the Niger Delta: Yesterday, Today and Tomorrow, as it marks its third Foundation Day? History provides the answer to this question. The Niger Delta is part of the Federal Republic of Nigeria – a federation that is the product of our history. Mineral oil from the Niger Delta accounts for some 90% of Nigerian annual income. Yet that region is patently under-developed. In the days when cocoa, palm produce, cotton, groundnuts, hides and skins, were Nigeria's major export commodities, fifty percent of revenue derived from the exportation of these commodities went to the regions that produced them. In the case of mineral oil, the percentage is twelve and a half.

Oil exploration has polluted the waters and land of the Niger Delta, such that fishing – a major occupation of the peoples – is no longer as productive as it used to be. Youth restiveness and militancy in the region are partly because of the degradation of the land and waters of the Niger Delta. These restiveness and militancy, which sometimes manifest in the kidnapping of oil workers (European and Nigerian), and other forms of violence have become a source of concern to the federal government, as they result in a fall of the quantity of oil produced per annum. A fall in the quantity of oil adversely affects the nation's annual production. This in turn results in diminution of the money derived from oil production. That is why what happens in the Niger Delta is of concern to all of Nigeria. That is why, so I dare to guess, this Discourse has been put in place. Once upon a time, the peoples of the Niger Delta were on their own – separate, independent. Then came British colonisation of what we now call Nigeria, of which the Niger Delta is a part. What happens in the Niger Delta, especially in the oil sector, is of major concern to the Federal Government of Nigeria and Nigeria as a whole. This Discourse is partly proof of the point here made. It is History that explains why it is that a university in Oyo State considers it necessary to put a panel together for a Discourse on the Niger Delta. As of the year of this Discourse, Nigeria depends on the oil that comes out of the Niger Delta for its very existence. Yet that region is bereft of many facilities which other parts of the country enjoy – hence youth restiveness and militancy in the Delta region, with their attendant consequences. These consequences constitute a national problem. It is this problem that explains our gathering here at Lead City University, Ibadan, to rub minds on the subject The Niger Delta: Yesterday, Today and Tomorrow. The Isaac Boro and Ken Saro-Wiwa phenomena can have no meaning except in the context of history of the Niger Delta in Nigeria. Having made these preliminary remarks, we can now go to that aspect of the Discourse that has been assigned to me, namely, *The Emergence of the People and Politics of the Niger Delta.*

The Emergence of the Niger Delta Peoples

It is common knowledge that geographical and environmental factors play a key role in the history of human groups. This has been very true for the peoples of the Niger Delta. Time will not permit me to go into the details of the varying ecological zones within the Niger Delta itself. It is enough to say that whereas the entire Delta region, from the west (roughly the region of the Benin River) to the East (roughly region of the Andoni River), appears to be the same ecological zone with its seemingly endless rivers and creeks through which the waters of the Niger-Benue River system are emptied into the Atlantic Ocean, there are differences in the vegetation and soil types which have played a decisive role in the evolution of the peoples of the region. Professor E.J. Alagoa, a leading historian of the Ijọ of the Niger Delta, divides the region into three – the Western Delta, the Central Delta and the Eastern Delta. The Western Delta is characterised by salt water mangrove swamps in which agricultural production is very limited. The Itsẹkiri and Ijọ peoples who live in these areas have had to depend for food crops on the Central Delta and their hinterland neighbours. The Central Delta is in the fresh water zone and so could produce water yam, cassava, cocoyam, plantain, bananas, sugar cane, maize, ọkro, peppers. The vegetation of this area is characterised by high trees, oil palms and raffia palms, unlike the salt water zone where the dominant vegetation is the mangrove tree. The eastern Delta is similar to the western Delta in vegetation.

What has been the historical significance of the vegetational differentiation to which we have just drawn attention? Mutual interdependence among of the peoples who live in the area. The only means of movement on the waters of the Niger Delta in times past was the canoe. Canoes cannot be made out of the mangrove tree because it is much too hard. The central Delta provides the timber for canoe-making. It also provided certain food crops as indicated earlier. The salt water mangrove swamp dwellers were great fishermen. They also produced local salt from the aerial roots of the mangrove tree and from evaporation of salt water. Wherever the right type of clay was available, the people engaged in pottery and produced utensils for storage, cooking, eating and even grinding.

Whereas all the Niger Delta folk are engaged in fishing, the salt water dwellers were greater fisher folks than the fresh water dwellers who had to devote time to both farming and canoe-making. From ancient times, therefore, intra-and cross-Delta trade was a regular feature of life among the peoples of Niger Delta. Agricultural production from the Central Delta was never enough to meet the food requirements of all the Niger Delta. Therefore trade between the "water people" and the upland peoples (hinterland peoples) developed at an early stage. The Delta states of history came to be described as "The trading States of the Niger Deltas." This description was ascribed to them because of their involvement first in the Atlantic slave trade and then the palm produce trade of the 19th century. The truth, however, is that these two later trades came after that trade which was necessary for the basic survival of the peoples of the Niger Delta.

European Commercial Activities in the Niger Delta: Europeans first came in contact with the Niger Delta peoples in the late 15th century. It used be assumed that it was the coming of Europeans into this area that stimulated trade in the region. While the advent of European traders and the demand for slaves undoubtedly gave a new fillip to the trade of the region, we have just established the fact that for the peoples of the Niger Delta, intra-Delta and Delta-hinterland trade were necessary for their survival. Indeed, we can go on to state that what the demand of European trade did was to expand the Delta-hinterland trade that had been going on for centuries before the Europeans came. Trade followed already existing trade routes even as new ones emerged. Unquestionably, however, the Atlantic slave trade, which threw the Niger Delta peoples into the vortex of international trade had a great impact on the history of these peoples. They became well known in Europe and the Americas at a much earlier date than many other peoples in present day Nigeria.

The involvement of the Niger Delta peoples in international trade had the effect of transforming the various groups into what have become known in history as "City States" or "Trading States" of the Niger Delta. The works of K. O. Dike, E. J. Alagoa and G. I. Jones provide the details of this transformation. A major aspect of the transformation which took place was the emergence of the office of *amayanabo* or king in the Eastern Delta. In that part of the Niger Delta, land was scarce. Persons who found land suitable for habitation therefore occupied a special position in the settlement which developed on that land. Indeed the amayanabo was seen as the "owner", and therefore controller of the land. His lineage in time became the royal lineage which produced and still produces the head/leadership of the settlement. It was settlements of this type which grew to become the city-states of the Eastern Delta. The need to control the trade with the Europeans, and to organise trade with the hinterland, gradually increased the powers vested in the head of the settlement and, in time, transformed him into a ruler, a king, of a state that occupied a small area, but which had to be well organised to ensure success in trade.

We cannot go into the details here. But we must indicate that the transformation affected other aspects of the emergent state. Trade was organised by families. In the Eastern Niger Delta these families became known as “Wari” or “Houses.” The “House” as it emerged, was made up not only of persons related by blood, but also of persons who willingly decided to throw in their trading fortunes with a chosen family, as trade hands. In time, the House became a trading corporation presided over by the Head of the House.

The challenges of Delta-European trade, and the Delta-hinterland trade, which fuelled the former, affected the choice of who led the Houses and who led the state. Thus, although the *amayanabo* had to come from the royal lineage, the person who emerged as *amayanabo* was chosen on the basis of demonstrated ability as a trader and leader, including leadership in war, since competition for trade resulted from time to time in wars between states. Similarly, the person chosen to be the Head of the House was chosen on the basis of proven ability and service. And the *amayanabo's* “council of state” – if one may use the term – was made up of the Heads of the various Houses.

Two points need stressing here. **One**, the persons who held offices were elected by the people; they were deliberately chosen. They did not inherit their offices. **Two**, once chosen, however, they did wield real power. Thus the *amayanabo* had the power to regulate the trade between his people and the Europeans, to stipulate the conditions that had to be met by European traders who operated in his state. Similarly, the Heads of Houses had the responsibility of ensuring that the trade of their Houses prospered. The city-states that emerged include Nembe, Kalabari, Ubani (Bonny), Okrika, and later Opobo. Each of these was a sovereign entity and dealt with European traders as such. Relations between them were as between independent states.

No city-states of the type we have described here arose in the Central Delta, and among the Ijọ of the Western Delta. The Ijọ groups in this part of the Niger Delta did not have the challenge of European trade that served as the catalyst that transformed the *amaokosowei* (the town elder) into the *amayanabo* of the Eastern Delta state. However, in the Western Delta there emerged the Itsẹkiri kingdom which was on all fours with the city-states of the Eastern Delta, except that because of its different historical circumstance, the kingship was hereditary, and certain families produced certain offices of states. Details about the Itsẹkiri kingdom are available in my own works given in the bibliography at the end of this chapter.

In the years of the slave trade which flourished between the sixteenth and mid-nineteenth centuries, the Delta states and the Itsẹkiri kingdom became very wealthy and well known in Europe and the Americas, wither the slaves they sold were taken. Their wealth was seen in the kind of houses they built, the state they kept and their general life style. In terms of relations between them and their hinterland neighbours, there was no doubt that they had the balance of advantage. All Europeans goods first came to them. In terms of arms and ammunition, they had a virtual monopoly, and this meant that in the days of the slave trade, they could use their ammunition to terrorize the hinterland. Although I personally argue that in the days of the Atlantic slave trade the Delta states did not routinely wage wars against their hinterland neighbours for the purpose of obtaining slaves, they did both promote and facilitate wars in the hinterland through their control of arms and ammunition, and they were certainly the beneficiaries of increased wars in the hinterland, since such wars provided slaves for sale.

Their location at the coast made them the recipients of slaves that came from the hinterland for shipment to Europe, the West Indies and the Americas. In the three and a half centuries of the slave trade, the Delta peoples enjoyed dominance in trade that has left an abiding impression about their standing in comparison with their hinterland neighbours from among whom, so the Delta people saw it, their slaves came! In the Eastern Delta, these hinterland peoples were the Igbo and the Ibibio. In the Western Delta they were the Urhobo. I have argued in some of my writings that the actual enslaving (the taking of persons as slaves, the consequences of war, capture or trickery) was done more by the hinterland peoples themselves than by the Delta peoples; that once trade in slaves became profitable, the judicial system in the hinterland was abused, such that offences that did not before this time carry banishment or selling into slavery began to attract that punishment; that in my view what the Delta peoples did was to buy slaves of hinterland origin far more than they actually enslaved people of the hinterland. Additionally, the point should be made that the slaves who found their way to the Eastern Delta States came from much further in the hinterland than Igboland or Ibibioland. Be all this as it may, the Delta peoples are accustomed to saying that the hinterland peoples were their slaves. In terms of inter-group relations, therefore, the Delta peoples saw themselves as superior to their hinterland neighbours in the period before the effective establishment of

British rule. This feeling of superiority was to be gradually undermined and then reversed in the colonial period of Nigerian history and since Independence, as we shall see presently.

The European Trades in Palm Produce: As is well known by now, the Atlantic slave trade was effectively suppressed by the middle of the 19th century, although some slave trade did go on up to the 1860s in some parts of the Niger Delta. For the Delta peoples, the suppression of the slave trade resulted in a major re-ordering of their economic activities. The details of this re-ordering have become well known. The Delta coastal traders remained the middlemen between the hinterland producers and the European exporters as they had always been. In some ways, indeed, the new trade strengthened the position of the Delta peoples vis a vis the hinterland. Because the new trade was organised on a "trust system," it was the coastal traders who, having received goods in trust from their European customers, advanced part of these goods as trust to their hinterland customers. This gave them something of a strangle hold over the hinterland oil producers. Also, because of the nature of the palm produce trade, Delta traders began to establish depots in the hinterland and to marry hinterland women to strengthen relations with that hinterland. In a sense, then, the trade in palm produce had the effect of increasing social and other contacts between the Delta peoples and their hinterland neighbours. These increase contacts were not, however, always peaceful. As existing works make quite clear, the years of trade in palm produce saw considerable tension and conflict between Delta traders and hinterland producers. In the context of today's assignment, the point that has to be made under this sub-head is that this trade in palm produce did not, in itself, lead to a reversal in the balance of relations as between coast and hinterland peoples. The Delta states and the Itsẹkiri kingdom retained their preeminence.

British Colonisation of Nigeria and the Beginning of the Emergence of Niger Delta Politics

The details of how Britain colonised Nigeria in the period from 1850 to about 1914 are available in various works, including my own *The Fall of Nigeria*. In the Niger Delta, what became obvious to the British was that if they were to effectively control the trade of the region, they needed also to control the politics. This end was attained in the years 1885-1900, by which year the Niger Delta region had become effectively incorporated first into the Oil Rivers Protectorate (1885), then the Niger Coast Protectorate (1891) and then the Protectorate of Southern Nigeria (1900). This development lies at the very root of Niger Delta politics. The evidence available to us indicates that the Eastern Niger Delta sold more slaves in the slave trade era than any other part of West Africa. Similarly, when the trade in palm produce replaced the trade in slaves, this same region exported more palm produce to Europe than any other part of West Africa. This was because, among other factors, the Niger Delta peoples had full control of their trade in their own hands, namely, the hands of their chosen rulers. First the colonial state and then the Nigerian nation-state took this full control from their hands and so undermined their economic well being. Their interests could no longer be determined by their own local rulers. A distant authority in the person of a British administrative officer began to call the shots in matters affecting their economic welfare. Niger Delta politics from that time till now has been concerned with how to muster the political muscle that would guarantee its economic well being.

Administrative Arrangements and the Fortunes of the Niger Delta Peoples: If we had the time, we would at this point have gone into the various administrative arrangements which the British put in place and how these affected the Niger Delta peoples. Because we don't have the time or space, we take a rather giant leap from 1900 to 1939. In that year, the British divided Southern Nigeria into two regions – Eastern Region and Western Region. The North remained undivided. As it turned out, these two regions created in 1939 each had one ethnic group that was numerically larger than the others put together. Thus it happened that in the Western Region, the Yoruba constituted the majority, while the Itsẹkiri, the Ijọ, the Urhobo, the Isoko, the Ndosimili and Ndokwa constituted part of the minority groups in that region. In the Eastern Region, the delta peoples also became a minority in a region in which the Igbo predominated. For centuries the Delta people had been dominant in this part of what became Nigeria. All of a sudden, the wheels of fortune changed and they became the underdog in the politics of the region to which they belonged. It was a bitter pill to swallow. This was the beginning of the minority status which attaches to the Niger Delta peoples in Nigeria even till this date, and which is a key element in the politics of the region.

The Politics of Decolonisation: As Nigeria sought to regain independence from Britain, the minorities in the North, West and East became restive. The Political Parties which emerged - the Northern People Congress (NPC), the National Council of Nigeria and the Cameroon's (later National Council of Nigeria Citizens – (NCNC) and the Action Group (AG) turned out to be dominated by the larger ethnic groups (Hausa-Fulani, Yoruba and Igbo), even though the minorities joined one or the other. Partly for this reason and partly because of observable neglect in the provision of much needed infrastructural development, the minorities began to agitate for their own states. As early as 1947 Chief Harold Dappa Biriye, and others like-minded, established the Niger Delta Congress to agitate for a separate region for the Niger Delta. No one heeded their agitation. Other similar efforts also failed right up to Independence. Why? Because unless some of the majority groups supported the minorities, none of them could actualize their political dreams. No one who is not a minority can know how it feels to be denied just rights. It is this deprivation of just rights that lies at the heart of Niger Delta politics.

State Creation as a Strategy of War: In 1963 the minorities of the Western Region were given their own state, the Mid-West Region (later Bendel State). But even in that region the Delta peoples were again a minority! Then came the national crisis of 1996-67, following the revenge coup or 1967. When it looked like civil war would erupt, Lt. Col. Yakubu Gowon, as he was at the time, created twelve states, among them South Eastern State and Rivers State which had Ijọ in them. It was clear that Gowon created the states – South Eastern State and Rivers State – to detach them from Ojukwu's Biafra. Nor can anyone argue about the fact that the naval base which the Federal Government had thereafter in Port Harcourt was an important factor in the prosecution of the war against Biafra. Additionally, Nigeria needed the oil wells in the Delta region for financing the war. But what happened after the war? Decree No 13 of 1970 provided for revenue allocation such that the states got far less than they used to get before the war! Just at the time when the new sates needed funds to settle down, their revenue expectations were frustrated by the new arrangement. From that time until now the matter of revenue allocation has continued to be a sore point in Delta politics.

Oil Exploitation and its Impact on Niger Delta Politics: As at 1966/67 oil contributed only 18.26% to Federal Government revenue. In the fiscal year 1989/00 oil contributed 97.24% of Federal Government revenue. Most of this oil came from the "belly" of the Niger Delta. Since independence, various efforts have been made to plough back some of the revenue derived from oil to the areas of production. Bodies like OMPADEC and now NDDC have been set up to enhance the development of the Niger Delta region. And the vexed debate on 'Resource Control" constitutes evidence that no satisfactory solution has yet been found as to what share of oil revenue should be made available to the oil-producing Niger Delta peoples. Rather than face up to this issue, it is being assumed that the problems of the Niger Delta are the same as those of all oil-producing areas. They are not. To oil pollution, gas flaring and the destruction of the ecosystem must be added the high cost of, say building a good road in the Niger Delta region. To that must also be added the difficulties of water transportation, etc. The truth is that the soul of the Nigerian nation has, of today's (2008) date, very little place for the peoples of the Niger Delta. There can be no question at all that the peoples of the Niger Delta feel neglected by their own nation. If gas flaring was going on in the heart of Yorubaland, Hausaland or Igboland, would it have been ignored for this long? What did Odi do to be leveled to the ground by the Nigerian Army in peace time? Have not other people killed police men on duty? Did they receive the Odi treatment? When the Jedo (a town near Wari) incident took place, resulting in the death of many of those who were taking advantage of the vandalisation of pipe lines, the Federal Government refused to give any aid to the families of the dead, on the ground that the Jedo people were guilty of sabotage. International organisations rushed in aid. Nigeria refused to do so! Niger Delta people are expendable. When inter-communal fights lead to deaths and destruction of property in other parts of Nigeria, the Federal Government usually rushes in aid. But not so if the area affected is the Niger Delta! It is difficult to resist the conclusion that the Federal Government's attitude to the oil-rich region of the Niger Delta has tended to be informed by the fact that the Delta is peopled by minorities. This breeds added resentment which, undoubtedly, constitutes a major ingredient of the politics of the region.

Conclusion

What has been said in this presentation is not all that can be said. I have merely been asked to address the emergence of the peoples and politics of the Niger Delta. It is with that emergence that I have concerned myself. The nature of the politics of the Niger Delta is another matter. Nothing in what I have said is to be construed to mean that we of the Niger Delta do not have our own share of responsibility for the proper development of our own peoples. We cannot pretend that what money has been made available has actually gone into meaningful development. We know that it has not; that certain functionaries of government have been busy enriching themselves at our expense. We are guilty of neglecting the socio-economic development of our peoples, who wallow in unspeakable poverty and degrading conditions of living. In 2008 we still have persons who live in homes with walls made of cardboard! And that in a region of heavy rainfall. The fault is not in our stars, nor always with the Federal Government, that we are underlings! The truth is that because of the terrain in which we live, the bulk of our country men and women have no idea how bad things are with us, as witness the reactions of the Senators who visited the Niger Delta recently. Without such knowledge, it is difficult for policy formulators to come up with well-reasoned policies designed to positively impact the lives of our peoples.

What is the conclusion of the whole matter? This. History has made the peoples of the Niger Delta minorities in Nigeria. In that Nigeria, politics have tended to be a winner-take-all affair. Since the winners thus far have, at Federal level, been from the majority groups in the land, they have not been fully able to enter into the plight of the Niger Delta peoples. Youth restiveness and militancy are partly explicable in terms of this reality, but also in terms of the fact that the weakening of the powers of the leaders closest to the peoples has left the latter with little control over their own peoples. There is also the fact of fallen standards of education which make our youths unable to compete favourably with their better educated counterparts from the more favoured parts of the country. My plea? This: minority groups are Nigerians too. And where, as is the case with the Niger Delta region, these minority groups live in an area that yields ninety percent of the nation's wealth (as at 2008), they deserve a fairer deal than they have gotten thus far. Does Nigeria have the heart to put this fairer deal in place? That is the challenge of the future.

BIBLIOGRAPHY

- Alagoa, E. J. *The Small Brave City-State: A History of Nembe-Brass in the Niger Delta*, Ibadan and Madison, Ibadan University Press and the University of Wisconsin Press, 1964.
- Alagoa, E. J., *A History of the Niger Delta* Ibadan, Ibadan University Press, 1972.
- Anene, J.C. *Southern Nigeria in Transition,* London, Cambridge University Press, 1966.
- Azaiki, Steve, *Inequities in Nigerian Politics*, Ibadan, Y. Books, 2007.
- Dike, K.O. *Trade and Politics' in the Niger Delta*, London, Oxford University Press, 1956.
- Ikime, Obaro, *Merchant Prince of the Niger Delta*, London, Heinemann Educational Books, 1961.
- Ikime, Obaro, *Niger Delta Rivalry*, London, Longmans, 1969.
- Ikime, Obaro, *The Fall of Nigeria*, London, Heinemann Educational Books, 1977.
- Ikime, Obaro (Editor) *Groundwork of Nigerian History,* Ibadan, Heinemann Educational Books, Nigeria Ltd., 1980 (see chapters on the Western Niger Delta).
- Ikime, Obaro,*History, The Historian and The Nation*, Ibadan, Heinemann Educational Books, (Nigeria) Plc., 2006 (see Chapters 5, 9, 10).
- Jones, G. I. *The Trading States of the Oil Rivers*, London, 1963.
- Ogbogbo, C.B.N. "Nigeria-Niger Delta Relations" in Akinwunmi, Olayemi et. al (Editors), *Inter-Group Relations in Nigeria During the 19th and 20th centuries.*

13

HISTORY, CHANGING PATTERNS OF LEADERSHIP AND THE CHALLENGE OF DEVELOPMENT IN THE NIGER DELTA REGION*

Introduction

My choice of subject has been determined by what has become, for me, a major preoccupation, namely, getting my countrymen and women to come to a realisation that History holds the key to our understanding of how Nigeria has come to be what it is. "Without History," someone has written, "we have no knowledge of who we are or how we came to be, like victims of collective amnesia groping in the dark for our identity."[1] The utter disregard of our governments and peoples for our history has never ceased to amaze me. Even in an intellectual community such as that where this lecture is being delivered, there be many who have no knowledge of the history of their own people, let alone the history of the entire nation. Indeed, I have heard many say to me that History is a useless discipline! Nigeria is the only nation known to me that does not teach its history to its citizenry! Many of those who rule Nigeria today, have little or no knowledge of the history of those over whom they

*This was a lecture under the auspices of the Niger Delta University's Institute for Delta Studies, on 19 February, 2009.

exercise governance. Consequently, various governments have made mistakes that would have been easily avoided, had they paid appropriate regard to the history of the peoples that constitute the Nigerian nation-state. The Niger Delta problem, which is now the greatest talking point of our nation, is a product of history, and it is my earnest hope that you, my listeners, will at the end of this presentation, appreciate the place of history in the Niger Delta problem.

History and the Changing Fortunes of the Niger Delta Region

From the late 15th to the middle of the 19th century, the City States or Trading States of the Eastern Niger Delta and the Itsẹkiri kingdom of the western Niger Delta were among the most prosperous entities in the area that was to become Nigeria. They owed their wealth to their location along the coastline of what is now Nigeria, and their middleman role in the trade between European merchants and the peoples in the Delta hinterland. First, it was the trade in slaves, then the trade in palm and other produce. Bonny, for example, was reported to be the leading slave trading state in West Africa and metamorphosed into the leading palm produce trading state in the same region. Bonny, Nembe, Kalabari, Okirika, and the Itsẹkiri kingdom – each of these was an independent entity. Their fortunes were in the hands of their rulers, and what some have described as the "trading corporations" (the *wari* of the Eastern Delta) that made up each state. In the Eastern Delta, the rulers, known as *Amayanabo,* had to come from the founding lineage, and had to be persons who had proven themselves as successful traders, war leaders and good managers of men. In other words, leadership in the Niger Delta was not simply a matter of heredity. Proven service and merit were crucial elements in the choice of leadership.[2] Indeed as K.O. Dike's *Trade and Politics in the Niger Delta* and my own *Merchant Prince of the Niger Delta* show very clearly, in the heady days of the trade in palm produce, emphasis was laid far more on the ability to secure the economic well being of the state than on hereditary titles.[3] E. J. Alagoa's work makes it clear that it was wealth from trade that enabled certain individuals found dynasties in states like Bonny, Elem Kalabari and Nembe. Leadership was conferred on these persons because of demonstrated abilities.[4] We can therefore claim that in the period up to the 19th century, a major determinant of the fortunes of the Niger Delta States was the quality of leadership of each state. Because each of the states was small in size and population, it was easy enough to identify those who could lead effectively, and to give them the mantle of leadership.

As is well known, the fortunes of the Niger delta peoples and states began to change dramatically for the worse as from the 1880s when the British systematically established their colonial rule over the Niger Delta region. Apart from Lagos which fell to the British in 1851, the Niger Delta region was the first part of what became Nigeria to become part of the British Empire. This was not altogether surprising. Just as their location at the coast had brought the Niger Delta states into the vortex of European commerce, so that same location facilitated their fall to the British.[5] First, it was the Oil Rivers Protectorate (1885), then the Niger Coast Protectorate (1891), then the Protectorate of Southern Nigeria (1900) and then the Colony (of Lagos) and the Protectorate of Southern Nigeria (1906).Finally came the amalgamation of Northern and Southern Nigeria 1914.[6]

The effect of the developments summarised above on the fortunes of the Niger Delta region was profound. For a while, in the years 1880 - 1914, the people of the Niger Delta region saw themselves being used as local agents of British imperialism – as guides, political agents, interpreters, court messengers and court clerks as the British moved into the hinterland from the coast. The use the British made of Delta personnel in the early years of their move into the hinterland conferred on the coastal Delta region a form of transient dominance during the early years of colonial rule. Why do I use the word transient? Because as the British moved into the hinterland, so their merchants gradually moved into that hinterland for the purpose of trade. Also, the British began to build roads which linked the hinterland to the coast, thereby permanently destroying the middleman role that the coastal Delta peoples had played for centuries in hinterland trade with Europeans, and so completely undermining the basis of Delta economic prosperity. By the end of the third decade of the 20th century, whatever advantage the Delta peoples had enjoyed since the coming of the British disappeared. Their years of dominance were over, and the years of decline – economically and politically – were about to begin.[7]

Two other points need to be made. The first is that as the British established their rule over the Delta region and eventually all of Nigeria, so control over the region passed into British hands. Because the fame and fortunes of the Niger Delta depended on the control which their leaders had over the economy of the states, loss of that control meant loss of the fame and fortunes of the Delta States. In other words, the poverty and neglect of the Delta region, which has become a major issue in our time, set in with the coming of British colonial rule. The second and related point has to do with the seat of power. Until the advent of colonial rule, the seat of power – political and economic – was within each state. The choice of who wielded power lay with the people. Colonial rule altered all that. The effective power base moved from the various states to the headquarters of the colonial administration, and the headquarters of the divisions or districts into which the area was divided for administrative purposes by the British.[8] The people had little or no say in the choice of who ruled them at local government level until the 1950s! Indeed the Amayanbos of the eastern Delta States and the Olu of the Itsẹkiri (as he was until 1952 when his title was changed to Olu of Warri) were excluded from the 'native councils' and "native courts" which the British established.[9] Legal, formal leadership ceased to be inherent in the traditional institutions of the people. "Government" became increasingly distant from the people who could no longer impose sanctions on those who ruled over them, as a means of ensuring that they performed the duties expected of them. The people lost control over those in whose hands their fortunes and development lay.

The amalgamation of 1914 did not materially alter the status quo of the Niger Delta region. In 1939 the British decided to split Southern Nigeria into two – what became known as Western Region and Eastern Region.[10] The Delta region was by this arrangement split into two – the Ijọ of the Eastern and part of the Central Delta, as well as the Ogoni and other groups, belonged to the Eastern Region, while those groups referred to as the Western Ijọ, the Itsẹkiri, the Isoko, Urhobo, and parts of Ndosimili and Ndokwa, belonged to the Western Region. As always, the British did what they did for reasons of administrative convenience. Their interests, not the interests of the peoples of the respective regions, determined their action. We will not here concern ourselves with the issue of why the British broke Southern Nigeria into two, while leaving the much larger Northern Nigeria intact. Those interested in details can read existing works on the history of Nigeria under colonial rule.[11] In the context of this presentation, the vitally important point is that it was with the creation of Western Nigeria and Eastern Nigeria that the minority status of the Niger Delta region first became manifest. In the

Southern Nigeria of the pre-1939 years, the Yoruba and the Igbo were in the same region, and so there did not exist one single ethnic group that could lord it over all the others. In each of the two regions carved out of Southern Nigeria in 1939, there was one dominant ethnic group – Yoruba in the West and Igbo in the East. Nigeria moved into the period of the politics of decolonisation and then into independence with the Niger Delta peoples as minority groups both in the East and the West. The discrimination, deprivation, neglect, oppression and marginalisation about which these people cry out today were thus initially the product of colonial administrative arrangements. Thus, it was history that turned the Delta states that were once leading political and economic entities, into oppressed and impoverished peoples. As C.B.N. Ogbogbo so aptly puts it: "the status of the [Niger Delta] region...shrunk from being a major international player to an inconsequential local participant."[12] The Niger Delta people became oppressed minorities before they became oil producing communities. Tragically for us – for I am a Deltan – the fact that Nigerian oil wealth is located in the bowels of the Delta increased the oppression and neglect our people have suffered. The "majority groups" – Hausa-Fulani, Yoruba and Igbo – have fed fat on the wealth that comes from our land and waters, while ignoring our welfare, because they control the reins of the central government. Perhaps my listeners can begin to appreciate why I have titled this section "History and the Changing Fortunes of the Niger Delta Region." We need to know that history if we are to understand how things have come to be as they are, even as we seek to tackle the problems that confront us in the present.

History and Changing Patterns of Leadership

Leadership is a key factor in the development of a people, for "leadership is that which moves persons and organisations towards the fulfillment of their goals."[13] A leader is "one who leads others to the accomplishment of a common goal." Edmund Haggai of the famous Haggai Institute has stated that 'leadership is the discipline of deliberately exerting special influence within a group to move it toward goals of beneficial permanence that fulfill the group's real needs."[14] Even as we speak, a major challenge of leadership in the Niger Delta is the identification of the real needs of the common man in the region, and seeking to meet those needs in the areas, for example, of housing, education, health, transportation, power supply, etc. Let us therefore move on to an examination of how history has resulted in changing patterns of leadership and how the changing pattern of leadership has affected the development (or is it lack of development?) of the Niger Delta region.

Pre-Colonial Leadership: It was in the pre-colonial period that leadership was closest to the people. As already indicated, leadership in the pre-colonial period of the Niger Delta was in the hands of those who could ensure the prosperity of each state. The Amayanabo's council was made up of heads of "Houses" each of whom was an accomplished trader and war canoe "lord." In post-1848 Itsẹkiriland where there was no Olu, the leading men of the kingdom who dealt with the British were the most successful traders of their day. Jaja, a former slave, became king of Opobo because of his proven ability in trade and the management of men. Undoubtedly, development in that age was closely tied to the calibre of the men who held leadership positions.

Leadership in the Colonial Period: The colonial period was characterised by a series of amalgamations of Nigerian peoples who had, until that time, been completely autonomous. Additionally, colonial rule meant that ultimate authority was not in the hands of Nigerians, but in the hands of the British colonial officers. In the Niger Delta, colonial rule brought with it the virtual exclusion of the erstwhile leaders of the people from the local government system (by whatever name it was called) that the British established. Those who were appointed to the native councils or native courts where not responsible to the people and had very limited power for initiating local development. It was the British Divisional and District Commissioners, later Residents, District and Assistant District Officers, who called the shots. And development in the colonial period was tied to the plans of the British for the effective exploitation of the Nigerian peoples for the benefit of Great Britain. In colonial Nigeria, the Niger Delta was only relevant in so far as the ports of Forcados, Burutu, Warri, Sapele, Calabar and Port Harcourt were available to the British for the evacuation of produce. Throughout that period, for example, Patani, one of UAC's river ports, was only accessible by water. To travel to Port Harcourt by road one had to traverse Igbo land. Development in that period was not tied to the needs of our peoples but the needs of the British Consequently, little effective development took place outside the main centres of British political and economic activities. Even within the centres of British activities, development was geared towards the "beneficial needs" of the British rather than of our peoples.

Leadership in the Period of Decolonisation: For the purpose of this presentation, I regard the period of decolonisation as the years between 1952 and 1960 – the years of the Macpherson Constitution (1952); the Lytleton Constitution (1954) and the Independence Constitution (1959). Considerations of space and time compel me to assume that the main political developments of this period are so well known that I can afford not to discuss them in extenso. I had said earlier that it was with the creation of Western and Eastern Regions in 1939 that the minority status of the Niger Delta peoples was institutionalized. The politics of decolonisation deepened our institutionalization as minorities, and resulted in that developmental neglect and deprivation which have been our lot. A major feature in these years was the emergence of three political parties, each dominated by the same ethnic groups that dominated the three regions. The Northern People's Congress (N.P.C.) was by its very name a regional party that made no effort to contest elections outside the Northern region. The Action Group (A. G.) metamorphosed from a Yoruba cultural organisation, the Egbe Omo Oduduwa, and was to become mainly a Yoruba party, though it had as member such a prominent non-Yoruba personality as Chief Anthony Enahoro. The National Council of Nigeria Citizens, was at its beginning the most national in outlook. In 1952 its leader, the late Dr. Nnamdi Azikiwe, was denied the opportunity of being elected by the Western House of Assembly into the House of Representatives by what was clearly Yoruba chauvinism. Frustrated by this experience, Azikiwe went to his home base in the East and helped to create a crisis which led to the dissolution of the Eastern House of Assembly, and therefore the removal of Professor Eyo Ita, a Vice-President of the N.C.N.C. and the Leader of Government Business in the East until the Zik-inspired crisis. Eyo Ita, an Efik, resigned from the N.C.N.C. and formed the United National Independence Party (U.N.I.P.) made up largely of the non-Igbo members of the Eastern House of Assembly and their sympathisers. Even though right into Independence the N.C.N.C. continued to enjoy a measure of support in certain parts of Yorubaland, Edo, Urhobo and Isoko areas, as from 1952, that party began to be increasingly seen as an Igbo-dominated party.[14]

In 1956 the Western and Eastern Regions became self-governing. The attainment of self-rule by these two regions worsened the majority/minority syndrome in the two regions where the Niger Delta people were minorities. A major feature of Nigerian politics from those years into Independence has been the winner-take all stance of the party in government. For the Delta peoples this translated into observable neglect in terms of infrastructural and other developments.

What was the state of leadership in the Niger Delta region in these years? The traditional rulers at grassroots increasingly found themselves only able to wield non-constitutional powers. Local government which had slipped from their control under British colonial rule was not restored to them, even though they were held in high esteem by their peoples. Elected councils became instruments of local government. Such councils were heavily influenced by the political party in power in the region. By the 1950s there had risen a new crop of leaders in the region, namely, the party politicians, who contested elections into the Regional Houses of Assembly and the House of Representatives. Needless to say, this new class of leaders' could only bring about development in their own areas to the extent to which they could influence their parties at regional headquarters. On the whole, this new crop of leaders did not achieve much for the Niger Delta before independence.

This is the appropriate place to pay tribute to Chief Harold Dappa – Biriye, who led like-minded colleagues in founding the Niger Delta Congress in 1957. The main concern of this party was to urge the colonial government to create a separate political unit (region) for the Niger Delta. Although this aim was not realised due, among other factors, to the opposition of the majority groups, it helped in no small measure to draw the attention of the colonial authorities to the plight of the Niger Delta peoples, and so contributed to the setting up of a Commission of Inquiry to look into the fears of the minorities, and the means of allaying them, headed by Sir Henry Willinck.[15] Although the Commission confirmed the fears of the Niger Delta peoples, it did not recommend the creation of a separate State for the Niger Delta region. Instead, it recommended the setting up of a Niger Delta Development Board (NDDB) that would handle the problems of the Niger Delta. This Board, which was set up in 1959 and which operated up to the end of the civil war, did not achieve much in terms of development before it became moribund at the end of the civil war.[16] I suggest that one reason why the NDDB failed was that it was a federal government agency which had no real roots among the Niger Delta peoples. The leadership of the NDDB did not derive from the peoples of the Niger Delta that it was supposed to serve, and the Federal, West Regional and East Regional Governments with which the NDDB had to relate had no real commitment to the development of the Niger Delta. By the eve of Independence when the NDDB was established, the leadership that mattered was not in the hands of the peoples of the Niger Delta. Consequently, their development suffered notable neglect.

Leadership and Development Since Independence: If the politics of decolonisation worsened the marginalisation of the Delta Region by the powers that be, the first ten years of independence which saw Nigeria's first military coup, which in turn led on to the civil war, laid the foundation for that increased exploitation of the Niger Delta region by the federal government without any pay back. This led me to conclude in another work that "the soul of the Nigerian nation has had little place for the peoples of the Niger Delta."[17]

In terms of the attitude of the Federal and Regional governments, Independence did not bring with it any positive change in the years 1960-1966, except that the Midwest Region was created in 1963. As all who have studied the politics of the creation of that region would agree, the Midwest Region was created not out of a desire to do justice to the minority groups of the then Western Region, but out of the determination of the unholy alliance of the N.P.C. and the N.C.N.C. to emasculate the Action Group and reduce the influence of its leader, Chief Obafemi Awolowo. At any rate, the peoples of the Niger Delta remained a minority even in the Midwest, where the Edo became the new majority ethnic group.

Then came the creation of the twelve state structure by General Yakubu Gowon on the eve of the civil war. The Eastern Region was split into three: the East Central State to which majority of the Igbos belonged, the South Eastern State for the Efik, Ibibio, and other non-Igbo groups, and the Rivers State to which the Eastern Delta peoples belonged. The nation which had turned a deaf ear to the agitation of the people of the Niger Delta for their own state since 1957, suddenly granted their request. Why? Because the Federal Government was anxious to remove the South-Eastern and Rivers States from Ojukwu's Biafra and so win their loyalty to the Federal Government. In retrospect we can argue that state-creation in 1968 was far more part of the diplomacy of war than it was an act of justice and respect for the wishes of the Niger Delta peoples. Even so, it was a welcome development, in so far as it gave some hope to the Delta peoples that they would shortly be in a position to have a much greater say in the determination of their own destiny. This proved to be a forlorn hope.

Most commentators agree that in declaring session, Ojukwu was encouraged by the knowledge of the wealth that would be available to Biafra from the oil wells of the Eastern Delta! Conversely, Gowon was determined that the wealth accruing from the oil wells of the Niger Delta should be in federal hands rather than Biafran hands.[18] And there can be no doubt at all that the Nigerian civil war was fought and won using oil money derived from the Niger Delta. “To keep Nigeria one is a task that must be done” was the Federal Government’s radio jingle of the civil war years. The task could not have been done but for funds which Gowon’s government obtained from the oil which came from the bowels of the Niger Delta.

What was Nigeria’s “thank you” to the Niger Delta? It was “the Petroleum Decree No.5 of 1969, which stated inter alia that the ownership and control of all petroleum in, upon, or under any land within 200 miles limit of the Exclusive Economic Zone (EEZ) is vested in the Federal Government of Nigeria.”[19] The Federal Military Government thus deprived the Delta peoples of the ownership of their God-given resources. That was not all. Decree 13 of 1970 radically altered the revenue allocation formula as between states and federal government. In the 1950s when the agricultural products of three regions accounted for Nigeria’s export earnings, the percentage that went to the region was 50%. In the post-war arrangements, oil producing areas were to get a percentage that ranged between 1.5% and 3%. In the sharing of funds from the Distributable Pool, 50% was to be distributed on the basis of equality of all states and 50% proportionately on the basis of population.[20] Since the population of the Hausa-Fulani, Yoruba and Igbo states was higher than that of states to which Delta people belonged, this meant that even in the sharing of Federal Government funds derived from the Niger Delta Region, the Niger Delta peoples got less than the Hausa-Fulani, Yoruba and Igbo peoples! History had created a situation in which the Military took over political power in 1966. History had created the civil war which further entrenched military rule. Military rule was necessarily unitary in nature, given the command structure of the Army. In Nigeria’s forty eight years (as of 2008) as an independent nation, the Army has ruled it for nearly thirty years. All the military Heads of State but one have been from the Northern part of the country which does not produce one teaspoonful of oil. The other non-northern military head of state is

Yoruba. None of these heads of state rose above the selfish interests of the majority groups to purse a policy of just and equitable development. Nigeria, on paper a Federal state, has tended to pursue a policy of "fiscal unitarism" which enables the Federal Government to control the bulk of the nation's wealth, and to deny the Niger Delta, from where 90% of the nation's wealth was then derived, a fair share of revenue and development.

In 1996 Nigeria was made up of thirty six states and the Federal Capital Territory (FCT). Of these states twenty seven are not oil producing. Of the remaining nine, Imo State and most of Ondo State (both of which produce some oil) do not belong to the Niger Delta terrain and so do not have the same challenge of development. Were the principle of economic viability applied, quite a number of these states would not have been created. As it is, since every state can receive from the Distributable Pool 50% of available funds on the principle of equality of states and the other 50% on the basis of population, these non-oil producing states depend for their existence on revenue derived from oil controlled by the federal government. The more the number of states, the less the revenue that accrues to each state from the Distributable Pool. What this has meant for the Niger Delta peoples is that they have received less revenue as more states have been created since 1970. Even as of the date of this lecture, there are agitations for more states to be created. Were such states to be created, the states of the Niger Delta will logically suffer loss of revenue.

Permit me here to make a point which some might consider facile. In the last administration, the President was himself Minister for Petroleum. In the present administration we now have a Petroleum Minister who is from the northern part of our country. Was our mineral oil flowing from the Chad basin, the Lagos lagoon or from the heartland of Igbodom, will the President chose an Ijọ man as Petroleum minister? But then we, Deltans, are minorities. For that reason, we are expected to be content when given a junior minister. That history, which made us minorities, continues to haunt us and to deprive us of just rights. The loss is ours, but the shame is that of the Federal Government that can be this insensitive. Clearly, thus far, leadership at the federal level has failed to rise up to the challenge of equitable development. A ministry has now been created to pay attention to the Niger Delta. Will the "Big Three" allow the ministry to work for equitable development? We wait to see.

Day after day we hear talk about that militancy which has caused the attention of the international community to be focused on the Niger Delta region. It is easy enough to condemn the youths of the Niger Delta and their methods. It is not my purpose in this presentation to go into details of militancy in the Niger Delta from Isaac Boro's "Niger Delta Republic" to Kenle Saro-Wiwa's Movement for the Survival of Ogoni People (MOSOP), to the youth groups currently in operation in the Niger Delta.[21] It is clear that the youths are reacting to the increasingly degrading conditions in which they and their people have had to live and are living. Existing works provide all the horrid details of what oil exploration and exploitation have done to the land, waters, and atmosphere of the Niger Delta.[22] How is it the Federal Government has been unable to stop gas flaring all these yes, whereas the oil companies know that in their home countries such a phenomenon would not be tolerated? Why have the Federal and State Governments been so easily satisfied by the tokenism of the oil companies? Is it not because the oil companies line the pockets of the officials who then turn a blind eye on their activities? I repeat: leadership both at federal and state levels has failed to live up to the responsibility and challenge of equitable development.

The Niger Delta problem has been with us since the 1950s. There was the Niger Delta Development Board which ceased to function by the end of the civil war. It was re-established in 1976 and metamorphosed into the Niger Delta Basin Development Authority (NDEDA) in 1978. It is instructive that in 1978, ten other river basin development authorities were set up alongside the NDEDA.[23] The message was clear enough: there is nothing special about the Niger Delta. There are rivers elsewhere in the country whose basins needed development. But those river basins did not produce the mineral oil that provided the revenue upon which Nigeria depended. What happened in 1978 was part of the mindless insensitivity that has characterised federal government attitude to affairs of the Niger Delta region.

The NDEDA was followed by Oil Mineral Producing Area Development Commission (OMPADEC) in 1992. And OMPADEC was succeeded by the Niger Delta Development Commission (NDDC) in 1999.[24] On the face of it, the Federal Government has constantly sought to do something about the Niger Delta through these various commissions. That we are still talking about Niger Delta problems today is the evidence that these various efforts have failed to provide adequate and lasting solutions to the Niger Delta problem. Commentators have drawn attention to the manner in which members of these Boards were appointed, poor funding, external interference and intervention from high places.[25] Since most of what the Boards have had to do involves the award of contracts, the so-called "Nigerian Factor "has seen to it that these contracts were awarded to favourites who did not have to perform.

Let me make myself clear. I am not saying that these bodies have not done anything. They have. It is clear, however, whatever they have done has not been enough. Permit me here to raise just one issue. Take the state of the road from Warri to Port Harcourt. Agreed that a dual carriage way is now being built. Those of us who use that road have seen how the NDDC has often intervened to repair sections of the road. This road is a federal road. There are federal roads in other parts of the country for which the Federal Government is responsible – hence the Federal Road Maintenance Agency (FERMA). When the NDDC intervenes to make the Warri-Port Harcourt road passable, it expends funds which could be used for other purposes. It does so because FERMA does not rise up to its responsibility. We are here once again dealing with the issue of leadership and how responsive that leadership is to problems of the Niger Delta region.

Justice demands that we remind ourselves that since 1967 when the Rivers State was created; since 1991 when Delta State was carved out of the former Bendel State, and Akwa Ibom State was carved out of the Cross River State, and since 1996 when Bayelsa State was carved out of the Rivers State, there has been leadership in the hands of indigenes of the Niger Delta region. The same is true for the local governments in the various states. Granted that the states of the Niger Delta region have not received the quantum of funds that they ought to receive, were the derivation principle more equitable, it is a moot question whether the governors, commissioners, local government chairmen and councillors have devoted ALL of the funds allocated to them to the development of their areas of authority. Here, we are faced with a phenomenon to which we hardly pay attention. We talk about democracy. And we see democracy almost only in terms of political parties and elections. Once elections are held and persons are voted (or "vote" themselves) into office, we consider that democracy is at work. Democracy entails far more than political parties, elections, parliament (by whatever name called) ministers and such like paraphernalia.

Democracy has to work within the context of a political culture developed over time. Political culture is "the set of attitudes, beliefs, and sentiments which give order and meaning to a political process and which provide the underlying assumptions and rules that govern behaviour in the political system. It encompasses both the political ideals and the operating norms of a polity."[26] As Walter Rosenbaum reminds us, political culture has to do with both the individual and the collectivity, i.e. the people as a group, and has an essentially psychological focus. At the personal level, political culture has to do with "all the important ways in which a person is subjectively oriented towards the essential elements in his political system... ***what he feels and thinks about the symbols, institutions, and rules that constitute the fundamental political order of his society and how he responds to them***" (emphasis mine). At the level of village, town, linguistic group, state or nation, political culture determines how the people evaluate their political institutions and officials, how they respond to policy decisions by government(s). It determines to which unit or group a member of the polity feels "a strong loyalty, obligation and duty." It involves one's perception of "the rules of the game." Rosenbaum points out that the rules of the game are not necessarily identical with the laws of the land. In other words, in the context of political culture, it is possible to obey all the laws and yet fall foul of "the rules of the game."[27] Nigeria is yet to evolve these "rules of the game". That is why our political leaders and politicians can and do get away with all manner of misdemeanor to the detriment of the body politic, the Niger Delta included.

The unspeakable corruption which has marked our practice of democracy thus far has been possible only because the rules of the political game – which are established by a political culture – have not yet been laid down. Undoubtedly, the creation of states in the Niger Delta region has facilitated the development of the region. We can all see that. But we can also see that loads of our money have been siphoned into private bank accounts by fellow Deltans who have held and are holding political office. Leadership, even at state and local government levels, has also failed us. This failure has been the more damnable, more despicable, because those involved are our flesh and blood. Nor is that all.

When it comes to relations between oil companies and various Delta communities, leaders of different hues – traditional rulers, youth leaders, self-proclaimed leaders, leaders chosen by the various fora in operation, local government chairmen, state commissioners and others more highly placed – have sacrificed the general good on the altar of personal greed. In the event, the oil companies have been enabled to turn a blind eye on the problems of the area – deforestation, forest degradation, pollution of the waters and atmosphere, poverty, unemployment, inter and intra-communal clashes, youth restiveness, threat to lives and properties, displacement of villages and communities, fear and insecurity, increased cost of living.[28] Permit me to quote from Dr. Steve Azaiki:

> How do we expect development when people cause problems in their communities? and use them to garner the communal wealth for themselves in order to own a fleet of cars, houses, foreign bank accounts and to send their children overseas while the suffering masses are overwhelmed by the existential politics of daily survival?[29]

Do we not know that there be quite a number of Deltans whose new-found wealth has come to them at the cost of the blood of our youths? Are there not "big men" behind some of the kidnappings about which we read in the newspapers? Can such "barons" be genuinely committed to ordered development which could make their much advertised leadership positions obsolete? So help us, God. If we are to be true to ourselves we have to admit that the Niger Delta crisis is largely the result of the failure of leadership at all levels.

The Challenge of Development

I am not an expert in planning. I do however, have certain ideas which I would like to share in and with this Forum. I have heard of a Master Plan for the Niger Delta. But I have not seen it, let alone read it. What follows are my thoughts, some of which, I hope, may be useful as we all brainstorm.

1. Collective Leadership: It is my view that for the Niger Delta to enjoy planned development, we need collective leadership at the state and local government level. Some of this already exists in the various bodies set up. My collective leadership groups would consist of youth leaders, community leaders, and traditional rulers in the various communities who would work with the state government officials, specialised government agencies and local government officials. The crucial point here will be that communities would be far more involved at the planning stage than they have been thus far. Each community should be able to call on its elite to be part of this involvement. My thinking is that instead of government telling the communities what it would do for them, the communities should be encouraged to tell the government what their needs are. When decisions are taken and projects initiated, the local communities, through their nominees, should be part of the monitoring of the projects.

2. Identifying The Needs: It is my earnest desire that there should be conducted a "census" of existing infrastructures and other amenities. Which of the various communities are now served by motorable, all season roads? Which communities need to be linked to existing roads? Which communities have schools, hospitals, health centres, maternity centres? Which communities have potable water supply? Which have electricity? My thinking is that when all the information has been gathered, it would be possible to identify the needs that exists in the area of infrastructures and amenities. State governments and local governments can then proceed each year to agree what can be done for specific communities such that over a period of time, basic needs would be met. If the state governments are consistent in following the agreed plan, communities would be willing to wait for their turn. The idea would be for state governments to be quite clear what can be done within an agreed time span, such that development is spread equitably in the rural areas. Here that collective leadership about which I spoke above should come into play.

3. Education: The difference between me and my age mates in the village is that I have education. Education is the vehicle for upward social mobility. I am currently teaching at the Niger Delta University on Wilberforce Island, Bayelsa State. The level of literacy of the undergraduates I am teaching is abysmally low. The same, I fear, is true for other institutions. In Amassoma village, the closest community to the university, a large number of children of school age are not in primary school. These children will be condemned to the same style of life as their illiterate parents are living. This is unacceptable. We must remember that we are minorities, and that the only way we can compete effectively with other groups is to have sound education. My cry is that government, communities as well as individuals with the resources, should build good schools in the difficult rural terrain of the Delta. If teachers are to be attracted to such schools, free accommodation in decent quarters should be provided, and the classrooms themselves should be learner friendly. Scholarships should be provided for bright but poor children. We need to invest heavily in the education of our children from primary to tertiary levels. In my own opinion, in the rural and even urban areas, education is in a crisis. We must now address that crisis. Government, churches, societies, individuals and, of course, the oil companies should join hands in tackling what is an urgent need in the Niger Delta. We have fallen behind our fellow Nigerians. The time to take urgent action is now. Government may need to set up a study group on the state of education in the Delta region, especially in the rural areas. We must lift up the level of living of our rural population through the provision of quality education. This will involve massive teacher training and re-training and the provision of modern teaching aids.

4. Health: Given the state of transportation facilities in the Niger Delta region, each state government will need to decide how health facilities can be sited such that people do not have to travel too far to reach a hospital, health centre, maternity centre, and so on. Once the "census" I spoke about earlier has been conducted, it should be possible to decide where to site health facilities in the rural areas, as in the towns, in an equitable manner. Local governments should be required to hire health workers, whose jobs would be to visit the rural areas and encourage healthier living habits. In oil-producing areas, government should require that oil companies be part of health projects by contributing an agreed sum annually.

5. Potable Water: There can be no doubt at all that provision of potable water is a crying need in many parts of the Niger Delta. Given the fact that the natural water supply in most parts of the region has been polluted as a consequence of oil exploration, there is a need for a comprehensive plan for the provision of potable water. This is an area in which government and the oil companies should put their heads together. The estates in which the oil company staff live have potable water. The people around them don't. If the governments of the various states, the Federal Government and its agencies and the oil companies can only muster the political will, mega water schemes can be in place, and potable water piped to the villages in the same way as crude oil is piped. It is "do-able." Those whose land provides the nation's wealth have a right to potable water.

6. Youth Employment: Part of the answer to youth restiveness is youth employment. This is an area that needs careful thought. It is a multi-sided problem. Part of the anger of the youths is that the workforce of the oil companies is loaded by persons from outside the oil-producing areas. This can be explained. Because senior positions in oil companies are occupied by non-indigenes of the area, it is the latter who sit on interviewing boards, and employ their own people. This practice needs to be deliberately halted. I have been talking to my students about the need to obtain requisite qualification to work in the oil companies. But the oil companies can be required by government not just to give scholarships to persons from oil producing areas, but to offer such scholarship holders specific and relevant training after graduation from universities. This is what many other companies do. Again, government must muster the will to put such a scheme in place. Appropriate training can also be provided for non-university graduates to fit them for certain kinds of work in the oil companies. It should be possible to negotiate a certain quota system with the oil companies.

Employment in the oil companies should not be the only way of providing employment. The region produces timber, fish, cassava, palm produce, plantains. Cannot plywood and other timber-related factories be set up in this area? Cassava-based industries are springing up outside the Delta. Why can't they be established in the Delta? Palm oil processing companies would have the needed raw materials. Indeed if the polluted soil can be chemically replenished, there are areas that can support palm plantations and factories. The truth is that both private enterprise and government as well as the oil companies have not set their minds on these areas of development. And I am pleading that the time to do so is now.

There is a season each year in which plantains and bananas are plentiful in the region. Universities in the region should begin research into how to preserve these products for export. Although I have no expertise in this area, I am persuaded that scientists can undertake research that can come up with results that, in the long term, can provide the basis for setting up industries that can use our plantains and bananas as base raw materials. Here as in other areas, government, universities, private enterprise and the oil companies can and should co-operate.

There is much talk about small scale industries in the country. How much of this talk is addressed to the youths of the Niger Delta? What schemes are on ground? Who is pushing these schemes? How much rural banking is there in the Niger Delta region? Questions, questions, questions. These questions are pointers to what is possible. The plea is for the development of the rural as well as non-rural areas in the oil-producing region. If we can find work for our youths in the villages, they will be encouraged to stay back and to refrain from that restiveness that has made the Niger Delta notorious.

7. **Housing:** Those who know the Niger Delta well will agree that the area of housing is a major challenge in the mosquito-infested region. I do not even know what to say under this head. The governments of states in the Niger Delta together with the Federal Government, the oil companies and others need to address this issue pointedly. How can we get the people who live in this difficult terrain to own better dwelling places? Perhaps a few pilot projects can be undertaken. Architects and developers can be brought together to study the terrain and see how cheap but durable housing can be found for the millions who live their lives in their miserable dwelling places. I have seen so-called houses, the walls of which are made of cellophane sheets! The challenges in this area are enormous. Those challenges should force us to react imaginatively. In this matter the people cannot help themselves. Help must come from outside. And I am saying that if the powers that be advert their minds to this problem, they can set up a study group that can come up with some kind of model for housing in this area. Of course all of this will cost money. But that money is in the bowels of the region. That is the justification for the expenditure that will be necessary for developing the kind of models being here advocated.

8. **Energy:** How many of the estates where the oil company workers live are without electricity? Wherever such estates are sited, electric power is provided. It follows that, given the political will, it is possible to provide electricity in the Niger Delta. Can you imagine what a difference it would make to the lives of the villagers of the Niger Delta if there were uninterrupted power supply? What is more, if industries are to be established in the rural areas of the Niger Delta, a steady supply of electric power is a sine qua non. In my view, enough money is being made out of the oil of the Niger Delta to justify whatever financial outlay will be necessary to provide electricity in the region. It could require the combined input of the federal and state governments as well as the oil companies to ensure electric power supply in the rural communities of the Niger Delta.

9. Security: When my friends at Ibadan hear that I am teaching at the Niger Delta University in Bayelsa State, their first reaction is that of apprehension! They hope I will not be kidnapped! Militancy has created a reputation for the Niger-Delta – a reputation of insecurity. The answer to militancy lies partly in putting into effect some of the projects suggested in this section of my presentation. Let me at this point dare to plead with the federal might to beware what methods it applies in cracking down on militancy. I am against violence and would wish our youths were putting their energies to more productive use. The Federal Government must, for its part, accept responsibility for that negligence that is partly responsible for youth restiveness in the Niger Delta. How can our youth see Abuja built with resources from their oil, look at their own environment and not be angry? Cannot the Federal Government and the oil companies build mini Abujas in different parts of the rural Niger Delta as a token of their gratitude to the region that produces the wealth of the nation? What did Odi do to be razed to the ground by the federal might? Odi youths killed some policemen. Have not policemen been killed in other parts of the nation, precisely in Lagos by members of Odua People's Congress? Why was Federal Government reaction to the Odi episode so vastly different from its reaction to police killings in Lagos? Because Odi is in the delta, and the Delta people are minorities. Because we are minorities, the Federal Government considers we are expendable, we are but cannot fodder! If the security position in the Niger Delta is to be improved, both sides must be persuaded to re-think their strategies.

By Way of Conclusion

I am not sure, as I draw this presentation to an end, what you will be taking away from it. One point that I have tried consistently to make is that the history of Niger Delta–Nigerian relations is that of the oppression of the former by the latter. The Nigerian nation, dominated by the Hausa-Fulani, Yoruba and Igbo, has turned a blind eye on the crying needs of the peoples of Niger Delta. We of the Niger Delta should brace up to the fact that we need to take our destiny in our own hands. The governments of the states within the Delta region should begin to undertake projects that will show the federal government what is possible. If we harness the resources now available to us prudently, we can undertake projects that can improve the quality of the lives of our peoples. Let us show the federal government what is do-able.

There is a lesson that we need to learn from Nigerian history. Each time a new state is created, a new majority group emerges which proceeds to unleash on the new minority all the oppression and deprivation about which it had complained when it was part of the minority. We have seen this phenomenon in the states in the Niger Delta region. The Ijọ, for example, never case to tell us that they are the fifth largest ethnic group in the country! Indeed, sometimes even the Federal Government speaks and acts as if once Ijọ demands are met, the Niger Delta is satisfied. This is a dangerous trend that can fuel even more tensions and conflict. There will always be majority groups in any region or state. The test of statesmanship is in ensuring that even the minorities have provided for them those infrastructures and amenities that make life meaningful. The majority groups in the Niger Delta will do well to pay due heed to the epigram that used to adorn lorries in the 1950s: *Live and let live.*

Thus far our leaders at every level have failed us. They have failed us because they do not see themselves as owing the positions they occupy to our goodwill. Many have bought their positions, and are merely recouping their investment. Character and proven ability which were important in traditional society no longer count in today's situation. Because of the poverty of our peoples, the rich can buy their way into office. Once in office they have little regard for the people they are paid to serve. The Niger Delta problem cannot be solved without a change in the attitude of those who lead at the various levels, most especially in the Niger Delta itself. Our governors, our civil servants, our commissioners, our traditional rulers, our local government chairmen and their councillors, our teachers at all levels and all others who lead in one way or the other must come to accept that self-enrichment never translates into societal prosperity. So long as the larger society is impoverished and discontented, so long will there be disaffection and tension that can erupt without notice into violence. The rich can never enjoy their wealth in the face of pervading insecurity. We need a radical change in the attitude of our leaders to their own people. When our own people ignore our real needs, to whom do we cry? By all means let us seek greater federal government commitment to the development of the Niger Delta region. Let us, at the same time, husband and expend the resources presently available to us in such a manner that they would uplift the standard of living of our peoples.

You would have observed that I have said nothing about resource control. This is not because I do not consider the subject important for this discourse. Of course, it is crucially important. The Federal Government has cheated us of resources that properly belong to us. The derivation argument could go on endlessly. In the meantime, I urge the Federal Government to do what it can do without constitutional amendments and tortuous legislation, namely, intervene meaningfully in specific areas of infrastructural and other development. It must also change its attitude to the oil companies that have not sufficiently invested in the re-building of the region they have devastated. As Azaiki put it "Although the activities of oil operators take place in territories belonging to [the Niger Delta] states, they are prevented by law from penalising polluters and destroyers of the environment"[30] The Federal Government can intervene in a number of the areas of action to which attention has been drawn in this presentation.

Mr. President has created a ministry to look after the affairs of the Niger Delta region. As we do not yet have details as to how the ministry will function, it is difficult to comment meaningfully. This one thing I am willing to say. The creation of the ministry is some indication that Mr. President seeks to depart from the old grooves. Let the point be made, however, that what will determine whether or not the creation of the ministry is worthwhile is how it functions and what it achieves. We wait to see.

NOTES

1. Ikime, Obaro, *History, The Historian and the Nation (The Voice of a Nigerian Historian)*, Heinemann Educational Books (Nigeria PLC, Ibadan, 2006), Chapter 10.
2. See Alagoa E. J. *A History of the Niger Delta*, Ibadan University Press, Ibadan, 1972.
3. Dike K.O. *Trade and Politics in the Niger Delta*, Oxford University Press, London, 1956.
4. Ikime, Obaro, *Merchant Prince of the Niger Delta*, Heinemann Educational Books, London, 1968.
5. See for example, Alagoa E. J. *A History of the Niger Delta*, Onyoma Research Publications, Port Harcourt, 2005, 117-118.

6. See Ikime, Obaro, *Niger Delta Rivalry*, Longman, London, 1969, Chapters 4 and 5.
7. The issue here summarised is discussed in detail in Afigbo, A.E., *The Warrant Chiefs,* Longman, London, 1972.
8. Anene, J.C. *Southern Nigeria in Transition*, Chapter 6.
9. Crowder, Michael, *The Story of Nigeria*, Faber and Faber, London, 1978, Chapter 14.
10. Crowder, *The Story of Nigeria*, Chapter 14.
11. Ogbogbo, C.B.N., "Nigeria – Niger Delta Relations 1960-1967" in Akinwumi, Olayemi et al (Editors), *Inter-Group Relations* in *Nigeria During the Nineteenth and Twentieth Centuries*, Aboki Publishers, Makurdi-Ibadan-Abuja, 2006, p. 560.
12. Bennis, Warre, *On Becoming a Leader*, Addison-Wesley, Menlo, California, 1989.
13. See for example, Crowder, Michael, *The Story of Nigeria*, Chapter 15.
14. Ogbogbo, C.B.N., "Nigerian-Niger Delta Relations" p. 555.
15. Azaiki, Steve, *Inequalities in Nigerian Politics*, Y-Books, Ibadan, 2007, p. 62.
16. Ikime, Obaro, *History, The Historian and The Nation*, p. 220.
17. See for example, Osaghae, Eghosa E., *Crippled Giant, Nigeria Since* Independence, Hurst & Company, London, 1998, Chapter 3.
18. Ikime, Obaro, *History, The Historian and the Nation,* p. 220.
19. Azaiki, Chapter 5.
20. Azaiki, p. 63.
21. Azaiki, Chapter 6.
22. Azaiki, pp 116-120.
23. Azaiki, p. 63.
24. Azaiki, p. 63.
25. For a detailed discussion of political culture, see Ikime, Obaro, *History, The Historian and The Nation*, Chapter 8.
26. Azaiki, Chapter 6.
27. See *The Encyclopedia of the Social Sciences.*
28. Rosenbaum, Walter, *Political Culture*, Thomas Nelson, London, 1975, quoted in Ikime, Obaro, *History, The Historian and The Nation*, p. 170. The reader may like to read Chapter 8 of the book entitled: *The Past in the Present: History and the Evolving Political Culture of Nigeria.*
29. Azaiki, p. 92.
30. Azaiki, p. 88.

14

GOD, HISTORY, THE AMALGAMATION OF 1914 AND THE NIGERIA OF 2013*

I am particularly delighted that some people consider the memory of the traditional historian of Benin, Jacob Egharevba, worth celebrating on a regular basis. All of us who studied History at university level, when History was regarded as a subject worth studying, remember the name Jacob Egharevba. His Book, *A Short History of Benin*, was a must read for all History Honours students. Today, I will not be surprised if that book is no longer on the list of books that students of Nigerian History in our universities are required to read. This is part of the tragedy that has befallen historical studies in our nation. Nigeria must be the only country in the world that does not, compulsorily, teach her history to her citizens! Whether Nigeria knows it or not, she is the poorer for this neglect of her history.

It is not my intention, to dwell at any length on Egharevba's *A Short History of Benin*. That this lecture is being delivered as a memorial to Chief Egharevba is evidence of the high regard in which he is held in this ancient city of Benin. The opening sentence of the book says:

*Lecture delivered at the 2013 Jacob Egharevba Memorial Lecture, Institute for Benin Studies.

> Many, many years ago, the Benin came all the way from Egypt to found a more secure shelter in this part of the world after a short stay in the Sudan and Ile Ife, which the Benin people call Uhe.

The Bini are negroid; the Egyptians are Caucasian, though it is said they were negroid before the Arab conquest of the seventh century. Did the Bini migrate from Egypt before the seventh century A.D.? "Many, many years ago," was Egharevba's Sudan the same Sudan we know today? Why did the Bini choose to stay in Ile Ife? For how long did they stay there? What means of transportation was available for the migrating Binis as they journeyed from "Egypt" to the Sudan and then to Ile Ife, before settling in Benin? How was it they found no "more secure shelter" until they got to Benin? The value of books like Egharevba's is that they raise issues and questions which force the academic historian to dig deeper. Given the location of Benin in the 1930s when Egharevba published the first edition of his book, one may be permitted to state that a claim to Egyptian origin was safe, in so far as Egypt was so far away that there was absolutely no chance of that country seeking to lay any claim whatsoever on Benin! Is it, likewise, possible that some of the claims by some Nigerians to have "come" from Benin were made for the same reason, namely, a link with a famous power or "civilisation", but one so far away that it could not lay claim to the groups that link their origins to her? Were such claims made as a warning to nearby neighbours not to dare attack the groups making the claim, lest the might of Benin descend on these neighbours? In these questions and the challenges they throw up lie part of the value of the work of traditional historians. For this reason, we celebrate the works of such historians and study them to learn as much as we can from them. Egharevba did not offer service to Benin alone. He offered service to History and historical studies in our country. I salute his memory.

I have been led to title this lecture **"God, History, the Amalgamation of 1914 and the Nigeria of 2013."** Some in this audience may consider this a peculiar title. I just pray and hope that at the end of the lecture, the reason for the unusual title would have become obvious.

One more preliminary point. I am not about to engage in a learned discourse. I have not come to Benin to present new research findings! I am not here to seek to win the applause of my fellow academic historians. Indeed, my academic historian colleagues, if any be in the audience, may, at the end of this lecture, pass a verdict of "so what?", on what you are about to hear! That is their entitlement! I am here to sing an old song, a song I have been singing for over thirty years without any impact on my nation. Nigeria is a relatively new nation-state. We are still very much in the process of nation-building. One of the greatest problems confronting us in this process is that of inter-group relations. The song I have been singing for nearly four decades is that History holds the key to our understanding of inter-group relations; that without knowledge of that history, we are indeed like "victims of collective amnesia groping about in the dark"; that in this matter of inter-group relations, what History teaches us is that we are not dealing with saints and sinners, but with sinners all! All who find themselves in vantage positions vis-à-vis their neighbours exploit those positions to the maximum! If then, we be sinners all, then the clarion call for repentance must ring forth. It is my submission that the needed repentance has to be based on knowledge of ourselves; and History holds the key to that knowledge, though Nigeria may not acknowledge this truth. Now, we can proceed with the lecture.

Of God

The Holy Bible opens with these words: "*In the beginning God created the heaven and earth*" (Genesis 1:1). In Psalm 24:1 we read, *The earth is the Lord's, and all its fullness, the world and those who dwell therein.* And in Psalm 50:12b: *For the world is mine* [i.e. the Lord's]. By His grace, I am a child of God. I believe in Him and in His Son Jesus Christ, as revealed in His Word. I believe that God created our earth. I believe that all who dwell on this earth- you and I – have been created by God and are subject to Him. I believe that He who created our earth is fully in charge of it, even when it does not appear to us that this is so. Why do I take this position? Again we go to His word: *Are not two sparrows sold for a copper coin? And not one of them falls to the ground apart from* [i.e. unless it is] *your Father's will* (Matthew 10:21). The Creator of the world, including our Nigeria, is in full charge of it. Hear Him in Isaiah 14:24.

> The Lord of Hosts has sworn saying, "Surely, as I have thought, so it shall come to pass. And as I have purposed, so it shall stand."

I believe God. I believe that as He has spoken, so it shall indeed come to pass. For as we read in Isaiah 14:27: *For the Lord of hosts has purposed, and who will annul it?* What God has purposed no one can annul. Meaning what? Meaning that whatever our politicians have done, are doing and will do, God's purpose for putting Nigeria together the way He has done, will come to pass – in the fullness of time. He, not man, will bring it to pass. Man can only be His agent.

Come with me to another declaration that God has made. In Daniel 4, we have the story of how God dealt with King Nebuchadnezzar. Permit me to reproduce verses 29-32.

> **29** At the end of the twelve months, he [Nebuchadnezzar] was walking about the royal palace of Babylon.
> **30** The King spoke, saying, Is it not this great Babylon, that I have built for a royal dwelling by my mighty power and for the honour of my majesty?
> **31** While the word was still in the king's mouth, a voice fell from heaven: "King Nebuchadnezzar to you it is spoken: the Kingdom has departed from you!"
> **32** And they shall drive you from men, and your dwelling shall be with the beasts of the field. They shall make you eat grass like oxen; and seven times shall pass over you, UNTIL YOU KNOW THAT THE MOST HIGH RULES IN THE KINGDOM OF MEN AND GIVES IT TO WHOMEVER HE CHOOSES (my capitalization).

God rules over the affairs, over the kingdoms, over the nations, of the world. Was it you, was it I, who took General Abacha from Aso Rock? Do we still remember that incident? God is God. He will do what He will do, how and when He will do it. He is God over the nations that He has created. He is God over Nigeria, whether we acknowledge it or not! And He will take Nigeria where He will take it!

God and History: God decided in His sovereignty that He would make a covenant with Abraham and his seed – and He did. All of the Old Testament is a record of how God dealt with His people, the Jews, and the latter's relations with the other nations of the then world. The God who blessed Abraham and his descendants, nevertheless allowed them to become slaves in Egypt for hundreds of years. Then, suddenly God said:

> 7 I have surely seen the oppression of my people Who are in Egypt, and have heard their cry because of their taskmasters, for I know their

> sorrows.
> **8** So I have come down to deliver them out of the hands of the Egyptians...
> – Exodus 3:7-8

God took His people from Egypt all right. But it took forty years before they got to the Promised Land. And even in that land, they had to constantly contend for possession with their enemies. Even now, Israel, the nation of the Jews, is surrounded by enemies and they, the Jews, have to be constantly on the alert. They have fought many wars in their history. My purpose in this lecture is not to bore you with a recapitulation of these wars. That is not necessary for our purpose. All I want to draw to your attention is that God is interested in History. Read from Exodus to the end of the Old Testament. What do you find? God constantly reminded His people that "with a strong hand the Lord has brought you out of Egypt" (Exodus 13:9). "For I am the Lord who brought you up out of the land of Egypt, to give you the land of Canaan and to be your God" (Leviticus 25:38). Over one hundred times, in the Old Testament, God and His prophets kept telling His people: Remember your past; recall your experiences – both pleasant and unpleasant; learn lessons from your walk with Me. Look back upon your past, your history. Look back. Remember. Recall. Learn. God, the Creator of heavens and the earth is, for that reason, the Chief History Maker! We ignore our nation's history at our own peril, for it is in that history we can gain understanding as to why things are as they are. God is God of History, for nothing happens that God does not know; and that which He has purposed, no one, nothing, can annul. I hope I can persuade you, as we go along, that this is an eternal truth.

Of History

We cannot, in this lecture, engage in a disquisition on History. We must, however, draw attention to certain truths about History that can help us understand the problems which have confronted and are confronting us as Nigerians. What is History? The reader is here reminded of our answer to that question at page 169. Perhaps a look at the situation will help to establish the profundity of the definition given on that page. One of the problems, with which we have to grapple as a nation, is the ethnic factor. Whether all Nigerians agree with me or not, I am fully persuaded that one of President Goodluck Jonathan's greatest problems had [as at 2013] to do with the fact that He is not Hausa-Fulani, not Igbo, not Yoruba, not even Edo! How can this man from the backwoods of Nigeria be President? How dare he want to rule Nigeria for as long as eight years? Who exactly is he? Why is the "North" so concerned that Jonathan should not have a second term? My answer is that the "North" cannot conceive of the possibility of one of their number not being in Aso Rock for as long as sixteen years! If Jonathan has a second term, he could be succeeded by an Igbo for eight years. This would mean that the "Northerners" have to wait till 2023! Unthinkable, for those who see themselves as "born to rule," a frame of mind which is the outcome of our history.

How do I tie this in with the definition of History I have chosen? The point has been repeatedly made in a number of the earlier chapters to the effect that the ethnic groups that are struggling to rule Nigeria in our time did not exist as ethnic groups till the late 19th and into the 20th century. It is History that created our ethnic groups. For all the groups that now make up Nigeria, it was the coming, first of the colonial state of Nigeria, and then the nation-state which we are still building, that brought about competition for development, office-holding, survival, etc, and so forced groups that had hitherto acted as separate socio-political entities to come together to struggle for both recognition and development. So? It is History – the emergence of "Nigeria" as a colony of Britain, that challenged our various socio-political entities that hitherto operated independently to seek linkage with others (especially those who spoke the same or similar language) because it was believed that the new groups – today's ethnic groups – could better compete with other groups that were also "amalgamating"! That is what we mean when we say that it is history that created Nigeria's ethnic groups.

What about the Islam/Christianity divide, and all that that has meant for our nation? Geography and History created the Islam/Christianity divide. In the heat of the religious differences which rock our politics today, we tend to speak and even act as if the "Southerners" deliberately chose Christianity while the "Northerners" chose Islam! Of course, this was never the case. The South is Christian as a consequence of what we sometimes describe as a "historical accident", and the North is Muslim also as a result of a "historical accident." Islam came to Kanem-Borno, the first part of what is now Nigeria to become Muslim, via the trans-

Saharan trade routes, which linked North Africa to the Western Sudan. It was through the same routes that Islam was introduced to some of the Hausa states. On the other hand, Christian missionaries came via the Atlantic Ocean to the coastal parts of what became Nigeria, as part of the British effort to put an end to the slave trade, at a time when the British economy was no longer as dependent on slave labour as it had been before the Industrial Revolution.

Christianity brought with it western European education. Islam brought with it Muslim education. This is what explains the South/North dichotomy in both religion and education. In the heat of our political differences, especially as from the period of decolonisation, we forget these "accidents of history," and think and speak as if we in the South are inherently superior to our brothers of the North in terms of "education"! Yet it is a historical fact that before the "South" produced her first educated elite, the "North" through Uthman dan Fodio, Muhammad Bello and others had produced learned treatises on Islamic religion and governance! "It just happened" that they wrote in Arabic and not in English! Had we been colonised by an Islamic power rather than a European power, the "North" would have been the educationally advantaged part and the South educationally disadvantaged! Are my listeners beginning to see the significance of the definition of History that I have chosen to use in this lecture?

As for the "North", the fact that they have controlled the Federal Government for some forty-four out of Nigeria's fifty-three years as a nation-state bred in them a "born to rule" mentality. Clearly, the cry on their part that Jonathan should not stand for election as President in 2015 is born out of the fear that the "North" may not get back to Aso Rock till 2019 or 2023! Again it is History that provides the answer as to why the North feels the way it does. But we must leave that till we discuss the Amalgamation of 1914. It is History that has produced the mindset of "Northern" politicians. It is necessary that that mindset be understood even as our nation passes through changing phases of evolution.

Before we move on to the issue of the Amalgamation of 1914, it is necessary to address a fallacy, itself a product of History, that has bugged North-South relations. Nigerian scholars of the Sokoto Jihad, do not, to my mind, sufficiently dwell on the truth that the success of the Sokoto Jihad meant the superimposition of a foreign religion and culture on what became the Sokoto Caliphate. Whereas leaders of the

Sokoto Caliphate and latter day politicians see the "Southerners" as persons who have imbibed a foreign European culture, they see their Islamic culture as indigenous to the "North," and are proud of it. Thus Sharia law, a body of laws based on Islamic concepts is, for the Muslim, a matter of pride, while British or received law based on the British legal system, is evidence of imperialistic enslavement! The truth, of course, is that both the "South" and the "North" have been victims of imperialistic enslavement, albeit by different powers and at different times. History, properly taught and learnt, should provide some of the understanding that is needed for our multifarious peoples to live together in a new multi-national state, our differences notwithstanding. Such understanding is necessary if we are to get rid of the derogatory epithets we have foisted on our fellow countrymen.

Because the Amalgamation of 1914 has acquired a unique significance in our history, it is easy to forget that there were many amalgamations before it. Every single clan, polity, kingdom, etc, is a product of a degree of amalgamation. The traditions of origin of our peoples, which speak about founding fathers who had **x** number of sons who founded **n** number of villages or even kingdoms, actually encapsulate series of amalgamations found necessary for better meeting the challenges with which the founding fathers of our peoples had to deal. As already indicated, the ethnic groups as we have them today emerged in response to historical developments which require new socio-political alignments for survival. This was the burden of my Inaugural Lecture as President of the Historical Society of Nigeria, way back in 1982. And even as we speak, new alliances, new alignments, are taking place in answer to the challenges of the politics in Nigeria today.

It was in 1900 that Frederick Lugard proclaimed a Protectorate of Northern Nigeria into being – even before he and his successors had brought the area so proclaimed under British colonial rule through military conquest. The concept of "Northern Nigeria" thus dates back to 1900 - as recently as that! In the South, the British, who had been trading along the coastal part since the days of the Atlantic slave trade, began to feel the need for some political authority to back up their trade. In 1849 John Beecraft was appointed British consul for the Bights of Benin and Biafra, to promote and protect British trade. As the scramble for Africa became more intense in the 1880s, the British, having signed various types of treaties with the rulers of our coastal states, proclaimed the Protectorate of the Oil Rivers in 1885. This protectorate covered the coastal areas from Calabar to the Benin River in the Itsẹkiri kingdom, and an undefined hinterland. In 1891 the name of the Protectorate was changed to Niger Coast Protectorate. Its headquarters remained in Calabar. The Niger Delta States, each of which had been autonomous till this time, were brought under a single foreign authority which divided the area into "Divisions" and "Districts" without their consent. This involved varying degrees of amalgamation.

In what came to be known as Yorubaland, Lagos had been bombarded into submission by the British for reasons to do with the suppression of the overseas slave trade in 1851. In 1861 the British proclaimed a colony over Lagos. The trade of Lagos, whether in the days of the slave trade or the new trade in forest products, depended on what came from the hinterland, occupied by various Yoruba-speaking kingdoms. Because war is always disruptive of trade, the British in Lagos, began to get involved with the Yoruba hinterland. Their aim? To bring the wars to an end and thereby enhance the trade of the region. This was how British authority spread from Lagos to the Yoruba hinterland, necessitating an amalgamation between the Lagos colony and its hinterland. The upshot was "The Colony and Protectorate of Lagos". This was in 1896.

In 1901 the Niger Coast Protectorate became known as the Protectorate of Southern Nigeria. This was the first time that the expression "Southern Nigeria" was applied to a part of what became Nigeria in 1914. It is necessary here to draw attention to the fact that the Yoruba country was NOT part of the Southern Nigeria of 1901! Yorubaland then still belonged to the Colony and the Protectorate of Lagos. There were thus three Protectorates in Nigeria in the years 1900-1913, each headed by a "Governor" as in the case of the Colony and Protectorate of Lagos or by a High Commissioner as in the case of the Northern and Southern Nigeria Protectorates.

In 1906 there came yet another amalgamation. The Colony and Protectorate of Lagos and what became known as the Protectorate of Southern Nigeria in 1901 were amalgamated into the "Colony and Protectorate of Southern Nigeria", with Sir Walter Egerton as Governor and Commander-in-Chief. The new "Colony" was divided into three Provinces - Western Province made up of Lagos and the former Protectorate of Lagos (i.e. Yorubaland); Central Province with Warri as headquarters (the Itsẹkiri, Urhobo, Western Ijọ, Isoko, Ndosomilli, - i.e.

Aboh, Ndokwa, the Benin territories, Agbor, Asaba, Onitsha, belonged to this Province); Eastern Province, with Calabar as headquarters (to which province belonged all the eastern coastal states and their Igbo and Ibibio hinterland). Each of these Provinces was headed by a British Officer, known as the Provincial Commissioner. As usual, the amalgamation was undertaken without consultation with the Nigerian peoples. One pressing reason for the 1906 amalgamation was financial. The Colony and Protectorate of Lagos was engaged in the building of a railway line to the North. This was too expensive for the revenue of the protectorate to carry. In contrast, what was then known as the Protectorate of Southern Nigeria, with ports dotting its littoral, was comparatively more buoyant. Since both territories were controlled by the British, it made sense, from the viewpoint of the latter, to amalgamate them, so that the resources of the former Niger Coast Protectorate could be used to aid the development of Lagos and the Yoruba hinterland. With the 1906 amalgamation, so we can argue, "Southern Nigeria" encompassed the coastline from Lagos to Calabar and the hinterland.

The Amalgamation of 1914

It was Fredrick Lugard who proclaimed a Protectorate over "Northern Nigeria" in 1900. He proceeded through military conquest to bring the Sokoto Caliphate, Borno and parts of "the Middle Belt" under British rule in the years 1900-1906. His successors continued the work he began and between 1906 and 1912 ensured the subjugation of virtually all of the "Middle Belt". Because Ilorin was part of the Sokoto Caliphate, insofar as an emirate was established there, when Ilorin fell to the British, it became part of "Northern Nigeria"; so did Kabba a Yoruba group.

I have, in some of my writings, drawn attention to the significance of what the British did in the "Middle Belt". The peoples of this "Belt" had successfully withstood the Sokoto Jihad of the 19th century, and so were not part of the Sokoto Caliphate. Then came the British and conquered parts of this "Belt" and created "emirates" where none had existed! The Middle Belt peoples have not forgotten how the British thus "enslaved" them, by bringing parts of their territory into the Caliphate. Remember part of our definition of History? "It is the events recorded in history that have generated all the motions, the values, the ideals that make life meaningful, that have given men something to live for, struggle over, die for." "Middle Belt" - "North" relations constitute proof of this truth. We shall have cause to return to this issue later. For now, it is enough to draw attention to the fact that Lugard's "Northern Nigeria" included all the area north of the Niger-Benue river system, plus Ilorin and Kabba, south of the Niger, and part of Yorubaland, that would otherwise have been part of the Colony of Southern Nigeria in 1906. It is this fact of history that explains the struggle by the Action Group, in the 1950s and early 1960s, for the return of Ilorin and Kabba territories to the former Western Nigeria; it is this fact which ultimately saw the emergence of Kwara State. History holds the key to this development. Let us return to the amalgamation story. Amalgamation was not the brain child of Lugard. It was the British Colonial Office that reached the decision that the amalgamation of Northern and Southern Nigeria was necessary. Lugard was appointed to carry out that decision.

The compelling reason for amalgamation was economic development, including the building of a South-North railway system. Wrote Michael Crowder:

> The Northern Protectorate was running at a deficit, which was being met by a subsidy from the Southern Protectorate, and an imperial grant-in-aid from Britain of about £300,000 a year. This conflicted with the age-old colonial policy that each territory should be self-subsisting.... it was felt that the prosperous Southern Protectorate could subsidise its northern neighbour until such time as it became self-supporting.*

As at 1913, the North was dependent on the South for part of its revenue, despite its land mass and population. As we deliver this lecture, the "Northern States" are being partly funded by mineral oil revenue from the Niger Delta. Yet that North considers that it should (nearly always?) control political power at the centre. Why? Because, as we shall see presently, Lugard's amalgamation was such that favoured the North. Forgive me, as I keep repeating the refrain: History holds the key to our understanding of how things have come to be as they are.

The amalgamation of 1914 involved two parts that were unequal

*Crowder, Michael, *The Story of Nigeria,* London, Faber and Faber, 1978, p. 196.

in size and population. As Lugard prepared for amalgamation, certain suggestions were put before him. C.L. Temple, who was to become Lieutenant Governor of the North under Lugard, proposed that Nigeria be broken into seven provinces: the North into three – Hausa State, Benue Province, Chad Territory; the South into four – Lagos Colony, Western, Central and Eastern Provinces. E.D. Morel, then editor of the *African Mail*, who was familiar with the Nigerian area advocated that four provinces be established: Northern, Central, Western and Eastern – the first two above the Niger-Benue River system, and the last two below the river system. Lugard rejected both suggestions and proceeded with a lopsided amalgamation such that Northern Nigeria included not only the area north of the Niger-Benue river system, but also the Yoruba of Ilorin and Kabba territories south of the Niger-Benue. The North was thus larger in area and population than the South. As the British, through the amalgamation of Northern and Southern Nigeria, thus consolidated their colonial hold over Nigeria, the seeds of future discord between the two constituent but unequal parts of Nigeria were sown. Permit me to be cynical for a moment. Is it this discord that our nation plans to celebrate in 2014? Was the Nigerian nation born in 1914? Exactly what are we set to celebrate a few months hence? How much of our history will inform the planned celebrations? Without knowledge of that history, let me remind this distinguished audience, we became victims of collective amnesia, groping around in the dark. Is that why our nation, fifty-three years old, is at it is?

What Made the Amalgamation of 1914 Possible and What Should We Celebrate in 2014?

A senior colleague of mine declared in a recent lecture on the subject of the Amalgamation of 1914, that what happened in 1914 was a territorial amalgamation. Our peoples were not and could not have been amalgamated. They had no say in what happened in 1914. At any rate, a nation-state evolves over time; it cannot be decreed into being! All the nations of our world have had to undergo this evolution, and I believe that we will eventually get there. Nigeria became independent in 1960. So, we cannot claim that in 2014 we would be one hundred years old as a nation. We would actually be fifty-four years old! So, I ask: Is there anything to celebrate in 2014? If there is, what is it?

The answer to my last question is found in what made theAmalgamation of 1914 possible, for it is that which makes 1914 a significant date for our dear country, Nigeria. As Lugard prepared to execute the Amalgamation of 1914, he did not have to worry about defining the external boundaries of "Northern Nigeria" and "Southern Nigeria." Those boundaries had been settled through a series of negotiations between Britain and France and Britain and Germany in the course of the last two decades of the 19th century. It is the size of amalgamated Nigeria as of 1914 that is significant in what happened in that year. What do I mean?

The amalgamated British colony of Nigeria was, and has remained, the largest collectivity of the black man in the world! Elsewhere, we had territories which were British protectorates or colonies which were never amalgamated – Northern and Southern Rhodesia, for example, which regained independence as two separate nations. The role Nigeria plays today in West Africa, the African Union, the British Commonwealth, the United Nations, where we are seeking a permanent seat on the Security Council, is based in part, on the truth that we are the largest black nation of the world. The fact that despite the ineptitude and corruption in certain government circles and even among some of our business class, many advanced economies are still investing in Nigeria is due to the size of our market, itself the product of the size of our nation and its population. There is also the fact that Nigerians are found in considerable numbers in many countries of the world, holding their own in various professions – again partly the consequence of our large population made possible by the size of our nation.

There may be some listening to me, who are saying to themselves that all I have just be saying is fortuitous. It just happened that the British and the French and Germans settled for the boundaries as they were in 1914. It just happened that the British Government decided to amalgamate Northern and Southern Nigeria for their economic benefit. Even were we to grant such a retort, the Amalgamation of 1914 still had the result to which attention has been drawn. Permit me, to state as my conviction, that with God there are no accidents. With Him, things do not just happen. He says to us in His word that "the Most High rules in the Kingdom of men" (Daniel 4:32c); He says, "Surely, as I have though, so it shall come to pass. And as I have purposed, so it shall stand" (Isaiah 14:24). Nigeria has the size it has because God so ordained it. That is why we fought a civil war to keep Nigeria one. That is why, despite all we are experiencing now as a nation, I am fully persuaded that God will take us to that destination that He has purposed for us, using whom He will use. I have absolutely no doubt in my mind that God's will for Nigeria will most assuredly come to pass. He has not made us the largest back nation of the world for nothing. His purposes will be established – in His time.

The Amalgamation of 1914 and the Nigeria of 2013

It is not my intention, in this section of the lecture, to take you through the ninety-nine year period covered by the years 1914-2013. What I have decided to do is to draw attention to a number of developments or incidents in the context of the theme of this lecture.

Limited Amalgamation: The amalgamation of 1914 was not undertaken for the benefit of our people – economic or political. It was undertaken to save the British tax payer from subsidising the cost of administering Northern Nigeria. The British did not unify the North and South in 1914. Lugard promised to respect the Islamic institutions of the caliphate. This meant that there was no concerted effort to introduce and develop western European education in the North, despite the fact that Britain was the colonising authority. By contrast in the south, even as at 1914, some degree of western European education was already in place and this was to develop apace in the years ahead. This explains the difference in western European education between the North and South. It was for this reason that as late as the 1960s and 1970s different levels of performance were put in place for admission of persons seeking admission to our federal universities. Provision had to be made for "educationally disadvantaged" areas. So a Southerner who scored 58% could miss admission while a Northerner with 48% was admitted. The amalgamation of 1914 and the terms thereof were still affecting developments in the 1960s!

Despite amalgamation, North and South did not have the same law-making institution until the Richards Constitution which came into effect in 1945, thirty-one years after amalgamation. The reason why it took this long for the colonial state to have a common Legislative Council was the British penchant to pander to the desires of the North. So, North and South were amalgamated, yet kept apart! It was not the business of Britain to build a united Nigeria. In the circumstances, differences between North and South persisted and were to vitiate efforts at proper unification of Nigeria, even after independence.

The North/South divide remained untouched until 1939 when Governor Bourdillon divided the smaller South into two – Western Province and Eastern Province. I will not bore you with the untenable reasons advanced by Governor Bourdillon for breaking the south into two, while leaving the North intact. I must, however, draw attention to the long-term impact of what happened in 1939. In the West, the Yoruba had a greater population than all the other groups - Edo, Urhbo, western Igbo, Itsẹkiri, Isoko, western "Ijọ", Aboh, Ndokwa put together. In the East the Igbo likewise had a larger population that all the other groups – the Eastern Ijọ, Efik, the Ibibio, the Ekoi and others. In each of the three regions, therefore, there was a dominant group which could lord it over the minority groups. The politics of Nigeria were played out in the context of this majority/minority syndrome. The point we are underlining in this presentation is that the 1914 amalgamation and British colonial policy in Nigeria thereafter were not designed to lay a solid foundation for the emergence of a united Nigerian nation-state. Colonialism is not designed for such ends!

At this point, we remind ourselves that it is History that has created all the human groupings and all the loyalties that attach to these. It was historical development that gave rise to the Hausa-Fulani of the North, the Yoruba of the West and Igbo of the East. In the regions over which these groups enjoyed majority status, their interests, rather those of all other component units of respective regions, became their main concern. The consequence was unequal development which bred tension between the majority ethnic groups and the minorities. A major challenge in Nigeria's nation-building remains that of fair and equitable development.

Lingering impact of the Amalgamation of 1914: In 1914 Lugard refused suggestions that the North and South be broken into smaller units. In 1939 the North remained as at 1914. The South was broken into two regions. This placed the North at a distinct advantage. As new loyalties developed around the new Western and Eastern regions, whatever southern solidarity there was up to 1939 was destroyed. East and West began to compete for federal appointments as from 1952. By 1960 when Nigeria regained independence, the North was clearly advantaged in terms of population vis-à-vis the West and the East. It was thus the amalgamation of 1914 which ensured Northern dominance of the Federal Government at independence and in the years before the military coup in January 1966. Even so, however, the North sought an ally in the south. That ally turned out to be from the East. The fact that the East participated in a coalition government with the North, led to East-West tension, which further strengthened the North at the expense of a South that could not work together, thanks to the breakup of the South in 1939, and the new loyalties that had developed around the regions created in that year. Many (if not all) in today's audience who are forty-six years and below have no knowledge of what I am talking about at this point in the lecture. They were not born as at 1966, and though many have gone through university education, and some are even major players in politics, business, the civil service, the army, the police, the customs and so on, they have no knowledge of the history of their country. Nigeria does not believe that her history should be taught to her citizens. For this reason, there be many who take sensitive decisions about our country in utter ignorance of the historical experiences of our various peoples. For example, in some of our state-creation exercises, some of our peoples have been included in states in which they never will be able to have one of their sons or daughters elected a local government councillor because the larger percentage of their kinsfolk are in a neighbouring state. Such peoples see themselves as enslaved. A little inquiry about the past would have averted mistakes of this type.

In the period of decolonisation, the political parties which piloted us into independence became increasingly seen as regional parties. The Northern People's Congress (N.P.C.), led by Ahmadu Bello, Sardauna of Sokoto, as its name implies, was a Northern party which sought no membership from the South. Yet, because of the size of the North, it had the largest number of seats in the House of Representatives at independence. The National Council of Nigeria and the Cameroon, later National Council of Nigerian citizens (N.C.N.C) and led, in the 1950s, by Dr Nnamdi Azikiwe, began as a national party. By 1953, however, it began to be seen as an Igbo-dominated party, even though it continued to have some following in the West. The Action Group (A.G.) led by Chief Obafemi Awolowo metamorphosed into a political party from a Yoruba cultural organisation, Egbe Omo Oduduwa, and was seen as a party for the Yoruba. Like the N.C.N.C., the A.G. also had some membership from outside Yorubaland. Ethnic and regional factors were thus very much at work as Nigeria moved into independence. Both of these factors were a product of historical developments in the period after the amalgamation of 1914.

In each of the three regions into which Nigeria was divided as at 1960, there were groups that felt oppressed and neglected. In the North the peoples of the Middle Belt began an agitation for the creation of the Middle Belt State. In the West, the people of Benin and Delta Provinces wanted a state created for them. In the East we had the Calabar-Ogoja-Rivers State Movement. Even though the British agreed that there was good reason for the agitation for the creation of more states, the 1914 structure as amended in 1939, which left Nigeria lopsided in terms of its constituent parts, lived on into independence. In 1963 only one state was created – the Midwest Region. Ironically, this region was carved out of the Western Region, the smallest of the three regions. The NPC and NCNC, which controlled the Federal Government, left the regions they controlled untouched, and broke the West into two – to reduce the area over which Awolowo and the Action Group had control! Naturally, the Yoruba felt ill-used. Inter group relations between Nigeria's peoples and regions in the period of decolonisation and early years of independence were thus marked by tension and hostility. The house that Britain built was in trouble.

The Nigerian Civil War, 1967-1970: It is not my intention to dwell at any length on this subject except to make a few comments, relevant to the formulation of the title of this lecture. One, on the eve of the civil war, General Yakubu Gowon, the military Head of State, announced the creation of twelve states – North Western, North Central, Kano, North Eastern, Kwara and Benue-Plateau from the old North, and Western, Lagos, Midwest, East Central, Rivers, South Eastern from the old South. Nigeria hailed this development because it met some of the demands that different groups had been making. It is my personal view that the twelve-state structure, which represented a major dismantling of the 1914/1939 structure, was really part of Gowon's war strategy. Civil war was looming. The Igbo were threatening to take Eastern Nigeria (1939 creation) out of Nigeria. By creating Rivers and South-Eastern States, Gowon hoped these areas would throw in their lot with the Federal Government, and thereby isolate the East Central State, the Igbo heartland. In the process, the monolithic North created in 1914 was dismantled on paper. The non-Hausa, non-Fulani peoples were given a separate state and Kwara state was carved out, thereby giving the Yoruba three states.

The above is one side of the coin. There is the other side. As of 1967, the Nigerian nation-state was only seven years old. But Nigeria as an entity was fifty-three years old. History had created a fifty-three year old entity called Nigeria. Nigeria's famous civil war cry was: To keep Nigeria one is a task that must be done! History had created a political entity called Nigeria. Some degree of loyalty had been built up around this Nigeria. Our soldiers fought (and many of them died) to ensure that this Nigeria was not broken up. History created that loyalty.

It was only on 30 May, 1967, that Ojukwu declared secession and proclaimed the establishment of the Republic of Biafra. The Nigerian civil war began on 6 July, 1967. Biafra was five weeks old! But History had produced the Igbo of East Central State hundreds of years before. Therefore, loyalty to Ojukwu's Biafra was really strong among these Igbo, his kinsmen. The Ijọ, Efik, Ibibio, etc., who were the oppressed minorities of the former Eastern Region, could not be expected to feel the same loyalty for Biafra as the Igbo did. History saw to that. That is why it was that the South Eastern State and Rivers State were more easily overrun by the Federal Forces than the East Central State. Ojukwu had hoped to fund the war with oil money from Rivers State in particular. The Federal Government quickly denied him that source of funds by militarily occupying the oil-region. Even so, the civil war that erupted lasted for two and a half years. Hundreds of thousands of Biafran soldiers fought and died for a Biafra that did not exist when they were born! That is how profound the consequences of historical developments can be.

It is also History that explains the fact that throughout the civil war, coastal trade went on between the coastal East and the rest of coastal Nigeria! It was dangerous to engage in that trade, but it went on nevertheless. Similarly, overland trade went on between the southerly parts of Northern Nigeria and Biafra through well-established routes. We can claim that "northern" cattle were used to feed Biafra soldiers for quite a while! The truth is that trade between peoples north of the Niger/ Benue river system and those to the south of it had gone on for centuries before "Nigeria" came into being. The coming into existence of Nigeria merely enhanced already existing commercial activities. The civil war clearly reduced this trade. It did not kill it. The pull of History explains this phenomenon.

The amalgamation of 1914 brought the colonial state of Nigeria into being. The nature of that amalgamation as well as the colonial policies of Britain in the years 1915-1959 created problems of relationship between our multifarious peoples in the years 1960-1966. Those problems partly explain the thirty-month civil war fought between 1967-1970. That civil war was evidence that the new nation-state of Nigeria had not yet moulded its component units into a homogenous socio-political entity. That could hardly have been achieved in seven years! Yes, we fought a civil war. That civil war did not kill the concept of the "Nigeria" that came into being in 1914. Indeed, we can claim that successive governments since 1970 have been seeking to perfect "the idea of Nigeria," seeking to build up a citizenry that can yield instinctive loyalty to the Nigerian nation-state.

Given the title of this lecture, permit me to remind us that "the Most High [God] rules over the kingdom of men." That God let the civil war "happen." That same God ensured that the civil war did not result in the break-up of Nigeria. Why? Let me dare to say that it was because it was HE who allowed Nigeria to be put together in 1914! 1914 did not just happen. He who allowed Nigeria to be together in 1914, ensured that Nigeria should remain. The civil war was to teach us sanguine lessons. I fear, however, that we have not yet learnt those lessons well. But, glory be to God, what He has begun, He will perfect. Nigerians will rise and build their nation just like the Jews did under Nehemiah.

Since the Civil War: It is now forty-three years plus since our civil war ended. The nation-building process is still on. Part of that process has been the creation of more states. In 1976 the number of states was increased to nineteen. In 1991 a thirty state structure was put in place, and in 1996 the number of states increased yet again- to thirty-six. And, as we all know, there is, even now, agitation for the creation of more states.

One argument in support of the creation of more states is that it brings government and development closer to the people, and reduces, in the process, the possibility of one ethnic group lording it over smaller ones. There is some force in this argument. Let us, however, examine what has happened thus far. Is it not true that each time states are created, we have the emergence of new majority groups and minority groups? Do not the new majority groups proceed to visit on the new minorities the same evil as had been visited on them (the new majority groups) when they were minority groups in a larger, former state, thereby providing the explanation for the never-ending demand for the creation of more states? What is the explanation for this? Our political leaders have not, thus far, found it possible to accept, as their governing principles, the concepts of justice, fairness and equitable development. Government is not yet seen as an instrument for ensuring the welfare of the governed. It is seen more as an avenue for the self-enrichment of those in office as well as the enrichment of their favoured ones. And why is this so? Because the heart of man is desperately wicked.

Come with me, I pray, into God's word:

> And God saw that the wickedness of man was great on the earth, and every imagination of the thoughts of his heart was only evil continually (Genesis 6:5 KJV)

In the above words we find the real explanation of why Nigeria is still as it is. The evil we resent, we are quite happy to visit on others. "Self" rules those who hold political office; our legislators all become millionaires; some of our senior civil servants perfect the art of corrupting even the ministers. Of course, there are exceptions to these generalisations. These are those who fear the Lord God. But, alas, they are too few. We still need God's intervention to change these hearts of stone to hearts of flesh. And God has given us a condition for that intervention in 2 Chronicles 7:14:

> ...If my people, which are called by my name shall humble themselves, and pray, and seek my face, and turn from their wicked ways, then I will hear from heaven and will forgive their sin, and will heal their land. (KJV)

As God had declared, so it stands forever. The fate of our nation is not in the hands of our politicians alone. It is also in your hand, in my hand. Are there any Nigerians who are truly called by the name of Jesus Christ? Then let them know that it is they who can call down the hand of God upon our nation. But – let them know that they must meet God's conditions. As for me, I am fully persuaded that God will act when He will act – and we shall see and wonder. God is God of History – and He will make History in, and for, Nigeria.

Let us return to secular history. What do we see in a thirty-six state Nigeria? What I see is the continuing impact of 1914 and 1939. In the 1914 amalgamation arrangement, the advantage belonged to the North in terms of size and population. And the Hausa-Fulani were the favoured ones in government. Our first Prime Minister, whose party, the N.P.C. did not win one vote in Southern Nigeria was, nevertheless, Prime Minister over all of Nigeria.

By the end of the civil war, the cream of senior Igbo military officers were dead. The Yoruba had very few senior military officers. The bulk of the rank and file of the Army was from the "Middle Belt." Because Northern politicians had cleverly pushed their sons into the army, it was these army officers of Northern origin who headed most of the military regimes – Yakubu Gowon, Murtala Mohammed., Buhari, Babangida, Abacha, Abubakar. Only Olusegun Obasanjo was the southern military officer who governed Nigeria. When we had a civilian "interregnum" in the years 1979-1983, the civilian President was Shehu Shagari – from the North! The "born to rule" mentality of the North is thus a product of our history since independence. As indicated earlier, the determination of the North to ensure that President Jonathan should not contest the 2015 election is because the "North" wants to return to "Aso Rock." The "North". "The North". "The North" – despite state creation and the dismantling of the "North" thereby? The 1914 amalgamation is still influencing the politics of 2013!!

What about the "South" of 1914? That "South" died in 1939. In the politics of decolonisation and the early years of independence, East and West (the South) were in fierce competition. The East eventually entered into a coalition with the North to teach Awolowo and the West a lesson! East-West co-operation has not been a major feature of our political life. We have had a Northern Elders Forum. Has there ever been a Southern Elders Forum? We have a Northern Governors Forum, where is its southern counterpart? None. What we have is a South-South Governor's Forum; a South-East Governor's Forum, a South-West Governor Forum. These three hardly act in unison. How do we explain the difference between the North and the South? I believe that the Sokoto caliphate which emerged in the 19th century, the role which Ahmadu Bello, the Sardauna of Sokoto, played in Northern Nigeria up to his demise in 1966, the enforced subjection of large area of the "Middle Belt" to Sokoto by the British, all of these, products of History, explain Northern solidarity. It is therefore no surprise that in the group of 7 governors who are anti-Jonathan, six are from the North. "It figures" as the Americans would say. So, History holds the key to a great deal of our national politics. The less we know of that history, the less understanding of Nigerian politics we have. It is ninety-nine years since amalgamation. The ghost of amalgamation continues to haunt our national politics.

By Way of Conclusion

I said at the beginning of this lecture that my fellow academics would probably return a verdict of "so what?" on this lecture. They may be saying in their hearts, "so what, men? What's new in all you have said?" The "facts" on which this lecture is based are not new. What I consider can be regarded as new, is what I have been led to do with these facts! This leads me to ask you, fellow academic historians: How do you teach Nigerian History to your students? Do you endeavour to link past history with present events, or do you teach history for history sake? Believe me in the context of Nigeria, to teach Nigerian History for history sake is to teach it for nothing sake! Again this is a song I have been singing for many years. Yet, even as I speak, I do not know how many of my colleagues teach Nigerian History, relating it to the issues with which our nation is grappling today. Unless we do that without standing History on its head, our nation will continue in the fallacy that History is a useless discipline. The fault, sometimes, is not in our stars but in ourselves that we are underlings. Historians look to yourselves, even as the battle to persuade our nation to give History its proper place in our educational system continues. Let us write the kind of History that our peoples can read and readily see the relevance of our subject for themselves and for our nation - without offending the international canons of historical scholarship to which we subscribe.

For the non-historians among us, you may be asking yourselves, what really does History do for us? Let me begin by saying that knowing the history of your country enables you fulfil one of the commandments of the God of heaven and earth: "for I say, to every man that is among you, not to think of himself more highly than he ought to think", (Romans 12:3). Often we tend to be proud because we find ourselves in an advantaged position vis-à-vis others. If you go into History, you are likely to find that it was historical circumstances that enabled you to be what you are, not that there is anything inherently superior in you. When you let history instruct you, you are humbled thereby, and saved from looking down on others.

What is true for the individual is true for collectivity. The coastal peoples of Nigeria are always proud of their early links with Europeans, as compared with their hinterland neighbours. For centuries they were the dominant party in coast-hinterland relations. Even after the coming of the British, the coastal peoples still had an advantage for a while. Then the tide changed. The hinterland was opened up by the British, and the coastal peoples lost their middlemen positions. The dominance passed on to the hinterland peoples. In the Eastern Region, it was the Igbo who eventually became the majority. We find this changing fortunes in other parts of the country. History teaches one abiding lesson: no condition is permanent. History enables us to understand why things are as they are. That understanding reduces arrogance and destroys stereotypes. It enables us live in love and understanding with our fellow countrymen and women.

Take, for example, North-South relations. There is nothing inherently inferior in the peoples of the North. I had three Northerners in my class at Ibadan. All three of them made Second Class (Lower Division) Honours Degree in History, like the bulk of the Southerners in the class. It was an accident of History that gave us western European education while giving the North Islamic education. Isn't it ironical that the British, out of respect for Islamic traditions, not only created a North that was larger than the south, but also kept the North undivided till just before the civil war? That gave them control of the Federal Government. That together with other developments to which attention has been drawn in this lecture is responsible for the attitude of the North that control of the Federal Government is theirs for the asking. Man being what he is, I am fully persuaded that if the South had the advantage which the North enjoyed up to 2011, Southern attitude would have been the same as that which we, Southerners, now condemn among our Northern brothers. The truth is that unregenerate man is essentially selfish. And it is this selfishness that explains the tensions in which we find ourselves today. Those tensions can be more easily resolved if we accept that "no condition is permanent" is one of the lessons of History. Understanding the issues makes the search for a solution easier. And History provides a major key to understanding how things are as they are. Learn that history. Get that understanding. And inter-group relations should be easier to manage.

I could hold forth on this issue for the next hour. But there is no need to, after what has been said earlier. All nations of the world have passed through their turmoils. Some have fought their civil wars. Others have fought wars of unification. Empires have risen and fallen. Today's high and mighty can be brought down by changing historical circumstances. What we are going through in our time - in the now - is but a phase in our development. We will, under God, move on to higher ground, as God raises up men and women whom He will use to do what only He can cause to be done. In the meanwhile, let us remember that the God about whom I have spoken is the Creator and Sustainer of heaven and earth; that as He has spoken, so it stands. Man – you and I – have our roles to play; and I plead that we play those roles in humility and love, always remembering that many of the developed countries had to pass through our present stage of evolution as a comparatively new nation-state; always remembering that one of the unchanging lessons History has to teach is that no condition is permanent.

I know not whether what I have said in this lecture has given you any better understanding of how and why your country and my country is as it is. I know not whether you consider that knowledge of history can do you any good in the context of Nigeria. If by the grace of God, I have said just one thing that you consider helpful in terms of your understanding of the affairs of our great country, I would consider that the purpose of my coming has been fulfilled.

AS WE END

CAN ANYTHING GOOD COME OUT OF HISTORY?

At page 184 we have recorded the views of a committee which the United States of America set up to look into the issue of teaching history in schools. The reader is requested to read again the eight points adduced by that Committee in defence of why history should be taught in American schools – in 1988. Permit me to reproduce here, the eighth point in their report:

> History is full of situations which are influenced by ideas as well as by character or leadership. **The student who properly grasps the role of ideas and forces as well as character and leadership should be able to better appreciate the problems of his nation and better play his role within that nation.** (my emphasis).

Paul Gagnon tells us (see p. 184) that when students ask him why they should study History, he tells them that the answer is found in one word: "judgment". He continued: "We need [judgment] most in the profession of citizen, which like it or not, exercise it or not, we are all born into". And my comment on Gagnon's very clear statement about the value of History is that "History provides training for living." Because History provides training for living, it cannot be a useless discipline.

The claim made above for History may not be acceptable to, or accepted by, all. It is, nevertheless, true. The reality is that we do not usually pause to ask ourselves why we react the way we do to the issues with which we have to contend in life. In our sub-conscious, our reactions are based on some experience in our past or something we have been told about the past. That past – the subject matter of historical inquiry – is always with us. To the extent to which this is true, to that extent is it true to declare that whether we are conscious of it or not, we are products of History and our lives are being constantly impacted by historical events, historical developments. Given this reality, History cannot be the useless discipline the powers that be in Nigeria declared it, judging from the way they have dealt with the subject of History in the last four decades. History has a value, a place, in the life of every nation. By its very nature, History is not, cannot be, a useless discipline.

"Historical events," declares Robert V. Daniels (see p. 3), have created all the basic human groupings – countries, religions, classes and all the loyalty that attach to these." Let us apply this to our country. To Daniel's "human groupings" we can add what we now call "ethnic nationalities" in Nigeria. At an earlier stage, these groupings were labelled tribes. Later the tag "tribe" was regarded as derogatory. So it was changed to "ethnic groups." Then even later, it was argued that some of the groups we labelled ethnic groups were larger in population than some countries. So we coined the name "ethnic nationalities" for what we used to call tribes or ethnic groups. We may never have thought about it, but these changes in nomenclature were our reaction to historical events and historical developments. What is more, as we have said in a number of times in this work, even these "ethnic nationalities" did not exist at the "beginning" – whenever that "beginning" was!

I am today an Isoko man. But I was not always Isoko! Before I began to call myself Isoko, I knew myself as Ẹrohwa, one of the smaller polities in today's Isokoland. It was within the colonial state of Nigeria that "Isokodom" emerged. It was a product of historical development, the response to a new challenge of identities in a new setting in which being Ẹrohwa did not, could not, confer the same benefits as being Isoko! What is true for me is true for every single Nigerian. The myriads of "ethnic nationalities" which today compete for recognition, positions, offices, development, etc, emerged in their present forms as a result of the coming into being of the colonial state of Nigeria and the policies of our colonial masters. As late as the beginning of the 19th century, today's Igbo, Yoruba, Hausa, Fulani, Ijọ, Ekiti, Tiv, Ebira, Urhobo, Kanuri,

Idoma, etc, did not exist as we know them today. Each of these "ethnic nationalities" emerged as a consequence of a series of "amalgamations" forced on what were earlier on smaller socio-political entities, each of which was independent of its neighbours before the establishment of British colonial rule over what became Nigeria! This is what Daniel means when he says "Historical events have created the basic human groupings and all the loyalties that attach to these." How can it be argued in the sight of the truth of Daniel's and our own assertions based on historical facts, that that History which produced Nigeria's multifarious ethnic nationalities, which we sometimes also refer to as peoples, is a useless discipline – with no value for our nation? Daniel drives his point home when he states: "It is the events recorded in History that have generated all the emotions, the values, the ideals that make life meaningful, that have given men something to live for, struggle over, die for."

A common definition of History is that it is a study of change over time. The reader would have observed that I have stated a number of times in the body of this work that No Condition is Permanent! Let me illustrate what I mean from slices of Nigerian History. Once there was a Kanem-Borno empire, the first empire to arise in what became Northern Nigeria. That empire, led by the ancestors of today's Kanuri, encompassed for lengths of time a number of the Hausa states in present day Nigeria. The Kanem-Borno empire was the first centre of Islam in what became Nigeria, at a time when Sokoto did not exist as a settlement! When in the 19th century Uthman Dan Fodio's forces attacked part of Borno's territories, the Shehu of Borno argued that it was not permitted for an Islamic state to attack a fellow Islamic state in the course of a jihad. Sokoto's reply was that because Borno had allied with some of the non-Islamic peoples against whom the jihadists had fought, it (Borno) had lost the immunity that would have been due to her. In the upshot, what became Hadeija and Katagum emirates, which were previously parts of Borno, were lost to the Sokoto Caliphate that was established as a consequence of the Uthman dan Fodio-led jihad. How did this little bit of history affect Northern Nigeria in the 20th century? At independence, the Sardauna of Sokoto, a descendant of Uthman dan Fodio, was premier of Northern Nigeria. The Governor was the Shehu of Borno, a descendant of the Elkanemi line of rulers of the Borno empire. This development was not fortuitous. It was a deliberate game of balancing for the sake of peace – Sokoto decided to give some recognition to Borno! Live and Let Live – another sentence the reader would have found in the body of the work. As you read this book, the Sokoto Caliphate does not exist qua caliphate. Why not? Because the colonial state of Nigeria and the Nigerian nation state which succeed it were not and are not, Islamic states. Today there is a Sokoto State and there is a Sultan of Sokoto. But the Sultan of Sokoto is not the Head of Sokoto State; it is the Governor of Sokoto State who is head! History brings about change and History is a study of the changes that it brings about! Knowledge of that History enables us to understand why things are as they are, and so equips us to deal with the present, a present which has grown out of the past, and which is therefore influenced by that past.

Once upon another time there was what was known as the Old Oyo empire, the largest geo-political entity in what we now call Yorubaland has ever known. The Old Oyo empire had not only some of the Yoruba kingdoms as vassal states, it also had non-Yoruba groups like Nupe, Borgu, etc, as well as some areas in today's Benin Republic. Like all empires, the Old Oyo empire collapsed in the 19th century in the military turbulence that characterised "Yorubaland." That collapse led to population movement from Old Oyo. Some of those who left Old Oyo settled in Ibadan, then an Egba settlement; others wondered farther afield and settled in what became Modakeke on land which belonged to Ile-Ife. The Ife-Modakeke problem arose out of this situation. In the meantime, Ibadan, having received a large influx of adventurer-immigrants from Oyo, grew into a strong military power, which gave birth to a new empire – an Ibadan empire.

Ile-Ife is regarded by the Yoruba as the cradle of Yoruba culture and civilisation – The Source, as it has been christened. The Yoruba wars of the 19th century shook even The Source, whose power and reputation were not based on military might but her mythical standing. In one of the wars that erupted between Ife and Modakeke over payment of land rent, Modakeke not only defeated Ife in war, but forced the Ooni into exile. It required the military might of Ibadan, with a mixed population of Egba, Oyo and Ife groups, to step into the situation and restore the Ooni to his throne – at a price. Ile-Ife became vassal to Ibadan for a while! Indeed No Condition is Permanent. In the Ife-Modakeke tensions and conflicts of the 20th century, the past was influencing human behaviour in the then new circumstances. Did the political leadership of Oyo State at the time know the strand of history we have just discussed above? If they did, did they bring it to bear on the situation at hand? The Ife obviously stood on their rights as the land owners to whom rent was due from the Modakeke settlers. The Modakeke could argue that after more than 100 years of settlement, they merited a new arrangement with regard to rent payable; they could even argue that they were where they are by right of conquest, having defeated the Ife in war and driven the Ooni into exile! Clearly there was a need for both parties to reach a new understanding. One of the claims made for History is that it deepens understanding. While understanding may not totally remove inter-group tensions, it can reduce them, and leave the way open for a "live and let live" relationship. History can thus be used to silence the guns and to promote peaceful co-existence.

Let us look at another slice of "Yoruba" history. The British authorities took advantage of the Yoruba wars of the 19th century to move into Yorubaland as peace brokers. Peacemaking soon gave way to the British occupation of Yorubaland. In the process of this occupation, the British built up what my late friend and colleague, J.A. Attanda, christened The New Oyo Empire. The British took the position that in the immediate past the Alaafin of Oyo was the ruler of all of Yorubaland. They therefore began to regard the Alaafin as the most senior of all the Yoruba monarchs. In the Native Court System which the British established, they established a Native Court of Appeal in Oyo to which appeals from other native courts in Yorubaland were to go, including appeals from the native court in Ile-Ife! In a manner of speaking, therefore, the Ooni was brought under the Alaafin by a British fiat. No appeal ever went from Ife to Oyo, obviously because the Ife could not see themselves being subject to the Alaafin. It was this development – created by History – which led to the struggle between the Ooni of Ife and the Alaafin of Oyo as to who should preside over the meetings of traditional rulers in the Old Oyo State. The struggle flowed over to the people and so worsened Ife-Oyo relations. History holds the key to an understanding of the struggle for primacy between the Ooni and the Alaafin, a struggle which was not terminated until the creation of Osun State put an end to the Ooni and the Alaafin being in the same state. The British colonial authorities thought they were acting in line with the history of the Yoruba before their coming. Because they were mistaken in their understanding of that history, they introduced a new tension into Ife-Oyo relations. This is what I describe as an unintended result of British colonial rule. In this regard, it is necessary to state that the unintended results of government policies sometimes impact more on inter-group relations than the intended results.

What happened to Ife-Oyo relations also happened elsewhere. For example, in my area of initial research, Itsẹkiri-Urhobo Relations, the appointment of an Itsẹkiri, Ọmadọghọgbọnẹ (the Dore of British records) as Paramount Chief of Warri Province, an area there were a total of six different ethnic nationalities had the effect of worsening Urhobo-Itsẹkiri relations. Encouraged by the arbitrary paramountcy which the British thus conferred on Chief Dọghọ (shortened form of the name), the Itsẹkiri went on to agitate for a change of the title of their ruler from Olu of Itsẹkiri to Olu of Warri in 1936. The British, this time, turned down the request of the Itsẹkiri. Later, in the period of decolonisation, Chief Obafemi Awolowo, leader of the Action Group and Leader of Government Business in the old Western Region, who also held the portfolio of Minister of Local Government and Chieftaincy Affairs, allowed political party affiliation to becloud sound judgment. Even though the other peoples in the then Warri Province opposed the Itsẹkiri demand that their ruler be styled Olu of Warri, Awolowo went on to grant the demand, to favour the Itsẹkiri, a majority of whom belonged to the Action Group and to side-line the Urhobo, majority of whom supported the National Council of Nigeria and the Cameroons (N.C.N.C.), the Opposition Party in the then Western Region. Riots broke out as a consequence of Awolowo's action, and lives were lost. Itsẹkiri-Urhobo relations have still not fully recovered from the deep wounds, inflicted by Awolowo's action sixty four years ago! What made Awolowo's action so pernicious was that the other peoples of Warri Province made their opposition to the proposed change known to him when he visited the area before the change was announced. In some attempt to appease the other peoples of the province, the name Warri Province was changed to Delta Province. But the harm had been done.

Did History have anything to do with the Warri episode? Yes. Warri Province was a creation of History. It was History that resulted in the emergence of the different peoples who constituted the British-created Warri Province. On the part of Awolowo, his being Yoruba may have influenced his decision, party politics apart. The majority of the Yoruba live in kingdoms and their rulers' titles are attached to the kingdoms – Ooni of Ife, the Alake of Abeokuta, Awujale of Ijebu, Alaafin of Oyo, etc. In many of these cases, the names of the kingdoms were the same as the names of the British-created Provinces. Coming from that background, Awolowo may have thought that the opposition of the non-Itsẹkiri peoples was mere fuss! If rulers elsewhere in the Region were called after the names of their provinces, why not in Warri Province? The answer is that, Warri Province had a different history! Again, we recall Daniel's dictum: It is the events recorded in History that have generated all the emotions, the values, the ideals that make life meaningful, that have given men something to live for, struggle over, die for. Itsẹkiri-Urhobo relations since 1952 confirm the truth of the dictum. Developments elsewhere in

Nigeria do the same.*

In Chapter Seven we discussed the colonial administrative set up in Nigeria. In the process we drew attention to Governor Bourdillon's action in breaking the Southern Nigeria into two in 1939 – Western Nigeria and Eastern Nigeria, while leaving the much larger Northern Nigeria intact. We made the point that Bourdillon's action meant that in each of Nigeria's three regions one ethnic group was larger in population than all the other groups put together. In the post-1939 period, therefore, the history of our country was dominated by the struggle of the Hausa-Fulani in the North, the Yoruba in the West and the Igbo in the East to establish control over their respective regions. As for the Federal Government, the British delivered control of it to the North on a platter of gold

*A number of works exist on British colonial rule in Nigeria which provide details of the effect of colonial rule on relations among different Nigerian peoples.

REFERENCE

- Ikime, Obaro, *Niger Delta Rivalry: Itsekiri – Urhobo Relations and the European Presence, 1884-1936*, London, Longman Green and Co Ltd., 1969
- Afigbo, A. E. *The Warrant Chief System: Indirect Rule in South-Eastern Nigeria, 1891-1929*. London, Longman Group Ltd., 1972
- Atanda J. A., *The New Oyo Empire: Indirect Rule in South-Eastern Nigeria, 1891-1929*, London, Group Ltd., 1973
- Asiwaju, A. I., *Western Yorubaland Under European Rule 1889-1945: A Comparative Analysis of French and British Colonialism*, London, Longman Group Ltd., 1976.
- Fika, Adamu Mohammed, *The Kano Civil War and Bristish Over-Rule 1882-1940*, Ibadan, Oxford University Press, 1978.
- Igbafe, Philip Aigbona, *Benin Under British Rule: The Impact of Colonial Rule on an African Kingdom 1897-1938*, London, Longman Group Ltd., 1979.
- Abubakar Saád, "The Northern Provinces Under Colonial Rule 1900-1959" in Ikime, Obaro (Editor), *Groundwork of Nigerian History*, Ibadan, Heinemann Educational Books Plc, 1980.

because population-wise, the North being larger than the East and West combined, would always provide leadership at the federal level. It is not our intention to go into a recapitulation of what this meant for Nigeria. Rather we concentrate on how changing administrative arrangements resulted in new loyalties being built around these new arrangements, and how these new loyalties, the product of History, determined development in our country in the post-1939 era.

West-East relations became strained as from 1952 when elections were held in the aftermath of the Macpherson constitution. In the election in Lagos, Nnamdi Azikiwe, leader of the N.C.N.C. and an Igbo resident in Lagos, was elected into the Western House of Assembly, dominated by the Yoruba. One can argue that Azikiwe's victory in Lagos was one of the best things that happened to Nigeria and was a pointer to what was possible in the future. Tragically, as it turned out, "Yorubadom" ensured that it was not to be tolerated for an Igbo man to ride the political high waves in Yorubaland. Azikiwe's fellow N.C.N.Cers who were Yoruba turned against him and ensured he was not elected to the Federal Legislature from the West. Then Azikiwe resigned his seat in the Western House of Assembly, went to the East and wrested political leadership from Eyo Ita, an Efik and a Vice-President of the N.C.N.C! Ethnicity triumphed over nationalism. And this was only eight years before Independence. God did not create Northern, Western and Eastern Nigeria. History did. Man – the Nigerian species – needs to study the circumstances in which these three regions were created and the consequence of their creation for the Nigerian nation state that came into being on 01 October, 1960. Nigerians need to know the history of their country under colonial rule, if they are to understand the history of their country as a nation state. But how can they know this history if they are not taught it as they pass through their nation's educational system? Nigeria does not yet know it. Nigerians, especially those who have ruled the nation thus far, do not consider that History is of any value. Even so, we dare to declare that Nigeria ignores her history at her own peril. The lessons of History may be lost on Government. Nevertheless those lessons continue to influence human action.

Nigeria attained independence with ethnicity and regionalism riding high in our national politics. The unexpected coalition between Northern and Eastern Nigeria – two strange bed fellows in terms of their political philosophies, was evidence that our politicians were being led not by what was best for Nigeria but by how they could get into office and stay in office. The development and circumstances which, only five years into independence, in January, 1966, led to our first military coup and the emergence of our first Military Government, confirmed the immaturity of our political class. That that first coup was labelled as an "Igbo coup," rightly or wrongly, is added evidence of that ethnicity to which we have drawn attention. The majority of these killed in that coup – both military officers and politicians were Northerners. In July 1966, came a Northern coup, or a revenge coup as it was also labelled – regionalism in full parade. The revenge coup turned out to be the signal for the slaughtering of Igbo and Easterners in parts of Northern Nigeria. The slaughters in turn led to the Military Governor of the East Central State, Lt Colonel Odumegwu Ojukwu, to call on all Igbo outside the East to return home. As Nigerians watched in confusion and consternation, our country began to slide into war. On 27 May, 1967, the Consultative Assembly of the Eastern Region announced its decision to establish an independent state to be called the Republic of Biafra. Lt. Colonel Yakubu Gowon, who became Head of State following the counter coup, responded to the announcement made by the East by creating the twelve state structure. Three states were created in the East, the South East, the Rivers and the East Central State. The first two states are peopled by non-Igbo; the East Central State was the homeland of the Igbo. Gowon's aim was clear, win the support of the non-Igbo of Eastern Nigeria from where Nigeria's oil wealth came. On 30 May, 1967, Ojukwu announced the secession of Biafra from Nigeria. Gowon declared that the announcement was tantamount to an act of rebellion which had to be crushed. That is how Nigeria was plunged into a civil war which did not end till 12 January, 1970.

We have not engaged in the above presentation of how Nigerian civil war came about with the aim of apportioning blame to any group. Our concern is to look at History and the civil war. The war was fought between Eastern Nigeria and Northern cum Western cum Mid-Western Nigeria. Nigeria did not exist as Nigeria till 1914. Northern Nigeria came into existence in 1900 and remained so until Gowon's twelve-state structure in 1967. "Southern Nigeria" referred to a variety of territories! In 1914 it referred to the area south of Niger-Benue River system, other than the Yoruba groups of Kabba and Ilorin which were part of Northern Nigeria. Western and Eastern Nigeria came to existence in 1939 and so were twenty eight years old when the civil war broke out. The Midwest Region was only four years old! The point of emphasis in the context of this book is that which has been repeatedly made; it is History that created the various groups and regions that were involved in the Nigerian civil war. "The North" came to have meaning because History endowed it with a certain cooperate existence; the same is true for "The South", "Western Region," "Eastern Region," "Midwest Region," "Biafra," and the states created in 1967 and later. Group loyalties developed around each of these entities. Nigeria was certainly not a strongly united country when the civil war broke out at the end of May 1969. Yet throughout the war the radio kept reminding us: To keep Nigeria one is a Task that must be Done! And Nigeria bought into it. Biafra was only a few weeks old as a political entity. But hundreds of thousands of soldiers and unlucky civilians died for Biafra. The same is true for Nigeria. Despite the inter-ethnic rivalries, and injustices that marked our politics since decolonisation and independence, a loyalty had developed towards Nigeria, so much so, that hundreds of thousands of our soldiers died for their country, that country that did not exist even as a colonial-state till 1914 and as a nation-state till 1960! History holds the key to all that has been said in these closing paragraphs of this work. Dare I copy the Nigerian civil war jingle and declare:

> TO TEACH HISTORY TO ALL NIGERIANS WHO PASS THROUGH THE NATION'S EDUCATIONAL SYSTEM IS A TASK THAT MUST BE DONE?

As for you, the reader, you owe yourself a duty, in the light of what you have read in this book, to answer the question which constitutes the title of the book:

> CAN ANYTHING GOOD COME OUT OF HISTORY?

What is your answer?

APPENDIX 1A
MEMORANDUM PRESENTED BY THE HISTORICAL SOCIETY OF NIGERIA TO THE HON. MINISTER OF EDUCATION OF THE FEDERAL REPUBLIC OF NIGERIA

1. The Historical Society of Nigeria is extremely grateful to you, Mr. Minister, for granting us an appointment to discuss with you, matters relating to our Society, as well as matters relating to our nation.

2. In a letter Ref. HSN/OIK/30 of 6 August, 1984 addressed to you, Mr. Minister, the President of the Historical Society of Nigeria sought to intimate you with the work of the Society and the financial problems which now face the Society. In that letter the Society prayed for financial support from your Ministry. That prayer still remains, Mr Minister. But we have not sought audience with you, Sir, just for the purpose of begging for financial assistance. We wish to take the opportunity of this meeting to put before you, Mr. Minister, certain matters which we consider of importance in the life of our nation – matters which have bearing on our discipline.

3. **The Historian and the Nation.** The way Nigeria has operated thus far leaves us with the impression that the nation does not think that the historian has any meaningful role to play in the life of the nation. While there have been calls for authentic writing of Nigerian history, it appears as if Government considers that we already have a surfeit of trained, professional historians in the country, and that the writing of this much-called-for authentic history can be done without commensurate financial outlay. Both these assumptions, Mr. Minister, are in fact wrong. The

number of trained historians in Nigeria is hopelessly inadequate for the kind of research needed if all parts of the nation are to have their history properly written. For this reason, the Historical Society of Nigeria laments the fact that in recent years postgraduate scholarships have hardly been awarded by the Federal Government to persons seeking to study history. We realise the logic for giving priority to Science and Technology. We submit, however, that at no time in the life of any nation – developed or developing – can the study of its history be irrelevant. We must urge, therefore, that the Federal Government should have another look at this aspect of its policy, especially now that various universities in Nigeria are also unable to grant postgraduate scholarships due to financial stringency. Mr. Minister, we are constrained to observe that the call for the writing of authentic Nigerian History is not matched by any awareness of what the historian can do for his nation. Permit us to illustrate.

(i) Since independence various Governments – civilian and military – have set up various commissions and committees to look into specific aspects of the nation's life. We refer in particular to the Boundary Adjustments and State Creation. Both the adjustments of boundaries and creation of States affect relationships between different peoples of our country. The historians of our land are concerned, among other things, with the study of these relations over time. Yet when Government sets up commissions to look into these matters, historians are never formally associated with the work of such commissions. Rather, High Court Judges, Political Scientists, Civil Servants, etc. are appointed to serve on these commissions. We do not question the wisdom of using the category of persons indicated. But we do lament the consistent failure to include historians in such teams, for we are persuaded that the kind of insight a trained historian can bring to bear on the work of such teams can be of great benefit to the nation.

(ii) Recently, the present Military Government set up a Committee to advise it on Local Government in Nigeria. Local Government has a history. In addition to whatever work has been done by the political scientists, there is a growing number of historians who have worked on the subject of local government. We are persuaded that the contributions of one such historian would have been of immense benefit to the committee now presenting a report to the Federal Military Government on local government reforms.

(iii) In recent weeks some of the military governors have talked about re-naming streets in their states. After whom will these streets be named? We can use the naming of streets to create a sense of history among our peoples. In most cities there are many new streets, named after various persons, irrespective of whether such persons are worthy of being immortalized by naming streets after them. Why cannot such governors seek advice from historians who will be glad to offer their services? In this connection, it is important that we do not destroy history by obliterating names which in themselves represent important phases in our historical development. Again the historian can be of service here.

One can go on to list the other areas in which the services of the historian cannot but benefit the nation. But we do not wish to take too much time or space. Our main point of emphasis is that the nation cannot and should not continue to ignore the many-sided roles which historians can play in the life of our nation. The Historical Society of Nigeria offers itself to the service of the nation and is prepared at all times to serve as the liaison between government and the professional historians of Nigeria.

1. Creating Historical Awareness among Our People: We make bold to say, Mr. Minister, that Nigeria has not learnt how to create a sense of historical awareness among its multifarious peoples. The Muhammed-Obasanjo regime came up with the concept of national heroes and proceeded to select certain persons designated national heroes. Ask any Nigerian in the streets of our towns who these national heroes are. Few will remember any, other than, perhaps, Muhammed. Why? Because we as a nation have not learnt how to make our history come alive to our people. A few illustrations will do:

(i) In January 1966 a number of Nigerian leaders who fought for and obtained independence for us were killed in a military coup that toppled the First Republic. Tafawa Balewa, our first Prime Minister, was gunned down in a house in Lagos. Have we marked that house in any way? No. A simple plaque, saying "In this house Alhaji Tafawa Balewa, Nigeria's first Prime Minister, was killed in a military coup on 15th January, 1966" would set the school boy passing by asking questions. Who was this Tafawa Balewa? Where did he come from? Why was he killed? The answers to these questions would teach the young boy certain aspects of our history. What is true for Balewa is true for the Sardauna of Sokoto, Chief S.L. Akintola, Chief Okotie-

Eboh, etc., and true also for Aguiyi Ironsi, Fajuyi and so on.
(ii) Murtala Muhammed has been declared a national hero. He was gunned down at a particular spot in Ikoyi. Have we marked that spot? No. What a way to treat the memory of a national hero. Elsewhere in the world a memorial would be erected there so that he who runs may read and learn instant history.
(iii) Dimka who led the coup that toppled Muhammed was arrested at a given point in Eastern Nigeria. Is there any memorial marking that spot? No.
(iv) Many of the men who led Nigeria in the 1940s and 1950s are dead and forgotten by the nation they served. Where is Herbert Macaulay's house? Where is Eyo Ita's grave? Where is Mbonu Ojike's grave? Are the graves of Balewa, Okotie-Eboh, Sardauna of Sokoto, Muhammed, regarded as national monuments. Is it planned to erect any memorials to these persons in a national cemetery?

The Historical Society of Nigeria is persuaded that there are many inexpensive ways in which the nation can create in the citizenry a greater awareness and sense of history. We are ready at all times to offer our advice and services to the nation, if the nation will care to avail itself of our offer.

2. Preserving the Nation's Records. As historians, we depend on records for our work. The National Archives exist for the purpose of collecting and preserving the records of the nation, and making these available not only to historians, but to all researchers interested in their use. Year after year, the Historical Society of Nigeria has issued communiques crying against the neglect of our National Archives and the fact that the National Committee on the Archives has not met for over ten years. As of the time of this Memorandum there still exists no effective policy-making body for our National Archives outside whatever ministry it is located. As historians we call for a greater commitment on the part of the government to the development and improvement of the National Archives. Our society has held meetings with the staff of the National Archives and we plan to maintain close relations with the Archives. A new Archives law is long overdue. We plead with you, Mr. Minister, to add your voice to those crying out for a speedy enactment of a new Archives Law. We pledge to support measures aimed at the improvement of the National Archives of Nigeria.

3. Mr. Minister, what we have said thus far represents only some of the issues that bother us as professional historians. We cannot be sure that they fall within your portfolio. From our perspective, they all have to do with the education of our peoples – formal as well as informal. Where matters raised do not really belong to your ministry or department, we plead that you be so good to forward them to the appropriate Ministry or Department. For that purpose we will leave 10 copies of the Memorandum with your officials.

4. Permit us now, Mr. Minister, to raise the issue of financial assistance from your ministry contained in our letter HSN/0IK/30 of 6th August, 1984. The justification for the request for financial assistance is contained in the letter under reference and will not be repeated in writing here. It is enough for us to remind you, Sir, of these arguments in our oral presentation. The items are, however, indicated below:

(i) Annual Congress 1985	...	... N5,000.00
(ii) Subsidy towards publication of the Society's History of Nigeria for schools and colleges ...	...	N10, 000.00
(iii) Part-cost of organising a workshop on the teaching of Nigerian History in April 1985 ...	...	N15, 000.00
TOTAL	=	N30, 000.00

As we indicated in our letter, we know that the funds available to Government are limited. We are persuaded, however, that our projects are of sufficient significance to the nation to justify the above sum being expended on them. We therefore strongly urge you, Mr. Minister, to give our request favourable consideration.

5. To end, Mr. Minister, the Historical Society of Nigeria thanks you most sincerely for granting us audience. We hope that you have found the issues we have raised of some interest.

We apologize for taking your time, and thank you very much indeed for your patience .

Professor Obaro Ikime, FHSN
President, Historical Society of Nigeria,
for and on behalf of the Society.

Presented to the Hon. Minister of Education of the Federal Republic of Nigeria on this 10th day of September, 1984.

APPENDIX 1B
THE PLACE OF HISTORY IN NIGERIA'S SCHOOL SYSTEM AND THE NATION: MEMORANDUM PRESENTED TO THE HON. MINISTER OF EDUCATION OF THE FEDERAL REPUBLIC OF NIGERIA BY THE HISTORICAL SOCIETY OF NIGERIA
WEDNESDAY, 21 JANUARY 1987

1. In September 1986, the Historical Society of Nigeria presented a memorandum to the Minister of Education on the place of history and the historian in the nation's life. Early in 1986, the Society sought audience with the current Minister of Education to discuss the same issues. Unfortunately the Minister's schedule at that time was such that it was not possible for us to wait on him. Events and developments since that time compel us to address a fresh memorandum to you, Sir, on the subject of **The Place of History in Nigeria's School System and the Nation.**

2. At the time of writing this memorandum, History as a separate subject is not taught at the primary school or Junior Secondary School levels. Also, because N.C.E. graduates are now expected to teach only in the junior secondary schools, history is not to be taught in the Colleges of Education which train teachers up to the N.C.E level. At these levels of our educational system, Social Studies has replaced, or is to replace, History and Geography.

3. At senior secondary school level, History is one of the optional subjects that students can take. Our investigation reveals that fewer and fewer students are taking the History option.

4. At the time the History syllabus for the 6-3-3-4 system was being drawn up, our understanding was that Social Studies as a subject was not to be taught at the Senior Secondary school level. We now understand that Social Studies is to be taught at that level. The most likely result of this decision is that most of the pupils at the Senior Secondary school level will opt for Social Studies, since they had taken that subject at the Junior Secondary School level. This means that the students, who will offer history a completely new subject in the school curriculum at Senior Secondary School level, will fall even more than it already has.

5. Present policy is that no child who leaves secondary school at the end of the first three years would have learnt any Nigerian History worth talking about, since the History content of the Social Studies curriculum is negligible. Similarly all those who take the N.C.E. course would have no knowledge of Nigerian History if they did not take it at the secondary school level, and only a few would have taken it. Given present trends, less that 5% of the secondary school population in Nigeria would be taught History as a subject. What all of this adds up to is that Nigeria would soon become a country whose lettered citizens have no idea of their own history because national policy is deliberately making History irrelevant in the scheme of things. The Historical Society of Nigeria considers that it owes a duty to the nation to state in very clear terms that this aspect of the nation's policy is retrogressive and not in the best interests of the nation.

6. There is a long-term consequence of present policy which may not yet be obvious to policy makers. Unless there is a change of heart very few pupils will take history at the end of their secondary school careers. Indeed it is easy to envision a situation in which Social Studies ultimately replaces History in fact if not as a matter of law. Why? Both teachers and students complain that the History syllabus calls on them to do more work than a number of other subjects, like Government, for example. Social Studies, as already indicated, will be preferred because it is a carry-over from Junior Secondary School, while History gets into the curriculum only at the Senior Secondary School level. If and when History disappears as a subject being taught in our secondary schools, it will also disappear at university level. Nigeria must ask herself whether there is any country in the world where History has disappeared from the

entire educational system. Yet we seem anxious, through present policies, to achieve that singular distinction of becoming the first nation which would, as a matter of deliberate policy, ensure that History, including Nigerian History, is not taught to our citizens.

7. Present policy partly springs from the new national commitment to the promotion of science and technology and the de-emphasizing of the Arts. For the avoidance of doubt, we wish to state that the Historical Society of Nigeria is not in complete agreement with the new emphasis on science and technology. We need science and technology for national development. What baffles us is the nation's current posture which, by implication, creates the impression that History including Nigerian History, is irrelevant for national development. In this context, we feel constrained to state, Mr. Minister, that it is most unfortunate to conceive of education only in terms of training for a job and not in terms of training for living as well. We submit, that in terms of training for living, by which we mean preparing the citizen to live effectively and meaningfully in his society, with proper conception of what relations should be between him and his fellow citizens, as well as a full appreciation of how and why things have come to be as they are, History as a discipline has far more to offer than many subjects. Yet, for some strange reason, it is History that now stands the greatest danger of being eliminated from the nation's educational system. The essential training which History offers is that of training the individual to reach a balanced judgement of events on the basis of a thorough study and analysis of all the evidence available to him. This is crucial training. Yet, while the nation can see the relevance of Religious Studies, of Government, of Political Science, the nation is apparently unable to see the relevance of History. Mr Minister, the Historical Society of Nigeria is amazed that Nigeria is anxious to get rid of a subject which every other nation of the world insists on teaching to its citizenry from childhood. Towards the end of 1986 we received a submission which Historical Association of Great Britain made to the Education Secretary on the need to teach History to all up to the age of 16. That submission was made at the invitation of the Education Secretary. We attach a copy of that submission to this memorandum. In doing so, we need to warn that the needs of Great Britain are necessarily different from ours. What Nigeria needs is that all of its lettered citizenry should learn the history of their own country

and that even non-lettered population should, through adult education, acquire some knowledge of their own country. We need this in order to promote greater understanding among our people; we need it in order to understand our problems of nation-building; we need it if we are to have any meaningful input into Government's efforts at forging a truly united Nigeria. Within our knowledge, none of the great nations of the world, including the most technologically advanced, have abandoned the learning of their national history. In the light of this unquestionable truth, Nigeria must ask herself why she is so anxious to relegate her own national history to the background. In our view, Mr Minister, present policy is mistaken and ought to be reviewed.

8. Across the country, there is an on-going campaign against History. History teachers are among the first to be retrenched. Some states have given directives that history graduates be not employed. In the secondary schools, while no principal will ask an Economics graduate to teach English, it is common to find graduates of Economics teaching History. Teachers of History, our investigations reveal, are often over-burdened, because Ministries of Education are unwilling to recruit History teachers in sufficient numbers. The impression we get, Mr. Minister, is that in the school system of our land, History is regarded as an unwanted and useless subject, a subject which anybody can teach. We regret that this is so, and urge that this tendency be checked in the long term interest of the nation.

9. In keeping with the new emphasis on science and technology, the Federal Government has decided that no scholarship will be awarded for postgraduate training in Arts. How does this affect History? Given the increased fees that universities are charging for postgraduate training, present policy will have the result of reducing the number of postgraduate students in History. Overtime, therefore, this nation will cease to have persons working for the PhD in History. We submit that such a development will be a tragedy for this nation.

10. There is a mistaken impression that Nigeria has a large collection of historians already. Mr Minister, the nation needs to be told that as a matter of fact the number of professional historians who have worked on Nigerian History is quite small. There are less than ten historians of

Igboland, for example. Some states like Benue have very few professional historians. There are many parts of this country whose histories are yet to be professionally investigated. So long as this remains so, the Nigerian History we teach will be incomplete to the extent that the experiences of the unstudied parts will not inform our analysis and conclusions. We fear that the history of such parts may never be studied, given a situation in which Government policy has no place for the funding of postgraduate training in History. It serves little purpose to argue back that universities can fund such training. Some of our universities — the older ones in particular – are in no financial position to award postgraduate scholarships. We must therefore urge Government to take another look at this aspect of its policy.

11. Then there is the issue of overseas scholarship. Present policy is that the Federal Government of Nigeria does not award overseas scholarships except in the sciences. Teaching History at the university level necessarily involves the teaching of histories of other lands. We teach the History of Europe, of the Americas, of the West Indies, of the Near, Middle and Far East. We teach the history of these other lands because, especially with regard to the third world countries, we believe that their experiences, their problems and how they are tackled and are tackling them are of direct interest to us here in Nigeria. Our teaching of these other areas, however, is inadequate because there are very few Nigerian experts in these fields. Just as other nations fund the study of the history of Africa, so do we need funding to enable Nigerians study the history of other lands. To train such Nigerians adequately, they need to study overseas, given the situation in which our libraries do not contain the kind of materials that would support PhD thesis on different aspects of the history of these other lands. Even in the terms of Nigerians undertaking research in the history of other African countries, we need scholarships from Government. In other countries, experts in the history of given areas are consulted whenever Governments have to formulate policies dealing with such parts. In Nigeria the historians are hardly regarded as having anything to contribute in the formulation of our foreign and other policies. We doubt whether Government knows that there are Nigerian experts in the history of Sierra Leone, Ghana, North Africa and East Africa working in our universities. We know that the views of such experts have never being sought despite the fact that

we have various relations with these other parts of Africa. It is almost as if Government is saying "Can any good thing come out of History?" It is perhaps because of this situation that Government does not consider it worthwhile to fund historical research overseas. It is the view of the Historical Society of Nigeria that Government's attitude in this regard is regrettable. We urge reconsideration. It is not enough for Nigerian Academics to teach the history of other lands. We need Nigerians who are research experts in the history of these other lands. In order to produce such experts we need Government scholarships at postgraduate level. In making this submission we realise that Government resources are limited and, in fact, dwindling. Even so we take the view that two or three scholarships a year to enable us train Nigerians in the history of other lands will be worthwhile investment. We urge governments to give thought to this submission. The Historical Society of Nigeria would only be too willing to advice Government on what the priorities should be in this regard.

12. The belief that History is of little importance in the scheme of things in the nation is reflected in other ways. For example, although the federal government spends millions of naira on the promotion of cultural activities each year, the only regular investment it makes on history is the N1,500 subsidy it gives to the Historical Society of Nigeria each year. In the last fifteen years the total grants Government has made to our Society for special projects are less than N40,000. Yet the same Government insists that the historians of our land should come out with what they often describe as authentic history. Authentic history can only be produced through research, and research costs money. Given the fact that there are many areas and aspects of our nation's history still awaiting their historians, the Governments of our land need to fund historical research more deliberately.

13. Recommendations

In the light of all that has been said above, we wish to make the following recommendations for the consideration of Government:

i. That Nigerian History should be taught as a compulsory subject to all Nigerian children in primary and Junior Secondary Schools, despite the presence in the school curriculum of Social Studies which, we submit, is not an adequate replacement for History.

ii. Those Social Studies be not taught at Senior Secondary School in order to make it possible for subjects like Geography, History and so on, to be taught as specific subjects.

iii. That at Senior Secondary School, the present History curriculum already approved by the National Council on Education be taught.

iv. That because of the need to continue to research into the history of Nigeria, government should award an agreed number of scholarships for postgraduate studies in Nigerian History each year.

v. That in view of the need to build up a body of Nigerian experts in the history of other lands, the federal government should award a limited number of scholarships to Nigerian scholars anxious to specialise in non-Nigerian history.

Professor Obaro Ikime, F.H.S.N.,
President, Historical Society of Nigeria, for and on behalf of the Society.

INDEX

www.ingramcontent.com/pod-product-compliance
Ingram Content Group UK Ltd.
Pitfield, Milton Keynes, MK11 3LW, UK
UKHW022002190726
13853UKWH00004B/1679

9 789788 457855